RESTAURANTS & BARS

IMPRINT

PROJECT MANAGEMENT
Florian Kobler, Cologne

COLLABORATION
Sonja Altmeppen, Berlin
Christina Holona, Cologne

PRODUCTION
Ute Wachendorf, Cologne

DESIGN
Sense/Net, Andy Disl
and Birgit Eichwede, Cologne

GERMAN TRANSLATION
Nora von Mühlendahl,
Ludwigsburg

FRENCH TRANSLATION
Jacques Bosser, Paris

PRINTED IN ITALY
ISBN 978–3–8365–0376–1

© 2009 TASCHEN GMBH
Hohenzollernring 53
D–50672 Cologne
www.taschen.com

ARCHITECTURE NOW!

RESTAURANTS & BARS

Architektur heute! RESTAURANTS & BARS
L'architecture d'aujourd'hui! RESTAURANTS & BARS

Philip Jodidio

TASCHEN

CONTENTS

INTRODUCTION

FROTH ON THE SEA

What do restaurants and bars have to do with architecture? The *Architecture Now!* books have on occasion presented realizations in these categories, but appearances might dictate that a place for a meal or a drink would be closer to decoration in their essence than to the art of building. There is something to that argument and, indeed, much of what makes a great bar has to do with appearances and ephemera rather than with steel, glass, and concrete. And yet, there are spaces that mark the collective consciousness, that form our perception not only of a pleasant evening, but of space and time. Two New York restaurants and bars might be cited in this respect. One is surely the Four Seasons, located at 99 East 52nd Street in the Seagram Building. The spaces of the restaurant and its interior were designed by the building's architects Ludwig Mies van der Rohe and Philip Johnson and have remained almost unchanged since it opened in 1959. The New York City Landmarks Preservation Commission designated it an interior landmark in 1989. Despite soaring windows, the Four Seasons does not boast a great view, since it is located just above ground level on the Park Avenue side. Its food has been praised, but that too seems not to be the most significant aspect of its success. The main dining room of the Four Seasons is quite simply one of the great interior spaces of modern architecture, a quintessential expression of modernism, with the hint of classic grandeur that so often escaped less generous realizations. The great and mighty of New York and the world have passed through these spaces, and a kind of urban legend has grown around the Four Seasons. Hired in 1958 to create a cycle of paintings for the space, the artist Mark Rothko vowed to produce "something that will ruin the appetite of every son-of-a-bitch who ever eats in that room," a pledge he never carried out because the paintings were never delivered. And yet this story, like the huge Picasso tapestry hanging between the bar and dining room, has contributed to making a restaurant that is more than a flash in the pan. Because interiors are so often little in harmony with the buildings they occupy, and because the Four Seasons is an example of the harmonious integration of architecture and décor, this is nothing other than an example of great architecture. A second iconic New York restaurant and bar space no longer exists. Windows on the World, located on the northern side of the top floors (106 and 107) of the former World Trade Center, operated between late 1972 and September 11, 2001. Occupying a space of 4600 square meters, Windows on the World, with its décor by Warren Platner, offered a view of Manhattan that made it an even more exceptional space than altitude and décor alone could have ensured. Warren Platner (1919–2006), who was educated as an architect and worked with the likes of Raymond Loewy, I. M. Pei, and Eero Saarinen, defined the word "classic" as "something that every time you look at it, you accept it as it is and you see no way of improving it." Naturally, the catastrophic end of Windows on the World and the World Trade Center towers contributes to the lasting image of the restaurant and bar that looked down on all of Manhattan. Though not exactly in the same category of modernist purity as the Four Seasons, Windows on the World offered another hint at the intimate relationship that must exist between great restaurants and bars and architecture. A view of cities like Bangkok, Tokyo, Hong Kong, or New York can be what transforms what could be an ordinary space into a celebration of architecture. So too, however, can lights, colors, materials, furniture, and even music shape space and create what can only be described as a memorable architectural experience. A restaurant or bar hardly exists without its patrons or the smell of food, even though such locations are often carefully photographed without a soul in sight. A restaurant or bar that is successful not only in terms of its turnover, but also because its space somehow transcends the moment, or perhaps integrates it fully, is an expression of the full life of architecture. It is living architecture.

1
Ludwig Mies van der Rohe and Philip Johnson, Four Seasons Restaurant, 99 East 52nd Street, Seagram Building, New York, New York, USA, 1959

ROOM WITH A VIEW

Spectacular views are a mainstay of many restaurants and bars, ensuring success, whether in the rising cities of the East or the older cities of the West. The Jules Verne (Paris, France, 2007, page 210) by Patrick Jouin (Jouin Manku) is perched 125 meters above ground level in the mythical Eiffel Tower. In a sense, the design relies as much on the books of the famous French author as it does on the inevitable and remarkable views of the French capital. Rather than a panorama of the city, visitors arriving at the restaurant are greeted by a window that looks into the kitchen. With its staff of 47, this Alain Ducasse restaurant does indeed provide a view of its own, fitting the quality of the cuisine. Jouin mixes such modern elements as carbon-fiber chairs by Pininfarina with his own romantic ideas of Jules Verne's sense of adventure and travel beyond the limits of normal experience, to the center of the earth, to the bottom of the sea, or here, on the way to the moon.

The moon is also the theme of the Vertigo Grill and Moon Bar (Thailand, 2001, page 51), perched on the 61st-story roof of Thai Wah Tower 2 in central Bangkok. The work of Architrave, the in-house design arm of Banyan Tree Hotels, these facilities are located on what was originally planned as a helicopter landing pad atop the hotel. The design here is quite literally vertiginous, with only thin metal rails separating guests from what appears to be an endless drop into a sea of lights and activity. A military style organization allows the restaurant to move patrons inside in case of precipitation, but the whole point is to be outside, under the moon and above the vibrant city. Although its spaces are less exposed to the elements, SEVVA (China, 2007, page 29), by Tsao & McKown for Bonnie Gokson in the heart of Hong Kong's Central, also offers a 360° view of another Asian metropolis. With views on Norman Foster's Hong Kong and Shanghai Bank on prominent offer, the relationship between this restaurant and architecture becomes a matter of give and take between exterior and interior. The view, though, is undeniably architectural in the best sense of the word.

Fashion and architecture have been more and more intimately related in Tokyo with buildings such as Prada by Herzog & de Meuron, Tod's by Toyo Ito, or Dior by SANAA occupying prominent sites in the Minami Aoyama, Omotesando area. Recent arrivals in nearby Ginza combine fashion, architecture, and restaurants and bars, as is the case in the Chanel Tower, where star New York designer Peter Marino created the Alain Ducasse restaurant Beige (Tokyo, Japan, 2002–04, page 17). Though the view may not be quite as sweeping as that offered by the Jules Verne for Ducasse, Beige is 56 meters off the bustling Tokyo avenue and most patrons get more than an eyeful. The combination here of understated elegance and the sense of being very much involved in the fashion of the moment would seem to be a quintessential early 21st-century experience. Marino's obvious talent, visible also in the rest of the building and its façades, ensures that a high level is maintained in the architecture and décor, much as it is in the products of Chanel.

A rival of Chanel, Giorgio Armani has also installed himself on Ginza, with the help of the Italian architect Massimiliano Fuksas. The Armani Ristorante (Tokyo, Japan, 2005–07, page 125) located on the 10th floor of the Armani Ginza Tower, features a sublimated bamboo leaf pattern that ties together ideas of Japanese tradition with the forward-looking modernity of Armani. The 40-seat Armani *privé* bar also

2
*Warren Platner, Windows on the
World, formerly One World Trade
Center, 107th Floor, New York, New
York, USA, 1972 (image 1976)*

2

offers views of the city and neighborhood, combining the day and night dynamism of Tokyo with the strong fashion and design sense generated by Armani and Fuksas. The bamboo theme does create links to Japanese culture that may not always be present in other fashion-driven restaurants set on the same avenue and in the broader neighborhood. It should be noted, though, that even Japanese designers like Issey Miyake have always been more interested in being genuinely cosmopolitan than in evoking specifically Japanese themes. Tokyo today is undeniably cosmopolitan, thus restaurants like Beige and the Armani Ristorante fit right in with the mood of the times.

FUSION CUISINE

Cuisine has seen the most unexpected amalgamations of influences from East and West, mixing ingredients and tastes from Japan to Chile in a quest for new dishes. The same might be said of a good deal of recent restaurant architecture, where fusion is also the name of the game. Imagine a restaurant conceived to resemble the home of a collector of French and Chinese antiquities. Put it in a former warehouse in the Meatpacking District of Manhattan and, *voilà*, you have Buddakan (Christian Liaigre with Gilles & Boissier, New York, 2006). A below-grade banquet-style hall more out of an English country home than either France or China marks this spectacular restaurant as much as Chinese wall paintings. Add in cuisine that mixes European, Asian, and American elements, and cultural boundaries appear to dissolve.

The same architects (Gilles & Boissier) are also responsible for the Shanghai Lan restaurants (China, 2008, page 137) that occupy a four-story building near the Bund. Here, French and Chinese elements are juxtaposed on different floors, with the top level and its Baccarat chandeliers exuding that French "je ne sais quoi." Granted, France was present in Shanghai with other foreign concessionaries, but here past and present are mixed, as are cultures from opposite ends of the world.

Philippe Starck, who has often indulged in humor and surprise in his work, recently completed the S Bar at the intersection of Hollywood and Vine in Los Angeles (California, 2007, page 363). Meant to evoke the "urban, eclectic style of an artist's warehouse gallery," the bar has huge photographs of Versailles and a "flea-market style," with mismatched chairs and tables and upside-down lamps dangling from the ceiling. It might be said that Versailles and the flea markets of France do not have too much to do with Hollywood, but, then again, all here is appearance or a décor meant to plunge guests into another universe, where food is only part of the experience. A space by Starck is certainly always amusing and innovative. Here, France meets California with all the zest of the cultural melting pot. Modernity is no longer about minimalist spaces and emptiness; here it is overflowing with references and objects from other worlds.

Blits in Rotterdam (The Netherlands, 2005, page 9) by the celebrated Dutch designer Marcel Wanders certainly serves a mix of cuisines—Japanese, Latin American, and Mediterranean. But the fusion does not stop there. Wanders imagined Blits as a "restaurant like a theater" with a live performance stage, and a "love suite" table for two with a heart-shaped window. Mix and match, your choice, but the design does not stop with the food and drink.

3 + 4
Marcel Wanders, Blits
Rotterdam, The Netherlands, 2005

3   4

PARADISE NOW

Any self-respecting survey of recent restaurants and bars must certainly include some that are located in the proverbial tropical paradise: on a white beach under a palm tree looking out on aqua waters. Unfortunately, it is difficult to combine a concern for the quality of architecture and design and a good deal of the realizations that also fit the tropical paradise description. The work of Bel Lobo in Brazil might well be an appropriate exception to the rule. Her Quadrucci Restaurant (Buzios, Rio de Janeiro, 2008, page 73) is located on the edge of a mangrove swamp on the beach 180 kilometers east of Rio. With an obvious concern for preserving existing trees on the site and elements such as a wood roof and a maximum number of locally produced materials, the restaurant is admirably green. Though it might seem quite simple in its design, the space of Quadrucci does, indeed, succeed in generating the "magic" referred to by the architect. With its transparency and reflections, it takes in the light and air of the place, just as it does its vegetation. In the domain of restaurants, where artificiality often reigns sovereign, here there is a taste for the natural and an ability to weave nature into a restaurant, making Quadrucci a stunning work of architecture. Those who know Brazil's cities may not consider them as being quite so close to paradise as the name of Ipanema Beach might imply. Physically splendid, Ipanema is not always a safe place. And yet, here too, Bel Lobo has crafted a simple, quite natural restaurant (Stravaganza, Ipanema, Rio de Janeiro, 2004–05, page 19) located near the famous beach. This is, of course, more an urban place occupying an old city house than it is a beach restaurant, but the strength of Brazil's nature flows through Bel Lobo's work, even when she includes a "fake, sculpted tree made of metal and amber-colored lamps" on a wall of Stravaganze. If Ipanema was once a vision of paradise, perhaps this restaurant is a step toward reconquering its extravagant beauty.

The architect Ed Tuttle, who has worked on a large number of hotels, restaurants, and resort projects, for the Amanresorts amongst others, preferred not to have his recent projects specifically featured in this book, largely because he has so much work that he cannot handle any more. Born and raised in the United States, Tuttle created his Paris firm Design Realization in 1977 with Christian Monges. He designs furniture and accessories for his projects and insists on respecting both local culture and the impact on nature of his remarkable resort projects. He has recently added the Puri Beach Club and the Puri Naoki Japanese restaurant to his earlier Amanpuri (1988) resort located on the west coast of Phuket, Thailand's largest island. Here, there is a suggestion of Asian architecture, but the openness and fundamental modernity of the spaces and objects are clearly present. Ed Tuttle proves that it is entirely possible to reconcile the demands of a sophisticated hotel group with a delicate natural site and the even more complex requirements of good design and architecture.

ARTS AND CRAFTS

Though the natural connection between architecture, design, and cuisine often makes for the success of the best restaurants, some choose to add yet another element to the mix—contemporary art. The celebrated Pharmacy Restaurant in London, the brainchild of artist Damien Hirst and designer Mike Rundell (1997), certainly showed that contemporary art can enter the realm of cuisine with success, even though this restaurant has since closed. Karriere (Copenhagen, Denmark, 2007, page 177), run by the artist Jeppe Hein and his sister Lærke,

5

6

is another effort to bring art and, in this case, a bar together. Nor has Hein gone about it in a haphazard way. Calling on his own excellent knowledge of the cutting edge of contemporary art, he convinced artists Dan Graham, Olafur Eliasson, Ernesto Neto, Elmgreen & Dragset, Rirkrit Tiravanija, Maurizio Cattelan, and Douglas Gordon to participate in his venture. Complemented by a very active Web site and newsletter, Karriere clearly aims to revive the tradition of the culturally driven venues that played such an active role in the development of Paris as a center of modern art in the 20th century. Just as intriguingly, Jeppe Hein demonstrates a will to show that art can be part of everyday life.

Whereas Damien Hirst made his own work the central of attraction and theme of Pharmacy, a very different and more private intervention for the bar of a private London club shows that this type of interaction between art, design, and architecture is very much alive and well. With her presence in recent Venice Biennale events, Zaha Hadid has repeatedly treaded the fine line between architecture, design, and art with success. Her bar for Home House (London, UK, 2007–08, page 171) was designed using the latest computer and CNC techniques. Fabricated with resin, fiberglass, and fabric, her bar interacts with the "characteristic orthogonal programming of its Georgian envelope," redefining the space and in the same process posing very real questions about the relationship of art, architecture, and design, or about the very definitions of space and function.

CHIC AND DISCREET

Though designers like Philippe Starck seem to have gone further and further into a kind of baroque mixture of styles and types of objects, others have remained faithful to their own taste for discretion, for whatever reason. It will not come as a surprise that Kengo Kuma's Sakenohana restaurant (London, UK, 2007, page 223) makes use of a distinctly Japanese vocabulary and discretion. The architect says specifically that his client rejected the very idea of a "slick" solution, but he knew very well that with Kuma that would not have been a danger. However, the traditional Japanese wooden framework he used for the ceiling, or the bamboo shades, are certainly not expected solutions, even for those who know Japan. Kuma has found his own way between the demands of modernity and a respect for tradition, and this restaurant is a full expression of that synthesis, even if he did not design the building itself.

Approaching some of the same issues from an almost opposite point of view, Stephanie Goto, who had already worked with Tadao Ando on his Meatpacking District restaurant morimoto nyc in New York (2005–06, page 10), sought in her recent Corton restaurant (New York, New York, USA, 2007–08, page 147) to re-create the atmosphere of a Paris townhouse, but her carved white plaster walls are surely more discreet than the sometimes abundantly gilt atmosphere of old Paris homes. Though Corton was completed before the recent financial downturn, its subtle approach seems better suited to the coming times than to the boom years just past. Design and style are surely a matter of cyclical change, often ranging from minimal to excessive, but these changes are usually driven by external factors, the economy surely amongst them. A bet might be taken that 2009 and 2010 will see fewer new restaurants and bars than the preceding years, and that those that do see construction and opening will be as discreet and nonetheless stylish as their designers can make them, at least in the upper

5 + 6
Tadao Ando, morimoto nyc
New York, New York, USA, 2005–06

7
Stephanie Goto, Corton
New York, New York, USA, 2007–08

7

range of the types of locations being considered here. It is true, too, that some cultures, such as that of Japan, may well have such discretion inscribed in their genes, as it were, but the obvious nature of cyclical design movements remains.

Isay Weinfeld's London restaurant and bar Mocotó (2006–07, page 387) does not have a Japanese feel to it, particularly since the architect is Brazilian, but an extreme simplicity reigns in these high, airy spaces. It is interesting to note that such discretion may well require a greater effort on the part of clients to actually notice how much good design seems to almost disappear into successful details and décor. This restaurant, since closed, was almost diametrically opposite in its spirit to the glitzy restaurants and bars that one might readily associate with the go-go years of the early 21st century.

There are two restaurants in slightly different modes but by the same designer, Ilse Crawford of Studioilse, in the Grand Hotel in Stockholm (Sweden, 2007). Her Matbaren and Matsalen rooms, both for the chef Mathias Dahlgren, are in a decidedly Scandinavian mode, but Matsalen is more upscale. Her idea of mixing a Carlo Scarpa light fixture with a "classic Swedish kitchen lamp" demonstrates an eclectic taste that nonetheless results in a refined and understated atmosphere that again goes in the direction of suggesting that the trends of the future will move toward discretion rather than bombast and superficial glitter.

ROUGH AND TUMBLE

The opposite of chic and discreet might well be rough and tumble. Reusing old, often industrial spaces such as warehouses for restaurants and bars is, of course, a tried and true recipe for success. Most of the restaurants created in Manhattan's Meatpacking District, some already mentioned here, take on the existing early 20th-century industrial architecture and convert it into something decidedly more contemporary. The approach to existing architecture may vary, of course, but in the case of the Amorio Restaurant (Bellavista, Santiago, Chile, 2005–06, page 377), the architects, the Tidy brothers, were specifically asked by the clients to maintain the aged, "bohemian" atmosphere of the façades while completely reinventing the interiors. Clearly, in this instance, there is a kind of a chic cachet to a slightly run-down-looking brick façade, which has nonetheless had its ground floor painted white and a bright lighting system installed.

The Australian architect Cate Young invented her Water Bar in a listed building on Finger Wharf at Woolloomooloo Bay in Sydney (Australia, 2007, page 407). She took obvious advantage of one of the most positive elements often to be present in industrial spaces, which is to say large volumes—here under a 13-meter-high ceiling that has seen much of its original vocabulary maintained. Cate Young describes her reaction to this space in terms of its proximity to the water, but also in terms of its relation to the layered history of the country. "It was also a disembarking point for new migrants arriving in Australia and for socialites and millionaires taking passage on luxury liners. It saw industrial disputes, green bans, and arson attempts. Now, of course, it is considered Sydney's most impressive residential and entertainment quarter." With all of this in mind, she concludes: "But all the layers of history, all its pasts, cleverly conserved at the Finger Wharf in the bones

8

of the building and the sinews of its massive rigging, are embedded in one common element: water." The listed nature of the building naturally encourages such thoughts, but Cate Young is not referring here to a hastily renovated bar; she is explaining a real architectural reaction
to fundamentally charged spaces, ones that have history and presence, but which can still live thanks to her efforts.

MODERN IS AS MODERN DOES

Though spaces like New York's Four Seasons are hard to come by, certain restaurants or bars occupy spaces that may be iconic for
reasons of their immediate history, or perhaps because of their surprising design. The English architect Richard Rogers was closely involved
in two such restaurants, the first of which originally opened in 1987 just near Thames Wharf, the Hammersmith location of the offices of the
Richard Rogers Partnership. The River Café has long been a famous London eating-spot because of its location along the river in a green set-
ting, but also because a great architect and a reputed chef here offered their efforts to create a place where architecture, design, and food
came together at a very high level. A fire early in 2008 required a substantive refitting of the River Café (London, UK, page 121), a job entrust-
ed to Stuart Forbes, a long-time Rogers collaborator who had worked on such London projects as Heathrow Terminals 1 and 5 and the
Millennium Dome. A visible kitchen and a large, round wood-burning stove are features that bring the cuisine that much closer to patrons
without sacrificing anything of the mystique that made the River Café famous. Indicating his own involvement in the refurbishment, Richard
Rogers states: "Stuart and I set out to make distinctive but subtle changes—we have significantly remodeled the River Café while respecting
its visual identity and retaining its original elegance."

A second restaurant, located in Barcelona, Spain, also bears the mark of Richard Rogers, albeit in a somewhat more perched or
exposed situation. The Evo Restaurant (2005–06, page 131) sits 105 meters above the ground on the roof of the Hesperia Tower. Rogers and
his firm Rogers Stirk Harbour (with Alonso & Balaguer) created the structure of the pod in which Evo is located, but the interior work was done
by the Barcelona firm GCA. Their reaction to the "spectacular architectonic form" of the pod was to add circular platforms to resolve what they
perceived as difficulties in the circulation patterns, and to harmonize their intervention with the style of the renowned chef Santi Santamaria.

The architects Regine Leibinger and Frank Barkow (Barkow Leibinger Architekten) took on the not always gratifying task of creating a
campus restaurant, for a firm called Trumpf located near Stuttgart (Ditzingen, Germany, 2006–08, page 67). With seating for 700, this restaurant dwarfs most carefully designed eating places, and, in many respects, it may come closer to pure architecture than most of the restaurants published in this book. Working with the reputed engineer Werner Sobek, the architects pitched a cantilevered canopy over groups
of columns, evoking a "polygonal leaflike canopy." The open spaces of the restaurant bring to mind a less elaborated shed-type structure.
Here, Barkow Leibinger have employed an industrial logic to a facility of high quality that functions admirably well as an assembly space and
dining hall. For those who ask what the point of calling on famous engineers and architects might be for such a functional facility, the
answer can be found in the inventiveness and generous spaces proposed here.

8
Jakob+MacFarlane, Alvéole Bar
Fondation d'Entreprise Ricard, Paris,
France, 2007–08

9
Wonderwall / Masamichi Katayama,
Tokyo Curry Lab
Tokyo, Japan, 2007

9

Operating in a more purely commercial environment, the Portuguese architects Guedes + DeCampos have called on a honeycomb or expanded metal solution in creating the basic structure for the Ar de Rio Bar Restaurant (Vila Nova de Gaia, Portugal, 2008, page 165). Both the Barkow Leibinger project and this one demonstrate how the technology that allows materials to be stretched and perched in such spectacular ways also provides new possibilities for the architecture and design of such facilities as restaurants and bars. More precisely, in these two instances, the architectural part defines or even forms the restaurant space, flooding it with light, creating an impression of modernity that is confirmed from outside to inside.

The Paris-based architects Jakob+MacFarlane were responsible for the design of one of the more iconic and successful restaurants in their city—the Georges Restaurant atop the Centre Pompidou (2000). Using computer-assisted design, the architects had originally conceived their restaurant as being based on the original grid of the 1977 Piano and Rogers building. By imagining that this grid was deformed and stretched, they created extrusions that contained a private dining room and, in another instance, the restaurant washrooms and cloakroom. It is this space that the architects redesigned recently (2006, page 189) for the restaurant owners, the Costes family. Rather than restrooms, the volume now contains the Pink Bar, and, instead of deforming or extruding the old grid, Jakob+MacFarlane imagined that they were carving from a 3D matrix. Eight years after their original success on the top floor of the Pompidou Center, Jakob+MacFarlane have shown that their original design retains a good deal of flexibility and they have been able to bring the Pink Bar very much into the present.

There is a certain amount of architectural humor in the bulbous forms of the Pink Bar and the Georges Restaurant, but it is naturally mixed with the kind of functional efficiency that the Costes brothers demand in Paris and restaurant and bar owners everywhere hope for. The Tokyo Curry Lab (Tokyo, Japan, 2007, page 393) by Wonderwall shows a similar degree of humor mixed with unremitting efficiency and design rigor. An open bar fronting a single extended oval table, the two separated by colorful vials full of spices, the Tokyo Curry Lab is enlivened by graphics representing pigs and chickens chasing a stylized sauce boat. Neither minimal nor baroque, this design is comfortably situated in another register of modernity, one that transgresses building or design types, here combining an open counter with a closed dining room and calling on the vocabulary of an almost scientific laboratory. Hot chicken curry coming up.

DYNAMIC DUOS

Some of the more unusual concepts for restaurants or bars involve dual functions separated according to the passage of time. One of these, Set & Sekt Retail Store and Bar (Basel, Switzerland, 2007, page 85) by Buchner Bründler, was a temporary installation that involved the unexpected transition from a fashion shop during the day into a bar at night thanks to a system of white curtains to cover the clothes in the evening. Though this solution could easily be attributed to purely economic reasoning, it also speaks of different ways of living that imply that design must be flexible in the extreme, even accommodating seemingly opposed uses. The Peacock Clubs in Göteborg and Stockholm (Sweden, 2006 and 2007, pages 291 and 296) designed by OlssonLyckefors are designed for a nearly seamless transition from restaurant

10   11

to nightclub, turning furnishings into a dance floor with minimal intervention. These functions are clearly more closely related than that of Set & Sekt, but the need to conceive convertible objects focuses the attention of the designers from the outset on spaces that are to be in constant movement. Though the two initiatives are not strictly comparable, it might be noted that the original configuration of a restaurant designed by Mies van der Rohe and Johnson in 1959 has hardly been altered in 50 years, while these new spaces change once a day. Might it be that restaurants and bars have entered a time of multitasking, much as electronic devices like telephones are now called on to show movies, provide maps, and play music? Convertibility is also the concept underlying the unusual Neogama BBH Plug Bar (São Paulo, Brazil, 2006, page 219) by the talented architect Marcio Kogan, who is surely better known for his private houses. With its aligned bottles, the greeting desk of this advertising agency might well strike visitors as an unusual publicity ploy, but, in fact, the long desk makes a perfect bar should the need arise. Even more than the mixture of fashion shop and bar, this juxtaposition of a serious daytime job with a drink on the town might serve to demonstrate that function can be no more than a question of appearances, or of the inventiveness of the architect or designer involved.

CREATURES OF FASHION

It is clear that, in most instances, restaurants and bars do not obey the same rules as architecture itself. Often, but not always limited to interior spaces, these businesses do not need to take into account the heavy infrastructure of an entire building. A light effect, a carefully chosen chair, and not least a good meal might well suffice to create a successful restaurant. It is no accident that Americans and others speak of the "dining experience" when referring to restaurants precisely because they often propose a voyage in time and space as well as the cuisine that is their *raison d'être*. At a time of cosmopolitan travel and wafting cultural influences, it is not surprising to find sushi in a bar in Los Angeles that evokes a Paris flea market. Almost as much as fashion boutiques, restaurants and bars are creatures of fashion, coming and going much faster than the average 50-story tower or football stadium. This fact, of course, means that the reasoning and methods employed to make a restaurant or bar are quite different from those that come into play for a large building, even if some are designed by world-renowned architects. As potential victims of fashion, restaurants and bars may well be even more sensitive barometers of taste and the spirit of the times than larger, more expensive realizations. Multitasking, whether to shift between daylight and night functions, or perhaps to simultaneously evoke a bit of China and a bit of France, seems to be quite the thing for recent restaurants and bars. Inevitably, this sort of cultural or functional sampling, reminiscent of some trends in popular music, implies higher and higher degrees of superficiality. But there are no hard and fast rules. The carefully designed and engineered corporate dining hall imagined near Stuttgart by Barkow Leibinger has as much architectural content as any older purpose-built space, but, here again, the space is conceived from the outset for assemblies or other events. Flexibility is the rule as, indeed, it has been in architecture in general for some time.

In 1990, the late Kirk Varnedoe organized a seminal exhibition at New York's Museum of Modern Art entitled "High and Low: Modern Art and Popular Culture" tracing the influences that have in fact flowed back and forth between popular culture and its more high-browed

10 + 11
Philippe Starck, Le Meurice
Paris, France, 2007

alternatives. Might restaurants and bars be the low-brow expression of architecture—a place where influences and cultures can flow over spaces without fundamentally changing the shape of the times? Or are they rather a sort of Tokyo Curry Lab of experimentation, a way to look at what might be the shape of tomorrow. Since 1990, it would appear that the movement back and forth between expressions of popular culture, driven by the Internet and high culture, has accelerated or fluidified. While the Four Seasons remains as it was in 1959, Windows on the World, seemingly just as immovable a fixture on the New York scene, was blown away in an instant one early morning in 2001, just like the great building in which it was perched. It is certain that many trends of future "serious" architecture can be seen in these pages, an imperfect prediction of what buildings themselves will look like in a few years. If there ever was a real dominant style in architecture, this has not been the case since the glory years of the International Style. Starck's humorous eclecticism will and must continue to coexist with the kind of Zen rigor expressed by Kengo Kuma, for example. An Alain Ducasse restaurant does not have much to do with a frozen yoghurt stand, and yet they both offer food, and both are subject to different forms of fashion-driven demand. One requires more investment than the other, one is supposed to be more "serious" than the other, but these are variants on a single type, an ephemeral place whose space and appearance may be fashioned by what the philosopher George Santayana called "the oddest of possibilities masquerading momentarily as fact." Bars and restaurants are theater, with an audience, a stage, and a backstage with its kitchen, for example. They are made up of moveable décors sliding in and out according to the needs of the moment, their lighting adjusted to match the mood of the actors or the spectators.

As functional as they may be, restaurants and bars that do not stand on their own do not have to meet the same criteria as buildings. They are a meeting point between various human needs—for sustenance or companionship. They are places of meeting and interaction and the flow of clients or food and drink form a changing architecture of their own. At a moment when architects seek to render their buildings ever more flexible and ever less frozen into a given mode, restaurants and bars can and do serve as a laboratory. Small changes can give spaces multiple functions, while, aesthetically speaking, many different solutions can coexist at any given point in time. Though they do not always respond to the vital signs that permit them to be identified as architecture, restaurants and bars are like the froth on the sea that is the built environment. They move and change faster than the underlying currents; they provide a lightness and coloration that can well portend changes to come in the sea itself.

Philip Jodidio, Doha, Qatar, November 23, 2008

EINLEITUNG

SCHAUM AUF DEM MEER

Was haben Restaurants und Bars mit Architektur zu tun? Die Bände der Reihe *Architecture Now!* haben gelegentlich Beispiele aus diesem Bereich vorgestellt, aber man könnte annehmen, dass ein Ort zum Essen oder Trinken mehr mit Dekoration als mit wahrer Baukunst zu tun habe. Das Argument hat einiges für sich, und in der Tat hat das, was eine tolle Bar ausmacht, mehr mit Ausstattung und flüchtigen Eindrücken zu tun als mit Stahl, Glas und Beton. Und doch gibt es Räume, die das kollektive Bewusstsein beeinflussen, die unsere Wahrnehmung bestimmen – nicht nur von einem angenehmen Abend, sondern von Raum und Zeit. Zwei New Yorker Restaurants und Bars sind im Hinblick darauf zu nennen. Eins davon ist sicherlich das Four Seasons im Seagram Building, 99 East 52nd Street. Die Räume und die Innenausstattung dieses Restaurants stammen von den Architekten dieses Gebäudes – Ludwig Mies van der Rohe und Philip Johnson – und sind seit der Eröffnung des Lokals im Jahr 1959 nahezu unverändert geblieben. Die New Yorker Denkmalschutzbehörde stellte es 1989 unter Schutz. Trotz großzügiger Fenster erfreut sich das Four Seasons keiner besonderen Aussicht, da es nur knapp über Erdgeschossniveau an der Park Avenue liegt. Das Essen wird zwar gelobt, aber das scheint nicht der entscheidende Aspekt seines Erfolgs zu sein. Der große Speiseraum des Four Seasons ist ganz einfach einer der großartigen Innenräume der modernen Architektur, die Quintessenz der Moderne mit einer Andeutung von klassischer Grandeur, die weniger großzügigen Realisationen so häufig fehlt. Die Großen und Mächtigen von New York und der ganzen Welt haben diese Räume besucht und das Four Seasons zu einer Art städtischer Legende werden lassen. Der 1958 mit einem Gemäldezyklus für diesen Raum beauftragte Künstler Mark Rothko versprach, etwas zu produzieren, „das jedem Halunken, der jemals in diesem Raum isst, den Appetit verderben" würde – eine Drohung, die er niemals wahr machte, denn er lieferte die Bilder gar nicht ab. Und doch hat diese Geschichte, ebenso wie der riesige Wandteppich von Picasso zwischen Bar und Speiseraum, dazu beigetragen, dass dieses Restaurant über jeden Misserfolg erhaben ist. Weil Innenräume so häufig nicht mit dem Gebäude harmonieren, in dem sie sich befinden, und weil das Four Seasons ein Muster an harmonischer Integration von Architektur und Dekor darstellt, ist es nichts anderes als ein Beispiel für großartige Architektur.

Ein anderes New Yorker Restaurant mit Bar, das zur Ikone wurde, gibt es nicht mehr. Windows on the World, auf der Nordseite der obersten (106. und 107.) Geschosse des ehemaligen World Trade Center, existierte von Ende 1972 bis zum 11. September 2001. Mit seiner Ausstattung von Warren Platner nahm es eine Fläche von 4600 m² ein und bot eine Aussicht über Manhattan, die es noch ungewöhnlicher machte, als Höhe und Dekor es ihm ohnehin garantierten. Warren Platner (1919-2006), der Architektur studiert und mit Leuten wie Raymond Loewy, I. M. Pei und Eero Saarinen zusammengearbeitet hatte, definierte Klassik als „etwas, das man bei jeder Betrachtung so akzeptiert, wie es ist, und bei dem man keine Möglichkeit sieht, es zu verbessern". Natürlich trägt das katastrophale Ende von Windows on the World und der Türme des World Trade Center zum bleibenden guten Image des Restaurants hoch über Manhattan bei. Wenn Windows on the World auch nicht zur gleichen Kategorie der puristischen Moderne wie das Four Seasons gehörte, bot es doch eine Andeutung des intimen Verhältnisses, das zwischen großartigen Restaurants und Bars und der Architektur bestehen muss. Der Blick auf eine Stadt wie Bangkok, Tokio, Hongkong oder New York kann einen ansonsten durchschnittlichen Raum in einen Ort verwandeln, der die Architektur feiert. So können jedoch auch Licht, Farben, Materialien, Möbel und sogar Musik einen Raum gestalten und das bewirken, was sich nur als unvergessliches Architektur-

12 + 13
Peter Marino, Beige at Chanel Tower
Tokyo, Japan, 2002–04

12   13

erlebnis beschreiben lässt. Ein Restaurant oder eine Bar kann schwerlich ohne seine Gäste oder den Geruch des Essens existieren, auch wenn solche Plätze oft bewusst ohne eine Menschenseele darin fotografiert werden. Ein solcher Ort, der nicht nur wegen seines Umsatzes erfolgreich ist, sondern weil er über den Augenblick hinaus Bestand hat oder ihn vielleicht ganz ausfüllt, ist Ausdruck des prallen Lebens der Architektur. Er ist lebendige Architektur.

ZIMMER MIT AUSSICHT

Spektakuläre Ausblicke sind eine lukrative Attraktion vieler Restaurants und Bars, in den aufstrebenden Metropolen des Ostens ebenso wie in den alten Städten des Westens. Das Jules Verne (Paris, 2007, Seite 210) von Patrick Jouin (Jouin Manku) thront 125 m über Geländehöhe im legendären Eiffelturm. In gewisser Weise beruft sich die Gestaltung des Lokals ebenso auf die Bücher des berühmten französischen Schriftstellers wie auf die unvermeidliche und bemerkenswerte Aussicht auf die französische Hauptstadt. Besucher des Restaurants werden aber nicht vom Panorama der Stadt, sondern von einem Fenster zur Küche empfangen. Dieses Alain-Ducasse-Restaurant mit 47 Mitarbeitern bietet tatsächlich eine besondere Aussicht, der auch die Qualität der Küche entspricht. Jouin verbindet moderne Elemente wie Stühle aus Kohlefaser von Pininfarina mit seinen eigenen romantischen Vorstellungen von Jules Vernes Abenteuerlust und Reisen über die Grenzen menschlicher Erfahrungen hinaus zum Mittelpunkt der Erde, zum Grund des Meers oder, wie hier, zum Mond.

Der Mond ist auch das Thema des Vertigo Grill und der Moon Bar (Thailand, 2001, Seite 51) auf dem Dach des 61-geschossigen Thai Wah Tower 2 im Zentrum von Bangkok. Dieses Werk von Architrave, dem eigenen Architekturbüro von Banyan Tree Hotels, befindet sich hoch oben auf dem Hotel an einer Stelle, die früher als Helikopterlandeplatz vorgesehen war. Die Gestaltung ist hier sprichwörtlich schwindelerregend: Nur ein dünnes Metallgeländer trennt die Gäste vom scheinbar endlosen Fall in ein Meer aus Licht und Geschäftigkeit. Ein fast militärisch organisiertes System macht es bei Niederschlägen möglich, die Gäste schnell nach innen zu befördern, aber der Schwerpunkt liegt auf dem Aufenthalt im Freien, unter dem Mond und über der pulsierenden Stadt. Obgleich die Räume von SEVVA (China, 2007, Seite 29) von Tsao & McKown für Bonnie Gokson im Zentrum von Hongkong den Elementen weniger ausgesetzt sind, bietet es ebenfalls einen Rundblick, wenn auch auf eine andere asiatische Metropole. Mit der Aussicht auf Norman Fosters Hong Kong and Shanghai Bank im Angebot, wird das Verhältnis dieses Restaurants zu seiner Architektur zu einem Geben und Nehmen zwischen Innen- und Außenraum. Der Ausblick ist jedoch unbestreitbar architektonisch im wahren Sinn des Worts.

Mode und Architektur haben sich in Tokio immer enger verbunden mit Bauten wie z. B. für Prada von Herzog & de Meuron, Tod's von Toyo Ito oder Dior von SANAA, die prominente Grundstücke im Bereich Minami Aoyama, Omotesando, einnehmen. Neuere Gebäude im nahe gelegenen Stadtteil Ginza verbinden Mode und Architektur mit Restaurants und Bars, wie im Fall des Chanel Tower, wo der New Yorker Stararchitekt Peter Marino das Alain-Ducasse-Restaurant Beige (Tokio, 2002–04, Seite 17) gestaltete. Die Aussicht ist zwar nicht so umwerfend wie beim Jules Verne von Ducasse, aber immerhin liegt das Beige 56 m hoch über Tokios verkehrsreicher Avenue, wovon die meisten Gäste

14
Architrave, Vertigo Grill and Moon Bar
Banyan Tree Bangkok, Bangkok,
Thailand, 2001

14

durchaus profitieren. Hier scheint die Verbindung von zurückhaltender Eleganz und dem Gefühl, zur aktuellen Modewelt zu gehören, ein typisches Erlebnis des beginnenden 21. Jahrhunderts zu bieten. Marinos offensichtliches Talent ist auch am ganzen Gebäude und seinen Fassaden ablesbar und garantiert in Architektur und Ausstattung ein hohes Niveau – ebenso wie die Produkte von Chanel.

Ein Konkurrent von Chanel, Giorgio Armani, hat sich mithilfe des italienischen Architekten Massimiliano Fuksas ebenfalls in Ginza niedergelassen. Das Armani Ristorante (Tokio, 2005–07, Seite 125) im zehnten Geschoss des Armani Ginza Tower zeigt ein edles Muster aus Bambusblättern, das die Vorstellungen von japanischer Tradition mit der fortschrittlichen Modernität von Armani verbindet. Die Bar-Privé mit 40 Plätzen bietet ebenfalls Ausblicke auf die Stadt und die Nachbarbebauung und vereint Tokios Tag und Nacht herrschende Dynamik mit dem starken, von Armani und Fuksas erzeugten Bewusstsein für Mode und Design. Das Bambusmotiv stellt Verbindungen zur japanischen Kultur her, die in anderen modeorientierten Lokalen an der gleichen Avenue und in der weiteren Umgebung nicht zu finden sind. Es ist jedoch zu beachten, dass sogar japanische Designer wie etwa Issey Miyake eher darauf bedacht sind, sich als wahre Kosmopoliten zu geben, als speziell japanische Themen aufzugreifen. Tokio ist heute zweifellos kosmopolitisch, daher passen Lokale wie das Beige und das Armani Ristorante genau in die gegenwärtige Stimmung.

FUSION CUISINE

Die Kochkunst erfindet unvermutete Verbindungen von Einflüssen aus Ost und West; auf der Suche nach neuen Gerichten vermischt sie Zutaten und Geschmacksrichtungen von Japan bis Chile. Das Gleiche gilt für einen Großteil der neueren Restaurantarchitektur, in der ebenfalls Fusion die Bezeichnung für dieses Spiel ist. Stellen Sie sich ein Restaurant vor, das dem Haus eines Sammlers französischer und chinesischer Antiquitäten gleicht. Setzen Sie es in ein früheres Lagerhaus im Meatpacking District von Manhattan und, *voilà*, hier ist das Buddakan (Christian Liaigre mit Gilles & Boissier, New York, 2006). Eine Halle unter Geländeniveau im Stil eines Bankettsaals, eher aus einem englischen Landhaus als aus Frankreich oder China, charakterisiert ebenso wie die chinesischen Wandmalereien dieses spektakuläre Restaurant. Fügen Sie eine Karte hinzu, die europäische, asiatische und amerikanische Elemente mischt, und die kulturellen Grenzen scheinen sich aufzuheben.

Dieselben Architekten (Gilles & Boissier) zeichnen für die Restaurants Shanghai Lan (China, 2008, Seite 137) verantwortlich, die in einem viergeschossiges Gebäude nahe dem Bund residieren. Hier wurden französische und chinesische Elemente auf verschiedenen Etagen gegenübergestellt, wobei das oberste Geschoss mit seinen Baccarat-Lüstern eine Atmosphäre des französischen „Je ne sais quoi" verbreitet. Gewiss, Frankreich war unter den anderen ausländischen Niederlassungen in Shanghai präsent, aber hier wurden Vergangenheit und Gegenwart gemischt, ebenso wie Kulturen aus Ländern vom entgegengesetzten Ende der Welt.

Philippe Starck, der gerne humoristische und überraschende Elemente in seinem Werk präsentiert, hat kürzlich die S Bar an der Kreuzung von Hollywood Boulevard und Vine Street in Los Angeles (Kalifornien, 2007, Seite 363) fertiggestellt. Mit dem Ziel, den „urbanen, eklek-

15
Bel Lobo & Bob Neri Arquitetos,
Stravaganze Restaurant
Ipanema, Rio de Janeiro, Brazil,
2004–05

15

tischen Stil einer Kunstgalerie in einem Lagerhaus" heraufzubeschwören, zeigt diese Bar riesige Fotografien von Versailles und einen „Flohmarktstil" mit Stühlen und Tischen, die nicht zusammenpassen, und verkehrt herum an der Decke aufgehängten Lampen. Man könnte meinen, dass Versailles und die französischen Flohmärkte nicht viel mit Hollywod zu tun haben, aber auch hier ist alles Aufmachung oder Dekor,
das die Gäste in eine andere Welt versetzen soll, wobei das Essen nur einen Teil dieses Erlebnisses ausmacht. Ein Raum von Starck ist immer
amüsant und innovativ. Hier trifft Frankreich auf Kalifornien mit allen Reizen eines kulturellen Schmelztiegels. Modernität ist nicht mehr minimalistischer Raum und Leere; hier quillt sie über von Bezügen und Objekten aus anderen Welten.

Blits in Rotterdam (2005, Seite 9) des hochgelobten niederländischen Designers Marcel Wanders serviert zweifellos einen Mix aus japanischer, lateinamerikanischer und mediterraner Küche. Aber die Fusion ist damit nicht zu Ende. Wanders stellte sich Blits als ein „Restaurant
wie ein Theater" vor, mit einer Bühne für Livespektakel und einem „Liebessuite"-Tisch für zwei Personen mit einem herzförmigen Fenster.
Nach Belieben wird das Passende ausgesucht und zusammengestellt, aber das Design hört mit dem Essen und Trinken nicht auf.

DAS PARADIES VON HEUTE
Jede ernstzunehmende Übersicht neuer Restaurants und Bars muss natürlich auch einige in den sprichwörtlichen Tropenparadiesen
enthalten, an einem weißen Strand unter Palmen mit Blick auf das blaue Meer. Leider ist es schwer, ein Bewusstsein für qualitätvolle Architektur und Gestaltung in Bauten zu finden, die auch der Beschreibung vom tropischen Paradies entsprechen. Die Projekte von Bel Lobo in Brasilien bilden eine Ausnahme von dieser Regel. Ihr Restaurant Quadrucci (Buzios, Rio de Janeiro, 2008, Seite 73) liegt 180 km östlich von Rio
am Rand eines Mangrovesumpfs am Strand. Dieses offensichtlich mit Rücksicht auf den vorhandenen Baumbestand und mit Elementen wie
einem Holzdach und aus vielen vor Ort produzierten Materialien erbaute Restaurant ist bewundernswert naturverbunden. Obgleich es in seiner
Gestaltung ganz einfach wirkt, ist es der Architektin gelungen, dem Quadrucci die von ihr als „magisch" bezeichnete Atmosphäre zu verleihen.
Mit seiner Transparenz und seinen Spiegelungen bezieht es das Licht und die Luft des Orts ein und desgleichen seine Vegetation. Bei Restaurants herrscht oft Künstlichkeit vor; hier ist jedoch eine Vorliebe für das Natürliche zu erkennen, und die Natur ist auf gelungene Weise in das
Restaurant integriert, was das Quadrucci zu einem fantastischen Werk der Architektur macht. Wer die Städte Brasiliens kennt, wird sie nicht
so dicht am Paradies einordnen, wie der Name Ipanema es nahelegen könnte. Der Strand von Ipanema ist zwar landschaftlich herrlich gele-
gen, aber nicht immer ein sicherer Ort. Und doch ist Bel Lobo ein einfaches, ganz natürliches Restaurant (Stravaganze, Ipanema, Rio de
Janeiro, 2004–05, Seite 19) in der Nähe dieses berühmten Strands gelungen. Hier handelt es sich natürlich um einen eher urbanen Ort in
einem alten Stadthaus und weniger um ein Strandlokal, aber die eindrucksvolle brasilianische Natur durchdringt auch diesen Bau von Bel
Lobo – selbst wenn sie einen „künstlichen, plastischen Baum aus Metall und bernsteinfarbigen Lampen" an einer Wand des Stravaganze auf-
stellt. Wenn Ipanema einst der Vorstellung vom Paradies entsprach, so ist dieses Restaurant vielleicht ein Schritt zur Rückgewinnung seiner
extravaganten Schönheit.

16

Der Architekt Ed Tuttle, der eine große Zahl von Hotels, Restaurants und Ferienanlagen, u. a. für Amanresorts, geplant hat, wollte seine neueren Projekte nicht ausführlich in diesem Buch publiziert sehen, vor allem weil er so viel Arbeit hat, dass er keine mehr annehmen kann. Der in den Vereinigten Staaten geborene und aufgewachsene Tuttle gründete 1977 mit Christian Monges sein Pariser Büro Design Realization. Er entwirft Möbel und Accessoires für seine Projekte und respektiert regionale Kulturen wie auch den Einfluss der Natur auf seine bemerkenswerten Freizeitanlagen. Kürzlich hat er sein älteres Amanpuri-Ferienzentrum (1988) an der Westküste von Phuket, Thailands größter Insel, um den Puri Beach Club und das japanische Restaurant Puri Naoki erweitert. Hier findet man Anklänge an asiatische Architektur, aber die Offenheit und grundlegende Modernität der Räume und Objekte ist überall präsent. Ed Tuttle beweist, dass es durchaus möglich ist, die Bedürfnisse einer anspruchsvollen Hotelgruppe mit einem lieblichen Naturgelände und den noch vielschichtigeren Forderungen nach guter Gestaltung und Architektur zu versöhnen.

ARTS AND CRAFTS

Obgleich der natürliche Zusammenhang von Architektur, Design und Cuisine häufig den Erfolg der besten Restaurants ausmacht, wollen einige diesem Mix noch ein weiteres Element hinzufügen – zeitgenössische Kunst. Das berühmte Pharmacy Restaurant in London, geistiges Produkt des Künstlers Damien Hirst und des Designers Mike Rundell (1997), zeigt sicherlich, dass moderne Kunst mit Erfolg in den Bereich der Cuisine eindringen kann, auch wenn dieses Restaurant inzwischen geschlossen wurde. Karriere (Kopenhagen, 2007, Seite 177), geführt von dem Künstler Jeppe Hein und dessen Schwester Lærke, ist ein weiterer Versuch, Kunst und in diesem Fall eine Bar zusammenzuführen. Hein hat das Projekt sehr gezielt in Angriff genommen. Dank seiner hervorragenden Beziehungen zur zeitgenössischen Kunstszene überzeugte er die Künstler Dan Graham, Olafur Eliasson, Ernesto Neto, Elmgreen & Dragset, Rirkrit Tiravanija, Maurizio Cattelan und Douglas Gordon, sich an seinem Unternehmen zu beteiligen. Mit Unterstützung einer sehr aktiven Website und eines Newsletters strebt Karriere eindeutig eine Wiederbelebung der kulturellen Begegnungsstätten an, die im 20. Jahrhundert eine so aktive Rolle bei der Entwicklung von Paris zum Zentrum der modernen Kunst spielten. Ebenso engagiert will Jeppe Hein zeigen, dass Kunst Anteil am täglichen Leben haben kann.

Während Damien Hirst sein eigenes Werk zum Thema und Zentrum des Pharmacy machte, zeigt ein ganz anderer, individuellerer Beitrag zur Bar eines Londoner Privatklubs, dass diese Art der Interaktion von Kunst, Design und Architektur durchaus noch lebendig ist. Mit ihren Beiträgen zu den neueren Biennalen von Venedig hat Zaha Hadid wiederholt die fließende Grenze zwischen Architektur, Design und Kunst mit Erfolg überschritten. Ihre Bar für Home House (London, 2007–08, Seite 171) wurde mithilfe neuester Computer- und CNC-Technik geplant. Dieses aus Kunstharz, Glasfaser und Textilien gestaltete Lokal stellt einen Kontrast zum „charakteristischen orthogonalen Programm seiner georgianischen Hülle" dar, gestaltet den Raum neu und stellt zugleich sehr reale Fragen zum Verhältnis von Kunst, Architektur und Design – oder zu der wahren Definition von Raum und Funktion.

16
Jeppe Hein, Karriere
Copenhagen, Denmark, 2007

17 + 18
Kengo Kuma, Sakenohana
London, UK, 2007

17   18

SCHICK UND DISKRET

Obgleich Designer wie zum Beispiel Philippe Starck die barocke Mischung von Stilen und Objekttypen immer weiter getrieben haben, sind andere – aus welchen Gründen auch immer – ihrer eigenen Vorliebe für vornehme Zurückhaltung treu geblieben. Es ist nicht verwunderlich, dass Kengo Kuma bei seinem Restaurant Sakenohana (London, 2007, Seite 223) auf japanische Zurückhaltung und Formensprache zurückgreift. Der Architekt hat ausdrücklich erklärt, dass sein Auftraggeber eine „raffinierte" Lösung ablehnte, aber der wusste auch sehr wohl, dass bei Kuma diese Gefahr sowieso nicht bestand. Dennoch hatte man sicher das traditionelle japanische Holzfachwerk der Decke oder die Bambusschirme nicht erwartet, selbst Kenner Japans nicht. Kuma hat seinen eigenen Weg zwischen den Forderungen der Moderne und dem Respekt vor der Tradition gefunden, und das Restaurant ist ein klarer Ausdruck dieser Synthese, auch wenn das Gebäude selbst nicht von ihm stammt.

Stephanie Gotho verfolgt ähnliche Ziele von einem völlig anderen Standpunkt aus. Nachdem sie schon mit Tadao Ando an seinem Restaurant morimoto nyc im New Yorker Meatpacking District zusammengearbeitet hatte (2005–06, Seite 10), versuchte sie in ihrem neuen Restaurant Corton (New York, 2007–08, Seite 147), die Atmosphäre eines Pariser Stadthauses wiederzubeleben, obgleich ihre klaren, weißen Putzwände gewiss zurückhaltender sind als das manchmal überladene Ambiente der alten Pariser Wohnhäuser. Obgleich Corton vor der derzeitigen Finanzkrise fertiggestellt wurde, erscheint diese subtile Lösung weit besser geeignet für die kommenden Zeiten als für den Boom der vergangenen Jahre. Design und Stil unterliegen natürlich zyklischen, von minimalen bis zu gravierenden Veränderungen, aber diese gehen meistens von externen Faktoren aus, vor allem natürlich von wirtschaftlichen. Man könnte wetten, dass 2009 und 2010 weniger neue Restaurants und Bars entstehen werden als in den vergangenen Jahren und dass deren Ausführung und Eröffnung zurückhaltend sein werden – und dennoch so stilvoll, wie es ihren Designern nur möglich ist. Zumindest gilt das für die luxuriöseren dieser Lokale, die hier zur Debatte stehen. Es trifft auch zu, dass einige Kulturen, z. B. die japanische, diese Zurückhaltung quasi in ihren Genen haben, aber die Tatsache des zyklischen Wandels der Gestaltung bleibt trotzdem bestehen.

Isay Weinfelds Londoner Restaurant Mocotó (2006–07, Seite 387) hat kein japanisches Ambiente – der Architekt ist Brasilianer –, aber in diesen hohen, luftigen Räumen herrscht eine fast extreme Schlichtheit. Es ist interessant zu sehen, dass eine derartige Zurückhaltung auch von den Auftraggebern die Erkenntnis fordert, wie sehr gute Gestaltung in erfolgreichen Details und Dekors untergehen kann. Dieses inzwischen geschlossene Restaurant war in seiner Atmosphäre fast diametral entgegengesetzt zu den glanzvollen Lokalen, die man mit den sorglosen Jahren des frühen 21. Jahrhunderts verbinden kann.

Zwei in ihrer Art recht verschiedene, aber von der gleichen Architektin, Ilse Crawford von Studioilse, gestaltete Restaurants befinden sich im Grand Hotel in Stockholm (2007). Ihre Lokale Matbaren und Matsalen, beide von Mathias Dahlgren geleitet, sind entschieden skandinavisch, aber Matsalen ist vornehmer. Crawfords Idee, Carlo-Scarpa-Leuchten mit einer „klassischen" schwedischen Küchenlampe zu kombi-

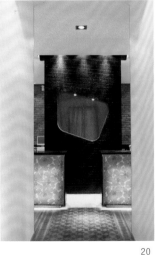

19

20

19 + 20
Tidy Arquitectos, Amorio Restaurant
Bellavista, Santiago, Chile, 2005–06

nieren, zeugt von einem eklektischen Geschmack, der trotzdem eine elegante und nicht aufdringliche Atmosphäre verbreitet, die wiederum darauf hinweist, dass der künftige Trend in Zurückhaltung und nicht in Protz und oberflächlichem Glanz bestehen wird.

EINFACH UND CHAOTISCH

Das Gegenteil von schick und diskret könnte einfach und chaotisch sein. Die Nutzung alter, häufig industrieller Bauten, z. B. Lagerhäuser, als Restaurants und Bars ist natürlich ein bewährtes und erfolgversprechendes Rezept. Die meisten der in Manhattans Meatpacking District entstandenen Restaurants, von denen einige hier schon erwähnt wurden, übernehmen die Industriearchitektur des frühen 20. Jahrhunderts und verwandeln sie in etwas Zeitgemäßeres. Der Umgang mit dem Bestand ist natürlich unterschiedlich, aber beim Restaurant Amorio (Bellavista, Santiago, Chile, 2005–06, Seite 377) wurden die Architekten, die Brüder Tidy, ausdrücklich gebeten, die altmodische, unkonventionelle Außenfassade zu erhalten, jedoch das Innere vollkommen neu zu gestalten. Natürlich ist dies ein schickes Detail bei einem leicht heruntergekommenen Backsteingebäude, in dem das Erdgeschoss weiß gestrichen und ein helles Beleuchtungssystem installiert wurde.

Die australische Architektin Cate Young gestaltete ihre Water Bar in einem denkmalgeschützten Gebäude am Finger Wharf in der Woolloomooloo-Bucht in Sydney (Australien, 2007, Seite 407). Sie nutzte eines der positivsten Kennzeichen des Industriebaus, die großen Räume – hier mit einer 13 m hohen Decke –, und erhielt weitgehend das ursprüngliche Formenvokabular. Cate Young beschreibt ihre Reaktion auf dieses Gebiet im Hinblick auf die Nähe zum Wasser, aber auch bezüglich der vielschichtigen Historie des Landes. „Es war ein Landeplatz für die neuen Einwanderer nach Australien wie auch für die oberen Zehntausend und die Millionäre, die auf Luxuslinern anreisten. Es hat Auseinandersetzungen mit der Industrie, Streiks und Brandstiftungen erlebt. Heute gilt es natürlich als angesehenes Wohn- und Unterhaltungsviertel." Und in diesem Bewusstsein endet sie: „Aber all die historischen Schichten, die ganze Vergangenheit, die am Finger Wharf klugerweise in den Knochen seiner Bauten und den Muskeln seiner massiven Anlagen erhalten blieben, sind in dem einen gemeinsamen Element Wasser enthalten." Die Tatsache, dass das Gebäude denkmalgeschützt ist, legt solche Gedanken natürlich nahe, aber Cate Young bezieht sich hier nicht auf eine im Schnellverfahren renovierte Bar; sie beschreibt die reale Reaktion einer Architektin auf mit Bedeutung aufgeladene Räume, die eine Geschichte und eine Gegenwart haben, aber dank ihrer Bemühungen auch in Zukunft weiterleben können.

MODERN IST, WAS DIE MODERNE MACHT

Obgleich Räume in der Qualität des New Yorker Four Seasons nur schwer zu finden sind, können bestimmte Restaurants oder Bars zu Ikonen werden aufgrund ihrer besonderen Geschichte oder vielleicht auch wegen ihrer erstaunlichen Gestaltung. Der englische Architekt Richard Rogers war an zwei solchen Restaurants stark beteiligt, von denen das erste, ursprünglich 1987 eröffnete, am Thames Wharf in Hammersmith liegt, wo sich auch das Büro von Richard Rogers befindet. Das River Café ist seit Langem ein berühmtes Londoner Speiselokal, sowohl wegen seiner Lage im Grünen am Fluss als auch, weil ein großartiger Architekt und ein renommierter Chefkoch durch ihre Bemühungen hier einen Platz geschaffen haben, wo Architektur, Design und Kochkunst sich auf hohem Niveau treffen. Ein Brand Anfang 2008 erfor-

21
Guedes + DeCampos, Ar de Rio Bar
Restaurant
Vila Nova de Gaia, Portugal, 2008

21

derte eine umfassende Renovierung des River Café (London, Seite 121). Damit wurde Stuart Forbes beauftragt, ein langjähriger Mitarbeiter von Rogers, der mit ihm an Londoner Projekten wie den Terminals 1 und 5 am Flughafen Heathrow und dem Millennium Dome zusammengearbeitet hat. Eine offene Küche und ein großer, runder, mit Holz beheizter Ofen sind Elemente, die den Gästen die Kochkunst näherbringen, ohne dass etwas von dem legendären Ambiente geopfert wurde, welches das River Café berühmt gemacht hat. Mit Hinweis auf seine eigene Beteiligung an der Renovierung erklärte Richard Rogers: „Stuart und ich wollten deutliche, aber subtile Veränderungen – wir haben das River Café entscheidend umgestaltet, jedoch seine visuelle Identität respektiert und seine ursprüngliche Eleganz bewahrt."

Ein weiteres Lokal in Barcelona, wenngleich an einem höheren oder exponierteren Standort, trägt ebenfalls den Stempel von Richard Rogers. Das Restaurant Evo (2005–06, Seite 131) liegt 105 m über Bodenniveau auf dem Dach des Hochhauses Hesperia. Rogers und sein Büro Rogers Stirk Harbour (mit Alonso & Balaguer) planten die Kuppel, in der sich Evo befindet, die Innenausstattung stammt jedoch vom Büro GCA aus Barcelona. Dessen Reaktion auf die „spektakuläre Architekturform" bestand darin, runde Plattformen einzufügen, um das ihrer Meinung nach problematische Wegesystem zu verändern und ihre Eingriffe mit den Vorstellungen des renommierten Küchenchefs Santi Santamaria in Einklang zu bringen.

Die Architekten Regine Leibinger und Frank Barkow (Barkow Leibinger Architekten) übernahmen die nicht immer dankbare Aufgabe, eine Kantine für die Firma Trumpf bei Stuttgart (Ditzingen, 2006–08, Seite 67) zu planen. Mit Plätzen für 700 Mitarbeiter lässt dieses Restaurant die sorgfältig geplanten Essräume klein wirken und kommt in mancher Beziehung einer rein architektonischen Lösung näher als die meisten in diesem Buch veröffentlichten Lokale. Die Architekten, die mit dem renommierten Ingenieur Werner Sobek zusammenarbeiteten, setzten über Stützengruppen ein auskragendes Vordach, ein „vieleckiges, blattartiges Dach". Die offenen Räume des Restaurants erinnern an eine weniger kunstvolle Shedkonstruktion. Hier haben Barkow Leibinger industrielle Formen für eine qualitätvolle Anlage verwendet, die als Versammlungs- und Speiseraum bewundernswert gut funktioniert. Diejenigen, die fragen, warum man berühmte Ingenieure und Architekten mit solch einer funktionalen Einrichtung beauftragen sollte, können die Antwort darauf in diesen fantasievollen und großzügigen Räumen finden.

In einer eher kommerziell genutzten Umgebung haben die Architekten Guedes + DeCampos sich beim Restaurant Ar de Rio (Vila Nova de Gaia, Portugal, 2008, Seite 165) auch für eine Waben- oder Streckmetallkonstruktion als Grundstruktur entschieden. Das Projekt von Barkow Leibinger und auch dieses demonstrieren, wie die Technik, die Materialien auf solch spektakuläre Weise strecken und aufeinandersetzen kann, auch neue Möglichkeiten für Architektur und Design von Restaurants und Bars schafft. Genauer gesagt, bestimmen oder bilden sogar in diesen beiden Beispielen die Architekten den Raum des Restaurants, erfüllen ihn mit Licht und erzeugen eine moderne Wirkung, die sich von außen nach innen fortsetzt.

22

Die Pariser Architekten Jakob+MacFarlane zeichnen für die Gestaltung eines erfolgreichen und zur Ikone gewordenen Restaurants in ihrer Stadt verantwortlich – des Georges hoch oben auf dem Centre Pompidou (2000). Ursprünglich hatten die Architekten mithilfe von CAD ihr Restaurant auf der Grundlage des Rasters des 1977 von Piano und Rogers entworfenen Gebäudes geplant. Indem sie dieses Raster veränderten und streckten, bildeten sie Ausformungen, die einen privaten Speiseraum und an anderer Stelle die Sanitäranlagen und Garderoben des Restaurants enthalten. Diesen Bereich gestalteten die Architekten kürzlich für die Besitzer des Restaurants, die Familie Costes, neu (2006, Seite 189). Anstelle der Toiletten liegt in dem Bereich jetzt die Pink Bar, und anstatt das alte Raster zu verändern oder zu strecken, hatten Jakob+MacFarlane die Idee, die Bar aus einer 3-D-Matrix auszuschneiden. 18 Jahre nach ihrem früheren Erfolg auf dem obersten Geschoss des Centre Pompidou haben sie gezeigt, dass ihr ursprünglicher Entwurf ein hohes Maß an Flexibilität hat, und es ist ihnen gelungen, die Pink Bar in die Gegenwart zu versetzen.

Die knolligen Formen der Pink Bar und des Restaurants Georges beinhalten eine ganze Menge architektonischen Humors, der natürlich mit der funktionalen Effizienz verbunden ist, welche die Gebrüder Costes in Paris und die Besitzer anderer Restaurants und Bars erwarten. Das Curry Lab in Tokio (2007, Seite 393) von Wonderwall zeigt ein ähnliches Maß an Humor, verbunden mit durchgehender Effizienz und gestalterischer Strenge. Mit einer offenen Bar und einem einzigen, langen, ovalen Tisch davor und farbigen, mit Gewürzen gefüllten Gefäßen dazwischen wird das Curry Lab belebt durch Grafiken, die Schweine und Hühner darstellen, die eine stilisierte Sauciere verfolgen. Dieses weder minimalistische noch barocke Design ist in einem anderen Bereich der Moderne angesiedelt, jenseits aller typischen Bau- oder Gestaltungsweisen. Hier wird eine offene Theke mit einem geschlossenen Speiseraum und dem Vokabular eines fast wissenschaftlichen Laboratoriums verbunden. Scharfes Hähnchencurry, kommt sofort!

DYNAMISCHE DUOS

Zu den eher ungewöhnlichen Konzepten für Restaurants oder Bars gehören Doppelfunktionen, die im Verlauf der Zeit wieder getrennt werden. Eine solche Lokalität, das Einzelhandelsgeschäft Set & Sekt mit Bar (Basel, 2007, Seite 85) von Buchner Bründler war eine vorübergehende Einrichtung, die den ungewöhnlichen Übergang von einem Modegeschäft am Tag in eine Bar bei Nacht mithilfe von weißen Vorhängen möglich machte, welche die Kleider am Abend kaschierten. Obgleich sich diese Lösung leicht mit rein wirtschaftlichen Gründen erklären lässt, zeugt sie auch von unterschiedlichen Lebensformen, die nahelegen, dass Gestaltung extrem flexibel sein und sich sogar praktisch entgegengesetzten Nutzungen anpassen muss. Die von OlssonLyckefors gestalteten Peacock Clubs in Göteborg und Stockholm (2006 und 2007, Seiten 291 und 296) sind für einen fast nahtlosen Übergang vom Restaurant zum Nachtklub vorgesehen, wobei das Interieur mit geringem Aufwand in eine Tanzfläche verwandelt wird. Hier sind die Funktionen sicher enger verwandt als bei Set & Sekt, aber die Forderung nach konvertiblen Objekten veranlasst die Designer, ihre Aufmerksamkeit schon bei Beginn der Planung darauf zu richten, dass solche Räume sich in ständigem Wandel befinden. Obgleich die beiden Projekte nicht wirklich vergleichbar sind, wäre anzumerken, dass ein von Mies van der Rohe und Johnson 1959 geplantes Restaurant sich in 50 Jahren kaum von seiner ursprünglichen Form entfernt hat, während diese neuen Räume

23 + 24
Johnsen Schmaling Architects,
Cafe Luna + Bar
Milwaukee, Wisconsin, USA, 2007–08

23   24

sich einmal täglich verändern. Kann es sein, dass für Restaurants und Bars eine Zeit des Multitasking begonnen hat, so wie elektronische Geräte, z. B. Telefone, heute Filme zeigen, Karten erstellen und Musik spielen können? Wandelbarkeit liegt auch dem Konzept der ungewöhnlichen Neogama BBH Plug Bar (São Paulo, 2006, Seite 219) des begabten Architekten Marcio Kogan zugrunde, der sicher durch seine Wohnhäuser bekannter geworden ist. Der Empfangstisch dieser Werbeagentur mit seinen aufgereihten Flaschen mag Besuchern als ungewöhnlicher Reklametrick erscheinen, aber tatsächlich funktioniert die lange Theke, wenn der Zeitpunkt dafür gekommen ist, perfekt als Bar. Stärker als die Mischung aus Modegeschäft und Bar, zeigt dieser Gegensatz zwischen der seriösen Tätigkeit am Tag und nachts „einen draufmachen", dass Funktion manchmal nur eine Frage der Ausstattung oder der Fantasie des betreffenden Architekten oder Designers sein kann.

GESCHÖPFE DER MODE

Es ist klar, dass Restaurants und Bars in den meisten Fällen nicht den gleichen Regeln folgen wie die Architektur. Häufig, aber nicht immer, auf Innenräume beschränkt, müssen diese Einrichtungen nicht auf die Infrastruktur eines ganzen Gebäudes Rücksicht nehmen. Ein Lichteffekt, ein bedacht ausgewählter Stuhl und nicht zuletzt eine gute Mahlzeit können durchaus genügen, ein erfolgreiches Restaurant zu begründen. Es ist kein Zufall, dass Amerikaner und andere bei der Erwähnung von Restaurants vom „Erlebnis des Speisens" sprechen, gerade weil sie häufig eine Reise in Zeit und Raum sowie eine bestimmte Küche zu ihrem Daseinsgrund erklären. In einer Zeit des kosmopolitischen Reisens und der Verbreitung kultureller Einflüsse erstaunt es nicht, Sushi in einer Bar in Los Angeles zu finden, die an einen Pariser Flohmarkt erinnert. Ähnlich wie Modeboutiquen sind Restaurants und Bars Geschöpfe der Mode, die viel schneller kommen und gehen als das durchschnittliche 50-geschossige Hochhaus oder das Fußballstadion. Dies bedeutet natürlich, dass die Argumente und Methoden zur Ausstattung eines Restaurants oder einer Bar ganz andere sind als die zum Bau eines großen Gebäudes, selbst wenn sie von weltberühmten Architekten gestaltet werden. Als potenzielle Opfer der Mode können Restaurants und Bars jedoch sensiblere Barometer für den Geschmack und den Geist der Zeit darstellen als größere und teurere Bauausführungen. Multitasking – ob eine Verschiebung der Funktionen vom Tag zur Nacht oder vielleicht eine Andeutung von China und Frankreich zugleich – erscheint für neuere Lokale durchaus annehmbar. Unweigerlich beinhaltet diese Art des kulturellen oder funktionalen Sampling, das an Trends in der Popmusik erinnert, ein immer größeres Maß an Oberflächlichkeit. Aber es gibt keine strengen und festen Regeln. Die nahe Stuttgart sorgfältig geplante und ausgeführte Firmenkantine von Barkow Leibinger enthält ebensoviel Architektur wie jeder ältere Zweckbau, aber auch hier ist der Raum von Anfang an gleichermaßen für Versammlungen und Events vorgesehen. Flexibilität ist die Regel, wie tatsächlich auch schon seit einiger Zeit in der Architektur allgemein.

1990 organisierte der inzwischen verstorbene Kirk Varnedoe eine bemerkenswerte Ausstellung im New Yorker Museum of Modern Art mit dem Titel „High and Low: Modern Art and Popular Culture". Sie ging den Einflüssen nach, die zwischen populärer Kultur und ihren intellektuelleren Alternativen hin- und herschwankten. Könnten Bars und Restaurants den gewöhnlicheren Ausdruck der Architektur darstellen – einen Ort, wo Einflüsse und Kulturen in Räume einfließen, ohne den gegenwärtigen Stand der Dinge grundlegend zu verändern? Oder sind sie eher eine Art experimentelles Curry Lab in Tokio, eine Möglichkeit zum Blick auf den Zustand von morgen? Es scheint, als ob das Hin und Her

25

25
Barkow Leibinger Architekten,
Campus Restaurant
Ditzingen, Germany, 2006–08

zwischen der vom Internet beschleunigten Popkultur und der Hochkultur sich seit 1990 immer schneller vollzieht oder fließender geworden ist. Während das Four Seasons noch so aussieht wie 1959, wurde Windows on the World, eine scheinbar unverrückbare Einrichtung der New Yorker Szene, eines Morgens im Jahr 2001 in einem Augenblick in die Luft gesprengt, so wie das ganze große Gebäude, in dem es untergebracht war. Gewiss sind auf den Seiten dieses Buchs viele Trends künftiger „ernsthafter" Architektur zu sehen, ein unvollkommener Ausblick darauf, wie Bauten in einigen Jahren aussehen werden. Sofern es denn überhaupt jemals einen wirklich dominanten Stil in der Architektur gab, was seit den glorreichen Jahren des Internationalen Stils nicht mehr der Fall gewesen ist. Starcks humorvoller Eklektizismus z. B. wird und muss weiterexistieren, ebenso die Zen-Strenge von Kengo Kumas Architektur. Ein Alain-Ducasse-Restaurant hat kaum etwas mit einem Stand gemein, der gefrorenen Joghurt verkauft, und doch bieten beide Lokale etwas zum Essen an, und beide unterliegen verschiedenen Formen des modebestimmten Bedarfs. Das eine erfordert höhere Investitionen als das andere, das eine ist angeblich „ernsthafter" als das andere, aber es handelt sich um Varianten desselben Typs, einen ephemeren Ort, dessen Raum und Aufmachung davon bestimmt werden sollten, was der Philosoph George Santayana als „die merkwürdigsten Möglichkeiten" bezeichnete, „die sich zeitweise als Fakten verkleiden". Bars und Restaurants sind Theater mit Zuschauern, einer Bühne und einem Bereich hinter den Kulissen, z. B. der Küche. Sie bestehen aus beweglichen Dekors, die entsprechend den momentanen Bedürfnissen verschoben werden und deren Beleuchtung der Stimmung von Schauspielern und Zuschauern angepasst wird.

So funktional sie auch sein mögen, Bars und Restaurants, die nicht in einem eigenen Gebäude liegen, müssen nicht die gleichen Kriterien erfüllen wie Bauwerke. Sie sind Treffpunkte für verschiedene menschliche Bedürfnisse – zur Ernährung oder zur Gesellschaft. Sie sind Orte der Begegnung und Interaktion, und der Durchlauf der Gäste oder der Speisen und Getränke erzeugt eine eigene, wechselhafte Architektur. Wenn Architekten versuchen, ihre Bauten noch flexibler und weniger festgelegt zu gestalten, können Restaurants als Laboratorien dienen. Kleine Veränderungen können Räumen vielerlei Funktionen verleihen, während, ästhetisch betrachtet, viele verschiedene Lösungen jederzeit nebeneinander existieren können. Obgleich sie nicht immer den Kriterien entsprechen, um sie als Architektur zu bezeichnen, sind Restaurants und Bars wie der Schaum auf dem Meer der gebauten Umwelt. Sie bewegen und wandeln sich schneller als die aktiven Strömungen darunter; sie erfreuen uns mit ihrer Leichtigkeit und Farbe, die durchaus Vorboten von Veränderungen des Meers sein können.

Philip Jodidio, Doha, Katar, 23. November 2008

INTRODUCTION

COMME L'ÉCUME SUR LA MER

Qu'est-ce que l'architecture a à voir avec les bars et les restaurants ? La série *Architecture Now !* a présenté à de nombreuses reprises des réalisations dans ce domaine, mais l'impact de l'apparence peut laisser penser qu'elles sont plus proches, par leur essence même, de la décoration que de l'art de construire. Cet argument est parfaitement recevable et une grande partie de la séduction d'un superbe bar, par exemple, est plus liée à son aspect et à ce qui s'y passe qu'à l'acier, au verre et au béton. Néanmoins, certains espaces de ce type ont marqué l'inconscient collectif et formaté notre perception non seulement de ce que doit être une soirée agréable, mais aussi de la configuration de l'espace et du temps dans certaines conditions. Deux bars et restaurants new-yorkais peuvent être cités à cet égard. Le premier, incontournable, est le Four Seasons, situé 99 East 52nd Street dans le fameux immeuble Seagram. Les volumes et les aménagements intérieurs conçus par les architectes de cette tour, Ludwig Mies van der Rohe et Philip Johnson, sont restés pratiquement inchangés depuis l'ouverture en 1959, et la Commission pour la préservation des monuments de la ville de New York a d'ailleurs classé son décor intérieur en 1989. Bien qu'il bénéficie de vastes parois vitrées, le Four Seasons ne peut se flatter d'une vue sublime puisqu'il se trouve juste au-dessus du rez-de-chaussée donnant sur Park Avenue. On a pu louer ses qualités gastronomiques, mais ce n'est pas là la raison la plus distinctive de son succès. La salle à manger principale du Four Seasons est tout simplement l'un des plus beaux espaces intérieurs de l'architecture moderne, une quintessence du modernisme, non sans quelques aspirations vers cette grandeur classique qui échappe si souvent à des réalisations moins généreuses. Les grands et les puissants de New York et du monde entier sont passés par ici et toute une légende s'est construite autour. Choisi en 1958 pour y réaliser un cycle de peintures, l'artiste Mark Rothko s'était juré de produire « quelque chose qui coupera l'appétit des foutus fils de p… qui viendront s'asseoir dans cette salle », une menace qu'il ne mit jamais à exécution car les toiles ne furent jamais livrées. Néanmoins, cette histoire et l'immense tapisserie de Picasso suspendue entre le bar et la salle à manger ont contribué à faire de la réussite de ce restaurant plus qu'un feu de paille. Parce que les intérieurs de restaurants s'accordent rarement avec les bâtiments qui les accueillent, et parce que le Four Seasons est un exemple d'intégration harmonieuse entre la construction architecturale et le décor, ce restaurant est de fait un exemple de grande architecture.

Un second restaurant-bar, qui fut longtemps une icône new-yorkaise, n'existe malheureusement plus. Le Windows on the World, inauguré fin 1972, se trouvait aux 106e et 107e étages de l'une des tours du World Trade Center. Occupant un volume de 4600 m^2 aménagé par Warren Platner, il offrait une vue sur Manhattan qui enrichissait d'une dimension d'exception la qualité de son décor. Platner (1919–2006), architecte de formation, avait travaillé avec, entre autres, Raymond Loewy, I. M. Pei et Eero Saarinen. Il définissait la qualité de « classique » comme « une chose qui, chaque fois que vous la regardez, est acceptée telle qu'elle est, et que vous ne voyez aucun moyen d'améliorer ». Naturellement, l'anéantissement des tours jumelles du World Trade Center a apporté une teinte particulière à l'image de cet endroit qui dominait tout Manhattan. Bien que n'appartenant pas à la même catégorie de purisme moderniste que le Four Seasons, le Windows on the World illustre un autre aspect de la relation intime qui peut se créer entre un grand restaurant et une architecture. Une vue sur la ville, que ce soit Bangkok, Tokyo, Hongkong ou New York, peut arriver par elle seule à transformer un lieu un peu ordinaire en une célébration de l'architecture.

26 + 27
Jouin Manku, Le Jules Verne
Eiffel Tower, Paris, France, 2007

28 + 29
Tsao & McKown, SEVVA Restaurant
Hong Kong, China, 2007

26   27

De même, la lumière, les couleurs, les matériaux, le mobilier, voire la musique peuvent donner forme à un espace et créer ce que l'on peut considérer comme une expérience mémorable de l'architecture. Un restaurant ou un bar existent difficilement sans leurs clients ou la présence de la nourriture, même si ces lieux sont généralement photographiés totalement vides. Ce n'est pas seulement le chiffre d'affaires qui fait leur succès, mais aussi l'espace qui transcende l'instant ou peut-être l'absorbe totalement dans une expression vitaliste de l'architecture. Il s'agit ici d'architecture vivante.

CHAMBRE AVEC VUE

Une vue spectaculaire est une des principales attractions capables d'assurer le succès d'un restaurant ou d'un bar, que ce soit dans une de ces villes en développement accéléré de l'Orient ou dans une vieille cité occidentale. Le Jules Verne (Paris, France, 2007, page 210) signé par Patrick Jouin (Jouin Manku) est perché à 125 m dans les hauteurs de la mythique tour Eiffel. En un sens, l'inspiration de ce projet s'appuie autant sur les œuvres du célèbre écrivain français que sur ses vues incontournables et somptueuses sur la capitale française. Mais plutôt que par le panorama parisien, les visiteurs qui accèdent à ce restaurant sont accueillis par une vaste baie qui donne sur la cuisine. Ce restaurant Alain Ducasse qui compte une équipe de quarante-sept personnes offre ainsi d'emblée une perspective originale sur la qualité de sa cuisine. Jouin mixe des éléments aussi contemporains que les fauteuils en fibre de carbone de Pininfarina et sa vision personnelle romantique du goût des voyages et de l'aventure de Jules Verne qui nous entraîne loin du quotidien vers le centre de la Terre, le fond des mers ou même la Lune.

La Lune est justement le thème du Vertigo Grill and Moon Bar (Bangkok, Thaïlande, 2001, page 51), perché au sommet des soixante étages de la Thai Wah Tower 2 au centre de la capitale thaïlandaise. L'intervention d'Architrave, agence intégrée de la société Banyan Tree Hotels, a porté ici sur ce qui aurait dû être un hélipad au sommet de l'hôtel. La conception est au sens propre quasi vertigineuse, car seuls de minces rambardes métalliques séparent les hôtes d'une chute dans l'océan de lumières et d'activités urbaines que la tour domine. Une organisation de style militaire permet de faire rentrer les clients à l'intérieur en cas de précipitations, mais l'intérêt est néanmoins de réserver une table à l'extérieur, sous la Lune, au-dessus de cette capitale vibrante. Bien qu'il soit moins exposé aux éléments, le SEVVA (Hongkong, Chine, 2007, page 29) par Tsao & McKown pour Bonnie Gokson en plein centre de la ville offre également un panorama à 360° sur la grande métropole asiatique. Avec des vues exclusives sur la tour de la Hongkong and Shanghai Bank de Norman Foster toute proche, la relation entre ce restaurant et l'architecture devient l'occasion d'un échange entre intérieur et extérieur. La vue est indéniablement architecturale au meilleur sens du terme.

À Tokyo, comme on le voit dans les immeubles, entre autres, de Prada par Herzog & de Meuron, de Tod's par Toyo Ito ou Dior par SANAA, qui occupent des emplacements prestigieux dans les quartiers de Minami-Aoyama et Omotesando, la mode et l'architecture sont de plus en plus intimement liées. Non loin, de nouveaux venus dans Ginza combinent mode, architecture, restaurants et bars, comme la tour

28

29

Chanel où l'architecte star new-yorkais, Peter Marino, a créé un restaurant d'Alain Ducasse, Beige (Tokyo, Japon, 2002–04, page 17). Bien que la vue ne soit pas aussi époustouflante que celle du Jules Verne à Paris, Beige se trouve quand même à 56 m au-dessus d'une avenue et la plupart des clients sont plus que comblés par la vue qui s'offre à eux. La combinaison d'une élégance discrète et du sentiment de participer pleinement à l'esprit du temps et de la mode semble être une de ces expériences nouvelles essentielles que nous a apporté le XXIe siècle. Le talent évident de Marino, que l'on peut aussi constater dans le reste du bâtiment et de ses façades, assure un remarquable niveau de qualité d'architecture et de décor qui fait pendant à celui des produits Chanel.

Concurrent de Chanel, Giorgio Armani s'est également installé à Ginza avec l'aide de l'architecte italien Massimiliano Fuksas. L'Armani Ristorante (Tokyo, Japon, 2005–07, page 125) installé au 10e étage de la tour Armani Ginza se distingue par un motif de feuille de bambou stylisé qui fait lien entre la tradition japonaise et la modernité résolue d'Armani. L'Armani Privé, bar de quarante places, offre également des panoramas sur la ville et le quartier, et associe le dynamisme diurne et nocturne de la capitale nippone à la force de la mode et du design générée par les créations d'Armani et Fuksas. Le thème du bambou jette certainement des ponts avec la culture japonaise laquelle n'est pas toujours présente dans les autres temples de la mode de la même avenue ou du quartier en général. On peut noter d'ailleurs que des concepteurs japonais comme Issey Miyake se sont toujours davantage intéressés au cosmopolitisme qu'à l'évocation de thèmes spécifiquement nippons. Aujourd'hui, Tokyo est indiscutablement cosmopolite, et des restaurants comme Beige ou l'Armani se trouvent exactement dans l'esprit du temps.

CUISINE FUSION

La cuisine actuelle se livre à l'amalgame des plus surprenantes influences de l'Orient et de l'Occident. À la recherche de nouveaux accords, elle mélange activement des ingrédients et des saveurs venus aussi bien du Japon que du Chili. On pourrait faire le même commentaire sur l'architecture de beaucoup de restaurants récents, qui s'est tournée elle aussi avec enthousiasme vers la fusion. Imaginez un restaurant conçu pour ressembler à la demeure d'un collectionneur d'antiquités françaises et chinoises, mélangez le tout dans un ancien entrepôt du quartier du Meatpacking à Manhattan et voilà le Buddakan (Christian Liaigre avec Gilles & Boissier, New York, États-Unis, 2006). La salle à manger souterraine, faisant davantage penser à la salle de banquet d'une *country house* anglaise qu'à la France ou à la Chine, symbolise ce restaurant aussi spectaculaire que ses fresques murales chinoises. Ajoutez une cuisine qui mixe ingrédients européens, asiatiques et américains, et les frontières culturelles semblent s'évanouir.

Les mêmes architectes (Gilles & Boissier) ont également à leur actif les restaurants Shanghai Lan (Shanghaï, Chine, 2008, page 137) qui occupent un bâtiment de quatre niveaux près du Bund. Les éléments français et chinois sont ici juxtaposés aux différents étages, le niveau supérieur et ses lustres de Baccarat exsudant un je-ne-sais-quoi de l'esprit français. La France était certes présente dans cette ville à l'époque des concessions, mais ici le passé et le présent se mélangent comme le font aujourd'hui les cultures des deux extrémités du monde.

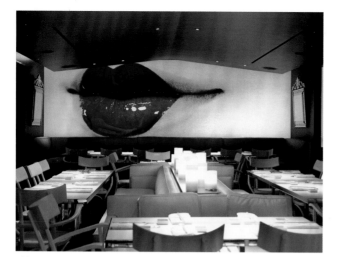

30

30
Philippe Starck, Katsuya Hollywood
Los Angeles, California, USA, 2007

31
Office dA, Banq
Boston, Massachusetts, USA,
2006–08

Philippe Starck, qui s'est souvent laissé aller à l'humour et au goût de la surprise, vient d'achever le S Bar au carrefour de Hollywood Boulevard et de Vine Street à Los Angeles (États-Unis, 2007, page 363). Voulant évoquer « le style urbain et éclectique d'un entrepôt de galerie d'art » ce bar est décoré de photographies grand format de Versailles et développe un style « marché aux puces » qui mélange sièges et tables d'origines diverses, et lampes suspendues par les pieds au plafond. On pourrait penser que Versailles et les marchés aux puces français ont bien peu de rapports avec Hollywood, mais là encore, tout réside dans l'apparence d'un décor censé plonger les hôtes dans un univers différent et pour lesquels la cuisine dispensée n'est qu'un des aspects de l'expérience. Un lieu conçu par Starck se veut innovant et amusant. Ici, la France et la Californie se rencontrent dans un *melting pot* culturel. Cette modernité ne s'intéresse plus au minimalisme ni au vide, mais au débordement de références et d'objets venus d'univers variés.

Le Blits à Rotterdam (Pays-Bas, 2005, page 9), dû au célèbre designer néerlandais Marcel Wanders, dispense lui aussi un mix de cuisines, notamment japonaise, latino-américaine et méditerranéenne, mais sa fusion va beaucoup plus loin encore. Wanders a voulu « un restaurant comme un théâtre », avec une scène de spectacles et une table « pour amoureux » pour deux avec fenêtre en forme de cœur. Mélangez, assortissez : ici le design ne s'arrête pas aux plats et aux boissons.

LE PARADIS ICI ET MAINTENANT

Toute étude un peu sérieuse sur les restaurants et bars contemporains se doit d'inclure certains d'entre eux récemment ouverts dans des paradis tropicaux, au bord d'une plage de sable blanc, sous un palmier et face à une mer turquoise. Malheureusement, le souci de la qualité de l'architecture et du design échappe à un grand nombre de réalisations dans ces lieux paradisiaques. Le travail de Bel Lobo au Brésil fait peut-être exception à la règle. Son restaurant Quadrucci (Búzios, Rio de Janeiro, Brésil, 2008, page 73) est situé sur une mangrove, à 180 km à l'est de Rio. Par son souci de préserver les arbres existants, son recours à certains éléments comme la toiture en bois et l'utilisation de matériaux de production locale, ce restaurant est admirablement « écologique ». Bien qu'il puisse sembler de plan assez simple, il réussit à générer la « magie » dont parle son architecte. Par ses transparences et ses jeux de reflets, il met à profit la lumière et l'air ambiants ainsi que la végétation. Dans le secteur des restaurants, l'artificiel règne souvent en maître, or on remarque ici un goût du naturel et un certain talent à introduire la nature qui font du Quadrucci une œuvre architecturale étonnante. Ceux qui connaissent les villes brésiliennes n'y trouvent pas toujours les connotations paradisiaques qu'évoque généralement le nom d'Ipanema. D'une extraordinaire beauté naturelle, Ipanema n'est en revanche pas très sûr, mais c'est là que Bel Lobo a dessiné un restaurant simple et assez naturel, le Stravaganze (Ipanema, Rio de Janeiro, Brésil, 2004–05, page 19), non loin de la célèbre plage. Il s'agit davantage d'une création urbaine aménagée dans une maison ancienne que d'un restaurant de plage, mais toute la puissance de la nature brésilienne anime le travail de cette architecte, même lorsqu'elle dresse « un faux arbre sculpté fait de métal et de lampes de couleur » sur un mur. Si Ipanema a pu représenter jadis une vision du paradis, ce restaurant annonce peut-être une première tentative vers la reconquête de son extravagante beauté.

31

L'architecte Ed Tuttle, qui a travaillé sur un grand nombre d'hôtels, de restaurants et de complexes de vacances, pour Amanresorts entre autres, n'a pas souhaité voir ses réalisations récentes publiées dans ce livre en partie parce qu'il est débordé au point de ne plus pouvoir accepter de nouvelle charge de travail. Né aux États-Unis où il a grandi, Tuttle a créé son agence parisienne Design Realization en 1977 en association avec Christian Monge. Il dessine certains meubles et accessoires de ses projets et insiste sur le respect des cultures locales et l'impact écologique de ses remarquables *resorts*. Il a récemment ajouté à son Amanpuri Resort (1988), sur la côte ouest de l'île de Phuket en Thaïlande, le Puri Beach Club et le restaurant japonais Puri Naoki. Si l'architecture japonaise y est suggérée, la modernité des espaces et des objets ainsi que le sentiment d'ouverture s'imposent nettement. Ed Tuttle montre qu'il est entièrement possible de concilier les attentes d'un groupe d'hôtels sophistiqués avec un site naturel sensible et les contraintes encore plus complexes de l'architecture et du design de qualité.

ARTS AND CRAFTS

Si le caractère naturel du lien qui semble exister entre architecture, design et cuisine fait souvent le succès des meilleurs restaurants, certain choisissent d'enrichir cette recette d'un autre ingrédient, l'art contemporain. Le célèbre Pharmacy de Londres, né des cerveaux de l'artiste Damien Hirst et du designer Mike Rundell (1997), a prouvé que l'art contemporain pouvait s'inviter avec succès à la table de la gastronomie, même si ce lieu a désormais fermé ses portes. Karriere (Copenhague, Danemark, 2007, page 177), dirigé par l'artiste Jeppe Hein et sa sœur Lærke est une autre tentative de réunir art et, dans ce cas précis, bar. Hein ne s'est pas lancé dans ce projet en aveugle. S'appuyant sur son excellente connaissance de l'art contemporain d'avant-garde, il a convaincu les artistes Dan Graham, Olafur Eliasson, Ernesto Neto, Elmgreen & Dragset, Rirkrit Tiravanija, Maurizio Cattelan et Douglas Gordon de participer à cette aventure. Complété par un site web très actif et une lettre d'information, Karriere a pour objectif affiché de faire revivre la tradition des lieux à prédominance culturelle qui ont notamment joué un rôle actif dans la puissance d'attraction de Paris, capitale de l'art moderne dans la première moitié du XXe siècle. Jeppe Hein démontre également sa volonté de prouver que l'art peut faire partie de la vie quotidienne.

Pendant que Damien Hirst faisait de son œuvre le centre d'attraction et le thème du Pharmacy, une intervention très différente et plus privée pour le bar d'un club londonien montrait que ce type d'interaction entre art, design et architecture se portait à merveille. Dans ses participations aux récentes Biennales de Venise, Zaha Hadid franchit à chaque fois les frontières entre ces trois formes d'expression. Son bar pour Home House (Londres, Angleterre, 2007–08, page 171) a été conçu à l'aide des toutes dernières techniques de CAO et d'usinage à pilotage numérique. En résine, fibre de verre et tissu, il entre en interaction avec « l'ordre orthogonal qui caractérise son enveloppe de style géorgien » et redéfinit l'espace en posant des questions très concrètes sur les relations entre la création artistique, architecturale et le design, ou sur les définitions mêmes de l'espace et de la fonction.

32 + 33
*Pacific Environments, Yellow Tree House
Hokianga Harbour, Northland, New Zealand, 2008*

34 + 35
*Zaha Hadid, Home House
London, UK, 2007–08*

32   33

CHIC ET DISCRET

Si des designers comme Philippe Starck paraissent s'engager de plus en plus loin sur la voie d'un mélange baroque de style et de types d'objets, d'autres sont restés fidèles – pour des raisons diverses – à leur goût personnel pour la discrétion. Ainsi est-ce sans surprise que le restaurant Sakenohana par Kengo Kuma (Londres, Angleterre, 2007, page 223) cultive à la fois un vocabulaire franchement japonais et les valeurs de la discrétion. L'architecte a d'ailleurs déclaré que son client avait rejeté le principe de toute solution « chic à la mode » et savait qu'avec lui ce risque était réduit. Néanmoins, l'ossature traditionnelle japonaise en bois utilisée pour le plafond ou les écrans de bambou ne sont certainement pas les réponses que l'on pouvait attendre, même pour les connaisseurs du Japon. Kuma a trouvé sa propre voie entre les exigences de la modernité et le respect de la tradition. Son restaurant est une expression pleine et entière de cette synthèse, même s'il n'est pas à l'origine du bâtiment lui-même.

S'intéressant aux mêmes enjeux mais d'un point de vue presque opposé, Stephanie Goto, qui avait déjà collaboré avec Tadao Ando pour son restaurant morimoto nyc dans le quartier du Meatpacking à New York (2005–06, page 10), a cherché à recréer l'atmosphère d'un hôtel particulier parisien dans son récent restaurant Corton (New York, États-Unis, 2007–08, page 147). Le plâtre blanc travaillé de ses murs est certainement plus discret que les dorures parfois surabondantes des élégantes demeures françaises. Bien que les aménagements aient été achevés avant le début de la crise financière, cette approche subtile semble plus appropriée aux temps à venir qu'aux années d'effusion économique qui viennent de prendre fin. Le design et le style connaissent eux aussi des évolutions cycliques, entre le minimal et l'excessif, qui sont généralement provoquées par des facteurs extérieurs auxquels appartient évidemment l'économie. On peut parier que 2009 et 2010 verront moins d'inaugurations d'établissements de restauration que les années précédentes et que ceux qui réussiront à ouvrir seront aussi discrets, et néanmoins stylés, que leurs créateurs auront pu le vouloir, du moins dans le segment supérieur de ce type de lieux, qui est l'objet de cet ouvrage. Il est vrai aussi que certaines cultures, comme celle du Japon par exemple, possèdent sans doute cette discrétion inscrite dans leurs gènes, mais l'évidence de la nature cyclique des mouvements stylistiques s'impose.

Le restaurant londonien Mocotó (Angleterre, 2006–07, page 387) par Isay Weinfeld n'a rien de japonais certes, ne serait-ce que parce que son architecte est d'origine brésilienne, mais une simplicité presque extrême règne dans ces vastes volumes aérés. Il est intéressant de noter qu'elle n'est pratiquement pas remarquée par la clientèle tant ce *good design* semble parfois s'effacer dans les détails et un décor particulièrement réussis. L'esprit de ce restaurant, qui a fermé depuis, était quasi diamétralement opposé à celui des divers établissement *bling-bling* que l'on pourrait associer aux « années folles » du début du XXIe siècle.

Deux restaurants de ton assez différent mais signés de la même architecte, Ilse Crawford de Studioilse, ont été réalisés pour le Grand Hotel à Stockholm (Suède, 2007). Le Matsalen et le Matbaren, animés par le chef Mathias Dahlgren, sont de style résolument scandinave, le premier dans une approche plus luxueuse. L'idée de Crawford de mélanger des luminaires de Carlo Scarpa à des « lampes de cuisine sué-

doise classiques » signale un goût éclectique qui crée néanmoins une atmosphère raffinée et retenue qui, redisons-le, va dans le sens de nouvelles tendances à la discrétion plutôt qu'aux paillettes.

LE BRUT ET LE VRAI

L'opposé du chic et de la discrétion pourrait bien être le brut et le vrai. La réutilisation d'anciens lieux, souvent d'origine industrielle comme les entrepôts, pour aménager des restaurants ou des bars est une recette abondamment utilisée avec succès. La plupart de ceux qui ont ouvert dans le Meatpacking District de Manhattan, dont certains ont été mentionnés plus haut, s'appuient sur une architecture industrielle existante du début du XXe siècle pour créer un décor nettement plus contemporain. L'approche peut varier bien sûr. Dans le cas du restaurant Amorio (Bellavista, Santiago, Chili, 2005–06, page 377), les frères Tidy, architectes, s'étaient vu demander par leur client de conserver l'atmosphère « bohème » des façades, mais de réinventer complètement l'intérieur. Malgré la peinture blanche du rez-de-chaussée et le puissant système d'éclairage installé, cette façade de brique, légèrement délabrée, n'est pas sans une sorte de chic.

L'architecte australienne Cate Young a installé son Water Bar dans un immeuble classé du Finger Wharf à Woolloomooloo Bay à Sydney (Australie, 2007, page 407). Elle a bénéficié de l'un des éléments les plus appréciés des volumes industriels, l'espace. Le plafond grimpe à 13 m de haut et la plupart des éléments de construction originaux ont été conservés. Cate Young décrit sa réaction à ce volume en termes de proximité de l'océan, mais aussi de relation avec l'histoire du pays : « C'était un des points de débarquement des nouveaux immigrants arrivant en Australie ou d'escale pour les paquebots de luxe de millionaires ou membres de la haute société. L'endroit a été témoin de conflits industriels, de manifestations contre les dévoiements de l'urbanisme, et de crimes. Maintenant il est considéré comme l'un des quartiers les plus recherchés de Sydney, aussi bien pour y habiter que pour sortir… Mais toutes les strates de cette histoire, tout ce passé, intelligemment conservés à Finger Wharf dans l'ossature de ce bâtiment et les recoins de sa charpente massive, sont liés par un élément commun : l'eau. » Le classement du bâtiment a certainement encouragé ce type de réflexion, mais Cate Young ne se réfère pas ici à un bar hâtivement rénové. Elle explique une réaction d'architecte devant un lieu fondamentalement riche de sens, qui possède une histoire et une présence, et qui peut poursuivre son existence grâce à ses efforts.

MODERNE DANS TOUS SES ÉTATS

Si des lieux comme le Four Seasons à New York sont difficiles à égaler, certains restaurants ou bars ont pris une valeur iconique pour des raisons tenant à leur histoire récente ou à l'étonnement qu'ils ont provoqué. L'architecte britannique Richard Rogers a participé à la création de deux restaurants de ce type. Le premier a ouvert ses portes en 1987 près du Thames Wharf à Hammersmith, non loin des bureaux de Richard Rogers Partnership. Ce River Café a longtemps été une célèbre adresse londonienne pour son agréable situation dans un cadre de verdure en bordure du fleuve, mais aussi parce qu'un grand architecte et un chef réputé avaient su joindre leurs efforts pour créer un lieu dans lequel architecture, design et cuisine atteignaient en chœur un niveau particulièrement élevé. Début 2008, un incendie a entraîné une

36
Isay Weinfeld, Mocotó Bar and
Restaurant
London, UK, 2006–07

37
Cate Young, Water Bar
Sydney, Australia, 2007

36

rénovation substantielle (Londres, Angleterre, page 121), tâche confiée à Stuart Forbes, collaborateur de longue date de Rogers qui avait travaillé sur des projets comme les terminaux 1 et 5 de Heathrow ou le Dôme du Millénaire. Une cuisine ouverte et une vaste cheminée ronde à feu de bois rapprochent ainsi le travail de préparation des mets de leurs consommateurs, sans rien sacrifier du mythe qui a rendu cet endroit célèbre. Signalant sa participation à cette rénovation, Richard Rogers a déclaré : « Stuart et moi avons pris le parti de changements clairs mais subtils. Nous avons significativement remodelé le River Café en respectant son identité visuelle et en conservant l'élégance de son origine. »

Un second restaurant, installé à Barcelone cette fois, porte lui aussi la marque de Rogers. Il se trouve dans un lieu nettement plus perché, ou exposé. L'Evo (Espagne, 2005–06, page 131) se trouve à 105 m au-dessus de l'entrée de la tour Hesperia. Rogers et son agence Rogers Stirk Harbour (avec Alonso & Balaguer) ont créé la structure en forme de soucoupe volante dans lequel est logé l'Evo, mais l'aménagement intérieur a été confié à l'agence barcelonaise GCA. La réponse de cette équipe à la « forme architectonique spectaculaire » a été d'ajouter des plates-formes circulaires pour résoudre certains problèmes de circulation et harmoniser leur intervention avec le style du célèbre chef Santi Santamaria.

Les architectes Regine Leibinger et Frank Barkow (agence Barkow Leibinger Architekten) ont pris en charge la tâche pas toujours gratifiante de créer un restaurant d'entreprise pour la société Trumpf, implantée non loin de Stuttgart (Ditzingen, Allemagne, 2006–08, page 67). La qualité de ce restaurant de sept cents places dépasse celle de nombreux établissements conçus pourtant avec soin. À de nombreux égards, il est peut-être plus proche d'une architecture pure que la plupart des restaurants publiés dans ce livre. Travaillant avec le célèbre ingénieur Werner Sobek, les architectes ont fixé un élément en porte-à-faux au-dessus d'un groupe de colonnes pour évoquer un « auvent polygonal en forme de feuille ». Très ouverts, les espaces intérieurs évoquent des structures d'entrepôt moins élaborées. Barkow Leibinger a appliqué une logique industrielle à cette installation de haute qualité qui fonctionne admirablement bien, que ce soit comme salle à manger ou salle de réunions. À ceux qui s'interrogeraient sur l'intérêt de faire appel à de célèbres architectes et ingénieurs pour un projet aussi fonctionnel, la réponse est donnée par l'inventivité et la générosité de ses espaces.

Opérant dans un environnement plus commercial, les architectes Guedes + DeCampos ont également fait appel à la solution du métal déployé en nid-d'abeilles pour créer la structure de base de leur bar restaurant Ar de Rio (Vila Nova de Gaia, Portugal, 2008, page 165). Comme chez Barkow Leibinger, ce projet montre comment la technologie permet d'étirer et de suspendre des matériaux de façon spectaculaire et offre de nouvelles possibilités d'architecture et de design à des lieux comme les restaurants et les bars. Plus précisément dans ces deux cas, l'intervention architecturale définit ou même donne forme à l'espace du restaurant, l'inonde de lumière, crée une impression de modernité qui se confirme au fur et à mesure que l'on se déplace de l'extérieur vers l'intérieur.

37

Les architectes parisiens Jakob+MacFarlane avaient été à l'origine de la conception de l'un des restaurants les plus iconiques et les plus à la mode de la capitale, le Georges, installé tout en haut du Centre Pompidou (2000). À l'aide de techniques de CAO, les deux architectes s'étaient appuyés sur la trame d'origine du bâtiment dessiné par Piano et Rogers en 1977. En imaginant la déformation et l'étirement de cette trame, ils avaient créé des extrusions contenant une salle à manger privée, les vestiaires et les toilettes. C'est ce dernier espace que les architectes ont récemment retravaillé (2006, page 189) à la demande des propriétaires des lieux, la famille Costes. À la place des toilettes, le volume contient maintenant le Pink Bar, et, au lieu de déformer ou d'extruder la trame ancienne, Jakob et MacFarlane ont imaginé de le sculpter dans une matrice en 3D. Huit ans après leur réussite initiale, les deux architectes montrent que leur projet autorisait une grande flexibilité et ont pu faire de ce « bar rose » un endroit on ne peut plus actuel.

Si l'on peut accorder un certain humour aux formes bulbeuses du Pink Bar et du Georges, ces derniers n'en répondent pas moins aux critères d'efficacité fonctionnelle que les Frères Costes attendent de leurs établissements parisiens et que visent tous les propriétaires de bars et de restaurants de par le monde. Le Tokyo Curry Lab (Tokyo, Japon, 2007, page 393) par Wonderwall témoigne d'un degré d'humour similaire mélangé à une rigueur de conception et d'efficacité sans concession. Composé d'un bar ouvert devant une unique et vaste table ovale, dont il est séparé par des ampoules de verre de couleur remplies d'épices, le Tokyo Curry Lab est animé par des œuvres graphiques représentant des porcs et des poulets à la poursuite d'une saucière stylisée. Ni minimaliste ni baroque, ce projet est confortablement installé dans un autre registre de la modernité qui transgresse les types de bâti et de conception, combinant un comptoir ouvert et une salle à manger fermée, et faisant appel à un vocabulaire de laboratoire scientifique. Une solution qui ne manque pas d'épices…

DUOS DYNAMIQUES

Certains des concepts les plus surprenants utilisés dans la conception de restaurants et de bars reposent sur la double fonction des lieux, qui varie selon les heures. L'un d'entre eux, le magasin et bar Set & Sekt (Bâle, Suisse, 2007, page 85), signé par l'agence Buchner Bründler Architekten était une installation temporaire qui transformait la nuit une boutique de mode en bar, grâce à un système de rideaux blancs masquant les vêtements le soir tombé. Si cette solution peut se justifier par des raisons purement économiques, elle exprime également une façon de vivre différente qui conditionne un design extrêmement souple, quitte à faire cohabiter des usages diamétralement opposés. Les Peacock Clubs de Göteborg et de Stockholm (Suède, 2006 et 2007, pages 291 et 296), conçus par OlssonLyckefors, facilitent ainsi une transition pratiquement sans rupture entre le restaurant et le night-club, transformant le mobilier en piste de danse grâce à une intervention minimale. Ces fonctions sont plus proches l'une de l'autre que celles de Set & Sekt, mais la nécessité de concevoir des objets convertibles a focalisé, dès le départ, l'attention des concepteurs sur ces espaces en mouvement constant. Bien que ces deux initiatives ne soient pas strictement comparables, on peut se rappeler que le Four Seasons new-yorkais conçu par Mies van der Rohe et Johnson en 1959 n'a pratiquement pas changé de configuration en cinquante ans, alors que ces deux lieux nouveaux modifient la leur une fois par jour. Il est possible que les restaurants et les bars s'orientent vers ce concept de multifonction, de même que les téléphones permettent de regarder des

38
Stuart Forbes, River Café
London, UK, 2008

films, étudier une carte ou jouer de la musique. La convertibilité est également le concept du très curieux Neogama BBH Plug Bar (São Paulo, Brésil, 2006, page 219) signé du très talentueux architecte Marcio Kogan, davantage connu pour ses résidences privées. Avec ses alignements de bouteilles, la banque d'accueil de cette agence de publicité pourrait passer pour une fantaisie de publicitaires, mais en fait, ce long comptoir arrive à se transformer en un bar parfait le moment venu. Plus encore que l'association de boutique de mode et de bar, cette juxtaposition de travail sérieux le jour et de possibilité d'y prendre un verre le soir montre que la fonction peut n'être rien de plus qu'un problème d'apparence ou d'inventivité de l'architecte ou du designer.

CRÉATURES DE LA MODE

Il est clair que dans la plupart des cas, les restaurants et les bars n'obéissent pas aux mêmes règles que l'architecture. Souvent, sans se limiter pour autant à l'espace intérieur, ces entreprises n'ont pas à prendre en compte les lourdes infrastructures de l'immeuble. Un effet d'éclairage, un siège bien choisi et bien sûr un bon repas peuvent suffire à créer un restaurant qui marche bien. Ce n'est pas par hasard si les Américains entre autres parlent de *« dining experience »* – l'expérience du moment du repas – lorsqu'ils se réfèrent à des restaurants qui proposent autant un voyage dans l'espace et le temps qu'une carte qui est leur première raison d'être. À une époque cosmopolite de voyages et de dispersion des influences culturelles, il n'est pas surprenant de trouver un bar à sushis à Los Angeles qui évoque un marché aux puces parisien. Presqu'autant que les boutiques de vêtements, les restaurants et les bars sont des créatures de la mode, qui apparaissent ou disparaissent beaucoup plus vite qu'une tour de cinquante étages ou un stade de football. Concrètement, ceci signifie que la réflexion et les méthodes utilisées pour réaliser ce type de lieu sont assez différentes de celles mises en œuvre pour un grand bâtiment, même dans le cas d'interventions d'architectes de réputation internationale. Victimes potentielles de la mode, les restaurants et les bars sont peut-être aujourd'hui des baromètres du goût et de l'esprit du temps, plus sensibles que certaines réalisations beaucoup plus coûteuses. Le concept de multitâches – changement de fonction entre le jour et la nuit – ou peut-être l'évocation simultanée d'un peu de Chine et d'un soupçon de France semble être l'idée à la mode. Inévitablement, ce type de *sampling* culturel ou fonctionnel, qui rappelle certaines tendances de la musique populaire, penche de plus en plus vers le superficiel. Mais il n'y a pas de règles. La cafétéria d'entreprise réalisée près de Stuttgart par Barkow Leibinger possède un contenu architectural aussi intéressant que n'importe quel espace fonctionnel construit auparavant, mais là aussi, elle a été conçue dès le départ pour s'adapter à des réunions ou d'autres types d'événements. La souplesse est de règle, ce qui est le cas de l'architecture en général depuis un certain temps.

En 1990, feu Kirk Varnedoe avait organisé une exposition marquante au Museum of Modern Art de New York intitulée « High and Low : Modern Art and Popular Culture » (Le haut et le bas : l'art moderne et la culture populaire), retraçant les influences qui vibrent en tous sens entre ces cultures. Les restaurants et les bars seraient-ils l'expression « populaire » de l'architecture, un lieu dans lequel les influences et les cultures pourraient survoler l'espace sans fondamentalement changer la forme du temps ? Ou sont-ils plutôt une sorte d'expérimentation à la Tokyo Curry Lab, une façon de jeter un œil sur la forme qu'il pourrait prendre demain. Depuis 1990, il semble que le mouvement d'avancée et

39
Marcio Kogan, Neogama BBH Plug Bar
São Paulo, Brazil, 2006

39

de recul entre les expressions d'une culture populaire propulsée par l'Internet et la haute culture se soit accéléré ou fluidifié. Alors que le Four Seasons est resté tel qu'il était en 1959, Windows on the World, qui pouvait sembler un monument de la scène new-yorkaise tout aussi inamovible, a disparu par un matin de 2001, emporté avec la tour sur laquelle il s'était perché. Il est certain que de nombreuses tendances de l'architecture « sérieuse » du futur sont représentées dans les pages qui suivent, prémonition imparfaite de ce que nous réserve l'avenir du bâti dans les années à venir. Il n'existe plus de style dominant en architecture depuis les glorieuses années du Style international. L'éclectisme humoristique de Starck continuera à exister, et à coexister avec la rigueur zen d'un Kengo Kuma, par exemple. Un restaurant d'Alain Ducasse n'a pas grand-chose à voir avec une baraque à frites, et pourtant, tous deux proposent de la nourriture, et tous deux sont soumis à différentes formes d'attente que la mode a orientées. L'un demande plus d'investissement que l'autre, l'un est supposé plus « sérieux » que l'autre, mais tous deux sont des variantes d'un même type, des lieux éphémères dont l'espace et l'aspect peuvent être mis en forme par ce que le philosophe George Santayana appelait « la plus étrange des possibilités se déguisant momentanément en fait ». Les bars et les restaurants sont des théâtres, avec leur public, leur scène et leurs coulisses, dont relève la cuisine. Ils sont faits de décors mobiles, évoluant selon les besoins du moment, leur éclairage réglé en fonction de l'humeur des acteurs ou des spectateurs.

Aussi fonctionnels puissent-ils être, les restaurants et les bars qui ne sont pas autonomes n'ont pas à se soumettre aux mêmes critères que les bâtiments. Ce sont des points de rencontre répondant à divers besoins humains, pour se nourrir ou échanger. Ce sont des lieux où l'interaction et le flux des clients, des plats et des boissons forment en soi une architecture animée. À un moment où les architectes cherchent toujours plus de souplesse dans leurs projets, en s'éloignant toujours plus des critères imposés par la mode, les restaurants et bars peuvent servir de laboratoires. De petits changements permettent à un espace de remplir de multiples fonctions tandis que, esthétiquement parlant, de nombreuses solutions différentes peuvent coexister en un lieu et moment donnés. Bien qu'ils ne correspondent pas en tout point à la définition d'une œuvre architecturale, les restaurants et les bars sont comme l'écume des vagues d'un océan, celui de notre environnement construit. Ils se déplacent et changent plus vite que les grands courants. Ils apportent une légèreté et une couleur qui pourraient bien présager des changements qui affecteront la mer tout entière.

Philip Jodidio, Doha, Qatar, 23 novembre 2008

3DELUXE-BIORHYTHM

3deluxe-biorhythm
Zehdenicker Str. 1
10119 Berlin
Germany

Tel: +49 30 24 34 27 91
Fax: +49 30 24 34 27 95
E-mail: biorhythm@3deluxe.de
Web: www.3deluxe-biorhythm.de

Nik Schweiger was born in 1965 in Freiburg. He worked as a craftsman in bars and fashion stores, before studying interior design and working in the offices of Philippe Starck in Paris and Matteo Thun in Milan. With the communication designers Andreas and Stephan Lauhoff and the designer Dieter Brell, in 1992, he created 3deluxe, a team of people from the fields of architecture, interior design, art, graphic design, media, and product design. Schweiger went on to create **3DELUXE-BIORHYTHM** in 2005 in Berlin, "as a vehicle for holistic projects that strike a balance between real and virtual spatial considerations, as well as those concerned with the community as a whole. These state-of-the-art endeavors are intended to appeal as much to the physical senses as they do to the intellect," according to Schweiger. Nik Schweiger and 3deluxe collaborated on the Leonardo Glass Cube (Bad Driburg, 2007).

Nik Schweiger wurde 1965 in Freiburg geboren. Er war als Handwerker in Bars und Modegeschäften tätig, studierte dann Innenarchitektur und arbeitete in den Büros von Philippe Starck in Paris und Matteo Thun in Mailand. Zusammen mit den Kommunikationsdesignern Andreas und Stephan Lauhoff und dem Designer Dieter Brell entstand 1992 3deluxe, ein Team von Architekten, Innenarchitekten, Künstlern, Grafikern, Medien- und Produktdesignern. 2005 gründete Schweiger in Berlin **3DELUXE-BIORHYTHM**, „zur Förderung holistischer Projekte, die einen Ausgleich schaffen zwischen realen und virtuellen Raumverhältnissen sowie solchen, die sich mit der Gemeinschaft als Ganzes befassen. Diese aktuellen Arbeiten sollen die Sinne wie den Intellekt gleichermaßen ansprechen", wie er schreibt. Schweiger und 3deluxe gestalteten gemeinsam den Glass Cube von Leonardo (Bad Driburg, 2007).

Nik Schweiger, né en 1965 à Freiburg, est d'abord intervenu comme artisan sur des projets de bars et des magasins de mode avant d'étudier l'architecture intérieure. Il a ensuite travaillé chez Philippe Starck à Paris et chez Matteo Thun à Milan. C'est avec les designers de communication Andreas et Stephan Lauhoff et le designer Dieter Brell qu'il a créé 3deluxe, agence composée de collaborateurs venus des domaines de l'architecture, architecture intérieure, art, design graphique, médias et design produit en 1992. Schweiger a ensuite créé **3DELUXE-BIORHYTHM** à Berlin en 2005, « véhicule de projets holistiques qui recherchent l'équilibre entre des considérations spatiales réelles et virtuelles, et d'autres concernant la communauté sociale dans son ensemble. » Selon sa présentation, « ces actions d'avant-garde veulent s'adresser autant aux sens qu'à l'intellect ». Nik Schweiger et 3deluxe ont collaboré au projet du Cube de verre Leonardo (Bad Driburg, 2007).

AU QUAI

Club La Nuit, Hamburg, Germany, 2007

Große Elbstr. 145 b-d, 22767 Hamburg, Germany, +49 40 38 03 77 30, www.au-quai.com
Area: 330 m². Client: Sylviane and Enzo Caressa. Cost: not disclosed

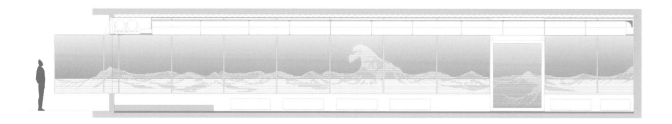

The brother and sister team, Sylviane and Enzo Caressa, opened La Nuit in October 2007. As their own publicity says: "These two combine French culture of style, the creative force of Italy, and the open-hearted spirit of the Mediterranean world with Hamburg's Hanseatic rigor." Collaborating with the Paris film team Moving Design, Philipp Walter and 3deluxe-biorhythm sought an interdisciplinary approach from the outset. Furnishings in Corian and teak in a white ambiance were selected to evoke the "atmosphere of a yacht by the water." An abstracted wave form runs along the wall to the dance floor and across the windows facing the port of Hamburg. Back-lit 3D computer-programmed lighting fixtures, complemented by organically shaped vases lit from the interior, give an impression of continual movement to the space. The films made by Moving Design are projected on a 16-meter span of the windows between the club and restaurant. This projection is clearly intended to interact with the graphic effects generated by the wave patterns in the design, again emphasizing the kind of movement one might well expect of a trend-setting club located in a port area. The interdisciplinary aspect of the work of 3deluxe is readily apparent in this combination of design, graphics, lighting, and film, as is the specificity of 3deluxe-biorhythm, the effort to seek "a balance between real and virtual spatial considerations."

Die Geschwister Sylviane und Enzo Caressa eröffneten La Nuit im Oktober 2007. In der Werbung heißt es: „Diese beiden verbinden französisches Stilgefühl, die Kreativität Italiens und das offene Gemüt der Mittelmeervölker mit Hamburgs hanseatischer Strenge." In Zusammenarbeit mit dem Pariser Filmteam Moving Design suchten Philipp Walter und 3deluxe-biorhythm von Anfang an nach einer interdisziplinären Lösung. Möbel aus Corian und Teak in einem weißen Ambiente wurden gewählt, um „die Atmosphäre einer Jacht am Wasser" zu beschwören. Ein abstrahiertes Wellenmuster läuft entlang der Wand zur Tanzfläche und über die Fenster, die zum Hamburger Hafen orientiert sind. Hinterleuchtete, dreidimensionale, computerprogrammierte Beleuchtungskörper, ergänzt durch organisch geformte, von innen beleuchtete Vasen vermitteln den Eindruck ständiger Bewegung. Die Filme von Moving Design werden auf eine 16 m breite Fensterfläche zwischen dem Klub und dem Restaurant projiziert. Diese Projektion soll bewusst in Interaktion mit den grafischen Effekten treten, die das Wellenmuster erzeugt. Dadurch wird wiederum eine Form der Bewegung betont, die man durchaus in einem am Hafen gelegenen, tonangebenden Klub erwarten kann. Der interdisziplinäre Aspekt der Arbeit von 3deluxe ist in dieser Kombination von Design, Grafik, Beleuchtung und Film leicht erkennbar, ebenso wie die spezifische Leistung von 3deluxe-biorhythm: das Bemühen um „einen Ausgleich zwischen realen und virtuellen Raumverhältnissen".

Frère et sœur, Sylviane et Enzo Caressa ont ouvert La Nuit en octobre 2007. Selon leur publicité : « Ils associent la culture française du style, la force créative de l'Italie et l'ouverture de cœur et d'esprit du monde méditerranéen à la rigueur hanséatique de Hambourg. » En collaboration avec l'agence française Moving Design, Philipp Walter et 3deluxe-biorhythm se sont attaché dès le départ à pratiquer une approche interdisciplinaire. Des meubles en Corian et teck dans une ambiance monochrome blanche ont été choisis pour évoquer « l'atmosphère d'un yacht ». Une vague abstraite se déroule le long du mur vers la piste de danse et traverse les fenêtres qui donnent sur le port de Hambourg. Un système de rétroéclairage en 3D piloté par ordinateur, complété par des vases de forme organique éclairés de l'intérieur, crée dans cet espace une impression de mouvement continu. Des films de Moving Design sont projetés sur les 16 m de baies séparant le club et le restaurant. Cette projection vient se placer en interaction avec des effets graphiques générés par le motif de vague du décor, et met en valeur le type d'animation auquel on peut s'attendre d'un club très à la mode dans une grande ville portuaire. L'aspect interdisciplinaire du travail de 3deluxe apparaît dans cette combinaison de design, de création graphique, d'éclairage et de film, bien dans l'esprit de cette spécificité de l'agence destinée à la recherche « d'un équilibre entre des considérations spatiales réelles et virtuelles ».

Above, an elevation shows the wall design. To the right, two images of the 3deluxe-biorhythm and Moving Design window projections in Club La Nuit.

Oben: Die Ansicht zeigt die Gestaltung der Wand. Rechts: Zwei Abbildungen der Fensterprojektionen von 3deluxe-biorhythm und von Moving Design im Club La Nuit.

Ci-dessus, une élévation du projet pour le mur. À droite, deux images d'exemples des projections de 3deluxe-biorhythm et Moving Design à travers les baies du Club La Nuit.

The terrace, designed by 3deluxe-
biorhythm, with its view onto the harbor and subtle lighting.

Die von 3deluxe-biorhythm gestaltete
Terrasse mit raffinierter Beleuchtung
und Ausblick auf den Hafen.

La terrasse au subtil éclairage, conçu
par 3deluxe-biorhythm. La vue donne
sur le port.

Above the terrace bar with its full-height glazing. To the right, a floor plan of Club La Nuit.

Oben: die voll verglaste Terrasse der Bar. Rechts: Grundriss des Club La Nuit.

Ci-dessus, le bar de la terrasse vitrée sur toute sa hauteur. À droite, le plan au sol du Club La Nuit.

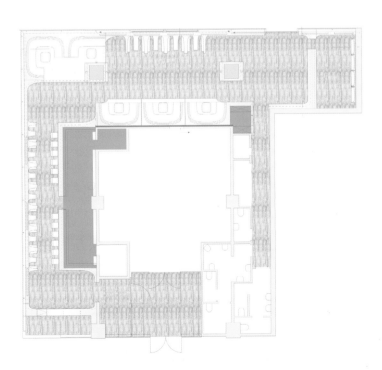

ARCHITECTUURBUREAU SLUIJMER EN VAN LEEUWEN

Architectuurbureau Sluijmer en Van Leeuwen
Kerkstraat 21
3581 RA Utrecht
The Netherlands

Tel: +31 30 231 87 61
Fax: +31 30 236 79 65
E-mail: info@architectuurbureau.nl
Web: www.architectuurbureau.nl

Michael A. van Leeuwen was born in 1959. He received his degree as an architect at the Delft University of Technology, Faculty of Architecture. He was an associate and founder of **ARCHITECTUURBUREAU SLUIJMER EN VAN LEEUWEN** (1988). Mariken van Nimwegen is a former employee of Architectuurbureau Sluijmer en Van Leeuwen with knowledge of historic ships. She was born in 1966, and attended the Utrecht School of Arts and participated in the Havenpost project. The work of Architectuurbureau Sluijmer en Van Leeuwen includes the Langerak housing project (Leidsche Rijn, Utrecht, 1998); Villa Lensink in't Hoff (Deventer, 2001); Villa Beukenburg (Groenekan, 2006); Albert Schweitzer School (Hoofddorp, 2007); the Havenpost Restaurant Divinatio (Utrecht, 2007–08, published here); Sterk House (Tjallebert, 2008); and the Twickel School (Hoofddorp, 2008), all in the Netherlands.

Der 1959 geborene Michael A. van Leeuwen erhielt sein Diplom an der Architekturfakultät der Technischen Universität Delft und wurde 1988 Partner und Mitbegründer des **ARCHITECTUURBUREAU SLUIJMER EN VAN LEEUWEN**. Mariken van Nimwegen, eine frühere Mitarbeiterin dieses Büros, kennt sich mit historischen Schiffen aus und beteiligte sich am Havenpost-Projekt. Sie wurde 1966 geboren und studierte an der Kunsthochschule Utrecht. Zu den Arbeiten des Büros Sluijmer en Van Leeuwen gehören Wohnbauten in Langerak (Leidsche Rijn, Utrecht, 1998), die Villa Lensink in't Hoff (Deventer, 2001), die Villa Beukenburg (Groenekan, 2006), die Albert-Schweitzer-Schule (Hoofddorp, 2007), das Restaurant Divinatio im Havenpost (Utrecht, 2007–08, hier veröffentlicht), das Haus Sterk (Tjallebert, 2008) und die Twickel-Schule (Hoofddorp, 2008), alle in den Niederlanden.

Michael A. van Leeuwen, né en 1959, est diplômé d'architecture de la Faculté d'architecture de l'Université de technologie de Delft. Il est associé fondateur du **ARCHITECTUURBUREAU SLUIJMER EN VAN LEEUWEN** (1988). Mariken van Nimwegen, ancienne collaboratrice d'Architectuurbureau Sluijmer en Van Leeuwen, possède des connaissances approfondies dans le domaine des vieux gréements. Née en 1966, elle a étudié à l'École des arts d'Utrecht et participé au projet du Havenpost. Parmi les réalisations de l'agence, toutes aux Pays-Bas : le Langerak, logements (Leidsche Rijn, Utrecht, 1998) ; la villa Lensink in't Hoff (Deventer, 2001) ; la villa Beukenburg (Groenekan, 2006) ; l'école Albert Schweitzer (Hoofddorp, 2007) ; le restaurant Divinatio au Havenpost (Utrecht, 2007–08, publié ici) ; la maison Sterk (Tjallebert, 2008) ; et l'école de Twickel (Hoofddorp, 2008).

THE HAVENPOST
RESTAURANT DIVINATIO

Utrecht, The Netherlands, 2007–08

Veilinghavenkade 14, 3521 AK Utrecht, The Netherlands, +31 30 294 12 26, www.divinatio.nl
Area: 250 m². Client: Parkhaven, Bouwfonds-Fortis. Cost: not disclosed

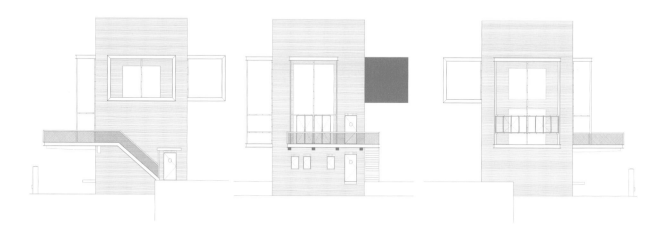

Restaurant Divinatio is situated in the Havenpost, a compact structure with five floors, located half on the quay and half in the water, just opposite the mooring point of the state yacht *De Utrecht*. The Havenpost offers access to the ship and space for volunteers and the crew. Divinatio occupies the first and second floors. The owner, a real estate developer, also uses the building to promote local projects. The Havenpost building was not allowed to exceed a footprint of 8 x 8.5 meters for reasons of local regulations. The "space boxes," projecting on all four sides in two different formats, offer a partial solution to the restrictive zoning requirements—creating special tables with a view for the restaurant and for persons wishing to see the historic harbor of Utrecht. A cellar partly below water level completes the structure. The architects explain: "Sturdy details were chosen to blend with the industrial harbor atmosphere—no slick window-frames but glass directly mounted on the steel profile. The layout refers to the environment of quays, harbors, and bridges."

Das Restaurant Divinatio liegt im Havenpost, einem kompakten, fünfgeschossigen Gebäude, das, teils am Kai und teils im Wasser, gegenüber vom Liegeplatz der Staatsjacht „De Utrecht" steht. Der Havenpost bietet Zugang zum Schiff sowie Räume für freiwillige Helfer und Besatzung. Das Restaurant nimmt die ersten beiden Geschosse ein. Der Besitzer, ein Immobilieninvestor, nutzt das Gebäude auch zur Werbung für lokale Projekte. Aufgrund der örtlichen Bauvorschriften war die Grundfläche auf 8 x 8,5 m beschränkt. Die auf allen vier Seiten in zwei verschiedenen Größen auskragenden Volumen bieten dem Restaurant einen gewissen Ausgleich für die strengen Bauvorschriften – sie enthalten Tische mit Ausblick auf den historischen Hafen von Utrecht. Ein teilweise unter Wasser liegender Keller vervollständigt die Anlage. Der Architekt erläutert: „Wir entschieden uns für robuste Details, die sich in die industrielle Hafenatmosphäre einfügen – keine schicken Fensterrahmen, sondern direkt auf die Stahlprofile montiertes Glas. Der Entwurf nimmt auf Kais, Hafen und Brücken Bezug."

Le Restaurant Divinatio est installé dans le Havenpost, petite construction compacte de cinq niveaux implantée à moitié sur un quai et à moitié dans l'eau, face au point d'amarrage du yacht De Utrecht, voilier classé patrimoine historique. Le Havenpost permet un accès au bateau et offre des installations destinées aux volontaires et à l'équipage. Le Divinatio occupe le rez-de-chaussée et le premier étage. Le propriétaire, un promoteur immobilier, utilise également les lieux pour promouvoir ses projets. L'emprise au sol du bâtiment ne pouvant dépasser 8 x 8,5 m, dimensions déterminées par la réglementation d'urbanisme, les « boîtes d'espace » de deux formats différents qui se projettent sur les quatre façades, sont une façon d'échapper en partie à cette contrainte. Elles permettent également d'installer des tables avec vue sur le port historique d'Utrecht. Une cave, réalisée en partie sous le niveau des eaux, complète le projet. Les architectes précisent : « Les finitions, d'aspect robuste, ont été choisies pour mieux se fondre dans l'atmosphère de ce port industriel : pas de menuiseries de fenêtre élégantes, mais des panneaux de verre montés directement sur un profilé en acier. Le projet se réfère à l'environnement du quai, des ports et des ponts. »

Above, elevations of the building show the strongly projecting window. Photos and a site plan to the right reveal how the structure fits into the harbor area—surprising in its form, and yet very much in scale with the neighboring architecture.

Oben: Die Ansichten des Gebäudes zeigen das stark auskragende Fenster. Rechts: Die Fotos und der Lageplan beweisen, dass das Gebäude sich gut in den Hafenbereich einfügt – mit einer erstaunlichen Form und doch durchaus im Maßstab der benachbarten Architektur.

Ci-dessus, ces élévations montrent la forte avancée des « fenêtres ». À droite, les photos et le plan du terrain montrent l'insertion de la construction dans la zone du port. Malgré sa forme surprenante, elle est parfaitement à l'échelle du cadre environnant.

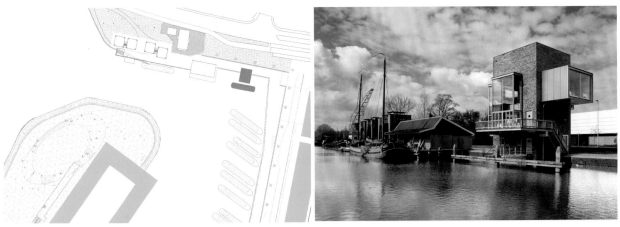

The restaurant interior opens broadly toward the port. The white leather chairs visible in these images are by Rolf Benz.

Der Restaurantbereich öffnet sich weit zum Hafen. Die auf diesen Bildern sichtbaren weißen Lederstühle stammen von der Firma Rolf Benz.

Vu de l'intérieur, le restaurant s'ouvre généreusement vers le port. Les sièges en cuir blanc sont de Rolf Benz.

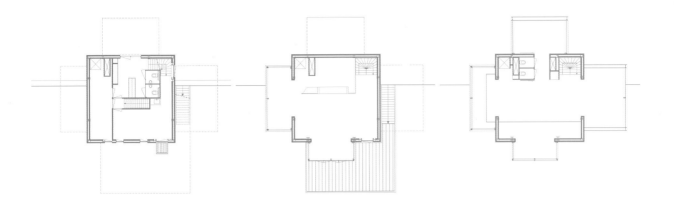

Floor plans show how the essentially square plan is rendered more lively by the projections. The image below gives an idea of the ample ceiling height.

Die Grundrisse zeigen, dass der überwiegend quadratische Plan durch die Auskragungen belebt wird. Die untere Abbildung vermittelt eine Vorstellung von der Höhe des Raums.

Ces plans de niveaux montrent comment le plan – essentiellement un carré – est animé par les différents éléments en projection. L'image ci-dessous donne une idée de la généreuse hauteur du plafond.

ARCHITRAVE

Architrave Design & Planning
Banyan Tree Holdings Ltd.
24A/B Cheong Chin Nam Road
Singapore 588747

Tel: +65 6849 5800
Fax: +65 6462 0187
E-mail: corporate@banyantree.com
Web: www.banyantree.com

Established in 1990, **ARCHITRAVE** is a sister company of Banyan Tree Hotels & Resorts. Under the leadership of Ho Kwon Cjan, the firm has designed hotels, resorts, spas, condominiums, retail malls, and golf and country clubs in Australia, the Middle East, China, India, Indonesia, Maldives, New Zealand, the Philippines, Seychelles, Singapore, Sri Lanka, and Thailand. Its "Asian-fusion influence and eco-friendly approach" has won Banyan Tree Hotels & Resorts several awards, including the President of Maldives Green Resort Award, the American Express and International Hotel Association Global Environment Award, and the 2007 Best Hotel (Luxury)/Hospitality Design Awards. Dharmali Kusumadi is the General Manager of Architrave Design & Planning. An Indonesian, who received his Technical Master's degree from Parahyangan Catholic University of Bandung, Indonesia, in 1984, he joined the Banyan Tree group in 1991. Ho Kwon Cjan is the Managing Director for Design Services of Banyan Tree Holdings Limited. He received his B.Arch degree from the University of Singapore and joined the family firm (his older brother Ho Kwon Ping is the Executive Chairman of Banyan Tree Holdings). He has designed numerous projects in Phuket, and worked on the Thai Wah Tower 2 project in Bangkok, Thailand, where the Vertigo Grill and Moon Bar (2001, published here) are located.

Das 1990 gegründete Büro **ARCHITRAVE** ist eine Schwesterfirma von Banyan Tree Hotels & Resorts. Unter der Leitung von Ho Kwon Cjan hat diese Firma Hotels, Freizeiteinrichtungen, Bäder, Wohnanlagen, Einkaufszentren sowie Golf- und Countryclubs in Australien, im Nahen Osten, in China, Indien, Indonesien, auf den Malediven, in Neuseeland, auf den Philippinen, den Seychellen, in Singapur, auf Sri Lanka und in Thailand geplant. Die „Verbindung von asiatischen Einflüssen mit umweltfreundlichen Lösungen" hat Banyan Tree Hotels & Resorts mehrere Auszeichungen eingebracht, u. a. den President of Maldives Green Resort Award, den American Express and International Hotel Association Global Environment Award und die 2007 Best Hotel (Luxury)/Hospitality Design Awards. Dharmali Kusumadi ist der leitende Direktor von Architrave Design & Planning. Der Indonesier schloss 1984 sein Technikstudium an der Katholischen Universität Parahyangan in Bandung, Indonesien, ab. 1991 begann er, für die Banyan-Tree-Gruppe zu arbeiten. Ho Kwon Cjan ist leitender Direktor der Planungsabteilung von Banyan Tree Holdings Limited. Er erhielt seinen B. Arch. an der Universität von Singapur und trat dann in das Familienunternehmen ein (sein älterer Bruder Ho Kwon Ping ist Geschäftsführer von Banyan Tree Holdings). Ho Kwon Cjan plante zahlreiche Projekte auf der Insel Phuket und arbeitete am Entwurf für den Thai Wah Tower 2 in Bangkok, Thailand, in dem sich der Vertigo Grill und die Moon Bar (2001, hier veröffentlicht) befinden.

Fondée en 1990, **ARCHITRAVE** est une société filiale de Banyan Tree Hotels & Resorts. Sous la direction de Ho Kwon Cjan, l'agence a conçu des hôtels, des complexes hôteliers, des spas, des immeubles en copropriété, des centres commerciaux et des clubs de golf et de sport en Australie, Chine, Inde, Indonésie, au Moyen-Orient, Sri Lanka, aux Maldives, Seychelles, Philippines, à Singapour, en Nouvelle-Zélande et en Thaïlande. Une « approche respectueuse de l'écologie et sensible à l'influence asiatique dans un esprit de fusion » a valu à Banyan Tree Hotels & Resorts de recevoir plusieurs prix, dont le Prix des complexes hôteliers écologiques du président des Maldives, l'American Express and International Hotel Association Global Environment Award, et les 2007 Best Hotel (Luxury)/Hospitality Design Awards. Dharmali Kusumadi est directeur général d'Architrave Design & Planning. Indonésien, titulaire d'un mastère en technologie de l'Université catholique Parahyangan de Bandoeng (Indonésie) en 1984, il est entré dans le groupe Banyan Tree en 1991. Ho Kwon Cjan est directeur en charge des services de conception de Banyan Tree Holdings Limited. Il est B.Arch de l'Université de Singapour et a rejoint la firme familiale (son frère aîné, Ho Kwon Ping, est président exécutif de Banyan Tree Holdings). Il a conçu de nombreux projets à Phuket, et travaillé sur celui de la Thai Wah Tower 2 à Bangkok, où se trouvent le Vertigo Grill et le Moon Bar (2001) publiés ici.

VERTIGO GRILL AND MOON BAR

Banyan Tree Bangkok, Bangkok, Thailand, 2001

21/100 South Sathon Road, Sathon, Bangkok 10120, Thailand, +66 2 679 1200, www.banyantree.com
Area: 627 m². Client: Thai Wah Plaza Limited
Cost: $210 000. Team: Dharmali Kusumadi, Ho Kwon Cjan

Located on the 61st-story rooftop of Thai Wah Tower 2 above the Banyan Tree Bangkok, the Vertigo Grill and Moon Bar must be amongst the most spectacular locations of this type in the world. Built on a former helipad, it offers an unobstructed 360° view of the Thai capital for approximately 120 guests. The area is divided into three sections—a dining courtyard, a private party lounge, and the Moon Bar. According to Sriram Kailasam, Director for Food & Beverages at Banyan Tree Hotels and Resorts: "The idea of the restaurant actually evolved from a guest's request to do something unique for a proposal to his girlfriend. So we had suggested doing it on the helipad. And then came the idea 'why not do a rooftop barbeque?' So we did, starting initially with just four or five tables, which were fully booked all the time. We then expanded to 10 to 15 tables, and converted an old storeroom into a kitchen on the rooftop. Eventually, due to popular demand, this was transformed into a restaurant which seats 120 and has a bar area." The impression of "Vertigo," a name derived from the Hitchcock movie, is heightened by wooden decks, deliberately set back from the edge with very thin metal railings that give the impression that the decks are floating independently of the outer parapet.

Der Vertigo Grill und die Moon Bar liegen auf dem Dach des 61-geschossigen Thai Wah Tower 2 oberhalb des Banyan Tree Bangkok und gehören zu den spektakulärsten Orten dieser Art in der Welt. Sie wurden auf einem früheren Helikopterlandeplatz errichtet und bieten etwa 120 Gästen einen Rundumblick auf die Hauptstadt Thailands. Die Fläche ist in drei Bereiche aufgeteilt – einen Speisebereich, eine private Partylounge und die Moon Bar. Sriram Kailasam, Direktor für Speisen und Getränke bei den BanyanTree Hotels & Resorts, erklärte: „Die Idee für das Restaurant entstand eigentlich aufgrund der Bitte eines Gastes um etwas Einmaliges für den Heiratsantrag an seine Freundin. So haben wir den Hubschrauberlandeplatz vorgeschlagen. Und dann kam uns die Idee, einen Grill auf dem Dach einzurichten. Das taten wir auch und begannen mit nur vier oder fünf Tischen, die immer ausgebucht waren. Wir erweiterten dann auf 10 bis 15 Tische und bauten einen alten Lagerraum zur Küche auf dem Dach um. Schließlich wurde das aufgrund der großen Nachfrage zu einem Restaurant mit 120 Plätzen und einer Bar." Die schwindelerregende Wirkung des „Vertigo" (engl. für Schwindel, Höhenangst und der Titel eines Hitchcock-Films) wird durch hölzerne Decks verstärkt, die absichtlich mit sehr dünnen Geländern von der Gebäudekante abgesetzt sind. Dadurch entsteht der Eindruck, als schwebten diese Terrassen frei über der äußeren Brüstung.

Situé au 61e niveau de la Thai Wah Tower 2, au-dessus du Banyan Tree Bangkok, le Vertigo est l'un des lieux les plus spectaculaires de ce type dans le monde. Construit sur une ancienne plate-forme pour hélicoptères, il offre à ses cent vingt couverts une vue à 360° sur la capitale thaïlandaise. Il est divisé en trois sections, une salle à manger en plein air, un salon pour réceptions privées et le Moon Bar. Selon Sriram Kailasam, directeur de la restauration du Banyan Tree Hotels and Resorts : « L'idée de ce restaurant vient en fait de la demande d'un client qui voulait un endroit exceptionnel pour faire sa proposition de mariage à son amie. Nous avons suggéré l'hélistation. Puis nous avons pensé : « Pourquoi pas un barbecue sur le toit ? », ce que nous avons fait en commençant avec quatre ou cinq tables, qui furent vite réservées en permanence. Nous nous sommes agrandis à dix puis à quinze tables, et avons transformé une pièce de stockage en cuisine sur le toit. Devant le succès, nous avons enfin transformé le tout en un restaurant de cent vingt couverts et un bar. » L'impression donnée par Vertigo (nom inspiré du film éponyme d'Hitchcock) est accentuée par les terrasses en bois qui ne sont séparées du vide que par une très mince rambarde métallique donnant l'impression qu'elles sont en suspension, indépendantes du garde-corps.

On the spectacular rooftop of the Vertigo Grill and Moon Bar, dining chairs are by Amewood and the dining tables by Architrave with Waipanai Co. Ltd. Outdoor lighting is designed by Architrave with C&P Lighting. The bar is by Architrave (Tara Fiber Ltd), and the bar stools are also by Architrave with Waipanai.

Der spektakuläre Vertigo Grill und die Moon Bar auf dem Dach sind mit Stühlen von Amewood und Tischen von Architrave mit Waipanai Co. Ltd. ausgestattet. Die Außenbeleuchtung gestaltete Architrave mit C&P Lighting. Die Bar plante Architrave (Tara Fiber Ltd.), und die Barhocker stammen ebenfalls von Architrave mit Waipanai.

Sur la spectaculaire terrasse du Grill and Moon Bar, les sièges sont d'Amewood et les tables d'Architrave (avec Waipanai Co. Ltd). L'éclairage extérieur a été conçu en collaboration avec C&P Lighting. Le bar a été dessiné par Architrave (Tara Fiber Ltd), ainsi que les tabourets (Architrave et Waipanai).

ASSADI + PULIDO

Felipe Assadi + Francisca Pulido Architects
Carmencita 262, oficina 202
Las Condes, Santiago
Chile

Tel: +56 2 234 5558
E-mail: info@assadi.cl
Web: www.felipeassadi.com

Felipe Assadi was born in 1971. He received his degree in Architecture from the Finis Terrae University (Santiago, 1996) and his M.Arch degree from the Pontificia Universidad Católica de Chile in Santiago in 2006. He teaches at the Andrés Bello University in Santiago. Francisca Pulido also received her architecture degree from the Finis Terrae University in 1996 and teaches at the Andrés Bello University. They created **ASSADI + PULIDO** in 1999 on an informal basis, incorporating the firm in 2006. Their work, concentrating on private residences for the moment, includes the Schmitz House (Calera de Tango, Santiago, 2001); Bar El Tubo (Lima, Peru, 2003–04, published here); Park Theater (Santiago, 2004): 20x20 House (Santiago, 2005); Gatica House (Rancagua, 2006); Russo Club (Talca, 2006); Serrano House (Santiago, 2006); Deck House (Alto Rungue, Santiago, 2006); and the Guthrie House (Santiago, 2007), all in Chile unless stated otherwise.

Felipe Assadi, geboren 1971, beendete 1996 sein Architekturstudium an der Universidad Finis Terrae und erhielt 2006 seinen M. Arch. an der Pontificia Universidad Católica de Chile (beide in Santiago). Er lehrt an der Universidad Andrés Bello in Santiago. Francisca Pulido studierte ebenfalls bis 1996 an der Universidad Finis Terrae und lehrt an der Universidad Andrés Bello. 1999 gründeten sie auf informeller Basis das Büro **ASSADI + PULIDO**, das 2006 als Firma eingetragen wurde. Zu ihren Projekten, die sich bisher auf Einfamilienhäuser konzentrierten, gehören das Haus Schmitz (Calera de Tango, Santiago, 2001), die Bar El Tubo (Lima, Peru, 2003–04, hier vorgestellt), das Teatro del Parque (Santiago, 2004), Haus 20x20 (Santiago, 2005), das Haus Gatica (Rancagua, 2006), der Klub Russo (Talca, 2006), das Haus Serrano (Santiago, 2006), das Haus Deck (Alto Rungue, Santiago, 2006) und das Haus Guthrie (Santiago, 2007), alle in Chile, sofern nicht anders angegeben.

Né en 1971, Felipe Assadi est diplômé en architecture de l'Universidad Finis Terrae (Santiago du Chili, 1996) et M.Arch de la Pontificia Universidad Católica de Chile de Santiago (2006). Il enseigne à l'Universidad Andrés Bello à Santiago. Francisca Pulido est également diplômée de l'Universidad Finis Terrae en 1996, et enseigne à l'Universidad Andrés Bello. Ils ont créé **ASSADI + PULIDO** en 1999 sur une base informelle, ne fondant leur agence qu'en 2006. Pour le moment, ils travaillent essentiellement au Chili et sur des projets de résidences privées, dont la maison Schmitz (Calera de Tango, Santiago, 2001) ; le bar El Tubo (Lima, Pérou, 2003–04, publié ici) ; le Teatro del Parque (Santiago, 2004) : la maison 20x20 (Santiago, 2005) ; la maison Gatica (Rancagua, 2006) ; le club Russo (Talca, 2006) ; la maison Serrano (Santiago, 2006) ; la maison Deck (Alto Rungue, Santiago, 2006) ; et la maison Guthrie (Santiago, 2007).

BAR EL TUBO

Lima, Peru, 2003–04

Ave. del Ejercito 650, Magdalena del Mar, Lima, Peru
Area: 200 m². Client: British American Tobacco, Lima, Peru. Cost: not disclosed

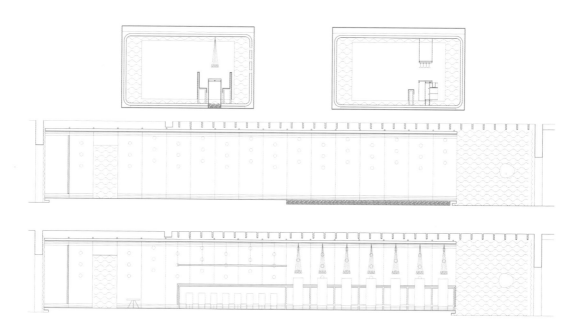

This bar, commissioned by Kent cigarettes, is located in the Puericultorio Pérez Araníbar building, a Neoclassical structure built in 1820 to house an orphanage. Considered to be part of the cultural heritage of Lima, the building is nonetheless partly abandoned. The architects used former classrooms on the second floor but determined that their intervention would not "acquire any relationship to the preexisting architecture." They inserted a tube into the space containing a bar and art gallery. This tube is independent of the floor, ceiling, and walls of the existing building and has perforations that admit a blue-violet light, accentuating the "idea of the floating element inside the building." A longitudinal bar, five sculptures, and large-format paintings provided by Peruvian artists further animate the space. The architects used steel, dry wall, white glossy epoxy paint, and lacquered medium-density fiberboard (MDF), focusing on "a very neutral and abstract aesthetic."

Diese von der Zigarettenfirma Kent in Auftrag gegebene Bar liegt im Gebäude Puericultorio Pérez Araníbar, einem neoklassizistischen Bau von 1820, der als Waisenhaus errichtet wurde. Obgleich er unter Denkmalschutz steht, ist er teils ungenutzt. Die Architekten wählten die früheren Klassenräume im zweiten Obergeschoss, beschlossen aber, dass ihr Eingriff „keinerlei Beziehung zur vorhandenen Architektur" haben sollte. Sie setzten eine Röhre in den Raum, die eine Bar und eine Kunstgalerie enthält. Diese Röhre ist unabhängig von dem Boden, der Decke und den Wänden des bestehenden Gebäudes und hat Aussparungen, die ein blauviolettes Licht einlassen, das „die Vorstellung von einem schwebenden Element im Gebäude" verstärkt. Eine längsgerichtete Bar, fünf Skulpturen und ein großformatiges Gemälde von peruanischen Künstlern beleben zusätzlich den Raum. Die Architekten verwendeten Stahl, Trockenwände, weißen, glänzenden Epoxidharzanstrich sowie lackierte, mittelschwere Spanplatten (MDF) und konzentrierten sich auf „eine sehr neutrale und abstrakte Ästhetik".

Ce bar commandité par les cigarettes Kent se trouve dans l'immeuble du Puericultorio Pérez Araníbar, un orphelinat de style néoclassique datant de 1820, en partie abandonné, bien que considéré comme appartenant au patrimoine culturel de Lima. Les architectes qui ont réutilisé les anciennes salles de classe du premier étage étaient déterminés à ce que leur intervention « soit sans relation avec l'architecture préexistante ». Ils ont inséré dans le bâtiment un tube contenant le bar et une galerie d'art, indépendants du sol, du plafond et des murs en place. Les ouvertures qui laissent pénétrer une lumière bleu violacé accentuent une perception « d'élément flottant à l'intérieur de l'immeuble ». Le bar très allongé ainsi que des sculptures et des peintures de grand format d'artistes péruviens contribuent à l'animation de l'espace. Les architectes ont utilisé de l'acier, des panneaux de plâtre, une peinture époxy brillante et du medium laqué pour renforcer l'effet « d'une esthétique abstraite et très neutre ».

Elevations, above, show the relatively simple design of the space—a long, fairly confined rectangular volume that is furnished in minimalist fashion.

Die Aufrisse oben zeigen die relativ schlichte Raumgestaltung – ein langes, ziemlich schmales, rechtwinkliges Volumen mit minimalistischer Möblierung.

Les élévations ci-dessus montrent la simplicité relative du plan du volume : un rectangle allongé, assez fermé, meublé de manière minimaliste.

The floor plan below shows how the main, rectangular volume is inserted into the existing architecture, with "satellite areas" spilling out into the older spaces, as seen in the photo on the lower right page.

Der Grundriss unten zeigt, wie der große, rechtwinklige Raum in die bestehende Architektur eingefügt ist. „Satellitenbereiche" ragen in die älteren Räume hinein, wie auf dem Foto auf der rechten Seite unten zu sehen ist.

Le plan au sol ci-dessous montre comment le volume rectangulaire principal s'insère dans l'architecture existante, et les « zones satellitaires » envahissent les volumes anciens (page de droite, en bas).

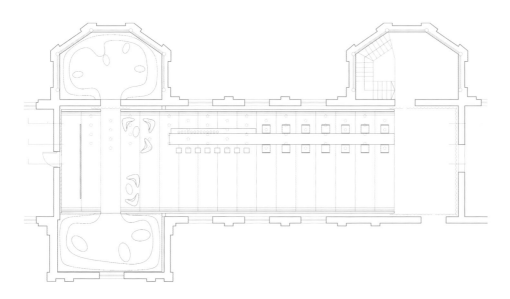

*Unexpected artworks liven the atmo-
sphere of the Bar El Tubo and
contrast in a willful manner with
the strongly rectilinear furniture.*

*Ungewöhnliche Kunstwerke beleben die
Atmosphäre in der Bar El Tubo und
bilden einen bewussten Kontrast zu
dem streng rechtwinkligen Mobiliar.*

*De surprenantes œuvres d'art créent
de l'animation dans le bar El Tubo
et forment un contraste voulu avec
le mobilier de style géométrique
marqué.*

AVROKO

AvroKO
210 Elizabeth Street, Floor 3
New York, NY 10012
USA

Tel: +1 212 343 7024
Fax: +1 212 343 1072
E-mail: info@avroko.com
Web: www.avroko.com

AVROKO describes itself as a "design and concept firm that is most notably defined by its lack of definition." The award-winning firm is headed by Kristina O'Neal, born in 1973 in Oregon City, Oregon (B. A. in Fine Arts, Cornell University, 1995); Adam Farmerie, born in Indianapolis, Indiana, in 1972 (B.Arch, Carnegie Mellon University, 1995); Greg Bradshaw, born in 1969 in San Diego, California (B.Arch, Carnegie Mellon University, 1992); and William Harris, born in 1973 in Binghamton, New York (B. A. in Fine Arts, Carnegie Mellon University, 1995). As well as Omido (New York, New York, 2006–07, published here), they have also completed PUBLIC (2003), Odea (2004), Sapa (2004), The Stanton Social (2005), Quality Meats (2006), European Union (2006), and Park Avenue (2007) restaurants in New York. Other work includes the Stone Rose (2008) and Bourbon Steak (2008) restaurants in Scottsdale, Arizona; and Lavo Restaurant in Las Vegas (Nevada, 2008). Additional projects include Double Crown (2008) in New York, RN 74 (2009) in San Francisco, and other restaurant, hotel, and retail concepts.

AVROKO beschreibt sich selbst als „Entwurfs- und Konzeptionsfirma, die sich vorwiegend über ihren Mangel an Definition definiert". Das preisgekrönte Büro wird geleitet von Kristina O'Neal, geboren 1973 in Oregon City, Oregon (B. A. Kunst, Cornell University, 1995), Adam Farmerie, geboren 1972 in Indianapolis, Indiana (B. Arch., Carnegie Mellon University, 1995), Greg Bradshaw, geboren 1969 in San Diego, Kalifornien (B. Arch., Carnegie Mellon University, 1992), und William Harris, geboren 1973 in Binghamton, New York (B. A. Kunst, Carnegie Mellon University, 1995). Ebenso wie das Omido (New York, 2006–07, hier vorgestellt) haben sie auch die Restaurants PUBLIC (2003), Odea (2004), Sapa (2004), The Stanton Social (2005), Quality Meats (2006), European Union (2006) und Park Avenue (2007) in New York ausgeführt, darüber hinaus auch die Restaurants Stone Rose (2008) und Bourbon Steak (2008) in Scottsdale, Arizona, und das Lavo in Las Vegas (Nevada, 2008). Weitere Projekte sind Double Crown (2008) in New York, RN 74 (2009) in San Francisco sowie Konzepte für Restaurants, Hotels und Läden.

AVROKO se présente comme une « agence de design et de conception qui se définit surtout par son absence de définition ». Elle est dirigée par Kristina O'Neal, née en 1973 à Oregon City, Oregon (B. A. en beaux-arts de l'Université Cornell, 1995) ; Adam Farmerie, né à Indianapolis, Indiana, en 1972 (B.Arch, Université Carnegie Mellon, 1995) ; Greg Bradshaw, né en 1969 à San Diego, Californie (B.Arch, Carnegie Mellon University, 1992), et William Harris, né en 1973 à Binghamton, New York (B. A. en beaux-arts, Université Carnegie Mellon, 1995). En dehors d'Omido (New York, 2006–07, publié ici), ils ont réalisé les restaurants PUBLIC (2003), Odea (2004), Sapa (2004), The Stanton Social (2005), Quality Meats (2006), European Union (2006) et Park Avenue (2007) à New York. Parmi leurs autres réalisations : les restaurants The Stone Rose (2008) et le Bourbon Steak (2008) à Scottsdale, Arizona, et le restaurant Lavo (2008) à Las Vegas, Nevada. D'autres projets sont Double Crown (2008) à New York, RN 74 (2009) à San Francisco et des concepts de restaurants, de boutiques et d'hôtels.

OMIDO

New York, New York, USA, 2006–07

1695 Broadway, 53rd Street, New York, NY 10019-5903, USA, +1 212 247 8110, www.hungryperson-sysco.com/omido/
Area: 204 m². Client: Charly Levy. Cost: not disclosed

Located at 1695 Broadway in Midtown Manhattan, Omido's design is derived by the architects from the meaning of its name in Japanese—which signifies both "shrine" and "small house." A glass-and-steel entrance area and opening wooden façade mark the exterior, while 10-centimeter-wide strips of Plyboo are used to clad the walls and ceiling, with gaps designed to enclose "votive candles." Old-fashioned "Edison" light bulbs are hung in glass globes above an Iroko wood sushi bar. A more specific reference to temples is made in the restaurant's private dining alcove, where the ceiling is lined with thousands of *omikuji*, written prayers in folded paper tied to ropes familiar to visitors of Japan. According to the architects, in this instance these "simulate the effect of a low cloud of feathers." Mixing wood and the *omikuji* with votive candles, the architects also leave certain brick walls exposed, linking the restaurant to its New York site despite its distant cultural references.

Den Entwurf für das in Midtown Manhattan, 1695 Broadway, gelegene Omido leiteten die Architekten von der japanischen Bedeutung seines Namens ab, der sowohl „Schrein" als auch „kleines Haus" bedeutet. Ein Eingangsbereich aus Glas und Stahl öffnet die Holzfassade; im Innern sind die Wände und Decken mit 10 cm breiten Streifen aus Bambus verkleidet, in deren Fugen sogenannte Votivkerzen untergebracht sind. Altmodische Glühbirnen in Glaskugeln hängen über einer Sushi-Bar aus Irokoholz. Einen eindeutigeren Bezug zu Tempeln stellt der intime Speisebereich des Restaurants her, wo die Decke mit Tausenden von *omikuji* überzogen ist – auf gefaltetes Papier geschriebenen, an Schnüren befestigten Gebeten, wie sie Besuchern von Japan bekannt sind. Nach Aussage der Architekten „simulieren sie" in diesem Fall „eine tief hängende Wolke aus Federn". Bei der Mischung aus Holz, *omikuji* und Votivkerzen haben die Architekten auch einige Backsteinwände sichtbar belassen, die das Restaurant, ungeachtet seiner Bezüge zur fernöstlichen Kultur, mit seinem Standort New York verbinden.

Installé au 1695 Broadway dans Midtown à Manhattan, Omido tire son concept du sens de ce mot japonais, qui signifie à la fois « petite maison » et « reliquaire ». Un espace d'accueil en verre et acier et une façade en bois qui peut s'ouvrir sur la rue signalent sa présence vers l'extérieur. Des bandeaux de Plyboo (contreplaqué de bambou) de 10 cm de large habillent les murs et le plafond. Des « chandelles votives » sont placées dans des niches correspondant à des interruptions dans ce bardage. Des ampoules électriques de style Edison sont suspendues dans des globes de verre au-dessus d'un bar à sushis en bois d'Iroko. Une autre référence spécifique à l'architecture des temples se repère dans une salle à manger privée en alcôve dont le plafond est doublé de milliers d'*omikuji*, prières écrites sur des papiers pliés et liés par des cordelettes, artefact familier pour ceux qui connaissent le Japon. Les architectes voulaient ici « simuler l'effet d'un nuage de plumes ». Tout en mêlant une multiplicité de ces références à une culture lointaine – essence des bois, *omikuji* et chandelles votives –, les architectes ont néanmoins laissé apparente la brique de certains murs, qui renvoie au vieux New York.

The façade of the restaurant opens onto the street, and its décor immediately gives a hint of the Asian cuisine to be enjoyed within.

Die Fassade des Restaurants öffnet sich zur Straße; das Dekor ist ein deutlicher Hinweis auf die darin angebotene asiatische Küche.

La façade côté rue s'ouvre sur le décor intérieur, ce qui donne une indication sur le type de cuisine asiatique servi.

A floor plan shows the main bar area—an open rectangle surrounded by seats. The atmosphere is dark and warm, dominated by the wood finish of the main surfaces.

Der Grundriss zeigt den großen Barraum – ein offenes, von Sitzgelegenheiten umgebenes Rechteck. Die Atmosphäre ist dunkel und warm und wird von den Holzflächen der Wände bestimmt.

Le plan montre la disposition centrale du bar, simple rectangle ouvert entouré de tabourets. L'atmosphère est chaleureuse, dominée par la présence de bois sombre sur la plupart des surfaces.

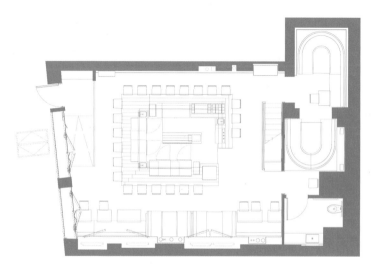

Thousands of omikuji, Japanese folded prayer papers, hang from the ceiling of the private dining alcove, seen
on the full page to the right.

*Tausende von omikuji, gefalteten
japanischen Gebetszetteln, hängen
von der Decke des privaten Speise-
raums, der auf der rechten Seite zu
sehen ist.*

*Des milliers d'omikuji, feuilles de
papier japonais sur lesquelles ont été
inscrites des prières, sont suspendus
au plafond de cette alcôve privée,
visible page de droite.*

Votive candles set in small openings
heighten the rather "religious" atmosphere of the space.

*In kleine Öffnungen gestellte Votiv-
kerzen verstärken die leicht sakrale
Atmosphäre des Raums.*

*Des chandelles votives posées dans
de petites ouvertures renforcent
l'aspect presque « religieux » de
l'atmosphère.*

BARKOW LEIBINGER ARCHITEKTEN

Barkow Leibinger Architekten
Schillerstr. 94
10625 Berlin
Germany

Tel: +49 30 31 57 12 0
Fax: +49 30 31 57 12 29
E-mail: info@barkowleibinger.com
Web: www.barkowleibinger.com

REGINE LEIBINGER was born in 1963 in Stuttgart, Germany. She studied Architecture in Berlin (Diploma, Technische Universität, 1989) and at Harvard University (M.Arch, 1990). She created a joint office with **FRANK BARKOW** in 1993. She has been a Visiting Professor at the Architectural Association (AA) in London (Unit Master, 1997–98), Cornell University, and Harvard University, and, since 2006, a Professor for Building Construction and Design at the Technische Universität Berlin. Frank Barkow was born in 1957 in Kansas City, USA, and studied Architecture at Montana State University (B.Arch, 1982) and at Harvard University (M.Arch, 1990). Barkow has been a Visiting Professor at the AA in London (Unit Master, 1995–98), Cornell University, Harvard University, and at the State Academy of Art and Design in Stuttgart. Their recent work includes Pavilions for Research and Production (Grüsch, Switzerland, 2001; 2004); TRUTEC Building (Seoul, Korea, 2006); a house in Berlin-Karlshorst (2007); a Gatehouse (Ditzingen near Stuttgart, 2007); and a Campus Restaurant (also in Ditzingen, 2006–08, published here), all in Germany unless stated otherwise.

REGINE LEIBINGER wurde 1963 in Stuttgart geboren. Sie studierte Architektur an der Technischen Universität Berlin (Diplom, 1989) und an der Harvard University (M. Arch., 1990). Mit **FRANK BARKOW** gründete sie 1993 ein gemeinsames Büro. Sie war Gastprofessorin an der Architectural Association (AA) in London (Unit Master, 1997–98), der Cornell University sowie der Harvard University und ist seit 2006 Professorin für Baukonstruktion und Entwerfen an der Technischen Universität Berlin. Frank Barkow wurde 1957 in Kansas City geboren und studierte Architektur an der Montana State University (B. Arch., 1982) und der Harvard University (M. Arch., 1990). Barkow war Gastprofessor an der AA in London (Unit Master, 1995–98), der Cornell University, der Harvard University und der Staatlichen Akademie der Bildenden Künste in Stuttgart. Zu ihren neuesten Projekten zählen Pavillons für Forschung und Produktion (Grüsch, Schweiz, 2001, 2004), das TRUTEC Building (Seoul, Korea, 2006), ein Wohnhaus in Berlin-Karlshorst (2007), die Hauptpforte der Firma Trumpf (Ditzingen bei Stuttgart, 2007) und ihr Betriebsrestaurant (ebenfalls in Ditzingen, 2006–08, hier veröffentlicht), alle in Deutschland, sofern nicht anders angegeben.

REGINE LEIBINGER, née en 1963 à Stuttgart, Allemagne, a étudié l'architecture à la Technische Universität de Berlin (diplômée en 1989) et à l'Université Harvard (M.Arch, 1990). Elle a créé son agence en association avec **FRANK BARKOW** en 1993. Elle a été professeur invitée à l'Architectural Association (AA) de Londres (Unit Master, 1997–98), aux universités Cornell et Harvard, et, depuis 2006, enseigne la conception et la construction à la Technische Universität de Berlin. Frank Barkow, né en 1957 à Kansas City, États-Unis, a étudié l'architecture à l'Université de l'État du Montana (B.Arch, 1982) et à l'Université Harvard (M.Arch, 1990). Barkow a été professeur invité à l'AA de Londres (Unit Master, 1995–98), aux universités Cornell et Harvard, et à l'Académie d'Art et de Design de Stuttgart. Parmi leurs récents travaux : pavillons pour la recherche et la production (Grüsch, Suisse, 2001, 2004) ; le TRUTEC Building (Séoul, Corée, 2006) ; une maison à Berlin-Karlshorst (2007) ; le pavillon d'accueil de Trumpf (Ditzingen, près de Stuttgart, Allemagne, 2007) et leur cafétéria (également à Ditzingen, 2006–08, publié ici).

CAMPUS RESTAURANT

Ditzingen, Germany, 2006–08

Cafeteria and auditorium, Johann-Maus-Str. 2, 71254 Ditzingen, Germany
Area: 1900 m² restaurant. Client: Trumpf GmbH + Co. KG. Cost: not disclosed. Team: Lukas Weder (Project Architect)
Façade: Werner Sobek Ingenieure, Stuttgart

This freestanding pavilion provides a new central cafeteria with seating for 700 for Trumpf's Stuttgart-based industrial campus and headquarters. Part of a newly landscaped park entrance, it is located between the new gatehouse entrance and the A81 freeway. When used for events, the space can seat 800. The main level of the pavilion is four meters below grade and is covered by a large canopy roof developed with the engineer Werner Sobek, giving the entire structure a relatively low profile despite its nine-meter central height. "The intention," say the architects, "was to create a polygonal leaflike canopy that achieves long spans (up to 20 meters) over groups of columns. This remarkable structure combines a steel frame and columns with a glu-laminated wood-cell infill." The columns are located so as to emphasize the cantilevered, hovering effect generated by the roof. CNC milling was used to create unique honeycomb joints. Overhead skylights allow natural lighting, while the glass façades are protected by rolling screens hidden in the floor. Closed exterior façades are clad in custom-made blue-cobalt ceramic tiles.

Dieser frei stehende Pavillon enthält eine neue, zentral gelegene Cafeteria mit Sitzplätzen für 700 Personen für die Hauptverwaltung und Fabrikationsstätte der Firma Trumpf bei Stuttgart. Er ist Teil des neu gestalteten Eingangsbereichs und liegt zwischen der neuen Hauptpforte und der Autobahn A 81. Bei Veranstaltungen kann der Raum auch Plätze für 800 Personen bieten. Das Hauptgeschoss des Pavillons liegt 4 m unter Bodenniveau und wird von einem großen Dach überdeckt, das in Zusammenarbeit mit dem Ingenieur Werner Sobek entwickelt wurde und dem Gebäude trotz seiner zentralen Höhe von 9 m eine relativ flache Silhouette verleiht. „Unser Ziel war ein vieleckiges, blattartiges Dach mit großer Spannweite (bis 20 m) über Stützengruppen. Die Konstruktion ist ähnlich wie ein Blatt aufgebaut und besteht aus Stahlträgern mit einer Sekundarkonstruktion aus Brettschichtholz", sagen die Architekten. Die Stützen sind so positioniert, dass sie die schwebende Wirkung des auskragenden Dachs mit aus CNC gefrästen Wabenelementen verstärken. Durch Oberlichter kann die künstliche Beleuchtung reduziert werden, während die Glasfassaden durch im Boden verborgene Sonnenschutzelemente geschützt werden. Die geschlossenen Außenfassaden sind mit eigens angefertigten, kobaltblauen Keramikfliesen verkleidet.

Ce pavillon indépendant, situé sur le campus industriel et siège de la société de Stuttgart Trumpf, abrite une cafétéria centrale de sept cents places. Partie intégrante des nouveaux aménagements paysagers de l'entrée, il se trouve entre le nouveau pavillon d'accueil et l'autoroute A81. Huit cents personnes peuvent y trouver place pour certaines manifestations. Le niveau principal est enterré à 4 m et recouvert d'un vaste toit en auvent (mis au point en collaboration avec l'ingénieur Werner Sobek), ce qui confère à cette structure un profil relativement surbaissé malgré sa hauteur de 9 m en partie centrale. « L'intention [des architectes] était de créer un auvent polygonal en forme de feuille se déployant sur longue portée (jusqu'à 20 m) au-dessus d'un ensemble de colonnes. Cette remarquable structure associe une ossature et des colonnes en acier à des remplissages en bois lamellé-collé. » Des techniques d'usinage à commande numérique ont servi à créer des jointures spécifiques en nid-d'abeilles. Des verrières zénithales ont permis de réduire les besoins d'éclairage artificiel, et les façades de verre sont protégées par des écrans enroulables dissimulés dans le sol. Les façades extérieures fermées sont habillées de carreaux de céramique bleu cobalt spécialement fabriqués pour ce projet.

The strong presence of the roof of the Campus Restaurant dominates as seen from ground level or from above.

Die Ansichten vom Erdgeschoss oder von oben zeigen die starke Präsenz des Dachs, von dem das Betriebsrestaurant beherrscht wird.

La forte présence de la toiture du restaurant du campus s'impose aussi bien au niveau du sol qu'en vue aérienne.

The roof slab is placed on a glass
base, formed by full-height glazing,
creating an interesting contrast
between heaviness and lightness.

Die Dachplatte ruht auf einer Basis
mit geschosshoher Verglasung und
bildet einen eindrucksvollen Gegensatz zwischen Schwere und Leichtigkeit.

La dalle du toit repose sur une base
en verre constituée par le vitrage
toute hauteur. Elle provoque un
contraste visuel intéressant entre
pesanteur et légèreté.

Above, the main dining space, with chairs designed by Jasper Morrison (SIM, Vitra), and tables by Alberto Meda (Media Click, Vitra). Below, left, a wall with shaped tiles designed by the architects (NBK Keramik).

Oben: Der große Speisesaal mit Stühlen von Jasper Morrison (SIM, Vitra) und Tischen von Alberto Meda (Media Click, Vitra). Unten links: Eine Wand mit Fliesen, die von den Architekten gestaltet wurden (NBK Keramik).

Ci-dessus, la salle principale : les sièges sont de Jasper Morrison (SIM, Vitra), les tables de Alberto Meda (Media Click, Vitra). Ci-dessous, à gauche, le carrelage du mur, dessiné par les architectes (NBK Keramik).

In the dining area, the serving islands were designed by Barkow Leibinger (Bernd Jurke GmbH).

Die Bedienungsinseln im Speisebereich wurden von Barkow Leibinger entworfen (Bernd Jurke GmbH).

Les îlots de service ont été conçus par Barkow Leibinger (Bernd Jurke GmbH).

BEL LOBO & BOB NERI ARQUITETOS

Bel Lobo & Bob Neri Arquitetos
Rua Marechal Pires Ferreira 66
Cosme Velho
Rio de Janeiro, 22241 RJ
Brazil

Tel: +55 21 3235 2000
E-mail: contato@belbob.com.br
Web: www.belbob.com.br

BEL LOBO was born in Rio de Janeiro in 1960. She graduated in 1984 from the Architecture and Urbanism School of Rio de Janeiro Federal University (UFRJ). She has worked on Salinas (beach fashion stores, Brazil, since 1994); Livraria da Travessa (bookstore chain, Rio de Janeiro, since 1995); Elle et Lui (fashion stores, Rio de Janeiro, since 2000); Farm (fashion stores, Brazil, since 2004); and completed the Elle et Lui Maison (furniture stores, Rio de Janeiro, 1999); H. Stern Home (jewelry store, Rio de Janeiro, 2004); and the Elle et Lui Home (gift stores, Rio de Janeiro, 2006). She has also completed the Zuka Restaurant (Rio de Janeiro, 2002); Bazzar Restaurant (Rio de Janeiro, 2003); the Cláudio Paiva Residence (Rio de Janeiro, 2007); and the Estação Cinema (Rio de Janeiro, 2007), all in Brazil. Although she works with her husband, the architect **BOB NERI**, two projects were designed entirely by Bel Lobo—the Stravaganze Restaurant (Ipanema, Rio de Janeiro, 2004–05) and the Quadrucci Restaurant (Búzios, Rio de Janeiro, 2008, published here), both in Brazil.

BEL LOBO wurde 1960 in Rio de Janeiro geboren. Sie beendete 1984 ihr Studium in der Abteilung für Architektur und Städtebau an der Universidade Federal do Rio de Janeiro (UFRJ). Sie hat für die Firmen Salinas (Läden für Bademoden, Brasilien, seit 1994), Livraria da Travessa (Buchladenkette, Rio de Janeiro, seit 1995), Elle et Lui (Modegeschäfte, Rio de Janeiro, seit 2000), Farm (Modegeschäfte, Brasilien, seit 2004) gearbeitet und folgende Bauten ausgeführt: Elle et Lui Maison (Möbelgeschäfte, Rio de Janeiro, 1999), H. Stern Home (Schmuckgeschäft, Rio de Janeiro, 2004) und Elle et Lui Home (Läden für Geschenkartikel, Rio de Janeiro, 2006). Zu ihren weiteren Arbeiten zählen die Restaurants Zuka (Rio de Janeiro, 2002) und Bazzar (Rio de Janeiro, 2003), das Wohnhaus Cláudio Paiva (Rio de Janeiro, 2007) und das Kino Estação (Rio de Janeiro, 2007), alle in Brasilien. Obgleich Bel Lobo mit ihrem Ehemann, dem Architekten **BOB NERI**, zusammenarbeitet, stammen die Restaurants Stravaganze (Ipanema, Rio de Janeiro, 2004–05) und Quadrucci (Búzios, Rio de Janeiro, 200, hier vorgestellt) von ihr allein.

BEL LOBO, née à Rio de Janeiro en 1960, est diplômée de l'École d'architecture et d'urbanisme de l'Université fédérale de Rio de Janeiro (UFRJ, 1984). Elle a travaillé pour les marques Salinas (boutiques de maillot de bain, Brésil, depuis 1994) ; et Farm (boutiques de mode, Brésil, depuis 2004) ; et, à Rio de Janeiro, pour la chaîne de librairies Livraria da Travessa (depuis 1995) ; et les boutiques de mode Elle et Lui (depuis 2000) ; et y a conçu les magasins de meubles Elle et Lui Maison (1999) ; la bijouterie H. Stern Home (2004) ; et les magasins de cadeaux Elle et Lui Home (2006). Elle a également réalisé, à Rio de Janeiro, le restaurant Zuka (2002) ; le restaurant Bazzar (2003) ; la résidence Cláudio Paiva (2007) et le cinéma Estação (2007). Bien qu'elle travaille avec son mari, l'architecte **BOB NERI**, elle a accompli seule les restaurants Stravaganze (Ipanema, Rio de Janeiro, 2004–05) et Quadrucci (Búzios, Rio de Janeiro, 2008, publié ici).

QUADRUCCI RESTAURANT

Búzios, Rio de Janeiro, Brazil, 2008

Rua dias Ferreira 233, Rio de Janeiro, RJ CEP 22431-050, Brazil, +55 21 2512 4551
Area: 240 m². Clients: Mario Fonseca, Eduardo Bellizzi, and Eduardo Sidi. Cost: $100 000
Team: Mariana Travassos (Designer), Carla Dutra (Architect)

The Quadrucci Restaurant opened in September 2008 in the beach town of Búzios, located 180 kilometers east of Rio. It is built on a mangrove swamp, near a beach called Manguinhos. "As for the materials," explains Bel Lobo, "it has a lot of mirrors and glass in order to bring the beautiful scenery from the surroundings inside the restaurant. It is quite a simple project," she states, "that aims to allow the natural beauty of the area to play the main role, as the reflections of the mirrors and glass participate in creating a magical place." A main concern in this project was to keep the existing trees as they were, not only preserving them, but also making them part of the project. The roof is made of wood and painted white to reflect the light. A deck follows the mangrove swamp along the side of the restaurant. An effort was made to use natural, locally fabricated materials.

Das Restaurant Quadrucci wurde im September 2008 in der 180 km östlich von Rio am Meer gelegenen Stadt Búzios eröffnet. Es wurde an einem Mangrovesumpf nahe einer Bucht namens Manguinhos errichtet. „Die Materialien", erklärt Bel Lobo, „bestehen zum großen Teil aus Spiegeln und Glas, um die schöne Landschaft der Umgebung in das Restaurant hereinzuholen. Es ist ein ganz schlichter Entwurf, welcher der natürlichen Schönheit des Gebiets die Hauptrolle zuweist, da die Reflexionen der Spiegel und des Glases dazu beitragen, einen zauberhaften Ort zu erzeugen." Hauptanliegen bei diesem Projekt war die Erhaltung des vorhandenen Baumbestands – und ihn nicht nur zu erhalten, sondern ihn zu einem Teil des Entwurfs zu machen. Das Dach besteht aus Holz und wurde weiß gestrichen, um das Licht zu reflektieren. Eine Terrasse führt am Restaurant entlang über den Mangrovesumpf. Soweit möglich, wurden natürliche, vor Ort produzierte Materialien verwendet.

Le restaurant Quadrucci a ouvert en septembre 2008 dans la ville balnéaire de Buzios, à 180 km à l'est de Rio. Il a été construit dans la mangrove, près de la plage de Manguinhos. « Pour les matériaux », explique Bel Lobo, « nous avons utilisé beaucoup de miroirs et de verre qui permettent au luxuriante environnement de pénétrer dans le restaurant. C'est un projet assez simple qui laisse le rôle principal à la beauté naturelle de l'endroit, et les reflets des miroirs et du verre participent à la création d'un lieu magique. » L'une des préoccupations principales a été de conserver les arbres existants tout en les faisant participer au projet. Le toit est en bois peint en blanc pour réfléchir la lumière. Une terrasse suit le profil de la mangrove sur un côté de l'établissement, et un effort a été fait sur le choix des matériaux naturels, travaillés localement.

The flowing decks of the restaurant run into its natural surroundings. Synthetic fiber poufs are designed by Bel Lobo as are the wooden benches.

Die auskragenden Terrassen des Restaurants leiten in die natürliche Umgebung über. Bel Lobo gestaltete die Hocker aus synthetischem Fasermaterial sowie die hölzernen Bänke.

Les terrasses suspendues du restaurant epousent le cadre naturel. Les poufs en fibre synthétique et les bancs de bois ont été dessinés par Bel Lobo.

CHRISTIAN BIECHER

CBA / Christian Biecher & Associés
14 rue Crespin-du-Gast
75011 Paris
France

Tel: +33 1 49 29 69 39
Fax: +33 1 49 29 69 30
E-mail: info@biecher.com
Web: www.biecher.com

CHRISTIAN BIECHER received his diploma as an architect from the École d'Architecture de Paris-Belleville in 1989. He worked as a designer for Bernard Tschumi Architects (Paris, New York, 1986–92) and was an Assistant Professor at Columbia University Graduate School of Architecture (1990–97). He created his own firm in Paris in 1992, and, more recently, his current firm CBA (Christian Biecher & Associés) in 1997. He won the Maison & Objet "Designer of the Year" Award in 2001. He is currently working on the Starship, a building for retail space and offices in Prague (Czech Republic); the interior design of the Hôtel Chambon de la Tour (Uzès, France, in progress); and the refurbishment of the former Budapest Stock Exchange into a center for retail, offices, and restaurants. Aside from the Fauchon restaurant and store (Beijing, China, 2006–07, published here), he has also designed spaces for the same firm in Paris (2008), Tokyo, and Casablanca (in progress). Biecher has also worked recently on interior design and furniture for Harvey Nichols stores in Hong Kong, Dublin (Ireland), and Bristol (UK). He has also designed numerous objects for such manufacturers as Christofle, Poltrona Frau, and Baccarat.

CHRISTIAN BIECHER erhielt sein Diplom als Architekt 1989 an der École d'Architecture de Paris-Belleville. Er arbeitete für Bernard Tschumi Architects (Paris, New York, 1986–92) und war Assistant Professor an der Columbia University Graduate School of Architecture (1990–97). 1992 gründete er ein eigenes Büro in Paris und 1997 seine jetzige Firma CBA (Christian Biecher & Associés). Er war 2001 Designer des Jahres in der Sparte Maison & Objet. Gegenwärtig arbeitet er an Starship, einem Geschäfts- und Bürogebäude in Prag (Tschechien), an der Innenausstattung des Hotels Chambon de la Tour (Uzès, Frankreich, im Bau) sowie an der Umgestaltung der früheren Budapester Börse in einen Komplex mit Läden, Büros und Restaurants. Außer dem Restaurant und Geschäft Fauchon in Peking (2006–07, hier veröffentlicht) hat er für die gleiche Firma Räume in Paris (2008), Tokio und Casablanca (im Bau) geplant. Kürzlich hat Biecher auch die Innenausstattung und Möblierung für die Harvey-Nichols-Geschäfte in Hongkong, Dublin und Bristol gestaltet, ebenso zahlreiche Objekte für die Produzenten Christofle, Poltrona Frau und Baccarat.

CHRISTIAN BIECHER est diplômé d'architecture de l'École d'Architecture de Paris-Belleville (1989). Il a travaillé comme concepteur chez Bernard Tschumi Architects (Paris, New York, 1986–92) et a été assistant professeur à la Graduate School of Architecture de l'Université Columbia (1990–97). Il a créé sa première agence à Paris en 1992, et son agence actuelle CBA (Christian Biecher & Associés) en 1997. Il a remporté le titre de « Designer de l'année » du salon Maison & Objet en 2001. Il travaille actuellement au projet Starship, immeuble de commerces et de bureaux à Prague (République tchèque) ; l'aménagement intérieur de l'hôtel Chambon de la Tour (Uzès, France, en cours) et la transformation de l'ancienne Bourse de Budapest en centre de commerces, de bureaux et de restaurants. En dehors du restaurant et magasin Fauchon de Pékin (Chine, 2006–07, publié ici), il a aussi conçu des espaces pour cette société à Paris (2008), Tokyo et Casablanca (en cours). Biecher a également travaillé récemment sur des projets d'aménagement intérieur et de mobilier pour les magasins Harvey Nichols à Hongkong, Dublin (Irlande) et Bristol (G.-B.). Il a également dessiné de nombreux produits pour des fabricants comme Christofle, Poltrona Frau, et Baccarat.

FAUCHON
Beijing, China, 2006–07

B1-F2 Shin Kong Place, 87 Jianguo Lu, Chaoyang District, 100020 Beijing, China, +86 10 6533 1266 8228, www.fauchon.com
Area: 1300 m². Client: Fauchon SAS. Cost: not disclosed
Team: Céline Trétout, Pascal Schaller, Xiao Dai, Régis Botta, Alexander Bartzsch

Originally established in Paris in 1886 on the Place de la Madeleine, where it is still located, Fauchon describes itself as the "house of luxury culinary goods." Its products are now sold in over 400 locations all over the world. The Beijing space is divided into three main areas—a gold room containing a bakery and coffee bar, a silver room with a restaurant, and the largest of the three, the black-and-white room with a gourmet grocery store. In this space, says the designer Christian Biecher, "small touches of timber, bamboo, and leather allude to the origins of Fauchon's products from far-away places." The entrance and circulation areas are pink, giving the whole a varied, bright color scheme. Describing the restaurant's colors and materials, he states: "The luminous and crystalline 'silver' melts into a pale pink evoking subtle Parisian elegance." As he describes the overall themes, Biecher says: "I was inspired by the idea of a home with rooms of varying atmospheres. The concept of luxury is expressed through the rigor of design and the quality of the materials, as well as the delicious profusion of foods displayed in a spirit of generosity and festivity." This glittering combination of transparent and opaque surfaces certainly evokes a sense of luxury.

Fauchon, gegründet 1886 in Paris, Place de la Madeleine, wo die Firma immer noch residiert, beschreibt sich selbst als „Haus der kulinarischen Luxusgüter". Ihre Produkte werden heute in über 400 Geschäften in der ganzen Welt verkauft. Die Pekinger Niederlassung ist in drei Bereiche unterteilt – einen goldenen Raum, der eine Bäckerei und Kaffeebar enthält, einen silbernen Raum mit einem Restaurant und, als größten, den schwarz-weißen Raum mit einem Delikatessengeschäft. Hier, sagt der Architekt Christian Biecher, „verweisen kleine Spuren von Holz, Bambus und Leder auf die Herkunft von Fauchons Produkten aus fernen Ländern". Der Eingang und die Verkehrsflächen sind in Rosa gehalten und geben dem Ganzen eine lebendige, leuchtende Farbe. Das Farb- und Materialschema des Restaurants beschreibt der Architekt wie folgt: „Das leuchtende und kristalline ‚Silber' verschmilzt zu einem blassen Rosa, das an subtile Pariser Eleganz erinnert." Zur Gesamtgestaltung sagt Biecher: „Ich war inspiriert vom Gedanken an ein Wohnhaus mit Räumen unterschiedlicher Atmosphäre. Das Konzept des Luxus wird durch die Strenge der Gestaltung und die Qualität der Materialien ausgedrückt, aber auch durch die großzügige, verschwenderische und festliche Zurschaustellung der Delikatessen." Diese glitzernde Kombination aus transparenten und opaken Flächen ruft natürlich eine luxuriöse Wirkung hervor.

Fondé à Paris en 1886 en bordure de la place de la Madeleine, où se trouve toujours son magasin principal, Fauchon se présente comme une « maison de gastronomie de luxe ». Ses produits sont aujourd'hui distribués dans plus de quatre cents magasins dans le monde entier. Celui de Pékin est divisé en trois zones principales : une salle dorée contenant une pâtisserie et un café, une salle argentée pour le restaurant et la plus grande des trois, une salle noire et blanche consacrée à l'épicerie. Dans cet espace, « des touches légères de bois, de bambou et de cuir rappellent l'origine des produits Fauchon venus de pays lointains », explique Christian Biecher. L'entrée et les circulations sont traitées en rose, en déclinaison du programme chromatique de l'identité de la marque. Décrivant la charte des couleurs et des matériaux, Biecher poursuit : « L'argent, lumineux et cristallin, se fond dans le rose pâle qui évoque avec subtilité l'élégance parisienne… Je me suis inspiré de l'idée d'une maison dont les pièces diffuseraient des ambiances différentes. Le concept de luxe s'exprime dans la rigueur du projet et la qualité des matériaux, ainsi que par la profusion des produits présentés dans un esprit de générosité et de festivité. » Cette combinaison scintillante de surfaces transparentes et opaques crée un fort sentiment de luxe.

The surprising colored design of the space seems to blend seamlessly with the packaging of many of the food items on sale in the store.

Die erstaunliche Farbgestaltung des Raums scheint sich nahtlos der Verpackung vieler der im Laden verkauften Lebensmittel anzupassen.

Les conditionnements de nombreux produits vendus dans le magasin semblent se fondre dans l'étonnante ambiance chromatique de l'espace.

Bright, pastel colors characterize the spaces, and lead the eye from the décor itself to the products of Fauchon.

Leuchtende Pastellfarben kennzeichnen die Bereiche und lenken das Auge vom Dekor zu den Produkten von Fauchon.

Des couleurs tantôt vives tantôt pastel mettent en valeur les volumes et guident le regard du décor vers les produits Fauchon présentés.

Ice Round cordless lamps (Neoz Lighting) are set on the tables in the main dining space. The wall mirrors (AMC2) and canapés (Ateliers du Lude) were designed by Christian Biecher.

Die kabellosen Leuchten Ice Round (Neoz Lighting) stehen auf den Tischen des großen Speisesaals. Die Wandspiegel (AMC2) und Sofas (Ateliers du Lude) wurden von Christian Biecher entworfen.

Des lampes sans fil Ice Round (Neoz Lighting) sont disposées sur les tables de la salle du restaurant. Les miroirs muraux (AMC2) et les canapés (Ateliers du Lude) ont été dessinés par Christian Biecher.

The table (HIF, Italy), Chaise Tulip (Cassina), and Chauffeuses (Drucker), as well as the bar stools (Ateliers du Lude, rear on the right page) were all designed by Christian Biecher.

Der Tisch (HIF, Italien), Chaise Tulip (Cassina), die Sessel Chaffeuses (Drucker) und die Barhocker (Ateliers du Lude, rechte Seite im Hintergrund) wurden von Christian Biecher entworfen.

La table (HIF, Italie), la chaise Tulip (Cassina), les Chauffeuses (Drucker) et les tabourets de bar (Ateliers du Lude, au fond, page de droite) ont été dessinés par Christian Biecher.

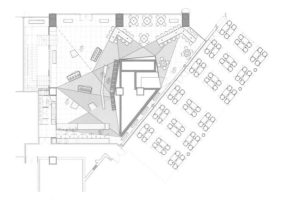

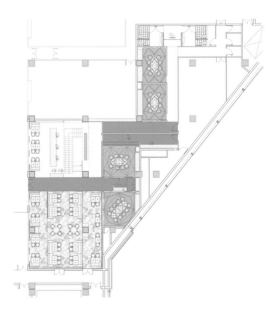

BUCHNER BRÜNDLER ARCHITEKTEN

Buchner Bründler Architekten AG Architekten RSA
Utengasse 19
4058 Basel
Switzerland

Tel: +41 61 301 01 11
Fax: +41 61 303 97 70
E-mail: mail@bbarc.ch
Web: www.bbarc.ch

BUCHNER BRÜNDLER ARCHITEKTEN was established by Daniel Buchner and Andreas Bründler in Basel in 1997. Born in Berneck, Switzerland, in 1967, Daniel Buchner graduated from the University of Applied Sciences in Basel in 1993, and worked for Morger & Degelo Architects in Basel before creating the present firm. He was a Guest Professor at the École Polytechnique Fédérale de Lausanne (EPFL) in 2008. Andreas Bründler was born in 1967 in Sins, Switzerland. He graduated from the University of Applied Sciences in Basel in 1993 as well and was a Guest Professor at the EPFL in 2008, working with Miller & Maranta Architects in Basel prior to establishing the current partnership with Buchner. They have built houses in Büren (2000–02); Blonay (2001–02); and Aesch (2003–04), all in Switzerland, and have recently completed the Set & Sekt Retail Store and Bar (Basel, 2007, published here). The pair are participating in the Ordos project curated by the artist Ai Wei Wei in Ordo (Mongolia) and are currently working on the residential and commercial "Volta Center" in Basel, renovating the City's youth hostel, and designing the Swiss Pavilion for Expo '10 in Shanghai (China).

Das Büro **BUCHNER BRÜNDLER ARCHITEKTEN** wurde 1997 von Daniel Buchner und Andreas Bründler in Basel gegründet. Der 1967 in Berneck, Schweiz, geborene Daniel Buchner erhielt sein Diplom 1993 an der Ingenieurschule Basel und arbeitete im Architekturbüro Morger & Degelo, bevor er die eigene Firma gründete. 2008 war er Gastprofessor an der École Polytechnique Fédérale de Lausanne (EPFL). Andreas Bründler wurde 1967 im schweizerischen Sins geboren, beendete ebenfalls 1993 sein Studium an der Ingenieurschule Basel und war Gastprofessor an der EPFL (2008). Er arbeitete bei Miller & Maranta in Basel und gründete dann das Büro mit Buchner. Dieses hat Wohnhäuser in Büren (2000–02), Blonay (2001–02) und Aesch (2003–04), alle in der Schweiz, gebaut und kürzlich Set & Sekt, ein Geschäft mit Bar fertiggestellt (Basel, 2007, hier veröffentlicht). Beide Partner haben an dem vom Künstler Ai Wei Wei kuratierten Ordos-Projekt in Ordos (Mongolei) teilgenommen und arbeiten gegenwärtig unter anderem an dem Wohn- und Geschäftshaus „Volta Zentrum" in Basel, dem Umbau der Jugendherberge in Basel, sowie am Schweizer Pavillon für die Expo '10 in Shanghai (China).

L'agence **BUCHNER BRÜNDLER ARCHITEKTEN** a été fondée par Daniel Buchner et Andreas Bründler à Bâle en 1997. Né à Berneck, Suisse, en 1967, Daniel Buchner est diplômé de l'Université des Sciences appliquées de Bâle (1993), et a travaillé pour l'agence Morger & Degelo à Bâle avant de créer l'agence actuelle. Il a été professeur invité à l'École polytechnique fédérale de Lausanne (EPFL) en 2008. Andreas Bründler, né en 1967 à Sins, Suisse, est diplômé de l'Université des Sciences appliquées de Bâle (1993), a été Professor invité à l'EPFL en 2008 et a travaillé pour les architectes Miller & Maranta à Bâle, avant de s'associer à Buchner. En Suisse, ils ont construit des maisons à Büren (2000–02) ; Blonay (2001–02) et Aesch (2003–04) ; et ont récemment achevé le Set & Sekt magasin et bar (Bâle, 2007, publié ici). Ils ont participé au projet Ordos sous la direction de l'artiste Ai Wei Wei à Ordos (Mongolie), et travaillent actuellement à la réalisation du centre commercial et résidentiel Volta à Bâle, à la renovation de l'auberge de jeunesse de Bâle, et à la conception du pavillon suisse pour Expo '10 à Shanghaï (Chine).

SET & SEKT RETAIL STORE AND BAR

Basel, Switzerland, 2007

Rümelinsplatz 5, 4001 Basel, Switzerland, +41 61 271 07 65, www.setandsekt.com
Area: 206 m². Client: Corinne Grüter. Cost: not disclosed
Collaboration: Tom Wüthrich (seating objects)

This was a temporary, one-year installation in a former market hall due to be transformed into a shopping mall. Intended to be used during the day as a shop for the clothes of designers Henrik Vibskov and Petar Petrov, the space was transformed into a bar in the evening with white curtains to cover the garments. The same curtains that the architects liken to a "silk cocoon" were used for fitting rooms in the fashion boutique. A steel counter was used as a sales desk in the day and as the bar at night with the bottles simply suspended from the ceiling. The bar and restrooms were painted black while the existing ceiling and its metal ducts were painted white. The architects opted to use Konstantin Grcic's Chair One because its "open metal grid fits perfectly into the scene."

Hierbei handelt es sich um eine einjährige Einrichtung in einer früheren Markthalle, die zu einem Einkaufszentrum umgebaut wird. Der Raum, in dem tagsüber Kleidung der Designer Henrik Vibskov und Petar Petrov verkauft wurde, verwandelte sich abends in eine Bar – mittels weißer Vorhänge, welche die Kleider verdeckten. Dieselben Vorhänge, die von den Architekten mit einem „seidenen Kokon" verglichen wurden, dienten zur Ausstattung der Modeboutique. Ein stählerner Tresen wurde tagsüber als Verkaufstheke und nachts als Bar verwendet; die Flaschen waren an der Decke aufgehängt. Bar und Toiletten waren schwarz gestrichen, die alte Decke und die Metallrohre weiß. Die Architekten entschieden sich für Konstantin Grcics Chair One, weil dessen „offenes Metallgitter hervorragend zur Szene passt".

Il s'agissait d'une installation temporaire mise en place pour un an dans un ancien marché qui devait être transformé en centre commercial. Conçu comme boutique pour les créations des stylistes de mode Henrik Vibskov et Petar Petrov, l'espace se transformait en bar pour la soirée, des rideaux blancs protégeant les vêtements. Ces mêmes rideaux que les architectes comparent à des « cocons de soie » servaient par ailleurs à délimiter les cabines d'essayage de la boutique. Un comptoir en acier qui servait de caisse pendant le jour se transformait en bar la nuit, les bouteilles étant suspendues au plafond. Le bar et les toilettes étaient peints en noir, le plafond et les conduites apparentes en blanc. Les architectes avaient choisi la chair One de Konstantin Grcic parce que « sa trame métallique ajourée était parfaitement adaptée à l'endroit ».

A floor plan (below) shows the full space, with the bar visible to the right. The stools are by Konstantin Grcic (Stool One, Magis). Above, the chairs, also by Konstantin Grcic (Chair One, Magis) are complemented by a Foto floor lamp designed by Thomas Bernstrand and Mattias Ståhlbom (Zero).

Unten: Der Grundriss zeigt den ganzen Raum mit der Bar auf der rechten Seite. Die Hocker stammen von Konstantin Grcic (Stool One, Magis). Oben: Die ebenfalls von Konstantin Grcic entworfenen Stühle (Chair One, Magis) werden ergänzt durch die Stehlampe Foto von Thomas Bernstrand und Mattias Ståhlborn (Zero).

Le plan au sol (ci-dessous) montre l'espace dans son entier et le bar visible à droite. Les tabourets sont de Konstantin Grcic (Stool One, Magis). Ci-dessus, les fauteuils, également de Konstantin Grcic (Chair One, Magis), avec le lampadaire Foto dessiné par Thomas Bernstrand et Mattias Ståhlbom (Zero).

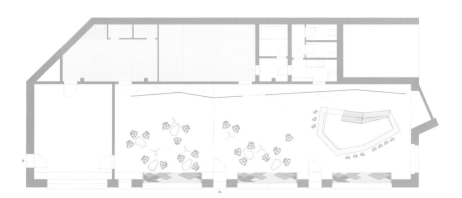

ARTHUR CASAS

Studio Arthur Casas SP
Rua Itápolis, 818
São Paulo, SP 01245-000
Brazil

Tel: +55 11 2182 7500
Fax: +55 11 3663 6540
E-mail: studio@arthurcasas.com
Web: www.arthurcasas.com

ARTHUR CASAS was born in 1961 and graduated as an architect from the Mackenzie University of São Paulo, Brazil, in 1983. He has concentrated on both interiors and constructions, developing residential and commercial projects with a distinctive vocabulary of forms. In 2008, Arthur Casas won the prestigious Red Dot Design Award, in Germany, for developing creative cutlery and dinner-set lines for Riva. He has participated in two Biennials of Architecture, in São Paulo, in 1997 and 2003, and in the Buenos Aires Biennial, in 2003 and 2005. His completed commercial projects include the Natura Store (Paris, France, 2005); Alexandre Herchcovitch store (Tokyo, Japan, 2007); Huis Clos Store (São Paulo, 2008); Cidade Jardim Mall (São Paulo, 2008); Zeferino Store, Oscar Freire Street (São Paulo, 2008); Kosushi Restaurant (São Paulo, 2008); C-View Bar and C-House Restaurant, Affinia Hotel (Chicago, Illinois, 2008); KAA Restaurant (São Paulo, 2008, published here); and the Jack Vartanian Store (New York, New York, 2008), all in Brazil unless stated otherwise.

ARTHUR CASAS, 1961 geboren, beendete 1983 sein Studium an der Mackenzie-Universität in São Paulo, Brasilien. Er hat sich auf Innen- und Außenarchitektur spezialisiert und Wohn- und Geschäftsbauten in einem charakteristischen Formenvokabular realisiert. 2008 erhielt Arthur Casas den renommierten deutschen Red Dot Design Award für die Gestaltung kreativer Bestecke und Essgeschirr für die Firma Riva. Er hat an den Architekturbiennalen 1997 und 2003 in São Paulo teilgenommen sowie 2003 und 2005 an den Biennalen von Buenos Aires. Zu seinen ausgeführten Projekten zählen die Geschäfte Natura (Paris, 2005), Alexandre Herchcovitch (Tokio, 2007), Huis Clos (São Paulo, 2008), die Cidade Jardim Mall (São Paulo, 2008), Zeferino in der Oscar-Freire-Straße (São Paulo, 2008), das Restaurant Kosushi (São Paulo, 2008), die Bar C-View und das Restaurant C-House im Affinia Hotel (Chicago, Illinois, 2008), das Restaurant KAA (São Paulo, 2008, hier veröffentlicht) und das Geschäft Jack Vartanian (New York, 2008).

ARTHUR CASAS, né en 1961, est diplômé en architecture de l'Université Mackenzie à São Paulo, Brésil (1983). Il se consacre à la fois à l'aménagement intérieur et à l'architecture, et met en œuvre dans ses projets résidentiels ou commerciaux un vocabulaire formel personnel. En 2008, ses lignes de couverts et de services de table pour Riva ont remporté le prestigieux prix allemand du Red Dot Design Award. Il a participé à deux biennales, la Biennale d'architecture de São Paulo en 1997 et 2003, et la Biennale de Buenos Aires en 2003 et 2005. Parmi ses projets réalisés : le magasin Natura (Paris, 2005) ; le magasin Alexandre Herchcovitch (Tokyo, 2007) ; le magasin Huis Clos (São Paulo, 2008) ; le Cidade Jardim Mall (São Paulo, 2008) ; le magasin Zeferino, rue Oscar Freire (São Paulo, 2008) ; le restaurant Kosushi (São Paulo, 2008) ; le bar C-View et le restaurant C-House à l'Affinia Hotel (Chicago, Illinois, 2008) ; le restaurant KAA (São Paulo, 2008, publié ici) et le magasin Jack Vartanian Store (New York, 2008).

KAA RESTAURANT

São Paulo, Brazil, 2008

Av. Juscelino Kubitschek, 279, Vila Olímpia, São Paulo, SP CEP 04543-010, Brazil, +55 11 3045 0043, www.kaarestaurante.com.br
Area: 683 m² (ground floor); 113 m² (mezzanine); 80 m² (kitchen). Client: not disclosed. Cost: not disclosed
Collaboration: Gica Meriara (Landscape Design)

Built on a long, narrow, 797-square-meter site, this new restaurant seeks to offer a refuge from the bustling streets of Brazil's largest city and to bring guests closer to the native environment of the country. A green vertical wall features plants from the Atlantic forest. At its base, a "water mirror" makes reference to the endangered Igarapés, or watersheds, of the region. A bar divides the space in two, with its generous shelves mounting up to the ceiling with "indigenous original objects that mimic the bottles, cups, and books." The roof of the restaurant is partly made with an automatically opening canvas that allows interior spaces to be transformed into an outdoor urban living room. According to the architect: "The furniture is contemporary and the philosophy of this place is about transporting the urban paulista (i. e. an inhabitant of São Paulo) to a green environment. It is an escape from the chaos."

Dieses neue, auf einem langen, schmalen, 797 m² großen Grundstück errichtete Restaurant will einen Rückzugsort von den hektischen Straßen der größten Stadt Brasiliens bieten und seinen Gästen die ursprüngliche Umgebung des Landes näherbringen. Eine vertikale grüne Wand zeigt Pflanzen aus dem Atlantischen Urwald. An ihrer Basis nimmt ein „Wasserspiegel" Bezug auf den gefährdeten Biotop Igarapés, das Gebiet der Wasserscheide in der Region. Eine Bar, deren hohe Regale bis zur Decke reichen und „originale einheimische Objekte, die Flaschen, Tassen und Bücher nachahmen", enthalten, teilt den Raum. „Ein Teil des Restaurantdachs besteht aus sich automatisch öffnendem Segeltuch, wodurch das Restaurant zu einem Aufenthaltsraum im Freien wird. „Die Möblierung ist zeitgemäß, der Charakter dieses Orts soll den Paulista (den Stadtbewohner von São Paulo) in eine grüne Umgebung versetzen. Es ist ein Rückzugsort aus dem Chaos."

Construit sur un long et étroit terrain de 797 m², ce nouveau restaurant propose en fait à ses clients un havre de paix où se protéger de l'animation des rues de la plus grande ville du Brésil et même de les rapprocher de l'environnement naturel de leur pays. Un grand jardin vertical met en scène des plantes de la forêt atlantique. À sa base, un miroir d'eau fait référence aux *igarapé*, les cours d'eau amazoniens actuellement en danger. Le bar divise l'espace en deux parties. De grands rayonnages toute hauteur présentent « des objets indigènes originaux qui imitent des bouteilles, des tasses et des livres ». Le toit est en partie fait d'une toile escamotable télécommandée qui permet de transformer les volumes intérieurs en une sorte de « salle de séjour urbaine en plein air ». « Le mobilier est contemporain et la philosophie du lieu vise à transporter les Paulistes (habitants de São Paulo) dans un environnement de verdure. Une échappée du chaos », précise l'architecte.

In the dining space, the ceiling light is by Rai de Meneres, the tables are designed by Arthur Casas (Taniguchi). The chairs at the bar are by Saarinen (Herança Cultural). The striped chairs are by Ronan & Erwan Bouroullec (Striped Sedia, Magis), while the armchairs below are by Arthur Casas (Casamatriz).

Die Deckenbeleuchtung im Speisesaal stammt von Rai de Meneres, die Tische wurden von Arthur Casas (Taniguchi) entworfen. Die Stühle in der Bar sind von Saarinen (Herança Cultural). Die gestreiften Stühle wurden von Ronan & Erwan Bouroullec entworfen (Striped Sedia, Magis), die Sessel unten stammen von Arthur Casas (Casamatriz).

Dans le restaurant, le luminaire est dû à Rai de Meneres, les tables ont été dessinées par Arthur Casas (Taniguchi), les fauteuils autour du bar sont de Saarinen (Herança Cultural), les chaises à lattes plastiques de Ronan & Erwan Bouroullec (Striped Sedia, Magis) et les fauteuils ci-dessous signés Arthur Casas (Casamatriz).

CL3

CL3 Architects Ltd.
7/F Hong Kong Arts Centre
2 Harbour Road
Wanchai, Hong Kong
China

Tel: +852 2527 1931
Fax: +852 2529 8392
E-mail: info@cl3.com
Web: www.cl3.com

William Lim Ooi Lee, the Managing Director of **CL3**, is an American citizen who was born in Hong Kong in 1957. He received his B.Arch (1982) and M.Arch (1983) degrees from Cornell University. He worked in Boston for five years before returning to Hong Kong, then worked for a developer there before joining CL3 in 1993. He has worked on all of CL3's projects since its creation in 1993. In 2006, CL3 Architects received an Asia Pacific Interior Design Award and a Hong Kong Institute of Architects' Award for its design of Vanke's sales office in Chengdu, China. The firm was responsible for both the architecture and the interiors of the three-story, 2000-square-meter facilities. CL3 has a staff of 56 and regional offices in Beijing, Bangkok, and Shanghai, and specializes in interior architecture. As well as The Racing Club and Nishimura Restaurants, published here, they have completed the Seibu Department Store (Hong Kong, 2000); a Tea House (Changsha, Hunan, 2003; winner of the American Institute of Architects, Hong Kong Chapter, Honor Award for Architecture 2003); Evian Spa (Shanghai, 2004); and are working on the restaurant of the Shangri-La Hotel in Chang Chun (ongoing), all in China.

William Lim Ooi Lee, leitender Direktor von **CL3**, ist amerikanischer Staatsbürger und wurde 1957 in Hongkong geboren. Er erhielt seinen B. Arch. (1982) und M. Arch. (1983) an der Cornell University. Danach arbeitete er fünf Jahre in Boston und dann wieder in Hongkong für einen Bauträger, bevor er sich 1993 an CL3 beteiligte. Seit der Gründung des Büros hat er an allen Projekten mitgearbeitet. 2006 erhielt CL3 einen Asia Pacific Interior Design Award und einen Preis des Hongkong Institute of Architects für den Entwurf des Verkaufsbüros Vanke in Chengdu, China. Das Büro war sowohl für die Architektur als auch für die Innengestaltung der dreigeschossigen, 2000 m² großen Einrichtung verantwortlich. CL3 hat 56 Mitarbeiter und unterhält Niederlassungen in Peking, Bangkok und Shanghai mit Schwerpunkt Innenarchitektur. Außer den hier vorgestellten Restaurants Racing Club und Nishimura hat das Büro folgende Projekte fertiggestellt: das Kaufhaus Seibu (Hongkong, 2000), ein Teehaus (Changsha, Hunan, 2003, ausgezeichnet vom American Institute of Architects, Hong Kong Chapter, Honor Award for Architecture 2003) und das Evian Spa (Shanghai, 2004). Zurzeit arbeitet das Büro am Restaurant des Shangri-La Hotels in Chang Chun (im Bau), alle in China.

William Lim Ooi Lee, directeur gérant de **CL3**, est un citoyen américain né à Hongkong en 1957. Il est B.Arch (1982) et M.Arch (1983) de l'Université Cornell. Il a travaillé à Boston pendant cinq ans, avant de revenir à Hongkong, où il a collaboré avec un promoteur avant de rejoindre CL3, en 1993. Il est intervenu sur tous les projets de l'agence depuis la création de celle-ci en 1993. En 2006, CL3 Architects a reçu le Asia Pacific Interior Design Award et un prix du Hongkong Institute of Architects pour les bureaux de vente de Vanke à Chengdu, Chine. L'agence avait été chargée à la fois de la conception architecturale et des aménagements intérieurs de ce projet de 2000 m². CL3, qui compte cinquante-six collaborateurs et possède des bureaux régionaux à Pékin, Bangkok et Shanghaï, s'est spécialisée en architecture intérieure. En dehors des restaurants Racing Club et Nishimura publiés ici, elle a signé le grand magasin Seibu (Hongkong, 2000) ; une maison de thé (Changsha, Hunan, 2003 ; Prix d'honneur 2003 de l'American Institute of Architects, Hongkong Chapter) ; l'Evian Spa (Shanghaï, 2004) ; et travaille actuellement sur le projet du restaurant du Shangri-La Hotel à Chang Chun (Chine).

THE RACING CLUB

Hong Kong, China, 2007

Hong Kong Jockey Club, Shatin Staff Quarters Blk 3 Chun Hang Court, New Territories, Hong Kong, China
Area: 892 m². Client: The Hong Kong Jockey Club. Cost: not disclosed
Team: Heather Wong, Aaron Wong, Jofi Ko

The ample spaces of the Racing Club allow for patrons to view flat-screen televisions (above, right). Smooth surfaces are carefully contrasted with more articulated volumes or cladding.

Oben, rechts: Die großzügigen Räume des Racing Club bieten genügend Platz zum Aufstellen von Flachbildfernsehern für die Gäste. Glatte Oberflächen stehen in bewusstem Kontrast zu stärker gegliederten Volumen oder zur Verkleidung.

Les généreux espaces du Racing Club laissent suffisamment de place pour disposer des téléviseurs à écrans plats (ci-dessus, à droite). Les plans lisses contrastent subtilement avec des volumes plus articulés ou des habillages.

Located at the Happy Valley Race Course in Hong Kong, The Racing Club is a new concept aimed at creating "a young, trendy nightspot with three main components: a bar, a restaurant, and a sushi bar." The Club is set in a 115-meter-long space, with three distinct areas—"sporty, elegant and colorful" for the bar; "dark and moody" for the restaurant; and white and "futuristic" for the sushi bar. The bar includes a multi-screen LED wall to display sporting events. A LED ceiling in the restaurant changes colors, while the tabletops in the sushi bar are made of cast acrylic with red rose petals. A surprising white wall also marks the sushi bar. "The detail is actually quite simple," says William Lim. "We laser cut the shapes onto aluminum panels finished with a white fluorocarbon coating, and backed them with a milky Plexiglas, which is installed 20 centimeters in front of the back wall. Then we put fluorescent lighting in between the Plexiglas and the back wall to achieve the glowing effect." As the architects go on to say: "The spaces are intended to complement each other and to make each stage of an evening a unique entertainment experience."

Der am Happy Valley Race Course in Hongkong gelegene Racing Club folgt einem neuen Konzept für ein „junges, trendiges Nachtlokal mit drei Hauptelementen: einer Bar, einem Restaurant und einer Sushi-Bar". Der Klub ist ein 115 m langer Raum mit drei verschiedenen Bereichen – einem „sportlichen, eleganten und farbigen" für die Bar, einem „dunklen und stimmungsvollen" für das Restaurant und einem weißen, „futuristischen" für die Sushi-Bar. Die Bar hat eine LED-Großleinwand zur Wiedergabe von Sportveranstaltungen, während im Restaurant eine LED-Decke die Farben wechselt. Die Tischplatten in der Sushi-Bar sind aus Gussharz mit roten Rosenblättern. Hier überrascht zudem eine weiße Wand. „Dieses Detail ist eigentlich ganz einfach", sagt William Lim. „Wir schnitten die Formen mit Laser aus Aluminiumtafeln, die mit einem weißen, fluoreszierenden Kohlenstoff beschichtet waren, und hinterlegten sie mit milchigem Plexiglas, das 20 cm vor der Rückwand installiert wurde. Dann setzten wir fluoreszierendes Licht zwischen Plexiglas und Rückwand, um die glänzende Wirkung zu erzielen. Die Räume sollen einander ergänzen und jede Phase eines Abends zu einem einmaligen Erlebnis machen."

Installé près du champ de course de Happy Valley à Hongkong, le Racing Club repose sur un nouveau concept de « lieu de nuit jeune et à la mode, dont les trois composants principaux sont un bar, un restaurant et un bar à sushis ». Le Club occupe un volume de 115 m de long divisé en trois zones distinctes : « style sportif, élégant et coloré » pour le bar, « sombre et plein d'atmosphère » pour le restaurant, blanc et « futuriste » pour le bar à sushis. Le bar est doté d'un mur d'écrans de LEDs qui diffusent des manifestations sportives. Dans le restaurant, le plafond éclairé également par des LEDs peut changer de couleur et les plateaux de table du bar à sushis sont en acrylique incrusté de pétales de roses rouges. Un étonnant mur blanc distingue également ce bar. « L'exécution est en fait assez simple », précise William Lim, « nous avons découpé au laser les formes dans des panneaux d'aluminium enduits de fluorure de carbone blanc, puis nous avons placé des éclairages fluorescents entre le Plexiglas et le mur du fond pour obtenir cet effet de luminescence… les espaces se complémentent pour faire de chaque étape de la soirée une expérience unique et différente ».

The bar contrasts with the vegetal or stalactite design for a ceiling fixture with a smooth glass surface and white marble floors. Below, the long, narrow floor plan.

Die Bar mit ihrer glatten Glasfläche und weißem Marmorfußboden bildet einen Gegensatz zur Deckenbeleuchtung in pflanzlicher oder stalaktitenartiger Form. Unten: Der lange, schmale Grundriss.

Le bar oppose un luminaire en forme de végétaux, ou de stalactites, à des surfaces planes habillées de verre et des sols en marbre. Ci-dessous, le plan au sol, étroit et tout en longueur.

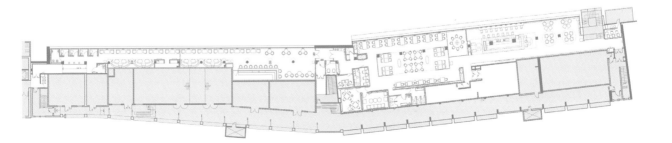

NISHIMURA RESTAURANT

Beijing, China, 2007

2/F, Shangri-La Hotel Beijing, 29 Zizhuyuan Road, Beijing 100089, China, +86 10 6841 2211 6719, www.shangri-la.com
Area: 499 m². Client: Beijing Shangri-La Hotel Ltd. Cost: not disclosed
Team: Jane Arnett, Joey Wan, Rain Ho, Alice Lei, Vani Cheung

CL3 designed both the Half-Wooden Sphere artwork (CSCEC Decoration Engineering) visible below, and the Glass Branch artwork on the right (also manufactured by CSCEC).

CL3 schuf sowohl das unten gezeigte Kunstwerk „Half-Wooden Sphere" (CSCEC Decoration Engineering) als auch das Werk „Glass Branch" rechts (ebenfalls von CSCEC).

CL3 a conçu à la fois la demi-sphère en bois visible ci-dessous et l'élément décoratif fait de branches de verre, à droite (tous deux réalisés par CSCEC Decoration Engineering).

This restaurant is located in the Shangri-La Hotel, Beijing. Its theme is the "natural garden" as reconstituted with wood, slate, rocks, pebbles, sand, bamboo, water, and dried tree branches. Three large artworks are made of engineered plywood sheet—"a giant wooden feature wall made of 1000 plywood sheets, with 2 punctured ovals, created by hand tooling the plywood sheets into shape; a large semi-sphere created by planes of plywood; a sushi counter with a 'wave' form enclosure made of bent plywood." The central wall is 9 meters long and 1.2 meters thick. Its plywood sheet structure is sanded and waxed, with two large oval openings allowing views through the restaurant.

Dieses Restaurant befindet sich im Shangri-La Hotel in Peking. Sein Thema ist ein „natürlicher Garten", der mit Holz, Schiefer, Felsbrocken, Kieselsteinen, Sand, Bambus, Wasser und trockenen Zweigen nachgebildet wurde. Drei große, aus Sperrholz gefertigte Kunstwerke schmücken es – „eine riesige, hölzerne Wand aus 1000 per Hand in Form geschnittenen Sperrholzplatten mit zwei ovalen Ausschnitten; eine große Halbkugel aus Sperrholzplatten, eine Sushi-Theke mit einer ‚wellenförmigen' Einfassung aus gebogenem Sperrholz". Die zentrale Wand ist 9 m lang und 1,2 m dick. Die Konstruktion aus Sperrholzplatten wurde geschmirgelt und gewachst; die beiden ovalen Ausschnitte bieten Durchblicke.

Ce restaurant se trouve dans l'hôtel Shangri-La à Pékin. Son thème est celui d'un « jardin naturel » reconstitué en bois, ardoise, rochers, graviers, sable, bambous, eau et branches d'arbres secs. Trois grandes pièces artistiques ont été réalisées en contreplaqué travaillé dans la masse : « Mille panneaux de contreplaqué, percés de deux ovales, formés à la main ; une grande demi-sphère également en panneaux de contreplaqué ; un comptoir pour sushis, pris dans une forme en vague, en contreplaqué courbé… » Le mur central mesure 9 m de long et 1,2 m d'épaisseur. La surface du contreplaqué est sablée et cirée et les deux grandes ouvertures ovales offrent des perspectives à travers le restaurant.

Narrow slat-shaped partitions rise to the ceiling, ensuring privacy for diners while also articulating the space. The Dry Woodstick artwork was designed by CL3 and fabricated by CSCEC.

Die Trennwände aus schmalen Lamellen reichen bis zur Decke und bieten Privatsphäre beim Speisen, aber sie gliedern auch den Raum. Das Kunstwerk „Dry Woodstick" wurde von CL3 entworfen und von CSCEC hergestellt.

Les étroites partitions en lattes de bois s'élèvent jusqu'au plafond et protègent l'intimité des clients tout en articulant l'espace. La composition de branchages Dry Woodstick a été conçue par CL3 et fabriquée par CSCEC.

A plywood laminated wall with an Oval 3D Sculpture was designed by CL3 (CSCEC) to lend the space a dynamism that it otherwise might have lacked. Below, the overall floor plan of the 499-square-meter restaurant.

Eine mehrschichtige Sperrholzwand mit der Skulptur „Oval 3D" wurde von CL3 (CSCEC) gestaltet, um dem ansonsten etwas eintönigen Raum etwas Dynamik zu verleihen. Unten: Der Gesamtgrundriss des 499 m² großen Restaurants.

Le mur en contreplaqué lamifié percé d'une sculpture ovale en trois dimensions a été conçu par CL3 (CSCEC) pour dynamiser un espace qui en avait besoin. Ci-dessous, le plan au sol de ce restaurant de 499 m².

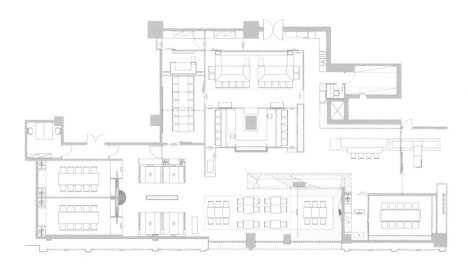

CONCRETE

Concrete Architectural Associates BV
Rozengracht 133 III
1016 LV Amsterdam
The Netherlands

Tel: +31 20 520 02 00
Fax: +31 20 520 02 01
E-mail: info@concreteamsterdam.nl
Web: www.concreteamsterdam.nl

Rob Wagemans was born in 1973. He created the interior design office **CONCRETE** Architectural Associates in 1997 with Gilian Schrofer and Erik van Dillen. Wagemans studied at the Academies of Architecture in Amsterdam and Utrecht and completed his studies with an M.Arch degree focusing on interior design. The firm, with a staff of 30, includes interior designers, product, communication, and graphic designers, as well as architects. The firm is divided into three divisions—Concrete Architectural Associates, Concrete Reinforced, and Studio Models + Monsters. Concrete worked with the architects UNStudio on the Mercedes-Benz Museum shops and restaurants (Stuttgart, Germany, 2006), while recent and current work includes the CitizenM Hotel, at Schiphol Airport (Amsterdam, The Netherlands, 2008); the Pearls and Caviar Restaurant (Abu Dhabi, UAE, 2008); VIP Lounge at Schiphol Airport (Amsterdam, The Netherlands, 2008); the Supperclub (Singapore, 2008, published here); the De Bijenkorf Kitchen (Amsterdam, The Netherlands, 2008, published here); and the Finca Pangola Eco Lodge (Costa Rica, 2009).

Rob Wagemans wurde 1973 geboren. Er gründete 1997 mit Gilian Schrofer und Erik van Dillen **CONCRETE** Architectural Associates, ein Büro für Innenarchitektur. Wagemans studierte an den Architekturakademien von Amsterdam und Utrecht und schloss sein Studium mit dem M. Arch. mit Schwerpunkt Innenarchitektur ab. Das Büro beschäftigt 30 Mitarbeiter, darunter Innenarchitekten, Produkt- und Kommunikationsdesigner sowie Grafiker und Architekten. Es besteht aus drei Abteilungen – Concrete Architectural Associates, Concrete Reinforced und Studio Models + Monsters. Concrete arbeitete mit den Architekten von UNStudio an den Läden und Restaurants des Mercedes-Benz-Museums (Stuttgart, 2006). Zu ihren neueren und in Arbeit befindlichen Werken zählen das CitizenM Hotel am Flughafen Schiphol (Amsterdam, 2008), das Restaurant Pearls and Caviar (Abu Dhabi, Vereinigte Arabische Emirate, 2008), die VIP-Lounge am Flughafen Schiphol (Amsterdam, 2008), der Supperclub (Singapur, 2008, hier vorgestellt), De Bijenkorf Kitchen (Amsterdam, 2008, hier vorgestellt) und die Finca Pangola Eco Lodge (Costa Rica, 2009).

Rob Wagemans est né en 1973. Il a créé l'agence d'architecture intérieure **CONCRETE** Architectural Associates en 1997 avec Gilian Schrofer et Erik van Dillen. Wagemans a étudié aux Académies d'Architecture d'Amsterdam et d'Utrecht et a obtenu un mastère en architecture d'intérieur. L'agence, constituée de trente collaborateurs, comprend des architectes d'intérieur, des designers produits, des concepteurs en communication et graphistes ainsi que des architectes. Elle compte trois départements : Concrete Architectural Associates, Concrete Reinforced, and Studio Models + Monsters. Concrete a travaillé avec l'agence d'architecture UNStudio sur le projet des boutiques et du restaurant du musée Mercedes-Benz (Stuttgart, Allemagne, 2006). Parmi ses réalisations récentes : le CitizenM Hotel à l'aéroport de Schiphol (Amsterdam, Pays-Bas, 2008) ; le restaurant Pearls and Caviar (Abu Dhabi, EAU, 2008) ; le salon VIP de l'aéroport de Schiphol (Amsterdam, 2008) ; le Supperclub (Singapour, 2008, publié ici) ; le restaurant De Bijenkorf Kitchen (Amsterdam, 2008, publié ici) et la Finca Pangola Eco Lodge (Costa Rica, 2009).

SUPPERCLUB

Singapore, 2008

331 North Bridge Road, Singapore, +65 8334 4080, www.supperclub.com
Area: 1300 m². Client: IQ Creative. Cost: not disclosed. Team: Rob Wagemans, Erik van Dillen, Jan Paul Shaltmeijer

The Supperclub is located in the Odeon Towers opposite the Raffles Hotel. Diagonal steel plates clad the entrance floor, with diagonal mirrors on the walls and ceiling, creating the "atmosphere of a theatre of the 1960s." Within, one space contains the Salle Neige, a two-story lounge modeled on a jewelry box. A black-painted open kitchen is centrally located. From this space, visitors can move to the Bar Rouge with an island bar and a red glass façade. These two spaces are separated by a "swing door" that can be opened to signify the transition from a supper area to the club. A purple *chambre privée* with a chrome steel bed in its center that can be used as a dance floor is set at the end of a corridor. A smoking room and "Supperdeluxe" private dining room and a *cave à vin* complete the project.

Der Supperclub liegt in den Odeon Towers gegenüber dem Hotel Raffles. Das Eingangsgeschoss ist mit schrägen Stahlplatten sowie Spiegeln an Wänden und Decke verkleidet, was eine „Theateratmosphäre der 1960er-Jahre" hervorruft. Innen gibt es die Salle Neige, eine zweigeschossige Lounge in der Form eines Schmuckkastens. Im Zentrum befindet sich eine schwarz gestrichene, offene Küche. Von hier aus können die Gäste weitergehen zur Bar Rouge mit einer Barinsel und einer roten Glasfassade. Diese beiden Räume sind durch eine „Schwingtür" verbunden, die als Übergang vom Speiseraum zum Klub geöffnet werden kann. Das in Violett gehaltene Chambre privée mit einer zentralen Fläche aus Chromstahl, die auch als Tanzfläche genutzt werden kann, liegt am Ende eines Korridors. Ein Rauchsalon sowie der private Speiseraum „Supperdeluxe" und ein Weinkeller vervollständigen das Angebot.

Le Supperclub se trouve dans les Odeon Towers, face à l'hôtel Raffles. Les panneaux d'acier posés en diagonale du sol de l'entrée, et les miroirs également en diagonale sur les murs et les plafonds créent « l'atmosphère d'un théâtre des années 1960 ». À l'intérieur, la « Salle Neige », est un *lounge* sur deux niveaux qui évoque une boîte à bijoux. La cuisine ouverte, toute noire, est implantée au centre. Plus loin s'ouvre un « Bar Rouge » à façade en verre rouge, avec un bar en îlot. Ces deux espaces sont séparés par une « porte battante » qui fait transition entre la section réservée au restaurant et le club. Une chambre privée, dotée d'un lit de chrome en son centre qui peut servir de piste de danse, se trouve à l'extrémité d'un corridor. Un salon pour fumeurs et une salle à manger privée « Supperdeluxe » avec cave à vin complètent le projet.

Below, the Bar Rouge has strong coloring that justifies its name, with a red glass façade and bar.

Unten: Die Bar Rouge hat mit einer roten Glasfassade und Bar eine kräftige Farbgebung, die ihren Namen rechtfertigt.

Ci-dessous, le Bar Rouge, dont le nom est justifié par la couleur du décor mais aussi de la façade transparente et du bar.

An entrance area features steel plates on the floor and diagonal mirrors on the ceilings and walls. Below, a dining space and another view of the Bar Rouge.

Der Eingangsbereich ist mit Stahlplatten auf dem Boden und diagonalen Spiegeln an Decken und Wänden ausgestattet. Unten: Ein Speiseraum sowie eine weitere Ansicht der Bar Rouge.

Le décor de l'entrée est constitué de miroirs posés en pointes de diamant sur le plafond et les murs et d'un sol en plaques d'acier. Ci-dessous, une salle du restaurant et une autre vue du Bar Rouge.

DE BIJENKORF KITCHEN

Amsterdam, The Netherlands, 2008

Dam 1, Amsterdam 1012 JS, The Netherlands, +31 20 552 17 00, www.bijenkorf.nl
Area: 1295 m². Client: de Bijenkorf. Cost: not disclosed
Team: Rob Wagemans, Melanie Knüwer, Charlotte van Mill, Erik van Dillen

Located in the de Bijenkorf department store, this restaurant is an open kitchen consisting of different cuisines from all over the world and the project is based on the idea of a light unpolished stainless-steel kitchen cupboard used to display foods and to provide seating. Seating areas are located on either side of this cupboard. Floors and tabletops are made of bamboo. In the kitchen area, a hot buffet is located on one side and three islands for cold dishes and juice on the other. A 30-meter-long cupboard wall on the hot buffet side is divided according to the different cuisines of the world. A number of different types of chairs made by Vitra, such as the Plastic Armchair DAW (Charles & Ray Eames) or a chrome bar stool, or InOut Chair, by Gervasoni, are provided for guests. A coffee bar and check-out counter are located at the entrance and exit of the kitchen. A roof garden with seating completes the project.

Dieses Restaurant im Kaufhaus De Bijenkorf besteht aus einer offenen Küche mit Speiseangeboten aus aller Welt. Der Entwurf basiert auf der Vorstellung von einem hellen Küchenschrank aus mattem Edelstahl zur Präsentation von Speisen und mit einem Angebot an Sitzplätzen. Diese sind zu beiden Seiten dieses Schranks angeordnet. Böden und Tischplatten bestehen aus Bambus. Im Küchenbereich befinden sich auf einer Seite das Büfett für warme Speisen, auf der anderen drei Inseln für kalte Gerichte und Säfte. Eine 30 m lange Schrankwand auf der Seite des warmen Büfetts ist in die verschiedenen Küchen der Welt aufgeteilt. Für die Gäste sind unterschiedliche, von Vitra produzierte Stuhltypen vorgesehen, z. B. der Plastic Armchair DAW von Charles & Ray Eames und der Barstuhl aus Chrom InOut von Gervasoni. Eine Kaffeebar und eine Kassentheke befinden sich am Ein- und Ausgang der Küche. Ein Dachgarten mit Sitzplätzen vervollständigt das Restaurant.

Implanté dans le grand magasin de Bijenkorf, le restaurant est doté d'une cuisine ouverte qui prépare des plats de différents pays du monde. Le projet repose sur une idée de mobilier de cuisine en acier inoxydable légèrement poli qui sert aussi bien à présenter les mets qu'à s'asseoir pour les consommer. Les zones de tables sont situées de part et d'autre de ce comptoir. Les sols et les dessus de table sont en bambou. La partie cuisine propose un buffet chaud d'un côté et trois îlots pour plats froids et jus de fruits et de légumes de l'autre. Un mur présentoir de 30 m de long côté buffet chaud est divisé en section illustrant les principales cuisines du monde. Des sièges de types différents fabriqués par Vitra ont été disposés, dont le modèle Plastic Armchair DAW de Charles & Ray Eames ou le tabouret de bar en acier InOut de Gervasoni. Le comptoir pour le café et la caisse ont été implantés près de la zone d'entrée et de sortie. Les clients peuvent également se rendre et s'asseoir dans le jardin aménagé sur le toit.

Carefully stacked and displayed food products (right page) set the tone for the dining space seen above. Dark ceilings contrast with the lighter floor cladding.

Effektvoll gestapelte und präsentierte Lebensmittel (rechte Seite) leiten zum oben sichtbaren Speiseraum über. Dunkle Decken bilden einen Gegensatz zum helleren Bodenbelag.

Des produits gastronomiques présentés avec soin (page de droite) donnent le ton du décor de la salle de restaurant (ci-dessus). Les plafonds sombres contrastent avec le revêtement de sol de couleur claire.

The cafeteria atmosphere seen in these images contrasts somewhat with the seated dining areas, adding to an overall impression of bustling, carefully designed spaces.

Die auf diesen Bildern erkennbare Atmosphäre der Cafeteria steht irgendwie im Kontrast zu den Speiseräumen mit Sitzplätzen. Alle Bereiche machen einen lebendigen, sorgfältig geplanten Eindruck.

L'atmosphère de cafétéria qu'illustrent ces pages contraste d'une certaine manière avec les zones de consommation, qui renforcent l'impression d'animation de ce lieu très vivant, étudié avec soin.

Designer furniture such as the Plastic Armchair DAW by Charles and Ray Eames, or chrome bar stools by Gervasoni (both manufactured by Vitra), contribute to the image of quality and thoughtful contrasts provoked by Concrete.

Designermöbel wie der Plastic Armchair DAW von Charles und Ray Eames oder die verchromten Barhocker von Gervasoni (beide von Vitra produziert) tragen zu der von Concrete angestrebten qualitätvollen Wirkung und den gewünschten Kontrasten bei.

Le mobilier de designers comme le Plastic Armchair DAW de Charles et Ray Eames, ou les tabourets de bar chromés de Gervasoni (tous deux fabriqués par Vitra), contribuent à donner l'image de qualité et offrir les contrastes voulus par Concrete.

ELECTRIC DREAMS

Electric Dreams AB
Alsnögatan 3
11641 Stockholm
Sweden

Tel: +46 736 55 32 92/+46 739 57 70 25
E-mail: info@electricdreams.se
Web: www.electricdreams.se

ELECTRIC DREAMS was founded in December 2006. Firm principals are Joel Degermark, born in 1973 in Stockholm, and Catharina Frankander, born in 1978 in Stockholm. Degermark received his B. A. in Design from Beckmans School of Design (Stockholm, 1999) and his M. A. in Product Design from the Royal College of Art (London, 2004). He co-founded and ran Yeti Design (1999–2006). Catharina Frankander received her B. A. in Architecture from the Architectural Association (AA) in London (2003) and her M.Arch degree from the Royal Institute of Technology (Stockholm, 2005). She worked with Klark Architects (1998–2005) and founded B+lu Architecture (2005–06). Their major projects include: Weekday Malmö Flagship Store (Malmö, 2006); Monki Götgatan Flagship Store (Stockholm, 2007); Pleasant Bar (Stockholm, 2007, published here); Kulturhuset Public Bathroom (Stockholm, 2007); Surgery in the Forest Dental Office (Stockholm, 2007); Monki Kompassen Flagship Store (Göteborg, 2007); B-Reel HQ (Stockholm, 2008); Atelier Exquise (office/retail, Paris, France, 2008); Monki Sergelgatan Flagship Store (Stockholm, 2008); B-Reel NYC offices (New York, New York, 2008); and the Vasa Museum permanent exhibition (Stockholm, 2008), all in Sweden unless stated otherwise.

ELECTRIC DREAMS wurde im Dezember 2006 von Joel Degermark, geboren 1973 in Stockholm, und der 1978 ebenfalls in Stockholm geborenen Catharina Frankander gegründet. Degermark erhielt seinen B. A. in Design an der Beckmans School of Design (Stockholm, 1999) und seinen M. A. in Produktdesign am Royal College of Art (London, 2004). Er war Mitbegründer und Leiter des Büros Yeti Design (1999–2006). Catharina Frankander absolvierte ihren B. A. in Architektur an der Architectural Association (AA) in London (2003) und ihren M. Arch. an der Königlichen Technischen Hochschule Stockholm (2005). Sie arbeitete bei Klark Architects (1998–2005) und gründete B+lu Architecture (2005–06). Zu ihren wichtigsten Projekten zählen: Weekday Malmö Flagship-Store (Malmö, 2006), Monki Götgatan Flagship-Store (Stockholm, 2007), die Pleasant Bar (Stockholm, 2007, hier veröffentlicht), die öffentlichen Toiletten im Kulturhuset (Stockholm, 2007), der Behandlungsraum des Dentalbüros Forest (Stockholm, 2007), Monki Kompassen Flagship-Store (Göteborg, 2007), der B-Reel-Hauptsitz (Stockholm, 2008), Atelier Exquise (Büros/Läden, Paris, 2008), Monki Sergelgatan Flagship-Store (Stockholm, 2008), die New Yorker Büros von B-Reel (2008) und die ständige Ausstellung des Vasa-Museums (Stockholm, 2008).

L'agence **ELECTRIC DREAMS** a été fondée en décembre 2006. Ses dirigeants sont Joel Degermark, né en 1973 à Stockholm (Suède), et Catharina Frankander, née en 1978 également à Stockholm. Degermark est B. A. en design de l'École de Design Beckmans (Stockholm, 1999) et M. A. en design produit du Royal College of Art (Londres, 2004). Il a cofondé et animé Yeti Design (1999–2006). Catharina Frankander est B. A. en architecture de l'Architectural Association (AA) de Londres (2003) et M.Arch de l'Institut royal de technologie (Stockholm, 2005). Elle a travaillé pour Klark Architects (1998–2005) et fondé B+lu Architecture (2005–06). Parmi leurs projets les plus importants : le magasin amiral Weekday (Malmö, Suède, 2006) ; le magasin amiral Monki Götgatan (Stockholm, 2007) ; le Pleasant Bar (Stockholm, 2007, publié ici) ; les toilettes publiques de la Kulturhuset (Stockholm, 2007) ; un cabinet dentaire (Stockholm, 2007) ; le magasin amiral Monki Kompassen (Göteborg, Suède, 2007) ; le siège de B-Reel (Stockholm, 2008) ; l'Atelier Exquise (boutique/bureaux, Paris, 2008) ; le magasin amiral Monki Sergelgatan (Stockholm, 2008) ; des bureaux pour B-Reel (New York, 2008) ; et l'exposition permanente du Vasa Museum (Stockholm, 2008).

PLEASANT BAR

Stockholm, Sweden, 2007

Kammakargatan 9, 11124 Stockholm, Sweden, +46 8 23 23 20, www.pleasant.se
Area: 65 m². Client: Pleasant Prospect AB. Cost: €300 000

The ceiling of the Pleasant Bar is covered with convex mirrors, a fact that Catharina Frankander attributes to her admiration for the Japanese artist Yayoi Kusama. "We like to build dreamlike worlds," she says. "It's about exaggeration: too much, too beautiful, too ugly, too many." Opened in June 2007, the Pleasant Bar is located in central Stockholm and has only five tables. A mixture of vintage chairs are painted glossy black, while the graphics, exterior glass illustrations, and urban forest wallpaper were created by Dizel & Sate. Frankander says: "As a starting point we worked with a fragmented fever dream, in which there was a place where the city meets an enchanted forest. The endless mirror-ball ceiling in the bar area permits secret spying on everyone else. The wall framing the bar interior forms a graphic element as well as a bottle stand, DJ stand, and narrow one-cocktail-only tables." Joel Degermark's Cluster Lamps for Moooi are placed above each table, while strands of fiber-optic threads are reflected in the bathroom ceilings and walls, "creating an endless sea of illuminated grass."

Die Decke der Pleasant Bar ist mit konvexen Spiegeln verkleidet – was Catharina Frankander mit ihrer Bewunderung des japanischen Künstlers Yayoi Kusama erklärt. „Wir lieben es, Traumwelten zu bauen", sagt sie. „Es handelt sich um Übertreibungen: zu viel, zu schön, zu hässlich, zu viele." Die im Juni 2007 eröffnete Pleasant Bar liegt im Zentrum von Stockholm und hat nur fünf Tische. Verschiedene klassische Stühle wurden glänzend schwarz gestrichen; die Grafiken, die Illustrationen an der verglasten Außenwand und die Urban-Forest-Tapete stammen von Dizel & Sate. Frankander sagt: „Als Ausgangspunkt nahmen wir eine Art Fiebertraum, in dem es einen Ort gab, wo die Stadt auf einen Zauberwald trifft. Die Decke aus zahllosen runden Spiegeln in der Bar macht das heimliche Ausspähen von jedermann möglich. Die Innenwand der Bar wie auch das Flaschenregal, das DJ-Pult und die schmalen Cocktailtische bilden grafische Elemente." Joel Degermarks Cluster-Leuchten für Moooi hängen über jedem Tisch, während sich an den Decken und Wänden der Toiletten faserartige Lichtstreifen spiegeln und „ein Meer aus erleuchtetem Gras" bilden.

Le plafond de ce bar est recouvert de miroirs convexes, ce que Catharina Frankander explique par son admiration pour l'artiste japonais Yayoi Kusama. « Nous aimons construire des univers de rêve », explique-t-elle, « tout est exagéré : trop, trop de tout, trop beau, trop laid ». Ouvert en juin 2007, le Pleasant, situé dans le centre de Stockholm, n'offre que cinq tables. Les chaises de diverses origines sont laquées en noir brillant et les éléments graphiques, comme les illustrations sur la façade de verre et le papier peint qui évoquent une forêt urbaine, ont été créés par Dizel & Sate. Catharina Frankander poursuit : « Nous avons pris pour point de départ un rêve fiévreux et fragmenté dans lequel on pourrait découvrir comme une forêt enchantée dans laquelle les citadins se rencontreraient. Le plafond en boules de miroir qui semble se multiplier à l'infini permet d'épier discrètement tout le monde. Le mur qui cadre l'intérieur du bar constitue un élément graphique, tout comme un rangement pour bouteilles, un stand pour le DJ et des tables étroites qui ne peuvent recevoir qu'un seul cocktail. » Des lampes Cluster de Joel Degermark pour Moooi sont disposées sur chaque table, et des torons de fibre optique se reflètent dans le plafond et les murs des toilettes « … créant une mer infinie d'algues illuminées ».

Within the Pleasant Bar, Threadlite Fibre Optics are used (left page). Above, custom-made graphics by Dizel & Sate. Below, tables and bar by Electric Dreams.

Für den Innenraum der Pleasant Bar wurden Leuchten der Marke Threadlite Fibre Optics verwendet (linke Seite). Oben: Eigens hierfür angefertigte Grafiken von Dizel & Sate. Unten: Tische und Bar von Electric Dreams.

Un éclairage en fibre optique Threadlite anime le plafond du Pleasant Bar. Ci-dessus, un décor graphique spécialement réalisé par Dizel & Sate. Les tables et le bar ci-dessous ont été dessinés par Electric Dreams.

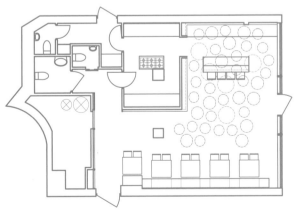

ELENBERG FRASER

Elenberg Fraser
374 George Street
Fitzroy
Melbourne, Victoria 3065
Australia

Tel: +61 3 9417 2855
Fax: +61 3 9417 2866
E-mail: mail@e-f.com.au
Web: www.e-f.com.au

ELENBERG FRASER was founded in 1998 by Callum Fraser and Zahava Elenberg. Elenberg received her B.Arch degree from the Royal Melbourne Institute of Technology University (RMIT) the same year. She created the firm Move-in in 2002 to propose complete "furniture packages" for clients in Australia and the United Arab Emirates. In 2003, she was named the Australian Telstra Young Business Woman of the Year. Callum Fraser has a "specific interest in sustainable design and the minimization of the effects of construction and building occupation on the environment." As the pair describe the originality of their firm, they state: "Combining the creativity of a design studio with the outcome-orientation of a commercial firm, we believe that design-driven and market-driven are not opposed to each other." After the Gingerboy Restaurant (Melbourne, 2006, published here), their ongoing projects in 2008 include the Elm Apartments, residential (South Melbourne); 401 St. Kilda Road, residential apartments (Melbourne); Batman Street, residential (Melbourne); Claremont Street, Lilli Apartments, residential (South Yarra, Melbourne); and another residential project at MacKenzie Street (Melbourne), all in Australia.

Das Büro **ELENBERG FRASER** wurde 1998 von Callum Fraser und Zahava Elenberg gegründet. Elenberg erhielt im gleichen Jahr ihren B. Arch. an der Royal Melbourne Institute of Technology University (RMIT). Sie gründete 2002 die Firma Move-in, die komplette „Möbelpakete" für Kunden in Australien und den Vereinigten Arabischen Emiraten anbot. 2003 wurde sie zur australischen Telstra Young Business Woman of the Year ernannt. Callum Fraser hat ein „besonderes Interesse an nachhaltigem Bauen und der Reduzierung der Auswirkungen von Bauten und der Bautätigkeit auf die Umwelt". Das Paar beschreibt die Besonderheit seines Büros wie folgt: „Wir verbinden die Kreativität eines Architekturbüros mit der Gewinnorientierung einer kommerziellen Firma und sind davon überzeugt, dass das Bemühen um gute Gestaltung nicht im Widerspruch zum Gewinnstreben steht." Nach dem Restaurant Gingerboy (Melbourne, 2006, hier vorgestellt) zählen zu ihren Projekten aus dem Jahr 2008 die Wohnanlagen Elm Apartments (South Melbourne), 401 St. Kilda Road (Melbourne), Batman Street (Melbourne), Claremont Street, Lilli Apartments (South Yarra, Melbourne) sowie ein weiteres Wohnbauprojekt in der MacKenzie Street (Melbourne), alle in Australien.

L'agence **ELENBERG FRASER** a été fondée en 1998 par Callum Fraser et Zahava Elenberg. Elenberg avait obtenu son B.Arch du Royal Melbourne Institute of Technology University (RMIT) la même année. Elle a créé l'agence Move-in en 2002 qui propose des « ensembles de mobilier » complets pour ses clients d'Australie et des Émirats arabes unis. En 2003, elle a été élue « Jeune femme d'affaires de l'année » en Australie. Callum Fraser « s'intéresse spécifiquement au design durable et à la réduction des effets de la construction et de l'occupation des bâtiments sur l'environnement ». Pour les deux associés : « Combinant la créativité d'un studio de design et une orientation sur la production qui est celle d'une société commerciale, nous pensons que l'axe design ou celui du marketing ne sont pas opposés ». Après le restaurant Gingerboy (Melbourne, 2006, publié ici), ils travaillent en 2008 sur des projets résidentiels comme Elm Apartments (South Melbourne) ; 401 St. Kilda Road (Melbourne) ; Batman Street (Melbourne) ; Claremont Street, Lilli Apartments (South-Yarra, Melbourne) ; et un autre projet résidentiel sur MacKenzie Street (Melbourne).

GINGERBOY RESTAURANT

Melbourne, Australia, 2006

27–29 Crossley Street, Melbourne VIC, Australia, +61 3 9662 4200, www.gingerboy.com.au
Area: 125 m². Client: Teague Ezard. Cost: $421 000
Collaborator: Lisa Jennings

Designed in three months and then built in three, the Gingerboy Restaurant has a bamboo bar made modern by the use of a back-lit acrylic with a digital print of Chinese characters between rows of bottles, and an open kitchen. Bamboo is also used as a flooring material, while, logically, the restaurant focuses on Asian cuisine. A random array of "dark bamboo poles with hundreds of interwoven point lights creates an atmosphere of airy night markets and an open night sky." These poles are arrayed on the ceiling and wall. In the dining area, the architects seek to evoke "an intimacy akin to the Shanghai tea rooms of the 1950s." Gold stainless-steel tiles on the exterior façade confirm this almost nostalgic reference. Victoria Ghost Chairs by Kartell and Charles Ghost Stools from the same manufacturer are used, while the high-gloss bamboo tables were custom-made.

Das in drei Monaten geplante und in drei Monaten ausgeführte Restaurant Gingerboy hat eine Bar aus Bambus, die durch eine hinterleuchtete Acrylwand mit einem Digitaldruck chinesischer Figuren zwischen Flaschenreihen und einer offenen Küche modernisiert wurde. Bambus wurde auch als Fußbodenbelag im Restaurant verwendet, das auf asiatische Küche spezialisiert ist. Eine freie Anordnung „dunkler Stangen aus Bambus mit Hunderten eingefügten Punktleuchten erzeugt eine Atmosphäre wie auf dunklen, nächtlichen Märkten unter freiem Himmel". Diese Stangen sind an der Decke und den Wänden angebracht. Im Speisebereich haben die Architekten versucht, „die Intimität der Shanghaier Teeräume aus den 1950er-Jahren" hervorzurufen. Goldfarbene Edelstahlplatten an der Außenfassade verstärken diesen eher nostalgischen Bezug. Eingerichtet wurde das Restaurant mit Stühlen von Victoria Ghost und Hockern von Charles Ghost, beide von Kartell produziert, sowie mit eigens angefertigten Hochglanztischen aus Bambus.

Conçu en trois mois et construit alors en trois, le restaurant Gingerboy possède une cuisine ouverte et un bar en bambou rendu très moderne par un panneau acrylique rétroéclairé sur lequel figure une reproduction numérique de caractères chinois qui apparaissent entre les alignements des bouteilles. Le bambou a également été choisi pour les sols et, logiquement, le restaurant propose une cuisine axée sur la gastronomie asiatique. L'implantation aléatoire « des tubes de bambou sombre supportant des centaines de points lumineux créent une atmosphère de marché nocturne et de ciel étoilé ». Ils sont disposés aussi bien contre les murs qu'au plafond. Dans la partie salle à manger, les architectes ont cherché à évoquer « une intimité proche de celle des salons de thé de Shanghaï dans les années 1950 ». En façade, un carrelage doré confirme cette référence nostalgique. Les sièges Victoria Ghost et les tabourets Charles Ghost sont édités par Kartell. Les tables en bambou vernis ultrabrillant ont été spécialement fabriquées pour le restaurant.

In the dining space, Victoria Ghost Chairs (Kartell) reflect LED point lights (Fairy Lights, Australia) and Sonny Track Lights (Euroluce). Charles Ghost Stools (Kartell) are lined up at the bar. Below, the restaurant seen from the street.

Im Speiseraum reflektieren die Victoria-Ghost-Stühle (Kartell) die LED-Punktstrahler (Fairy Lights, Australien) und Sonny-Track-Leuchten (Euroluce). Charles-Ghost-Barhocker (Kartell) sind in der Bar zu sehen. Unten: Blick von der Straße in das Restaurant.

Dans la salle à manger, les chaises Victoria Ghost (Kartell) reflètent les ponctuations lumineuses des LEDs (Fairy Lights, Australie) et des Sonny Track Lights (Euroluce). Des tabourets Charles Ghost (Kartell) entourent le bar. Ci-dessous, le restaurant vu de la rue.

STUART FORBES

Stuart Forbes Associates Ltd.
189c Putney Bridge Road
London SW15 2NY
UK

Tel: +44 208 704 09 71
Fax: +44 208 788 45 20
E-mail: stuart@stuartforbes.com
Web: www.stuartforbes.com

STUART FORBES graduated from the Royal College of Art in London with an M. A. in Architecture and Design Studies in 1989. He worked at Tinley Pike Shane, Richard Horden Associates, before entering the office of Richard Rogers in 1990. Forbes created his own firm, Stuart Forbes Associates, in 2006, after a 15-year career with Richard Rogers Partnership. He worked on the Millennium Dome and Heathrow Terminals 1 and 5 with Rogers. Current projects include the Blackrock Clinic Dublin (Ireland, 2007); Festival Pier London (UK, 2007); and a mixed residential and commercial scheme in Draycott Avenue (London, UK, 2007). He has also worked on the renovation of the River Café (London, 2008, published here) and on numerous residential projects, principally in London.

STUART FORBES beendete 1989 sein Studium am Royal College of Art in London mit einem M. A. in Architektur und Design. Vor seinem Eintritt in das Büro von Richard Rogers 1990 war er für Tinley Pike Shane und Richard Horden Associates tätig. Stuart Forbes gründete sein Büro, Stuart Forbes Associates, im Jahr 2006 nach 15-jähriger Partnerschaft mit Richard Rogers. Er arbeitete mit Rogers am Millennium Dome und an den Heathrow Terminals 1 und 5. Zu seinen aktuellen Projekten zählen die Klinik Blackrock in Dublin (2007), der Festival Pier London (2007) und ein Wohn- und Geschäftskomplex in der Draycott Avenue (London, 2007). Er hat auch die Sanierung des River Cafés (London, 2008, hier veröffentlicht) und zahlreiche Wohnbauten, vorwiegend in London, ausgeführt.

STUART FORBES, diplômé du Royal College of Art de Londres et M. A. en Architecture and Design Studies en 1989, a travaillé pour Tinley Pike Shane, Richard Horden Associates, avant d'entrer chez Richard Rogers en 1990. Après avoir travaillé quinze ans pour le Richard Rogers Partnership, pour lequel il est intervenu sur le Dôme du Millénaire et les terminaux 1 et 5 d'Heathrow avec Richard Rogers, il a créé sa propre agence, Stuart Forbes Associates, en 2006. Parmi ses projets actuels : la Clinique Blackrock (Dublin, Irlande, 2007) ; le Festival Pier (Londres, G.-B., 2007) ; et un projet mixte, résidentiel et commercial, sur Draycott Avenue (Londres, 2007). Il a également réalisé la rénovation du River Café (Londres, 2008, publié ici) et de nombreux projets résidentiels, principalement à Londres.

RIVER CAFÉ

London, UK, 2008

37 Thames Wharf, Rainville Road, London W6 9HA, +44 207 386 4200, www.rivercafe.co.uk
Area: 300 m². Client: The River Café Limited. Cost: £2 million
Collaboration: Richard Rogers

The River Café, located next to the offices of Richard Rogers (Rogers Stirk Harbour + Partners), is an emblematic London eating spot, where the star chef Jamie Oliver worked for three years. The site at Thames Wharf, Hammersmith, was purchased by Richard Rogers Partnership in 1983 as the location for the practice's new offices. Formerly an industrial complex, including a group of early 20th-century warehouses, the site includes the River Café, opened in 1987 in a green area on the bank of the Thames. A fire early in 2008 at the establishment provided an occasion for Stuart Forbes to redesign the 20-year-old restaurant, adding an open kitchen, private dining room, and cocktail bar. Visitors are greeted with a yellow Corian reception desk near the bar, while a wood-burning oven made in Italy is another new feature. Richard Rogers has stated: "Stuart and I set out to make distinctive but subtle changes—we have significantly remodeled the River Café while respecting its visual identity and retaining its original elegance."

Das neben den Büros von Richard Rogers (Rogers Stirk Harbour + Partners) gelegene River Café ist ein zum Symbol gewordenes Londoner Speiselokal, in dem der Starkoch Jamie Oliver drei Jahre gearbeitet hat. Das Grundstück am Thames Wharf in Hammersmith war 1983 von Richard Rogers Partnership für ihr neues Büro erworben worden. Zu diesem ehemaligen Industriegelände gehören mehrere Lagerhäuser aus dem frühen 20. Jahrhundert sowie das 1987 eröffnete River Café in einer Grünfläche am Ufer der Themse. Zu Beginn des Jahres 2008 bot ein Feuer in der Anlage Stuart Forbes die Chance, das 20 Jahre alte Restaurant umzugestalten und um eine offene Küche, einen privaten Speiseraum und eine Cocktailbar zu erweitern. Die Gäste werden an einer gelben Empfangstheke aus Corian neben der Bar begrüßt. Ein weiteres neues Element ist ein in Italien produzierter Holzofen. Richard Rogers hat erklärt: „Stuart und ich wollten deutliche, aber subtile Veränderungen – wir haben das River Café entscheidend umgestaltet, jedoch seine visuelle Identität respektiert und seine ursprüngliche Eleganz bewahrt."

Ouvert en 1987, le River Café, situé non loin des bureaux de Richard Rogers (Rogers Stirk Harbour + Partners), est l'un des plus célèbres restaurants londoniens. Le jeune chef star Jamie Oliver y a œuvré pendant trois ans. Le terrain de Thames Wharf, à Hammersmith, avait été acquis par Richard Rogers Partnership en 1983 pour les nouveaux bureaux de l'agence. Ancien complexe industriel qui comprenait un ensemble d'entrepôts du début du XXe siècle, le site comprend donc également le River Café édifié dans un espace vert en bordure de la Tamise. Un incendie survenu en 2008 a été l'occasion pour Stuart Forbes de rénover ce restaurant vieux de vingt ans. Il a créé une cuisine ouverte, installé un four à bois importé d'Italie, une salle à manger privée et un bar à cocktails. Les clients sont accueillis par un comptoir de réception en Corian jaune près du bar. Selon Richard Rogers : « Stuart et moi avons pris le parti de changements clairs, mais subtils. Nous avons significativement remodelé le River Café en respectant son identité visuelle, et en conservant l'élégance de son origine. »

Chairs are designed by Alberto Meda (Alias). "The Pass" counter was designed by SFA and manufactured in LG Hi-Macs. The wood oven was also designed by SFA, with an outer dome in fibrous plaster by Thomas & Wilson.

Die Stühle wurden von Alberto Meda entworfen (Alias). Die Theke „The Pass" wurde von SFA geplant und von LG Hi-Macs hergestellt. Auch der Holzofen mit einer Kuppel aus faserverstärktem Gipsputz von Thomas & Wilson wurde von SFA entworfen.

Les chaises ont été conçues par Alberto Meda (Alias). Le comptoir « The Pass » a été dessiné par SFA et fabriqué en LG Hi-Macs (acrylique massif). Le four à bois a également été conçu par SFA, sa coupole extérieure en plâtre fibreux étant l'œuvre de Thomas & Wilson.

DORIANA AND MASSIMILIANO FUKSAS

Studio Fuksas
Piazza del Monte di Pietà 30 / 00186 Rome / Italy
Tel: +39 06 68 80 78 71 / Fax: +39 06 68 80 78 72
E-mail: office@fuksas.it / Web: www.fuksas.it

MASSIMILIANO FUKSAS was born in 1944 in Rome. He received his degree in Architecture at the "La Sapienza" University in 1969. In 1967, he opened his own studio in Rome, followed by one in Paris in 1989. He won the 1999 Grand Prix d'Architecture in France, and has written the architecture column of the Italian weekly *L'Espresso* since 2000. He was the Director of the VIIth Architecture Biennale in Venice (1998–2000). He has worked with **DORIANA MANDRELLI FUKSAS** since 1985. She graduated from ESA (École Spéciale d'Architecture) in Paris, France, and has been responsible for Fuksas Design since 1997. The presence of Massimiliano Fuksas in France was notably marked by his work at the Médiathèque in Rézé (1986–91); the National Engineering School in Brest (1990–92); the Maison des Arts in Bordeaux (1992–95); and the Maximilien Perret De Vincennes High School in Alfortville near Paris (1995–98). His Cor-ten steel entrance for the caves at Niaux (1988–93) shows, as did the Maison des Arts in Bordeaux, that Fuksas has a sustained interest in contemporary art. In 1995–2001, they built the Vienna Twin Tower, a 150-meter-high headquarters for Wienerberger (Vienna, Austria). More recently, they completed the Ferrari Research Center (Maranello, Italy, 2001–04); the New Trade Fair (Milan, Italy, 2002–05); the Armani Ginza Tower (Tokyo, Japan, 2005–07); the Peres Peace Center (Jaffa, Israel, 1999–2008); the Zenith Music Hall (Strasbourg, France, 2003–08); the Mainz Markthäuser 11–13 (Mainz, Germany, 2003–08); the MAB Zeil (Frankfurt, Germany, 2000–09); and Armani Fifth Avenue (New York, USA, 2007–09). Ongoing work includes the Molas Golf Resort (Pula, Italy); the Euromed Center in Marseille (France); the French National Archives Center at Pierrefitte-sur-Seine (Paris, France); the Centro Congressi Eur (Rome, Italy); the Lyon Confluence (Lyon, France); and Terminal 3 International Shenzhen Bao'an Airport (Shenzhen, China).

MASSIMILIANO FUKSAS, 1944 in Rom geboren, beendete 1969 sein Architekturstudium an der Universität La Sapienza. 1967 eröffnete er ein Büro in Rom und 1989 ein weiteres in Paris. 1999 gewann er den französischen Grand Prix d'Architecture. Seit 2000 verfasst er die Architekturkolumne in der italienischen Wochenzeitung *L'Espresso*. Er war Direktor der VII. Architekturbiennale in Venedig (1998–2000). Seit 1985 arbeitet er mit **DORIANA MANDRELLI FUKSAS** zusammen. Sie erwarb ihr Diplom an der Ecole Spéciale d'Architecture in Paris und ist seit 1997 für Fuksas Design verantwortlich. Von den Arbeiten Massimiliano Fuksas' in Frankreich sind vor allem die Médiathèque in Rézé (1986–91), die staatliche Ingenieurschule in Brest (1990–92), die Maison des Arts in Bordeaux (1992–95) und die Schule Maximilien Perret De Vincennes in Alfortville bei Paris (1995–98) zu nennen. Der von Fuksas aus Cor-Ten-Stahl gestaltete Eingang zu den Höhlen von Niaux (1988–93) wie auch die Maison des Arts in Bordeaux zeugen von seinem anhaltenden Interesse an zeitgenössischer Kunst. 1995 bis 2001 baute er den Vienna Twin Tower, die 150 m hohe Hauptverwaltung der Firma Wienerberger in Wien. In neuerer Zeit wurden das Ferrari-Forschungszentrum (Maranello, Italien, 2001–05), die New Trade Fair (Mailand, 2002–05), der Armani Ginza Tower (Tokio, 2005–07), das Peres Peace Center (Haifa, Israel, 1999–2008), das Konzerthaus Zenith (Straßburg, Frankreich, 2003–08), die Mainzer Markthäuser (Markt 11–13, Mainz, 2003–08), das Einkaufszentrum MAB Zeil (Frankfurt am Main, 2000–09), und Armani Fifth Avenue (New York, 2007–09) fertiggestellt. In Arbeit befinden sich der Molas Golf Resort (Pula, Italien), das Euromed-Center in Marseille (Frankreich), das französische Staatsarchiv in Pierrefitte-sur-Seine (Paris), das Centro Congressi Eur (Rom), Lyon Confluence (Lyon) und der Terminal 3 des Internationalen Flughafens Shenzhen Bao'an (China).

MASSIMILIANO FUKSAS, né en 1944 à Rome, est diplômé d'architecture de l'université romaine La Sapienza (1969). Il ouvre sa propre agence à Rome en 1967, suivie d'une seconde à Paris en 1989. En 1999, il remporte en France le grand prix d'architecture et tient, depuis 2000, une rubrique d'architecture dans l'hebdomadaire italien *L'Espresso*. Il a été directeur de la VIIe Biennale d'architecture de Venise (1998–2000). Il travaille avec **DORIANA MANDRELLI FUKSAS** depuis 1985. Celle-ci, diplômée de l'ESA de Paris, est responsable de Fuksas Design depuis 1997. La présence en France de Massimiliano Fuksas a été marquée par plusieurs réalisations, dont la médiathèque de Rézé (1986–91), l'École nationale des ingénieurs de Brest (1990–92), la Maison des Arts de Bordeaux (1992–95) et le collège Maximilien-Perret à Alfortville, près de Paris (1995–98). Son entrée en acier Corten pour les grottes de Niaux (France, 1988–93) témoigne, comme la Maison des Arts de Bordeaux, de son intérêt profond pour l'art contemporain. En 1995–2001, le studio construit le Vienna Twin Tower de 150 m de haut, siège de Wienerberger (Vienne, Autriche). Plus récemment, ils ont achevé le Centre de recherches Ferrari (Maranello, Italie, 2001–04), les nouvelles installations de la Foire de Milan (Milan, 2002–05), la tour Armani Ginza (Tokyo, 2005–07), le Centre Pérès pour la Paix (Haïfa, Israël, 1999–2008); le Zénith à Strasbourg (2003–08); les Mainz Markthäuser 11–13 (Mainz, Allemagne, 2003–08); le MAB Zeil (Francfort, Allemagne, 2000–09); et Armani Fifth Avenue (New York, États-Unis, 2007–09). Parmi les projets en cours figurent le club de golf de Molas (Pula, Italie); le Centre Euromed à Marseille; les Archives nationales de France à Pierrefitte-sur-Seine (près de Paris); le Centro Congressi Eur (Rome); Lyon Confluence (Lyon); et le Terminal 3 International de l'aéroport de Shenzhen Bao'an (Shenzhen, Chine).

ARMANI RISTORANTE

Armani Ginza Tower, Tokyo, Japan, 2005–07

5–5–4 Ginza, Chuo-ku, Tokyo 104–0061, Japan, +81 3 6274 7005, www.armaniginzatower.com
Area: 384 m² (restaurant); 38 m² (privé bar); 70 m² (terrace). Client: Giorgio Armani
Cost: not disclosed. Interior and Furniture Design: Filippo Bich, Ana Gugic, Maria Lucrezia Rendace
Lighting Design: Speirs & Major Associates

Furniture and partitions for the
restaurant were also designed by
Doriana and Massimiliano Fuksas,
here creating a flowing continuity
that nonetheless affords patrons
a good deal of privacy.

Möblierung und Trennwände für das
Restaurant wurden ebenfalls von
Doriana und Massimiliano Fuksas
entworfen; sie erzeugen ein Raum-
kontinuum, das den Gästen dennoch
ausreichend Privatsphäre bietet.

Les meubles et les cloisonnements
ont également été conçus par Doriana
and Massimiliano Fuksas, pour créer
une continuité fluide tout en apportant une réelle intimité aux clients.

The 7000-square-meter, 12-story Armani Ginza Tower, set in the midst of one of Tokyo's most fashionable shopping districts, was designed by Doriana and Massimiliano Fuksas. The first shop in the world to sell the entire Armani line, the building includes a spa and a restaurant. The Italian restaurant is set on the 10th floor, and seats 120 people. Like the rest of the building, beginning with the façades, its décor is based on bamboo—here curving partitions based on a golden bamboo leaf theme are in evidence, giving each dining space a relatively high degree of privacy. Lighting work by Speirs & Major Associates heightens the glittering effect generated by the gold partitions and mesh surfaces. The 40-seat Armani *privé* lounge bar is located one floor up, with a terrace offering spectacular views of the city and floor-to-ceiling mesh screens that again create spaces where visitors can be on their own while still being in the midst of a fashionable location. Inspired both by the clothes of Armani and by Tokyo, "a city alive with continuous movement," as Fuksas says, the Armani Ristorante is certainly cosmopolitan in its décor, alluding in a metaphoric way to Japanese culture with its repeated bamboo themes.

Der 7000 m² große, zwölfgeschossige Armani Ginza Tower inmitten von Tokios modernstem Einkaufsbezirk wurde von Doriana und Massimiliano Fuksas geplant. Dieses Gebäude enthält das erste Geschäft, in dem die gesamte Armani-Kollektion angeboten wird, sowie ein Hallenbad und ein italienisches Restaurant. Letzteres befindet sich im zehnten Geschoss und hat Platz für 120 Gäste. Wie das gesamte Gebäude, von den Fassaden angefangen, ist auch das Restaurant mit Bambus ausgestattet – hier sind es gekrümmte Zwischenwände, die auf dem Symbol eines goldenen Bambusblatts beruhen und jedem Speisebereich ein recht großes Maß an Privatsphäre bieten. Die Lichtplanung von Speirs & Major Associates verstärkt den Glitzereffekt der goldenen Trennwände und Gitterflächen. Die 40 Personen fassende Bar Armani Privé liegt einen Stock höher und hat eine Terrasse mit großartigem Ausblick auf die Stadt sowie raumhohe Gitterwände, die den Gästen ebenfalls eine gewisse Privatsphäre bieten, während sie sich zugleich mitten in einem modischen Lokal aufhalten. Das Armani-Restaurant ist sowohl von der Kleidung Armanis als auch von Tokio inspiriert, „einer Stadt in ständiger Bewegung", wie Fuksas sagt. Es ist zweifellos kosmopolitisch in seinem Dekor und verweist mit den sich wiederholenden Bambusmotiven metaphorisch auf die Kultur Japans.

Conçue par Doriana et Massimiliano Fuksas, la tour Armani Ginza de 7000 m² sur douze niveaux se dresse au centre de l'un des quartiers de la mode et du luxe les plus élégants de Tokyo. Premier magasin au monde à proposer la totalité de la gamme des productions Armani, l'immeuble comprend également un spa et un restaurant italien de cent vingt couverts au neuvième étage. Comme le reste de l'immeuble, à commencer par les façades, le décor repose sur le bambou. Des cloisonnements incurvés très présents, inspirés d'une thématique de feuille de bambou dorée, permettent d'assurer un degré d'intimité assez élevé aux tables. L'éclairage, dû à Speirs & Major Associates, met en valeur l'effet lumineux de ces cloisons dorées et des surfaces en maillage métallique. L'Armani privé, lounge de quarante places, se trouve à l'étage supérieur d'où une terrasse vient offrir une vue spectaculaire sur la ville. Des écrans en maillage métallique allant du sol au plafond délimitent des espaces où les clients peuvent se sentir entre soi, installés au milieu de cet endroit si élégant. Inspiré à la fois par les vêtements d'Armani et par Tokyo « ville en mouvement continu », comme l'explique Fuksas, ce restaurant est cosmopolite par son décor, mais il fait aussi métaphoriquement allusion à la culture japonaise par la répétition de thèmes inspirés du bambou.

The round seating areas seen on the left page are clearly visible in the lower floor plan (below). Lighting and shimmering wall surfaces contribute to an atmosphere that is continuous, from the architecture to the furniture and object design.

Die auf der linken Seite abgebildeten runden Sitzbereiche sind im Grundriss des unteren Geschosses (unten) gut erkennbar. Die Beleuchtung und die glänzenden Wandflächen tragen zu einer einheitlichen, von der Architektur über die Möblierung bis zum Objektdesign erzeugten Atmosphäre bei.

Les alcôves rondes de la page de gauche apparaissent également sur le plan au sol (ci-dessous). L'éclairage et l'effet de vibration donné par les plans verticaux contribuent à créer une atmosphère qui s'appuie aussi bien sur l'architecture que sur le mobilier et le design des objets.

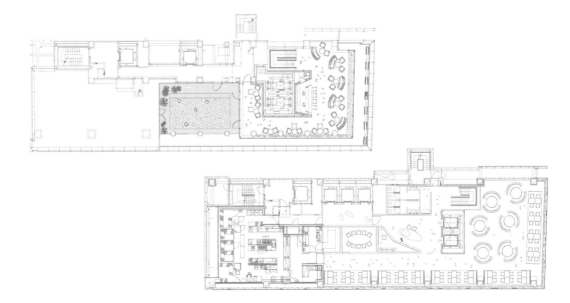

GCA ARQUITECTES

GCA Arquitectes Associats
C/ Valencia 289 bajos
08009 Barcelona
Spain

Tel: +34 934 761 800
Fax: +34 934 761 806
E-mail: info@gcaarq.com
Web: www.gcaarq.com

GCA ARQUITECTES ASSOCIATS was founded in 1986 by Josep Juanpere and Antonio Puig, while Josep Riu, Jesús Hernando, Jordi Castañé, Lluís Escarmís, Maria Vives, Francisco de Paz, and Carlos Aizpún became partners at later dates. Josep Juanpere was born in 1952 in Barcelona and studied at the Escuela Técnica Superior de Arquitectura (ETSA) Barcelona (1970–76). Maria Vives was born in 1974 in Barcelona and also studied at the ETSA (1992–98). The firm currently employs 120 people, specialized in architecture, interior design, graphics, landscaping, photography, and management, and has offices in Barcelona and Madrid. They do both private and government work, with projects ranging from office buildings to single-family homes, shopping centers, community facilities, and hotels and restaurants. They have carried out projects in Paris, London, Prague, and Lisbon, and shops in New York, Athens, Great Britain, China, and Taiwan. In Barcelona, they have worked on the Arts Hotel (1990–92); Gran Marina Hotel (World Trade Center, 2000–02); Prestige Hotel (2000–02); AC Barcelona Hotel (2002–04); Casa Fuster Hotel (2005); Olivia Plaza Hotel (2005–06); and the Hesperia Tower Hotel interior design. They have also focused on the restaurants of Sergi Arola, Carles Gaig, Fermí Puig, and Santi Santamaria, who is responsible for the Evo Restaurant published here.

GCA ARQUITECTES ASSOCIATS wurde 1986 von Josep Juanpere und Antonio Puig gegründet; Josep Riu, Jesús Hernando, Jordi Castañé, Lluís Escarmís, Maria Vives, Francisco de Paz und Carlos Aizpún kamen später als Partner hinzu. Josep Juanpere wurde 1952 in Barcelona geboren und studierte an der Escuela Técnica Superior de Arquitectura (ETSA) in Barcelona (1970–76). Maria Vives wurde 1974 in Barcelona geboren und studierte ebenfalls an der ETSA (1992–98). Gegenwärtig beschäftigt die Firma 120 Personen; es ist auf Architektur, Innenarchitektur, Grafik, Landschaftsplanung, Fotografie und Management spezialisiert und unterhält Büros in Barcelona und Madrid, die öffentliche und private Aufträge ausführen. Die Projekte reichen von Bürogebäuden, Einfamilienhäusern, Einkaufszentren und Gemeinschaftseinrichtungen bis zu Hotels und Restaurants und wurden in Paris, London, Prag und Lissabon ausgeführt, außerdem gestaltete GCA Geschäfte in New York, Athen, Großbritannien, China und Taiwan. In Barcelona haben sie das Arts Hotel (1990–92), das Gran Marina Hotel (World Trade Center, 2000–02), das Prestige Hotel (2000–02), das AC Barcelona Hotel (2002–04), das Casa Fuster Hotel (2005), das Olivia Plaza Hotel (2005–06) und die Innenausstattung des Hesperia Tower Hotel realisiert, ferner die Restaurants von Sergi Arola, Carles Gaig, Fermí Puig sowie Santi Santamaria, der auch für das hier vorgestellte Restaurant Evo verantwortlich sind.

L'agence **GCA ARQUITECTES ASSOCIATS** a été fondée en 1986 par Josep Juanpere et Antonio Puig, rejoints plus tard par Josep Riu, Jesús Hernando, Jordi Castañé, Lluís Escarmís, Maria Vives, Francisco de Paz et Carlos Aizpún. Josep Juanpere, né en 1952 à Barcelone, a étudié à l'École technique supérieure d'architecture (ETSA) de Barcelone (1970–76). Maria Vives, née en 1974 à Barcelone, a également étudié à l'ETSA (1992–98). L'agence emploie actuellement cent vingt collaborateurs spécialisés en architecture, architecture intérieure, design graphique, paysagisme, photographie et gestion, et possède des bureaux à Barcelone et Madrid. Elle intervient aussi bien pour une clientèle privée que publique, réalisant immeubles de bureaux, résidences familiales, centres commerciaux, équipements publics, hôtels et restaurants. Elle est intervenue à Paris, Londres, Prague, Lisbonne, et a aménagé des magasins à New York, Athènes, en Grande-Bretagne, Chine, et à Taïwan. À Barcelone, elle a travaillé sur les projets du Arts Hotel (1990–92) ; Gran Marina Hotel (World Trade Center, 2000–02) ; Prestige Hotel (2000–02) ; AC Barcelona Hotel (2002–04) ; Casa Fuster Hotel (2005) ; Olivia Plaza Hotel (2005–06) et l'intérieur du Hesperia Tower Hotel. Elle a également réalisé les restaurants de Sergi Arola, Carles Gaig, Fermí Puig, et de Santi Santamaria qui dirige le restaurant Evo publié ici.

EVO RESTAURANT

Hesperia Tower, Barcelona, Spain, 2005–06

Gran Vía, 144, 08907 L'Hospitalet, Barcelona, Spain, +34 934 135 030, www.restauranteevo.es
Area: 267 m². Client: Hesperia Hotels. Cost: not disclosed

The Evo Restaurant is located atop the Hesperia Tower designed by Richard Rogers (Rogers Stirk Harbour with Alonso & Balaguer). With its bright red-and-blue structural beams, the tower is certainly recognizable, but its most surprising element may be the volume conceived by the architect for the restaurant. Compared to a "flying saucer" that landed on top of the building, this glass-domed pod sits 105 meters above ground level. The 55-seat restaurant, whose décor was created by GCA, occupies three levels—with the tables on the second floor and the kitchen and private areas above. As the architects say: "The complexity of the interior design resides in harmonizing the spectacular nature of the architectonic space and reflects the detail and quality of chef Santi Santamaria's cuisine. Therefore circular platforms were created at different levels, which allow circulation while giving privacy and identity to the tables' locations." The perimeter walls are covered in screen-painted glass designed for the restaurant, while GCA created the carpet design. Structural stainless-steel lamps shaded with golden-colored fabric are used to resolve the lighting problems posed by the glass dome, casting a specific light on each table. Black lacquered wood furniture is used, with stools by Pedrali and Artifort chairs with upholstery by Gastón & Daniela.

Das Restaurant Evo liegt auf dem von Richard Rogers (Rogers Stirk Harbour mit Alonso & Balaguer) geplanten Hesperia Tower. Das Hochhaus fällt zweifellos durch seine leuchtend roten und blauen Tragbalken auf; sein wohl erstaunlichstes Merkmal ist jedoch das vom Architekten erdachte Volumen des Restaurants, vergleichbar mit einer „fliegenden Untertasse", die auf dem Dach des Gebäudes gelandet ist. Dieses mit einer Glaskuppel überdeckte Restaurant liegt 105 m über Geländehöhe und bietet Platz für 55 Gäste. Seine Ausstattung stammt von GCA. Es nimmt drei Geschosse ein – die Tische befinden sich auf der zweiten Ebene, die Küche und private Räume liegen darüber.[6] Die Architekten erklären hierzu: „Die Komplexität der Innenarchitektur steht im Einklang mit der spektakulären Architektur des Raums und entspricht in ihren Details auch der Qualität der Küche des Chefs Santi Santamaria. So wurden kreisförmige Plattformen auf verschiedenen Ebenen gebildet, die Umläufe ermöglichen, dem jeweiligen Umfeld der Tische jedoch Privatsphäre und Identität vermitteln." Die Außenwände sind mit für das Restaurant entworfenem gitterartig gestrichenem Glas verkleidet, der Entwurf der Teppiche stammt von GCA. Leuchten aus Edelstahl mit goldfarbenem Textilschirm dienen zur Lösung der durch die Glaskuppel bedingten Beleuchtungsprobleme und werfen auf jeden einzelnen Tisch ein besonderes Licht. Die Möblierung besteht aus schwarz lackiertem Holz, mit Hockern von Pedrali und Artifort-Stühlen mit einer Polsterung von Gastón & Daniela.

L'Evo se trouve au sommet de la tour Hesperia conçue par Richard Rogers (Rogers Stirk Harbour, avec Alonso & Balaguer). Cette structure métallique apparente en rouge et bleu vif se remarque de loin, mais son élément le plus étonnant reste sans doute le volume conçu par l'architecte pour le restaurant. Comparé à une soucoupe volante qui aurait atterri au sommet de la tour, cette capsule à coupole de verre se trouve à 105 m au-dessus du niveau du sol. Le restaurant de cinquante-cinq couverts, dont le décor est dû à GCA, occupe trois niveaux, la salle de restaurant occupant le second, sous la cuisine et les salles privées. Les architectes expliquent ainsi leur intervention : «La complexité de l'aménagement intérieur tient à l'harmonisation de la nature spectaculaire de l'espace architectonique à la qualité et à la présentation de la cuisine du chef Santi Santamaria. Des plates-formes circulaires ont été créées aux différents niveaux pour faciliter la circulation tout en assurant identité et intimité à l'implantation des tables.» Les murs périmétriques sont en verre sérigraphié spécialement réalisé pour le restaurant, et GCA a créé le dessin des moquettes. Des lampes en acier inoxydable structurel avec abat-jour en tissu doré résolvent les problèmes posés par la coupole de verre et projettent une lumière très particulière sur chaque table. Le mobilier est en bois laqué noir. Les tabourets sont de Pedrali, les sièges d'Artifort tendus de tissu de Gastón & Daniela.

The building was designed by Richard Rogers, with the pod that houses the Evo Restaurant visible in the images to the left, at the top of the tower.

Das Gebäude wurde von Richard Rogers geplant – einschließlich des runden Aufbaus für das Restaurant Evo auf dem Hochhaus, sichtbar auf den Abbildungen links.

L'immeuble a été conçu par Richard Rogers. Sur les images de gauche, la capsule dans laquelle est implanté le restaurant Evo, en haut de la tour.

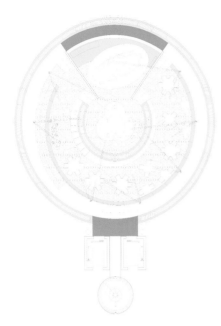

The round form of the restaurant allows for spectacular views of the city, as seen in these images.

Die runde Form des Restaurants ermöglicht spektakuläre Ausblicke auf die Stadt, wie auf diesen Abbildungen zu sehen ist.

Comme le montrent ces images, la forme ronde du restaurant lui permet d'offrir des vues spectaculaires sur la ville.

Overhead lighting, designed for the space, take over as night falls.

Oben angebrachte, für diesen Raum entworfene Leuchten entfalten bei Nacht ihre Wirkung.

Les grands luminaires spécialement conçus pour le restaurant prennent le relais quand le soleil se couche.

The pod-like form of the restaurant and the manner in which the facilities have been inserted into it are visible in the drawing to the right.

Die runde Form des Restaurants und die Art, wie die Einrichtungen darin untergebracht wurden, sind in der Zeichnung rechts zu erkennen.

La forme de capsule du restaurant et la manière dont les services techniques ont été insérés apparaissent clairement sur le dessin de droite.

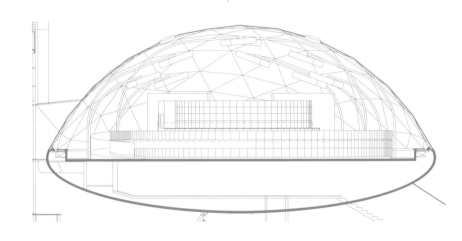

The UFO-like appearance of the restaurant's outer shell is visible in the night image to the right. Below, a broader view of the dining area, which seeks to blend with the rather surprising forms of the volume.

Rechts: Das einem Ufo ähnliche Erscheinungsbild der Außenhülle des Restaurants ist auf der Nachtaufnahme sichtbar. Unten: Ein Foto aus größerer Entfernung vom Speisesaal, der sich mit den erstaunlichen Formen des Volumens zu verbinden scheint.

L'aspect de soucoupe volante du restaurant se confirme dans cette image prise de nuit (à droite). Ci-dessous, une vue plus large de la salle de restaurant qui tend à se fondre dans ce volume assez surprenant.

GILLES & BOISSIER

Gilles & Boissier
18/20 rue du Faubourg du Temple
75011 Paris
France

Tel: +33 1 45 41 74 96
Fax: +33 1 45 41 58 39
E-mail: contact@gillesetboissier.com
Web: www.gillesetboissier.com

Patrick Gilles attended the École Nissim de Camondo in Paris (1990–95) before working in the office of Christian Liaigre from 1995 to 2002. He became the head of Liaigre's office in 2000. He created his own firm in 2002 (Agence Patrick Gilles) before creating **GILLES & BOISSIER** (2004) with Dorothée Boissier. Boissier attended the École Penninghen-ESAG, receiving her diploma in interior architecture in 1995. She then worked in the offices of Christian Liaigre (1995–98) and Philippe Starck (1998–2006). Gilles & Boissier presently have three architects, four interior designers, and an administrator. Their recent work includes the Buddakan Restaurant (with Christian Liaigre, New York, New York, 2006); the Wakiya Restaurant for Ian Schrager in the Gramercy Park Hotel (New York, New York, 2007); and the Hakkasan Restaurants in Istanbul, Abu Dhabi, and Miami. They have also designed a restaurant for Daniel Boulud in Beijing (Maison Boulud, 2008); the in Shanghai Lan restaurant (2008, published here); and the Canton Road Restaurant in Hong Kong (2008), all in China. Current work includes the W Hotel (Shanghai, Pudong, opening in 2010).

Patrick Gilles studierte an der École Nissim de Camondo in Paris (1990–95) und arbeitete danach von 1995 bis 2002 im Büro von Christian Liaigre, dessen Leitung er 2000 übernahm. Er gründete 2002 sein eigenes Büro (Agence Patrick Gilles) und 2004 zusammen mit Dorothée Boissier **GILLES & BOISSIER**. Boissier besuchte die École Penninghen-ESAG und erhielt 1995 ihr Diplom in Innenarchitektur. Danach arbeitete sie in den Büros von Christian Liaigre (1995–98) und Philippe Starck (1998–2006). Gilles & Boissier beschäftigen gegenwärtig drei Architekten, vier Innenarchitekten und eine Verwaltungskraft. Zu ihren neuesten Arbeiten zählen das Buddakan Restaurant (mit Christian Liaigre, New York, 2006), das Wakiya Restaurant für Ian Schrager im Gramercy Park Hotel (New York, 2007) und die Hakkasan Restaurants in Istanbul, Abu Dhabi und Miami. Sie haben auch ein Restaurant für Daniel Boulud in Peking geplant (Maison Boulud, 2008) sowie das Restaurant Shanghai Lan (2008, hier vorgestellt) und das Restaurant Canton Road in Hongkong (2008), alle in China. In Planung befindet sich das Hotel W (Shanghai, Pudong, Eröffnung 2010).

Patrick Gilles a étudié à l'École Nissim de Camondo à Paris (1990–95) avant de travailler pour Christian Liaigre de 1995 à 2002. Il a accédé à la direction de l'agence Liaigre en 2000, puis a créé sa propre structure en 2002 (agence Patrick Gilles) avant de fonder **GILLES & BOISSIER** (2004) avec Dorothée Boissier. Celle-ci a étudié à l'École Penninghen-ESAG, où elle a obtenu un diplôme d'architecte d'intérieur en 1995. Elle a ensuite travaillé dans les agences de Christian Liaigre (1995–98) et de Philippe Starck (1998–2006). Gilles & Boissier compte actuellement trois architectes, quatre architectes d'intérieur, et un gérant administratif. Parmi leurs réalisations récentes : le restaurant Buddakan (avec Christian Liaigre, New York, 2006) ; le restaurant Wakiya pour Ian Schrager au Gramercy Park Hotel (New York, 2007) et les restaurants Hakkasan à Istanbul, Abu Dhabi et Miami. Ils ont également conçu un restaurant pour Daniel Boulud, la Maison Boulud, à Pékin (2008) ; les restaurants du Shanghai Lan (Shanghaï, 2008, publié ici) et le restaurant Canton Road à Hongkong (2008). Ils travaillent actuellement au projet du W Hotel (Shanghaï, Pudong, ouverture prévue en 2010).

SHANGHAI LAN
Shanghai, China, 2008

102 Guang Dong Road, Shanghai, China, +86 21 6323 8029
Area: 6000 m². Client: Zhang Lan. Cost: not disclosed

Located just off the Bund in a four-story building formerly used by a foreign concessionary, this restaurant is owned by Mrs. Zhang Lan, who is also the owner of the South Beauty restaurant chain in China and Lan's Club in Beijing, designed by Philippe Starck. Lan contains a bar, tea room, Chinese and French restaurants, brightly colored VIP rooms, and a cafeteria. The restaurant is directed by the Belgian chef Yves Mattagne. Gilles & Boissier have intentionally varied the ambiances in the different spaces, ranging from active and festive to more calm and confidential. The lower three floors were designed in a Chinese style, while the top level and its covered terrace is decidedly French with its Baccarat chandeliers. Lan was imagined as a place to meet others and to find distraction from the urban environment. An interesting aspect of this large project is the variety of different atmospheres that Gilles & Boisier have succeeded in creating, while maintaining overall unity.

Dieses dicht am Bund gelegene Restaurant in einem viergeschossigen, früher von einer ausländischen Konzession genutzten Gebäude, ist im Besitz von Frau Zhang Lan, der auch die chinesische Restaurantkette South Beauty und der von Philippe Starck gestaltete Lan's Club in Peking gehören. Zum Shanghai Lan gehören eine Bar, ein Teeraum, ein chinesisches und ein französisches Restaurant, in fröhlichen Farben gehaltene VIP-Räume sowie eine Cafeteria. Chef des Restaurants ist der Belgier Yves Mattagne. Gilles & Boissier haben das Ambiente der verschiedenen Räume bewusst unterschiedlich gestaltet – von aktiv und festlich bis ruhig und intim. Die drei unteren Stockwerke sind im chinesischen Stil gehalten, während das oberste Geschoss und die gedeckte Terrasse mit Baccarat-Lüstern sehr französisch ausgestattet sind. Lan soll ein Ort sein, an dem man sich trifft und von der städtischen Umgebung entfernt ist. Ein interessanter Aspekt dieses großen Projekts ist die Tatsache, dass es Gilles & Boissier gelungen ist, unterschiedliche Atmosphären zu erzeugen, während gleichzeitig eine übergeordnete Einheit gewahrt bleibt.

Situé à proximité immédiate du Bund dans un immeuble de trois étages utilisé jadis par une concession étrangère, ce lieu appartient à Mme Zhang Lan, également propriétaire de la chaîne de restaurants South Beauty en Chine et du Lan's Club à Pékin, conçu par Philippe Starck. Le Shanghai Lan contient un bar, un salon de thé, des restaurants français et chinois, des salons pour VIP décorés de couleurs vives, et une cafétéria. Le restaurant est dirigé par le chef belge Yves Mattagne. Gilles & Boissier ont différencié les ambiances de ces différents lieux, passant d'une atmosphère active ou festive à des environnements plus calmes et plus intimes. Les trois niveaux inférieurs ont été traités en style chinois et le niveau supérieur et sa terrasse couverte en style résolument français symbolisé par des lustres de Baccarat. Shanghai Lan a été conçu comme un lieu de rencontre, où l'on peut oublier l'environnement urbain. L'un des aspects intéressants de cet important projet est la variété des atmosphères que Gilles & Boissier ont réussi à créer tout en maintenant une unité d'ensemble.

Left, the façade of Shanghai Lan seen in the evening. Above, the VIP Amber Mirror Corridor located on the second floor.

Links: Die Fassade des Shanghai Lan am Abend. Oben: Der VIP Amber Mirror Corridor im zweiten Geschoss.

À gauche, la façade du Shanghai Lan prise le soir. Ci-dessus, le corridor VIP à miroir d'ambre du premier étage.

A table located near the Chinese Screen Corridor on the first floor of Shanghai Lan.

Ein Tisch beim Chinese Screen Corridor im ersten Geschoss des Shanghai Lan.

Une table près du corridor d'écrans chinois au premier étage du Shanghai Lan.

Four details of the design work that has gone into creating the exceptional atmosphere of this very large establishment.

Vier Details des Entwurfs, der für diese sehr große Einrichtung eine außergewöhnliche Atmosphäre geschaffen hat.

Quatre détails du travail de décoration qui a permis de créer l'atmosphère extraordinaire de ce très vaste établissement.

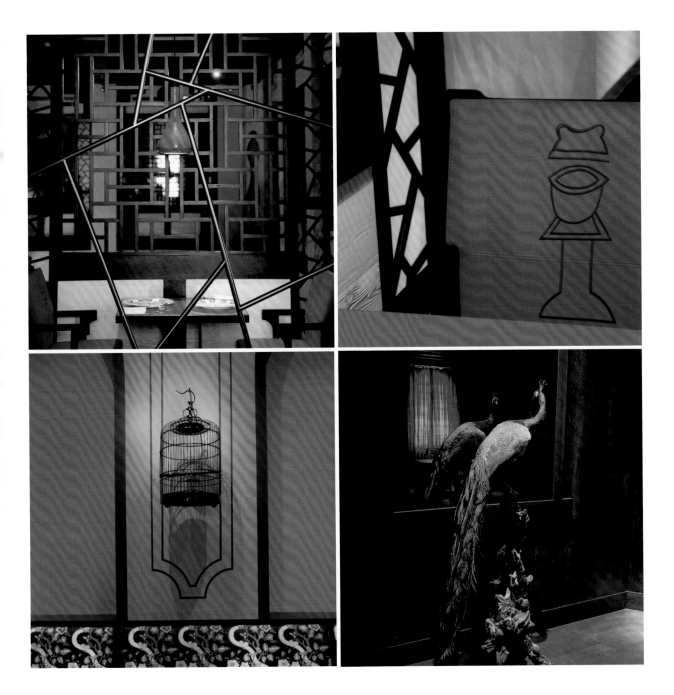

Four further details show the change in atmosphere that occurs as patrons go up through the different floors, to the upper terrace.

Vier weitere Details zeigen die Veränderung der Atmosphäre, wenn sich die Gäste durch die verschiedenen Ebenen zur oberen Terrasse begeben.

Quatre détails supplémentaires montrent le changement d'atmosphère que chaque client découvre en passant d'un étage à l'autre pour se rendre à la terrasse supérieure.

The French restaurant on the third floor certainly has a brighter, far less "oriental" feel, as befits the cuisine.

Das französische Restaurant im dritten Geschoss hat eine fröhlichere, weniger „orientalische" Atmosphäre, was zur Küche passt.

Le restaurant français du troisième étage offre une ambiance plus lumineuse, beaucoup moins « orientale » et mieux adaptée à la cuisine servie.

As opposed to the more unified, or even minimal atmosphere that held sway in restaurant design a number of years ago, Gilles & Boissier opt here for an eclectic approach that allows for varied colors and patterns as well as different materials.

Entgegen der einheitlicheren oder sogar minimalistischen Atmosphäre, die bis vor kurzem in der Restaurantgestaltung vorherrschte, entschieden sich Gilles & Boissier hier für eine eklektische Lösung mit unterschiedlichen Farben, Dekors und Materialien.

Par opposition à l'atmosphère uniforme voire minimaliste qui régnait il y a peu dans la conception de restaurants, Gilles & Boissier ont opté pour une approche éclectique qui s'autorise des couleurs, des matériaux et des motifs décoratifs variés.

Corton ▶

STEPHANIE GOTO

Stephanie Goto
One Union Square West
New York, NY 10003
USA

Tel: +1 212 475 5575
Fax: +1 212 475 0055
E-mail: goto@stephaniegoto.com
Web: www.stephaniegoto.com

STEPHANIE GOTO was born in 1974 in Los Angeles. She attended Cornell University (College of Architecture, Art and Planning, 1992–96). She worked for six years in the office of Rafael Viñoly in New York on such projects as Jazz at Lincoln Center Rose Hall; the Columbia University International Climate Prediction Center; and the University of Chicago Graduate School of Business. She also worked with New York architect David Rockwell on the Motown Museum in Detroit and restaurants in Miami and Philadelphia. Stephanie Goto created her own firm in 2004, proposing services ranging from architecture to graphics and lifestyle. In 2006 in New York, she completed the morimoto nyc Restaurant with Tadao Ando and the Buddakan Restaurant with interior designers Christian Liaigre and Gilles & Boissier. In both cases, she was the local designer working for Starr Restaurant Group. In 2007, she redesigned Monkey Bar (New York) and in fall of 2008 completed Corton (New York, New York, published here) for chef Paul Liebrandt and New York restauranteur Drew Nieporent. Current projects include the Aldea Restaurant in New York; a private residence in Los Angeles; an apartment in the Museum Tower in New York; redesign of Student Housing in Santa Barbara (Fontainebleau); and hotel and retail projects in New York and Asia.

STEPHANIE GOTO wurde 1974 in Los Angeles geboren. Sie studierte an der Cornell University (College of Architecture, Art and Planning, 1992–96). Danach war sie sechs Jahre im Büro von Rafael Viñoly in New York an Projekten wie dem Jazz in der Lincoln Center Rose Hall, dem Columbia University International Climate Prediction Center und der University of Chicago Graduate School of Business tätig. Sie arbeitete auch für den New Yorker Architekten David Rockwell am Motown Museum in Detroit und an Restaurants in Miami und Philadelphia. Stephanie Goto gründete 2004 ihr eigenes Büro, das Dienstleistungen in Architektur, Grafik und Lifestyle anbietet. 2006 entwarf sie in New York zusammen mit Tadao Ando das Restaurant morimoto nyc und mit den Innenarchitekten Christian Liaigre und Gilles & Boissier das Restaurant Buddakan. In beiden Fällen arbeitete sie als Designerin vor Ort für die Starr Restaurant Group. 2007 baute sie die Monkey Bar (New York) um, und im Herbst 2008 vollendete sie für den Küchenchef Paul Liebrandt und den New Yorker Restaurantbesitzer Drew Nieporent das Corton (New York, hier vorgestellt). Zu ihren aktuellen Projekten zählen das Aldea Restaurant in New York, ein privates Wohnhaus in Los Angeles, eine Wohnung im Museum Tower in New York, der Umbau eines Studentenwohnheims in Santa Barbara (Fontainebleau) sowie Hotels and Ladeneinrichtungen in New York and Asien.

STEPHANIE GOTO est née en 1974 à Los Angeles. Elle a étudié à l'Université Cornell (College of Architecture, Art and Planning, 1992–96), puis travaillé pendant six ans chez Rafael Viñoly à New York sur des projets comme Jazz au Lincoln Center Rose Hall ; le centre international de prévisions climatiques de l'Université Columbia ; et la Graduate School of Business de l'Université de Chicago. Elle a aussi collaboré à New York avec l'architecte David Rockwell sur le projet du Motown Museum à Detroit et des restaurants à Miami et Philadelphie. Elle a fondé sa propre agence en 2004, et propose des services allant de l'architecture à la création graphique et aux interventions sur les styles de vie. En 2006, à New York, elle a achevé le restaurant morimoto nyc avec Tadao Ando et le restaurant Buddakan avec les architectes d'intérieur Christian Liaigre et Gilles & Boissier. Dans les deux cas, elle jouait le rôle de designer de projet local pour le Starr Restaurant Group. En 2007, elle a réaménagé le Monkey Bar (New York), et, á l'automne 2008, a achevé le Corton (New York, publié ici) pour le chef Paul Liebrandt et le propriétaire de restaurants new-yorkais Drew Nieporent. Parmi ses projets actuels : le restaurant Aldea à New York ; une résidence privée à Los Angeles ; un appartement dans la Museum Tower à New York ; le réaménagement de logements pour étudiants à Santa Barbara (Fontainebleau) ; et des projets d'hôtels et de magasins à New York et en Asie.

CORTON

New York, New York, USA, 2007–08

239 West Broadway, New York, NY 10013, USA, +1 212 219 2777, www.cortonnyc.com
Area: 232 m² (121 m² dining room). Clients: Drew Nieporent (owner), Paul Liebrandt (chef, partner)
Cost: not disclosed

The well-known Manhattan restaurant Montrachet opened in this location in Tribeca (239 West Broadway) when the area was considered off the beaten track, and even a bit risky. Named, like its predecessor, after a top Burgundy wine (Château de Corton-André), Corton was redesigned entirely by Stephanie Goto, who envisioned it as a "salon of an urban house in Paris…" embodying "the spirit of a modern day *hôtel particulier*. A wall of green-gold wine bottles marks the vestibule, while white plaster walls hand-carved with abstract leaves and branches enfold the dining area that seats 65 guests. "Selected leaves are adorned in gold leaf," says Stephanie Goto, "giving the appearance of the leaves blowing or perhaps falling. Gold chandelier stems with glass egg-shaped jewels flecked in gold highlight corners of the room that is grounded by the chartreuse and green-gold banquettes and chairs. A veiled slot captures glimpses into the kitchen beyond as the softness of the room envelops, embraces, and sets an elegant stage to showcase the culinary experience." Much less flamboyant than Ando's Morimoto, Corton is very much in the spirit of understated luxury that may well be more in keeping with the times than some of the other extravagant restaurants that marked the early years of the 21st century in New York.

Das bekannte Manhattaner Restaurant Montrachet eröffnete an diesem Standort in Tribeca (239 West Broadway), als das Gebiet noch als abseits und sogar etwas gefährlich galt. Das wie sein Vorgänger nach einem berühmten Burgunderwein (Château de Corton-André) benannte Corton wurde von Stephanie Goto vollkommen umgestaltet; sie betrachtete es als „Salon eines Pariser Stadthauses, das den Geist eines modernen *hôtel particulier*" verkörpert. Eine Wand aus grün-goldenen Weinflaschen ziert das Vestibül, während sich im Speiseraum, der 65 Gästen Platz bietet, auf den weiß verputzten Wänden handgeschnitzte abstrakte Blätter und Zweige ausbreiten. „Bestimmte Blätter sind mit Blattgold geschmückt", sagt Stephanie Goto, „sodass es aussieht, als würden sie weggeweht oder zu Boden fallen. Goldene Lüster an Stielen mit runden, goldgetupften Glassteinen zieren die Ecken dieses Raums, der mit grünen und grün-goldenen Bänken und Stühlen ausgestattet ist. Ein verhängter Schlitz gewährt Einblick in die Küche – der delikate Raum umfasst, umarmt und bietet eine elegante Bühne für die Darstellung des kulinarischen Erlebnisses." Das Corton, weit weniger ausgefallen als Andos Morimoto, ist Ausdruck von zurückhaltendem Luxus, der vielleicht eher dem Zeitgeist entspricht als manch anderes extravagantes Restaurant aus den frühen Jahren des 21. Jahrhunderts in New York.

Le célèbre restaurant de Manhattan, Le Montrachet avait ouvert dans ce quartier de Tribeca (239 West Broadway) alors considéré comme loin de tout et même un peu dangereux. Nommé comme son prédécesseur d'après un grand vin de Bourgogne (Château de Corton-André), le Corton a été entièrement rénové par Stephanie Goto qui a pris pour référence le « salon d'une maison parisienne… » incarnant « l'esprit d'un hôtel particulier de nos jours ». Un mur de bouteilles de vin de couleur vert doré décore le vestibule. La salle à manger de soixante-quinze couverts est agrémentée de murs de plâtre ornés de feuillages abstraits sculptés à la main dans la matière. « Certaines feuilles sont dorées à l'or, précise S. Goto, pour donner l'apparence de feuilles agitées par le vent ou chutant. Des luminaires dorés, faits de tiges se terminant par des œufs de verre tachetés d'or, éclairent les angles de la pièce animée de banquettes et de sièges aux couleurs chartreuse et vert doré. Une meurtrière voilée permet de jeter un regard sur les cuisines. La douceur pénétrante de l'atmosphère de cette salle dresse une scène élégante pour le spectacle gastronomique. » Beaucoup moins flamboyant que le Morimoto de Tadao Ando, le Corton est dans l'esprit d'un luxe discret, peut-être davantage en accord avec l'époque que certaines créations extravagantes de restaurants qui ont marqué le début du XXIᵉ siècle à New York.

Below, chairs in the dining area are by Stephanie Goto (JC Furniture), while the mica finish on the main column is by Toby Nuttal. Right, the "relief wall" is by Silver Hill Atelier.

Unten: Die Stühle im Speisesaal stammen von Stephanie Goto (JC Furniture), der Glimmerüberzug der großen Säule von Toby Nuttal. Rechts: Die „Reliefwand" wurde von Silver Hill Atelier gestaltet.

Ci-dessous, les sièges de la salle à manger sont de Stephanie Goto (JC Furniture), la finition au mica de la colonne centrale est de Toby Nuttal. À droite, le « mur en relief » est dû au Silver Hill Atelier.

The chandelier visible here is by Takeshi Miyakawa. The custom "bottle wall" was designed by Stephanie Goto.

Der hier sichtbare Kronleuchter stammt von Takeshi Miyakawa, die „Flaschenwand" von Stephanie Goto.

Le lustre central est de Takeshi Miyakawa. Le « mur de bouteilles » a été spécialement conçu par Stephanie Goto.

A floor plan of the restaurant shows its "L" shape, with round tables in the open area and rectangular ones along the walls. The banquettes are by Munrod Interiors.

Der Grundriss zeigt die L-Form des Restaurants mit runden Tischen im offenen Bereich und rechteckigen entlang den Wänden. Die Sitzbänke stammen von Munrod Interiors.

Le plan du restaurant en forme de « L » montre l'implantation des tables rondes dans la partie centrale et des tables rectangulaires le long des murs. Les banquettes sont de Munrod Interiors.

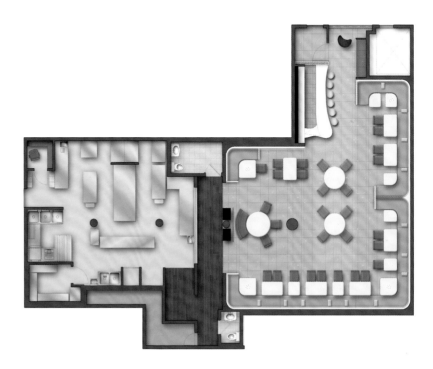

GRAFT

Graft – Gesellschaft von Architekten mbH
Heidestr. 50 / 10557 Berlin / Germany
Tel: +49 30 30 64 51 03-0 / Fax: +49 30 30 64 51 03-34
E-mail: berlin@graftlab.com / Web: www.graftlab.com

GRAFT was created in Los Angeles in 1998 "as a label for architecture, art, music, and the pursuit of happiness." Lars Krückeberg, Wolfram Putz, and Thomas Willemeit are the partners of Graft that today employ about 20 architects and artists in the USA, Europe, and Asia. Graft have offices in Los Angeles, Berlin, and Beijing. Lars Krückeberg was educated at the Technische Universität Braunschweig as an engineer (1989–96) and at SCI-Arc in Los Angeles (1997–98). Wolfram Putz attended the Technische Universität Braunschweig (1988–95), the University of Utah, Salt Lake City (1992–93), and SCI-Arc in Los Angeles (1996–98). Thomas Willemeit was also educated in Braunschweig (1988–97), and at the Bauhaus Dessau (1991–92), before working in the office of Daniel Libeskind (1998–2001). Two other partners have since joined the firm, Gregor Hoheisel (founding partner Graft Beijing, 2004) and Alejandra Lillo (Graft Los Angeles, 2004). Taking advantage of their German background combined with US training, Graft declare: "We can see an architecture of new combinations, the grafting of different cultures and styles." They have built a studio and house for the actor Brad Pitt in Los Angeles (California, 2000–03), and, working with Brad Pitt and William McDonough + Partners, Graft are the lead architects for the Pink Project and Make it Right initiative in New Orleans (Louisiana, 2007–). They designed the Hotel Q! in Berlin (Germany, 2002–04); and restaurants in the Mirage and Bellagio casinos in Las Vegas (Nevada, 2007–08) and in the Monte Carlo Hotel (Las Vegas, 2007–08, published here); and worked on several Luxury Resort Hotels in the Caribbean, including locations in the Turcs and Caicos and in the Dominican Republic. Work in 2008 includes the Emperor Design Hotel (Beijing); the Kinderdentist (Berlin), a children's dentistry; the Gong Ti Club (Beijing); Sichuan Airlines VIP Lounge at Terminal 3 (Beijing); and the Gingko Restaurant (Chengdu, 2008, published here).

GRAFT wurde 1998 in Los Angeles „als eine Gesellschaft für Architektur, Kunst, Musik and das Streben nach Glück" gegründet. Lars Krückeberg, Wolfram Putz und Thomas Willemeit sind die Partner von Graft, die heute etwa 20 Architekten und Künstler in den USA, Europa und Asien beschäftigen. Die Firma unterhält Büros in Los Angeles, Berlin und Peking. Lars Krückeberg studierte an der Technischen Universität Braunschweig Bauingenieurwesen (1989–96) und am SCI-Arc in Los Angeles (1997–98). Wolfram Putz studierte an der Technischen Universität Braunschweig (1988–95), der University of Utah in Salt Lake City (1992–93) und am SCI-Arc in Los Angeles (1996–98), Thomas Willemeit ebenfalls in Braunschweig (1988–97) und am Bauhaus in Dessau (1991–92), danach arbeitete er im Büro von Daniel Libeskind (1998–2001). Seither wurden zwei weitere Partner in die Firma aufgenommen: Gregor Hoheisel (Gründungspartner von Graft Peking, 2004) und Alejandra Lillo (Graft Los Angeles, 2004). Im Hinblick auf ihren deutschen Hintergrund in Verbindung mit ihrer Ausbildung in den USA erklären die Graft-Partner: „Wir vertreten eine Architektur der neuartigen Verbindungen, der Kreuzung – grafting – verschiedener Kulturen und Stile." Sie haben ein Atelier und Wohnhaus für den Schauspieler Brad Pitt in Los Angeles gebaut (Kalifornien, 2000–03) und arbeiten mit Brad Pitt und William McDonough + Partners als führende Architekten am Pink Project und der Initiative „Make It Right" in New Orleans (Louisiana, seit 2007). Außerdem haben sie das Hotel Q! in Berlin (2002–04) sowie Restaurants in den Kasinos Mirage und Bellagio in Las Vegas (Nevada, 2007–08) und im Monte Carlo Hotel (Las Vegas, 2007–08, hier gezeigt) geplant und für mehrere Luxusferienhotels in der Karibik gearbeitet, z. B. auf den Turks- und Caicos-Inseln und in der Dominikanischen Republik. Zu den Arbeiten von 2008 zählen das Emperor Design Hotel (Peking), der Kinderdentist (Berlin), der Gong Ti Club (Peking), die VIP-Lounge von Sichuan Airlines am Terminal 3 (Peking) und das Restaurant Gingko (Chengdu, 2008, hier veröffentlicht).

GRAFT, « label pour l'architecture, l'art, la musique et la recherche du bonheur », a été créé à Los Angeles en 1998. Lars Krückeberg, Wolfram Putz et Thomas Willemeit sont les associés de cette agence qui emploie aujourd'hui environ vingt architectes et artistes aux États-Unis, en Europe et en Asie, et possède des bureaux à Los Angeles, Berlin et Pékin. Lars Krückeberg a fait ses études d'ingénierie à l'Université technique de Brunswick, Allemagne (1989–1996) et à la SCI-Arc à Los Angeles (1997–98). Wolfram Putz a également étudié à la l'Université technique de Brunswick (1988–95), à celle de l'Utah à Salt Lake City (1992–93) et à la SCI-Arc à Los Angeles (1996–98). Thomas Willemeit a aussi étudié à Brunswick (1988–97) et au Bauhaus-Dessau (1991–92) avant de travailler auprès de Daniel Libeskind (1998–2001). Deux autres associés ont rejoint l'agence : Gregor Hoheisel (associé fondateur de Graft Pékin, 2004) et Alejandra Lillo (Graft Los Angeles, 2004). En s'appuyant sur cette formation à la fois allemande et américaine, Graft se propose « d'envisager une architecture de combinaisons nouvelles, la greffe de différents styles et cultures ». Ils ont construit un atelier et une maison pour l'acteur Brad Pitt à Los Angeles (2000–03) et collaboré avec lui et William McDonough + Partners sur les projets Pink et Make it Right à la Nouvelle-Orléans, dont ils sont les architectes en chef. Ils ont conçu l'Hotel Q ! à Berlin (2002–04), des restaurants pour les casinos Mirage et Bellagio à Las Vegas (2007–08) et du Monte Carlo Hotel (Las Vegas, 2007–08, publié ici) ; et travaillé sur plusieurs projets de complexes hôteliers de luxe dans les Caraïbes, les îles Turques-et-Caïques, et en République dominicaine. En 2008, leurs projets portent sur l'Emperor Design Hotel (Pékin) ; le Kinderdentist (Berlin), une clinique dentaire pédiatrique ; le Gong Ti Club à Pékin ; le salon VIP de Sichuan Airlines et le Terminal 3 (Pékin) ; et le restaurant Gingko à Chengdu (2008, publié ici).

BRAND STEAKHOUSE
Las Vegas, Nevada, USA, 2007–08

Monte Carlo Resort, 3770 S. Las Vegas Blvd., Las Vegas, NV 89109, USA, +1 702 693 8300, www.lightgroup.com
Area: 691 m². Client: MGM Mirage Design Group. Cost: not disclosed
Team: Asami Tashikawa (Project Manager), Stephen Beese (Project Manager), Brian Wickersham (Supervisor)

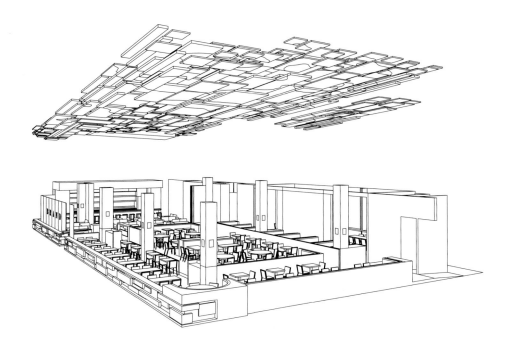

Located on the floor of the casino of the Monte Carlo Hotel in Las Vegas, this restaurant features a ceiling canopy "made of numerous panels wrapped in custom-printed fur creating a pixilated abstract cowhide pattern. Panels lit at various depths create a spectacular dusting glow that emanates from the ceiling," according to the architects. The facility includes a lounge and main dining room, together with space for private dining. Each area is distinct but not completely enclosed. Like the ceilings, the floors of the restaurants are of varying heights, emphasizing the changes of atmosphere imagined by Graft. Sliding glass panels and bronze curtains allow for variable divisions of the spaces according to customer demand. The architects say of this system: "Unexpected visual connections are thereby shared within, providing an array of opportunities for voyeurism and social contact."

Dieses auf dem Geschoss des Kasinos vom Monte Carlo Hotel in Las Vegas gelegene Restaurant hat an der Decke einen Baldachin „aus zahlreichen, mit speziell bedrucktem Kuhfell überzogenen Tafeln, die ein verwirrendes, abstraktes Muster bilden. Diese in unterschiedlicher Stärke beleuchteten Tafeln erzeugen ein spektakuläres, gedämpftes Licht, das von der Decke abstrahlt", sagen die Architekten. Zu der Einrichtung gehören eine Lounge und ein großer Speisesaal sowie Räume für private Einladungen. Alle Bereiche sind abgesondert, aber nicht völlig abgeschlossen. Wie die Decken sind auch die Böden der Restaurantbereiche unterschiedlich hoch, wodurch auch die von Graft beabsichtigte Änderung der Atmosphäre hervorgehoben wird. Glasschiebewände und bronzefarbene Vorhänge ermöglichen eine variable Aufteilung der Räume nach Bedarf. Die Architekten erläutern dieses System wie folgt: „Im Innern entstehen unerwartete visuelle Verbindungen, die vielfältige Gelegenheiten zum Sehen und Gesehenwerden und sozialen Kontakt bieten."

Installé dans le casino du Monte Carlo Hotel à Las Vegas, ce restaurant se distingue par un plafond « composé de multiples panneaux tendus de fourrure imprimée créant un motif de peau de vache abstrait pixellisé. Ces panneaux sont éclairés de différentes densités pour créer la lumière poudrée spectaculaire qui émane de ce plafond ». Ce grill comprend un salon, une salle à manger principale, ainsi que des espaces pour dîners privés. Chaque zone est distincte sans être entièrement fermée. Comme les plafonds, les sols sont de hauteurs différentes, ce qui souligne les changements d'atmosphère imaginés par Graft. Des panneaux de verre coulissants et des rideaux de bronze permettent de diviser l'espace selon les demandes des clients. Pour Graft : « Des connexions visuelles inattendues se déclenchent ainsi et offrent une multiplicité d'opportunités de regards et de contacts. »

Ceiling panels are in synthetic cowhide on aluminum honeycomb. Wall finishes are recycled leather on DJ Wall and Ponywall (EcoDomo LLC). Above, an axonometric drawing shows the ceiling and dining space.

Die Deckenplatten bestehen aus synthetischer Kuhhaut auf Aluminiumgitter. Die Wandverkleidung ist aus recyceltem Leder auf DJ Wall- und Ponywall-Systemen (EcoDomo LLC). Oben: Die Axonometrie zeigt die Decke und den Speiseraum.

Les panneaux du plafond sont en cuir de vache synthétique tendu sur une trame en nid-d'abeilles d'aluminium. Les murs des partitions et du podium du DJ sont en cuir recyclé (EcoDomo LLC). Ci-dessus, axonométrie du plafond et du restaurant.

The ample volumes of the restaurant are dominated by dark tones, with the active surface transitions of the ceiling giving a sense of movement to the space.

Die großzügigen Räume des Restaurants werden von dunklen Tönen beherrscht; die Übergänge an den Deckenflächen bringen Bewegung in den Raum.

Les amples volumes du restaurant sont traités dans des tonalités sombres, faisant transition avec les surfaces plus dynamiques du plafond qui confèrent à cet espace un sentiment de mouvement.

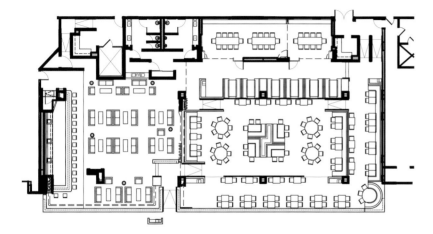

GINGKO BACCHUS RESTAURANT

Chengdu, China, 2008

12 Lin Jiang Zhong Lu, Chengdu, Sichuan, 610041, China, +86 28 8555 5588
Area: 1200 m² (1500 m² including kitchen). Client: GINGKO Restaurant Management Corporation
Cost: $1.5 million (interior construction and furniture); $60 000 (decoration)
Collaboration: Lighting Design: CDM Lighting Design Group; Still-Life Photography: Kevin Best

The surprising wallpaper prints in the restaurant are by Beijing Beiren Yuxin Offset.

Die ungewöhnlichen bedruckten Tapeten im Restaurant stammen von Beijing Beiren Yuxin Offset.

Les surprenants papiers-peints ont été réalisés par Beijing Beiren Yuxin Offset.

This spectacular restaurant is located on the fourth floor of the Gingko Restaurant building in Chengdu, the capital of Sichuan Province. Entered through elevators only, Gingko Bacchus seeks to be a "surrealistic blend of Western and Chinese restaurant and food culture." The main space is black, with an undulating wood ceiling and a pattern of stainless-steel inlay in the floor intended to emphasize the impression of a stream flowing through the restaurant. There are eight private dining rooms as well as an open dining and "show cooking" area. Photographs of vegetables are used to wallpaper the private dining rooms, each in a different color, ranging from green to red. Reproductions of Dutch still-life paintings blown up to full wall size are lit in a pattern that varies over time. Large reproductions of paintings representing Bacchus offer a more boisterous or emphatic note. These range from Caravaggio's depiction of *Bacchus as a Young Boy with a Fruit Basket*, to the *Triumph of Bacchus* by Velázquez. The architects explain: "The paintings are used in pixilated abstraction. The pixilated graphics are laser cut out of stainless-steel sheets. Through the laser cut pixels of the historical Bacchus paintings one sees the illuminated background of the vegetable wallpapers and Arcadian landscapes."

Dieses spektakuläre Restaurant liegt im vierten Geschoss des Gingko-Gebäudes in Chengdu, der Hauptstadt der Provinz Sichuan. Das nur über Fahrstühle erschlossene Gingko Bacchus versteht sich als „eine surrealistische Mischung aus westlichem und chinesischem Restaurant mit entsprechender Esskultur". Der Hauptraum ist in Schwarz gehalten, hat eine wellenförmige Holzdecke und auf dem Boden dekorativ angeordnete Edelstahleinlagen, die den Eindruck erwecken sollen, als flösse ein Strom durch das Restaurant. Es gibt acht private Speiseräume sowie einen offenen Bereich zum Essen und „Showkochen". Fotos von Gemüsesorten in verschiedenen Farben von Grün bis Rot dienen als Tapeten in den privaten Speiseräumen. Reproduktionen niederländischer Stillleben, die die ganze Wand bedecken, werden abwechselnd mit unterschiedlicher Wirkung beleuchtet. Große Reproduktionen von Gemälden mit Darstellungen des Weingottes Bacchus – von Caravaggios Wiedergabe des Bacchus als kleiner Junge mit einem Früchtekorb bis zum „Triumph des Bacchus" von Velázquez – verleihen den Räumen eine ausgelassene oder emphatische Note. Die Architekten erklären: „Die Gemälde sind in Form von Pixeln abstrahiert. Die in Pixel aufgelösten Grafiken wurden mit Laser aus Edelstahlblech geschnitten. Durch die Pixel der historischen Bacchus-Gemälde werden der beleuchtete Hintergrund der Gemüsetapeten und die arkadischen Landschaften sichtbar."

Ce spectaculaire restaurant est situé au quatrième étage de l'immeuble du Gingko Restaurant à Chengdu, capitale de la province du Sichuan. Accessible uniquement par ascenseur, le Gingko Bacchus a recherché « un mélange surréaliste de styles de restaurants et de cultures gastronomiques occidentales et chinoises ». L'espace principal est traité en noir sous un plafond en bois à profil ondulé. Un motif en acier inoxydable inséré dans le sol veut créer l'impression d'un ruisseau parcourant le volume. Huit salles à manger privées viennent se greffer sur une grande salle à cuisine ouverte. Des photographies de légumes en papier peint décorent les petites salles du restaurant, chacune traitée d'une couleur différente, allant du vert au rouge. Des reproductions de natures mortes hollandaises agrandies et occupant toute la surface des murs sont éclairées selon une programmation variable au fil du temps. De grandes reproductions de peintures sur le thème de Bacchus apportent une note plus animée ou plus emphatique. Elles vont d'une représentation d'un Bacchus en jeune garçon devant un panier de fruits par Le Caravage au *Triomphe de Bacchus* par Vélasquez. « Ces peintures sont des abstractions réalisées à partir de l'image numérisée. Les formes pixellisées sont découpées au laser dans une feuille d'acier inoxydable. À travers ces découpes de tableaux historiques, se perçoit le fond illuminé des papiers peints de légumes et de paysages arcadiens », expliquent les architectes.

Furniture is by the Dong Guan Ming
Hui Furniture Company, and lighting
design by the CD+M Lighting Design
Group.

Die Möbel stammen von Dong Guan
Ming Hui Furniture Company, die
Leuchten wurden von CD+M Lighting
Design Group entworfen.

Le mobilier vient de la Dong Guan
Ming Hui Furniture Company, et
l'éclairage a été conçu par le
CD+M Lighting Design Group.

The private dining rooms are colored in a transition from greens to reds with matching custom-made wall-paper featuring vegetables ranging from artichokes to chilies.

Die privaten Speiseräume sind in einem Farbspektrum von Grün bis Rot gehalten, die Tapeten mit Abbildungen von Gemüse wie Artischocken und Chilis wurden eigens dafür gefertigt.

Les salles à manger privées traitées dans des couleurs allant du vert au rouge sont décorées de papiers-peints assortis spécialement réalisés, qui reproduisent divers légumes comme artichauts et poivrons.

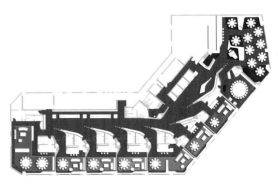

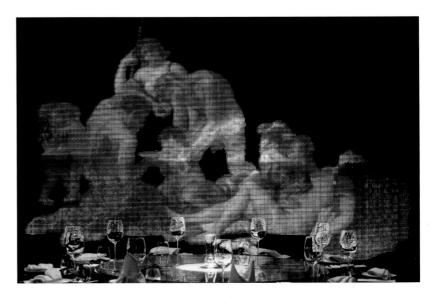

GUEDES + DECAMPOS

Guedes + DeCampos
Rua São Francisco 5, 3° andar
4050–548 Porto
Portugal

Tel/Fax: +351 222 010 451
E-mail: info@guedesdecampos.com
Web: www.guedesdecampos.com

Menos é Mais Arquitectos Associados was the name of the office created in Porto in 1994 by Cristina Guedes, who was born in Macau in 1964, and Francisco Vieira de Campos, born in Porto in 1962. Both graduated from the Faculdade de Arquitectura da Universidade do Porto (FAUP) respectively in 1992 and 1991. Before creating their own office, Cristina Guedes worked with Álvaro Siza, and Francisco Vieira de Campos with Eduardo Souto de Moura. Both lecture in the Architecture Department at the Lusíada University in Porto. Their built work includes Café do Cais (Porto, 1994); the Work Crafts Pavilion for FAUP (Porto, 1996); three bar pavilions (Vila Nova de Gaia, 1999); and, more recently, two industrial units for automobile components in the Autoeuropa Complex in Palmela (2004 and 2006); and the Ar de Rio Bar Restaurant (Vila Nova de Gaia, 2008, published here), all in Portugal. Most of their professional activity has resulted from public tenders, such as the Açores Contemporary Center of Art (Terceira, with João Mendes Ribeiro, 2007); or the Gaia Rope-Way Teleferic (Vila Nova de Gaia, 2007). They presently call their office **GUEDES + DECAMPOS**.

Menos é Mais Arquitectos Associados war der Name des 1994 von Cristina Guedes (geboren 1964 in Macau) und Francisco Vieira de Campos (geboren 1962 in Porto) in Porto gegründeten Büros. Beide studierten an der Faculdade de Arquitectura da Universidade do Porto (FAUP) bis 1992 bzw. 1991. Vor Gründung ihres eigenen Büros arbeitete Cristina Guedes bei Álvaro Siza und Francisco Vieira de Campos bei Eduardo Souto de Moura. Beide lehren an der Architekturabteilung der Universität Lusíada in Porto. Zu ihren ausgeführten Werken gehören das Café do Cais (Porto, 1994), das Ateliergebäude der FAUP (Porto, 1996), drei Bar-Pavillons (Vila Nova de Gaia, 1999) und zwei Industriebauten für Autozulieferer im Komplex Autoeuropa in Palmela (2004 und 2006) sowie die Bar und das Restaurant Ar de Rio (Vila Nova de Gaia, 2008, hier veröffentlicht), alle in Portugal. Die Mehrzahl ihrer Aufträge erhielten sie aufgrund öffentlicher Ausschreibungen, z. B. das Zentrum für zeitgenössische Kunst (Terceira, Azoren, mit João Mendes Ribeiro, 2007) oder die Seilbahn Gaia Teleferic (Vila Nova de Gaia, 2007). Ihr Büro heißt jetzt **GUEDES + DECAMPOS**.

L'agence **GUEDES + DECAMPOS**, fondée à Porto en 1994 par Cristina Guedes, née à Macau en 1964, et Francisco Vieira de Campos, né à Porto en 1962, s'appelait à l'origine Menos é Mais Arquitectos Associados. Tous deux sont diplômés de la Faculté d'architecture de l'Université de Porto (FAUP), respectivement en 1992 et 1991. Avant de créer cette agence, Cristina Guedes avait travaillé pour Álvaro Siza, et Francisco Vieira de Campos pour Eduardo Souto de Moura. Ils enseignent tous les deux au département d'architecture de l'Université Lusíada à Porto. Parmi leurs réalisations, toutes au Portugal : le Café do Cais (Porto, 1994) ; le pavillon d'ateliers de la FAUP (Porto, 1996) ; trois pavillons pour des bars (Vila Nova de Gaia, 1999) ; deux usines pour pièces d'automobile dans le complexe Autoeuropa de Palmela (2004 et 2006) et le bar restaurant Ar de Rio (Vila Nova de Gaia, 2008, publié ici). Une bonne partie de leur activité relève de la commande publique, comme le Centre d'art contemporain des Açores (Terceira, avec João Mendes Ribeiro, 2007) ou le téléphérique de Gaia (Vila Nova de Gaia, 2007).

AR DE RIO BAR RESTAURANT

Vila Nova de Gaia, Portugal, 2008

Av. Diogo Leite, 5, 4400 Vila Nova de Gaia, Porto, Portugal, +351 223 701 797, www.arderio.pt
Area: 108 m². Client: Ar de Rio. Cost: €200 000

Inside the restaurant, the architects selected the Ant Chair by Arne Jacobsen (Fritz Hansen), and designed the tables themselves (Veloso & Troca). The restaurant exterior is seen to the right.

Für den Innenraum des Restaurants wählten die Architekten den Ant-Stuhl von Arne Jacobsen (Fritz Hansen), die Tische entwarfen sie selber (Veloso & Troca). Rechts: Das Restaurant von außen.

Pour l'intérieur du restaurant, les architectes ont choisi la chaise «Fourmi (Ant Chair)» d'Arne Jacobsen (Fritz Hansen) et dessiné eux-mêmes les tables (Veloso & Troca). À droite, la façade du restaurant.

The architects explain: "The brief asked for a versatile space, protected from the seasonal changes of weather but open to the river breeze on warmer days." They based their scheme on an open honeycomb structure, with spans reaching 27 meters to create a covered esplanade. Essentially a long rectangular box formed from metal honeycomb, the restaurant offers various surfaces, including smooth glass and metal façades. The forms of the basic structure offer varying views of the water, and the lighting within changes in visible, evolving patterns. According to the designers: "The precision, rigor, and repetition of the structural module are complemented by its expressive possibilities: play with shadow and light, transparency, and opacity. The project," they conclude, "presupposes that the precarious equilibrium of its light structure almost falls into visual oblivion."

In der Erläuterung der Architekten heißt es: „Die Ausschreibung forderte einen vielseitig und unabhängig von der Jahreszeit nutzbaren Raum, der jedoch an warmen Tagen zur Brise vom Fluss geöffnet werden kann." Ihr Entwurf basiert auf einer offenen Wabenkonstruktion mit Spannweiten bis zu 27 m, die eine überdachte Esplanade bildet. Das im Wesentlichen aus einem langen, rechtwinkligen Kasten aus Metallwaben bestehende Restaurant zeigt unterschiedliche Fassaden aus geschliffenem Glas und Metall. Die Formen der Grundkonstruktion bieten verschiedene Perspektiven zum Wasser; die Beleuchtung im Innern wechselt in unterschiedliche Muster. In den Worten der Architekten: „Präzision, Strenge und Wiederholung des konstruktiven Moduls werden ergänzt durch ihre expressiven Möglichkeiten: das Spiel mit Schatten und Licht, Transparenz und Undurchlässigkeit. Der Entwurf setzt voraus, dass das prekäre Gleichgewicht seiner leichten Konstruktion so gut wie gar nicht ins Auge fällt."

Selon le descriptif fourni par les architectes : « Le cahier des charges demandait un espace polyvalent, protégé des changements de saisons ou de temps, mais ouvert sur la brise qui arrive du fleuve par beau temps. » Le projet repose sur une structure en nid-d'abeilles, présentant des portées de 27 m qui créent une esplanade couverte. À la base, boîte rectangulaire allongée également à trame métallique en nid-d'abeilles, le restaurant joue sur la différenciation des plans, comme dans ses façades en verre poli et métal. Les formes permettent d'offrir des vues variées sur le fleuve. L'éclairage intérieur se modifie de façon sensible selon des motifs changeants. « La précision, la rigueur et la répétition du module structurel sont complétées par ces possibilités d'expression : jeux d'ombre et de lumière, transparence et opacité. Ce projet présupposait que l'équilibre précaire de sa structure légère se fasse visuellement oublier », concluent les architectes.

The open honeycomb design of the walls allows for a generous view of the surroundings and creates unusual light patterns inside.

Die offene Wabenstruktur der Wände bietet großzügige Ausblicke in die Umgebung und erzeugt im Innern ungewöhnliche Lichteffekte.

Le motif en nid-d'abeilles ouvert de la trame des murs, laisse une excellente vision de l'environnement extérieur et provoque de curieuses projections lumineuses à l'intérieur.

Although metallic surfaces dominate the ceiling and some walls, the curving forms of the Jacobsen chairs, together with the changing light, contribute to the variety and relative warmth of the space.

Obgleich Metallflächen an der Decke und einigen Wänden dominieren, tragen die gekrümmten Formen der Jacobsen-Stühle im Verein mit dem wechselnden Licht zur Vielfalt und relativen Wärme des Raums bei.

Bien que les surfaces métalliques dominent au plafond et sur certains murs, les formes courbes des chaises de Jacobsen et les lumières changeantes contribuent à donner à la fois de la variété et une certaine chaleur à l'espace.

ZAHA HADID

Zaha Hadid Architects
Studio 9, 10 Bowling Green Lane
London EC1R OBQ, UK

Tel: +44 207 253 51 47 / Fax: +44 207 251 83 22
E-mail: mail@zaha-hadid.com / Web: www.zaha-hadid.com

ZAHA HADID studied architecture at the Architectural Association in London (AA) beginning in 1972 and was awarded the Diploma Prize in 1977. She then became a partner of Rem Koolhaas in the Office for Metropolitan Architecture (OMA) and taught at the AA. She has also taught at Harvard, the University of Chicago, in Hamburg and at Columbia University in New York. Well-known for her paintings and drawings, she has had a substantial influence, despite having built relatively few buildings. She has completed the Vitra Fire Station (Weil am Rhein, Germany, 1990–94); and exhibition designs such as that for "The Great Utopia" (Solomon R. Guggenheim Museum, New York, 1992). Significant competition entries include her design for the Cardiff Bay Opera House (1994–96); the Habitable Bridge (London, 1996); and the Luxembourg Philharmonic Hall (1997). More recently, Zaha Hadid has entered a phase of active construction with such projects as the Bergisel Ski Jump (Innsbruck, Austria, 2001–02); Lois & Richard Rosenthal Center for Contemporary Art (Cincinnati, Ohio, 1999–2003); Phaeno Science Center (Wolfsburg, Germany, 2001–05); and Central Building of the new BMW Assembly Plant in Leipzig (Germany, 2005). She has just completed Home House (London, UK, 2007–08, published here); the MAXXI National Center of Contemporary Arts in Rome (Italy, 2008); and is now working on the Guangzhou Opera House (Guangzhou, China, 2006–09); and the Sheik Zayed Bridge (Abu Dhabi, UAE, 2005–10). In 2004, Zaha Hadid became the first woman to win the coveted Pritzker Prize.

ZAHA HADID studierte Architektur an der Architectural Association in London (AA) von 1972 bis zum Erwerb des Diploma Prize 1977. Dann wurde sie Partnerin von Rem Koolhaas im Office for Metropolitan Architecture (OMA) und lehrte an der AA. Sie hat auch an der Harvard University, der University of Chicago, in Hamburg und an der Columbia University in New York gelehrt. Durch ihre Malereien und Zeichnungen wurde sie bekannt und hat beträchtlichen Einfluss ausgeübt, auch wenn sie nur relativ wenig gebaut hat. Ausgeführt hat sie u. a. die Feuerwehrstation von Vitra (Weil am Rhein, Deutschland, 1990–94) und Ausstellungsentwürfe, z. B. „The Great Utopia" (Solomon R. Guggenheim Museum, New York, 1992). Zu ihren bedeutenden Wettbewerbsprojekten zählen ihre Entwürfe für die Cardiff Bay Opera (1994–96), die bewohnbare Brücke (London, 1996) und die Philharmonie in Luxemburg (1997). In letzter Zeit hat für Zaha Hadid eine Phase des aktiven Bauens begonnen, mit Projekten wie der Bergiselschanze (Innsbruck, Österreich, 2001–02), des Lois & Richard Rosenthal Center for Contemporary Art (Cincinnati, Ohio, 1999–2003), des Wissenschaftszentrums Phaeno (Wolfsburg, 2001–05) und des neuen BMW-Werks in Leipzig (2005). Kürzlich fertiggestellt wurden das Home House (London, 2007–08, hier veröffentlicht) und das MAXXI, das Nationalmuseum für die Kunst des 21. Jahrhunderts in Rom (2008). Zurzeit arbeitet sie am Opernhaus für die chinesische Stadt Guangzhou (2006–09) und an der Scheich-Zayed-Brücke (Abu Dhabi, Vereinigte Arabische Emirate, 2005–10). 2004 erhielt Zaha Hadid als erste Frau den begehrten Pritzker-Preis.

ZAHA HADID a étudié à l'Architectural Association (AA) de Londres de 1972 à 1977, date à laquelle elle a reçu le Prix du diplôme. Elle devient ensuite partenaire de l'agence de Rem Koolhaas, Office for Metropolitan Architecture (OMA), et enseigne à l'AA ainsi qu'à Harvard, à l'Université de Chicago, à Hambourg et à l'Université Columbia à New York. Célèbre pour ses peintures et dessins, elle exerce une réelle influence, même si elle a assez peu construit pendant longtemps. Parmi ses réalisations anciennes : une casene des pompiers pour Vitra (Weil am Rhein, Allemagne, 1990–94) ; et des projets pour des expositions comme « La Grande Utopie » au Solomon R. Guggenheim Museum à New York (1992). Elle a participé à de nombreux concours, dont les plus importants sont le projet pour l'Opéra de Cardiff (Pays de Galles, 1994–96) ; un « Pont habitable » (Londres, 1996) ; et la salle de concerts philharmoniques de Luxembourg (1997). Plus récemment, elle est entrée dans une phase active de grands chantiers avec des réalisations comme le tremplin de ski de Bergisel à Innsbruck (Autriche, 2001–02) ; le Centre d'art contemporain Lois & Richard Rosenthal (Cincinnati, Ohio, 1999–2003) ; le Musée des sciences Phaeno (Wolfsburg, Allemagne, 2001–05) ; et le bâtiment central de la nouvelle usine BMW à Leipzig (Allemagne, 2005). Elle vient d'achever la Home House (Londres, 2007–08, publiée ici) ; le Centre national des arts contemporains de Rome, MAXXI (2008) ; et travaille maintenant à ses projets pour l'opéra de Guangzhou (Chine, 2006–09) et le pont Cheikh Sayed (Abu Dhabi, EAU, 2005–10). En 2004, Zaha Hadid a été la première femme à remporter le très convoité Prix Pritzker.

HOME HOUSE
London, UK, 2007–08

20 Portman Square, London W1H 6LW, UK, +44 207 670 2000, www.homehouseclub.com
Area: 158 m². Client: Home House Ltd. Cost: not disclosed
Team: Woody Yao, Maha Kutay, Melissa Woolford

This project marks the first intervention of Zaha Hadid in a London interior in over 20 years. Located on the ground floor of the Home House private members' club in a Georgian structure, this bar explores forms that Hadid has developed in recent years with her installations at the Venice Biennales, for example. As Zaha Hadid Architects state: "The furniture installations at Home House demonstrate a new type of living environment that continues the investigations of dynamic space making, creating a new open aesthetic that plays with the user's interaction." Unlike the temporary exhibitions in Venice, this installation is meant to be permanent and plays on the Georgian décor of Home House. CNC milling was used to create parts of the furniture, made with resin, fiberglass, and fabric. The bar is almost a pretext here for further exploration of Hadid's interest in redefining space and form. "A unique dichotomy is realized within Home House between this new formal language of morphology," say the architects, "and the dynamic forces and characteristic orthogonal programming of its Georgian envelope."

Dieses Projekt ist der erste Entwurf von Zaha Hadid für das Innere eines Londoner Gebäudes seit über 20 Jahren. Die im Erdgeschoss des georgianischen Home House untergebrachte Bar eines Privatklubs ist ein Versuch mit Formen, die Hadid in den letzten Jahren u. a. für ihre Installationen auf den Biennalen von Venedig entwickelt hatte. Wie Zaha Hadid Architects erklären, „zeigen die Möbeleinrichtungen im Home House einen neuen Typ des Wohnumfelds, der die Auseinandersetzung mit dynamischer Raumgestaltung fortsetzt und eine neue, offene Ästhetik erzeugt, die mit der Interaktion des Nutzers spielt". Im Gegensatz zu den befristeten Ausstellungen in Venedig soll diese Installation von Dauer sein und ist auf das georgianische Dekor des Home House bezogen. Teile der Möblierung wurden im CNC-Verfahren aus Kunstharz, Glasfaser und Stoff hergestellt. Die Bar wurde hier fast zum Vorwand für Hadids weitergehende Erforschung von Raum und Form. „Im Home House wurde eine einmalige Dichotomie zwischen dieser neuen, morphologischen Formensprache und den dynamischen Kräften und dem charakteristischen orthogonalen System seiner georgianischen Hülle realisiert", sagen die Architekten.

Ce projet marque la première intervention de Zaha Hadid en plus de vingt ans dans un intérieur londonien. Situé au rez-de-chaussée d'un club privé, le Home House, dans un immeuble de style géorgien, ce bar explore les formes que l'architecte développe depuis quelques années, en particulier dans ses installations pour la Biennale de Venise. Comme le précise l'agence : « Les installations de mobilier de Home House illustrent un type nouveau d'environnement dans le prolongement de nos recherches sur les espaces dynamiques, créant une nouvelle esthétique qui joue avec les interactions de l'utilisateur. » À la différence des installations temporaires vénitiennes, ce projet est de nature permanente et dialogue avec les éléments du décor géorgien. Des techniques d'usinage à pilotage numérique ont permis de créer des éléments de mobilier en résine, fibre de verre et tissu. Le bar est ici un quasi-prétexte à de nouvelles explorations de Zaha Hadid sur la redéfinition de l'espace et de la forme. « Une dichotomie spécifique s'organise dans le Home House entre ce nouveau langage morphologique, ses forces dynamiques et la programmation orthogonale caractéristique de son enveloppe ancienne de type géorgien », précise l'agence.

The flowing bar occupies the room in a surprising way, redefining its rectilinear volume.

Das fließende Volumen der Bar hat eine erstaunliche Wirkung und verändert den rechteckigen Raum.

L'espace fluide du bar prend possession de la pièce de manière étonnante et redéfinit son volume orthogonal.

Unexpected, and very present in the
room, the bar has an almost organic
presence that contrasts with the
walls—with their straight moldings—
and the small rectangular window-
panes that envelop it.

Die Bar zeigt eine unerwartete und
sehr eindrucksvolle, fast organische
Präsenz, die im Kontrast zu den ge-
radlinigen Wänden und den kleinen,
rechtwinkligen Fensterscheiben steht.

Surprenant et très présent, le bar
impose une présence quasi organique
qui contraste avec les murs aux mou-
lures orthogonales et les fenêtres à
petits bois.

JEPPE HEIN

Jeppe Hein Studio
Oranienstr. 185
10999 Berlin
Germany

Tel: +49 30 616 51 91 70
Fax: +49 30 616 51 91 79
E-mail: info@jeppehein.net
Web: www.jeppehein.net

JEPPE HEIN was born in 1974 in Copenhagen. He lives and works in Berlin and Copenhagen. He graduated from the Städelschule, Hochschule für Bildende Künste, Frankfurt (1999), and the Royal Danish Academy of Arts, Copenhagen (1997). His most recent solo exhibition was in 2008 at the ARoS Museum (Århus, Denmark). He is represented by the 303 Gallery in New York and was a cofounder of OTTO, a non-commercial exhibition forum in Denmark (www.artnode.dk/otto). With his sister Lærke, he is the founder of Karriere, a café/bar with site-specific artworks by international artists, located in Copenhagen (Denmark, 2007, published here). **LÆRKE HEIN**, born in 1982, is "an experienced bar and nightclub worker. She has extensive experience in the management of a number of Copenhagen's nightlife hot spots, and is responsible for the day-to-day management of the Karriere. Jeppe Hein's pieces, space, artwork, and audience are closely connected. He works with a wide range of materials and art forms: water, neon, fire, balls, cubes—and nothing at all. In the work *Invisible Labyrinth* (2005), visitors were invited to walk around in a large empty museum space wearing a headband fitted with sensors. When the sensor vibrated, it was an indication that the visitor had collided with the walls of the invisible maze, and a cue to change direction and find one's way through the empty space while gradually forming an idea of its "layout."

JEPPE HEIN wurde 1974 in Kopenhagen geboren; er lebt und arbeitet dort und in Berlin. Er studierte an der Städelschule, Hochschule für Bildende Künste, in Frankfurt (Abschluss 1999) und der Königlichen Dänischen Kunstakademie in Kopenhagen (Abschluss 1997). Seine jüngste Einzelausstellung fand 2008 im ARoS Museum (Århus, Dänemark) statt. Er wird von der 303 Gallery in New York vertreten und war Mitbegründer von OTTO, einem nichtkommerziellen Ausstellungsforum in Dänemark (www.artnode.dk/otto). Mit seiner Schwester Lærke eröffnete er 2007 Karriere, ein Café mit Bar in Kopenhagen, das ortsspezifische Kunstwerke von internationalen Künstlern ausstellt (hier vorgestellt). **LÆRKE HEIN**, geboren 1982, hat „Erfahrung in der Arbeit für Bars und Nachtklubs", das heißt in der Leitung von angesehenen Nachtlokalen in Kopenhagen, und ist verantwortlich für das Tagesgeschäft in Karriere. Jeppe Heins Aufführungen, Räume und Kunstwerke sind eng mit seinen Zuschauern verbunden. Er arbeitet in sehr verschiedenen Materialien und Kunstformen: mit Wasser, Neon, Feuer, Bällen, Kuben – und überhaupt nichts. Bei seinem Werk „Invisible Labyrinth" (2005) wurden die Besucher aufgefordert, in einem großen, leeren Museumsraum herumzugehen. Sie trugen ein Stirnband, das mit Sensoren ausgestattet war. Wenn so ein Sensor vibrierte, war dies ein Anzeichen dafür, dass der Besucher mit der Wand des unsichtbaren Labyrinths zusammengestoßen war und er die Richtung zu ändern und einen anderen Weg durch den leeren Raum zu suchen hatte, wobei er allmählich eine Vorstellung von dessen Gestaltung gewann.

JEPPE HEIN, né en 1974 à Copenhague, vit et travaille à Berlin et Copenhague. Il est diplômé de la Städelschule, Hochschule für Bildende Künste de Francfort (1999), et de l'Académie royale des Arts à Copenhague (1997). Sa plus récente exposition personnelle s'est déroulée en 2008 au ARoS Museum (Århus, Danemark). Il est représenté par la galerie 303 de New York et a été cofondateur d'OTTO, forum danois d'expositions non commerciales (www.artnode.dk/otto). C'est en compagnie de sa sœur Lærke qu'il a créé Karriere, un café-bar présentant des œuvres d'art spécialement créées par des artistes internationaux (Copenhague, 2007, publié ici). **LÆRKE HEIN**, née en 1982, possède une expérience approfondie de la gestion de restaurants et de bars, acquise dans un certain nombre de hauts lieux de la vie nocturne copenhagoise, et est responsable de la gestion quotidienne de Karriere. Les installations, œuvres, espaces et le public de Jeppe Hein sont étroitement liés. Il travaille à partir d'une importante gamme de matériaux et différentes formes artistiques : eau, néons, feu, boules, cubes, voire rien. Dans son œuvre *Invisible Labyrinth* (2005), les visiteurs étaient invités à se promener dans un vaste espace muséal vide en portant un serre-tête équipé d'un capteur. La vibration de celui-ci signalait au promeneur qu'il avait heurté les murs d'un labyrinthe invisible, et devait changer de direction pour trouver son chemin à travers l'espace vide et se former peu à peu une idée de son « plan ».

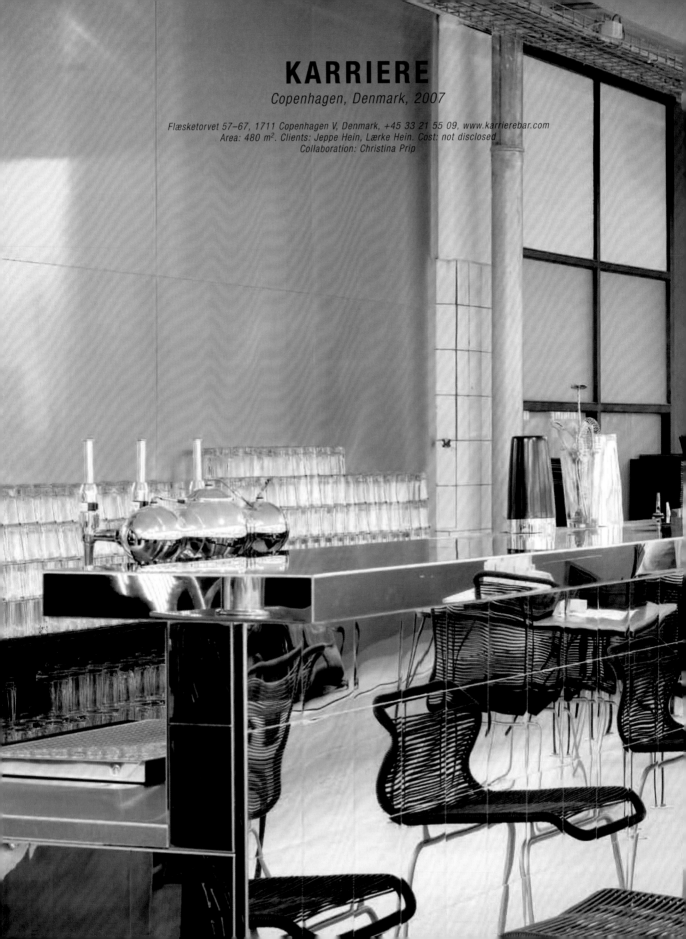

KARRIERE
Copenhagen, Denmark, 2007

*Flæsketorvet 57–67, 1711 Copenhagen V, Denmark, +45 33 21 55 09, www.karrierebar.com
Area: 480 m². Clients: Jeppe Hein, Lærke Hein. Cost: not disclosed
Collaboration: Christina Prip*

Karriere is a café/restaurant/bar located in the Flæsketorvet area of Copenhagen, unusual because it houses works of art by some of the most creative and socially interactive artists of the moment. There are works by Dan Graham, Olafur Eliasson, Ernesto Neto, Elmgreen & Dragset, Rirkrit Tiravanija, Maurizio Cattelan, and Douglas Gordon, amongst others. Founder Jeppe Hein's artistic contribution to Karriere is the bar counter itself. Twelve meters long and located in the center of the space, the bar counter gently sways from side to side. As Hein says: "Drinks and handbags are constantly sliding about a bit, causing slight bemusement: 'Hey! Have you just taken my drink?' Or, 'have I had a bit too much already?'" The Danish artist FOS designed the dining tables and small coffee tables for Karriere. Peter Kirkhoff Eriksen runs programs presenting artist talks, performances, and sound-based artworks, as well as preparing a newsletter on art available in pdf form on Karriere's Web site: www.karrierebar.com. The Heins have assembled a top team for the kitchen, including head chef Morten Haukaas, who has worked in London, Marseille, Lausanne, Siena, and Montreal. As Jeppe and Lærke Hein say: Karriere "is a venue with huge ambitions and the credentials to go with them: world-class artists across a range of artistic disciplines have defined the functions and design of the place, thereby making art part of a social space shared by a broad audience. At Karriere art is a natural part of meeting, eating, drinking, relaxing, and having fun, spurring communication, reflection, and play."

Karriere ist ein Café mit Restaurant und Bar im Bezirk Flæsketorvet von Kopenhagen und insofern ungewöhnlich, als es Kunstwerke von einigen der kreativsten und sozial engagiertesten Künstlern der Gegenwart enthält. Dort gibt es u. a. Werke von Dan Graham, Olafur Eliasson, Ernesto Neto, Elmgreen & Dragset, Rirkrit Tiravanija, Maurizio Cattelan und Douglas Gordon. Der künstlerische Beitrag des Gründers von Karriere, Jeppe Hein, ist die Theke in der Bar. Sie steht im Zentrum des Raums, ist 12 m lang und schwingt leicht von einer Seite zur anderen. Wie Hein sagt, „rutschen Drinks und Handtaschen immer irgendwo herum und schaffen Verwirrung. ‚Hey, hast du etwa meinen Drink genommen?' Oder: ‚Habe ich schon etwas zuviel getrunken?'" Der dänische Künstler FOS entwarf die Speisetische und die kleinen Kaffeetische für Karriere. Peter Kirkhoff Eriksen macht die Programme für Künstlergespräche, Aufführungen und Konzerte; er erstellt auch einen Newsletter für die Website www.karrierebar.com. Die Heins haben ein Topteam für die Küche gewonnen mit Küchenchef Morten Haukaas, der in London, Marseille, Lausanne, Siena und Montreal gearbeitet hat. Wie Jeppe und Lærke Hein sagen, ist Karriere „ein Schauplatz mit großen Ambitionen und damit verbundenen Voraussetzungen: Künstler von Weltklasse aus verschiedenen künstlerischen Disziplinen haben die Funktion und die Gestaltung dieses Orts bestimmt und dadurch Kunst zum Teil eines sozialen Bereichs gemacht, der von einem großen Publikum besucht wird. In Karriere ist die Kunst natürlicher Bestandteil der Begegnung, vom Essen, Trinken, Erholen und Spaßhaben; sie ist Anregung zur Kommunikation, zur Reflexion und zum Spiel."

Karriere est un café-restaurant-bar du quartier de Flæsketorvet à Copenhague. C'est un lieu curieux en ce qu'il accueille des œuvres d'art de certains des artistes les plus créatifs et les plus connus du moment comme, entre autres, Dan Graham, Olafur Eliasson, Ernesto Neto, Elmgreen & Dragset, Rirkrit Tiravanija, Maurizio Cattelan et Douglas Gordon. La contribution artistique de Jeppe Hein est ici le comptoir du bar de 12 m de long, implanté au centre de l'espace et de profil légèrement incliné. Comme le précise Hein : «Les boissons et les sacs à main glissent constamment, ce qui provoque un certain amusement : «Hé! C'est vous qui avez pris mon verre?» ou «J'en ai déjà pris un de trop?» «L'artiste danois FOS a conçu les tables et les tables basses. Peter Kirkhoff Eriksen anime des programmes de conférences d'artistes, des performances visuelles et sonores et édite une lettre d'information disponible en pdf sur le site www.karrierebar.com. Pour la cuisine, les Hein ont réuni une équipe de haut niveau dirigée par le chef Morten Haukaas qui a travaillé à Londres, Marseille, Lausanne, Sienne et Montréal. Comme ils l'expliquent : «Karriere est un lieu aux grandes ambitions et qui en a les moyens : des artistes de niveau international, choisis dans une gamme de disciplines artistiques variée, ont défini les fonctions et le design de l'endroit pour que l'art s'intègre à cet espace de socialisation ouvert à un large public. Pour Karriere, l'art fait naturellement partie de l'esprit de rencontre, de la cuisine, de l'agrément de prendre un verre, de se détendre et de se faire plaisir, en stimulant la communication, la réflexion et le jeu. »

Above, left, the Dividing Wall by Dan Graham with tables and benches by Bank & Rau (Meat and Tools). Above, right, the entrance to Karriere.

Oben links: „Dividing Wall" von Dan Graham mit Tischen und Bänken von Bank & Rau (Meat and Tools). Oben rechts: Der Eingang zum Karriere.

Ci-dessus, à gauche, le Dividing Wall de Dan Graham. Les tables et les bancs sont de Bank & Rau (Meat and Tools). Ci-dessus, à droite, l'entrée du Karriere.

Above, left, Johannes Wohnseifer, My Night is your Day. *Above, center, Robert Städter,* Pentaphone. *Above, right, Olafur Eliasson,* National Career Lamp. *Below,* Wallpainting *by Franz Ackermann and Rirkrit Tiravanija's* Elephant Juice.

Oben links: Johannes Wohnseifer, „My Night is your Day". Oben, Mitte: Robert Städter, „Pentaphone". Oben rechts: Olafur Eliasson, „National Career Lamp". Unten: „Wallpainting" von Franz Ackermann und Rirkrit Tiravanijas „Elephant Juice".

Ci-dessus, à gauche : My Night is your Day *de Johannes Wohnseifer. Ci-dessus, au centre :* Pentaphone *de Robert Städter. Ci-dessus, à droite :* National Career Lamp *d'Olafur Eliasson. Ci-dessous :* Wallpainting *de Franz Ackermann et* Elephant Juice *de Rirkrit Tiravanija.*

HOSOYA SCHAEFER

Hosoya Schaefer Architects AG
Reinhardstr. 19
8008 Zurich
Switzerland

Tel: +41 43 243 63 13
Fax: +41 43 243 63 15
E-mail: office@hosoyaschaefer.com
Web: www.hosoyaschaefer.com

HOSOYA SCHAEFER was founded by Markus Schaefer and Hiromi Hosoya in 2003. Hiromi Hosoya, who is of Japanese origin, has B. A. degrees in English Literature from Doshisha Women's University, Kyoto; in Fine Arts and Architecture from the Rhode Island School of Design; as well as an M.Arch from the Harvard GSD, where she worked on the *Harvard Guide to Shopping* in the team of Rem Koolhaas. She worked in the office of Toyo Ito in Tokyo (1998–2001) and in Rotterdam (2001–03) before cofounding Hosoya Schaefer. Markus Schaefer has an M.Arch degree from the Harvard GSD, where he also collaborated on the Koolhaas project and met Hosoya. He also has a Master's in Neurobiology from the University of Zurich. He worked in the office of OMA in Rotterdam from 1999 to 2003. Recent projects include a documentary movie *Cities in Motion* (with Condor Films, Zurich, 2007); *Second Planet* (with Condor Films, 2009–); MSG Office Building Hypercore (Milan, Italy, 2007); and the "La Rinascente" Department Store, also in Milan (2007). The firm won a ContractWorld Award 2008 for their first realized project, the AnAn Restaurant built for Autostadt, the theme park and communications platform for the Volkswagen Group in Wolfsburg (Germany, 2005–07, published here). Recently, the firm also won First Prize to design a new private airport in Saint Moritz-Samedan (Switzerland), and a master plan for the redevelopment of 230 hectares in Ljubljana, Slovenia, in 2008.

Das Büro HOSOYA SCHAEFER wurde 2003 von Markus Schaefer und Hiromi Hosoya gegründet. Hiromi Hosoya stammt aus Japan und hat einen B. A. in englischer Literatur von der Frauenuniversität Doshisha in Kioto, in bildender Kunst und Architektur von der Rhode Island School of Design sowie einen M. Arch. von der Harvard Graduate School of Design (GSD), wo sie im Team von Rem Koolhaas am *Harvard Guide to Shopping* mitarbeitete. Vor der Gründung von Hosoya Schaefer war sie im Büro von Toyo Ito in Tokio (1998–2001) und in Rotterdom (2001–03) tätig. Markus Schaefer hat einen M. Arch. von der Harvard GSD, wo auch er am Koolhaas-Projekt arbeitete und Hosoya begegnete. Er hat außerdem einen Mastertitel in Neurobiologie von der Universität Zürich. Von 1999 bis 2003 arbeitete er bei OMA in Rotterdam. Zu den neueren Projekten des Büros zählen der Dokumentarfilm *Cities in Motion* (mit Condor Films, Zürich, 2007), *Second Planet* (mit Condor Films, 2009–), das Bürogebäude MSG Hypercore (Mailand, 2007) und das Kaufhaus La Rinascente, ebenfalls in Mailand (2007). Das Büro gewann einen ContractWorld Award 2008 für sein erstes ausgeführtes Projekt, das Restaurant AnAn in der Autostadt der Volkswagengruppe in Wolfsburg (2005–07, hier vorgestellt). Kürzlich gewann das Büro erste Preise für einen neuen, privaten Flughafen in Sankt-Moritz-Samedan (Schweiz) und für einen Masterplan für die Sanierung eines 230 ha großen Gebiets in Ljubljana, Slowenien (2008).

L'agence HOSOYA SCHAEFER a été fondée par Markus Schaefer et Hiromi Hosoya en 2003. D'origine japonaise, Hiromi Hosoya est B. A. en littérature anglaise de l'Université de femmes Doshisha à Kyoto et B. A. en beaux-arts et architecture de la Rhode Island School of Design, et M.Arch de la Harvard GSD, où elle a collaboré au *Harvard Guide to Shopping* dans l'équipe de Rem Koolhaas. Elle a travaillé chez Toyo Ito à Tokyo (1998–2001) et à Rotterdam (2001–03), avant de fonder Hosoya Schaefer. Markus Schaefer est M.Arch de la Harvard GSD, où il a également participé au projet de Koolhaas et rencontré Hosoya. Il possède également une maîtrise en neurobiologie de l'Université de Zurich. Il a travaillé pour l'agence OMA à Rotterdam de 1999 à 2003. Parmi leurs projets récents figurent un film documentaire *Cities en Motion* (avec Condor Films, Zurich, 2007); *Second Planet* (avec Condor Films, 2009–); l'immeuble de bureaux MSG Hypercore (Milan, Italie, 2007) et le grand magasin La Rinascente, également à Milan (2007). L'agence a remporté le prix ContractWorld 2008 pour son premier projet réalisé, le restaurant AnAn construit pour Autostadt, parc à thème et plate-forme de communication du groupe Volkswagen à Wolfsburg (Allemagne, 2005–07, publié ici). Récemment, elle a aussi obtenu le premier prix pour la conception d'un nouvel aéroport privé à Saint-Moritz-Samedan (Suisse), et un plan directeur pour la rénovation d'un quartier de 230 ha à Ljubljana, Slovénie (2008).

ANAN RESTAURANT
Autostadt, Wolfsburg, Germany, 2005–07

Autostadt GmbH, StadtBrücke, 38440 Wolfsburg, Germany, +49 5361 40 61 16, www.autostadt.de
Area: 360 m². Client: Autostadt GmbH. Cost: not disclosed

Graphics were provided by Büro Destruct, Furi Furi Company, Fuyuki, GWG inc., Kentaro Fujimoto, Maniackers Design, Power Graphixx, and Yamafuji-Zuan.

Die Grafiken stammen von Büro Destruct, Furi Furi Company, Fuyuki, GWG inc., Kentaro Fujimoto, Maniackers Design, Power Graphixx und Yamafuji-Zuan.

Les éléments graphiques sont de Büro Destruct, Furi Furi Company, Fuyuki, GWG inc., Kentaro Fujimoto, Maniackers Design, Power Graphixx et Yamafuji-Zuan.

AnAn is a Japanese noodle bar for which Hosoya Schaefer was selected in a 2005 competition that stipulated that the restaurant should "represent in a small area, a piece of contemporary Tokyo." The architects proposed a series of distorted hexagonal cells for the floor and ceiling. These 3.5-meter-high cells made of 25-millimeter acrylic panels contain two counters, tables, vending machines, a coat-room, and a 3D menu column. They are covered with patterns produced by a selection of young Japanese graphic designers. The architects explain: "The entire project is based on just a few different angles allowing for an optimized range of formwork necessary to form the 2.5 cm thick acrylic panels. The space is conceived to be both transparent and filled with a range of different graphics and sensibilities creating a heterogeneous, urban whole."

AnAn ist ein japanisches Nudelrestaurant. Hosoya Schaefer erhielten den Auftrag nach einem Wettbewerb von 2005, der forderte, dass das Lokal „auf kleiner Fläche ein Stück des modernen Tokio wiedergeben" sollte. Die Architekten schlugen eine Reihe von verformten hexagonalen Zellen aus Plexiglas vor, die Boden und Decke untergliedern. Diese 3,5 m hohen Zellen aus 25 mm starken Acrylplatten enthalten zwei Theken, Tische, Automaten, Garderobe und eine Säule für die Speisen. Die Wände sind mit Mustern überzogen, die von ausgewählten jungen japanischen Grafikern stammen. Die Architekten erklären: „Der ganze Entwurf beruht auf nur wenigen verschiedenen Winkeln; daher war eine besondere Optimierung der Schalung notwendig, um die 2,5 cm dicken Acryltafeln zu formen. Das Lokal ist sowohl als Raum mit Durchblick geplant wie auch mit verschiedenen Grafiken und anderen künstlerischen Elementen ausgestattet, die ein heterogenes urbanes Ganzes bilden."

AnAn est un bar à nouilles japonais pour lequel l'agence Hosoya Schaefer a été sélectionnée à l'issue d'un concours organisé en 2005. Le cahier des charges stipulait que le lieu devait « représenter sur une petite surface, une partie du Tokyo contemporain ». Les architectes ont proposé une série de cellules hexagonales déformées pour le sol et le plafond. Ces cellules de 3,5 m de haut en panneaux d'acrylique de 25 mm d'épaisseur contiennent deux comptoirs, des tables, des distributeurs, un vestiaire et une colonne d'affichage des menus en trois dimensions. L'ensemble est décoré de motifs imaginés par une sélection de jeunes artistes graphistes japonais. « Le projet tout entier ne repose que sur quelques inclinaisons différentes seulement d'où la nécessité d'une gamme optimisée de coffrages pour fabriquer ces panneaux acryliques de 2,5 cm d'épaisseur. L'espace est conçu pour être à la fois transparent et décoré de toute une gamme d'éléments graphiques de sensibilités différentes pour créer un ensemble urbain hétérogène », expliquent les architectes.

A plan to the right shows the restaurant space. The custom-designed furniture is by Quinze & Milan with Hosoya Schaefer Architects.

Der Grundriss rechts zeigt den Restaurantbereich. Die hierfür entworfenen Möbel stammen von Quinze & Milan mit Hosoya Schaefer Architects.

Ci-contre, le plan du restaurant. Le mobilier a été spécifiquement conçu par Quinze & Milan en collaboration avec Hosoya Schaefer Architects.

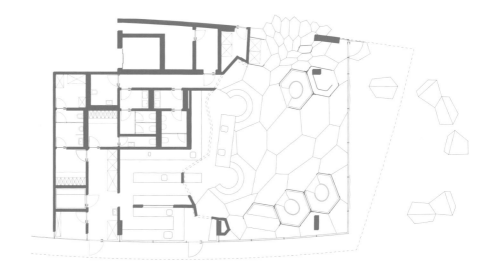

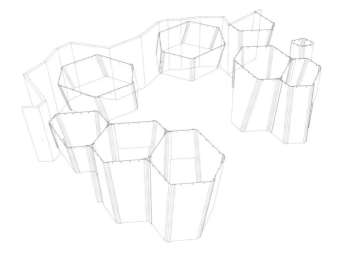

The graphics seem to fill the entire space, even beyond the surfaces on which they are inscribed.

Die Grafiken scheinen den ganzen Raum zu füllen, wirken sogar stärker als die Flächen, auf die sie aufgebracht sind.

Les éléments graphiques semblent remplir la totalité de l'espace, et même déborder des surfaces qui leur avaient été assignées.

JAKOB+MACFARLANE

Jakob+MacFarlane SARL d'Architecture
13–15 rue des Petites Écuries
75010 Paris
France

Tel: +33 1 44 79 05 72 / Fax: +33 1 48 00 97 93
E-mail: info@jakobmacfarlane.com / Web: www.jakobmacfarlane.com

DOMINIQUE JAKOB was born in 1966 and holds a degree in Art History from the Université de Paris I (1990) and a degree in Architecture from the École d'Architecture Paris-Villemin (1991). She has taught at the École Spéciale d'Architecture (1998–99) and at the École d'Architecture Paris-Villemin (1994–2000). Born in New Zealand in 1961, **BRENDAN MACFARLANE** received his B.Arch at SCI-Arc, Los Angeles (1984), and his M.Arch degree at the Harvard GSD (1990). He has taught at the Paris La Villette architecture school (1995–96), at the Berlage Institute, Amsterdam (1996), at the Bartlett School of Architecture in London (1996–98), and at the École Spéciale d'Architecture in Paris (1998–99). From 1995 to 1997, MacFarlane was an architecture critic at the Architectural Association (AA) in London. Jakob and Mac-Farlane founded their own agency in 1992 in Paris and were also cofounders with Emmanuelle Marin-Trottin and David Trottin of the exhibition and conference organizer Periphériques (1996–98). Their main projects include the T House (La-Garenne-Colombes, 1994, 1998); the Georges Restaurant (Centre Pompidou, Paris, 1999–2000, where the Pink Bar—2006, published here—is located); the restructuring of the Maxime Gorki Theater (Petit-Quevilly, 2000); the Renault International Communication Center (Boulogne, 2004); a docks project, the Docks Quai Rambaud (Lyon, 2004); and the Saint-Nazaire Theater (2004). Recent work includes the Alvéole Bar, Fondation d'Entreprise Ricard (Paris, 2007–08); the transformation of a former Paris dock warehouse into the French Institute of Fashion (2007–09); and the FRAC Centre in Orléans (2009–), all in France.

DOMINIQUE JAKOB wurde 1966 geboren und hat ein Diplom in Kunstgeschichte von der Université de Paris I (1990) sowie in Architektur von der École d'Architecture Paris-Villemin (1991). Sie hat an der École Spéciale d'Architecture (1998–99) und an der École d'Architecture Paris-Villemin (1994–2000) gelehrt. Der 1961 in Neuseeland geborene **BRENDAN MACFARLANE** erhielt den B. Arch. am SCI-Arc in Los Angeles (1984) und den M. Arch. an der Harvard Graduate School of Design (1990). Er hat an der Architekturhochschule Paris-La Villette (1995–96), am Berlage Institute in Amsterdam (1996), an der Bartlett School of Architecture in London (1996–98) und an der École Spéciale d'Architecture in Paris (1998–99) gelehrt. Von 1995 bis 1997 arbeitete MacFarlane als Architekturkritiker an der Architectural Association (AA) in London. Jakob und MacFarlane gründeten ihr eigenes Büro 1992 in Paris und waren mit Emmanuelle Marin-Trottin und David Trottin auch Mitbegründer der Ausstellungs- und Konferenzorganisation Periphériques (1996–98). Zu ihren wichtigsten Projekten zählen die Maison T (La-Garenne-Colombes, 1994, 1998), das Restaurant Georges (Centre Pompidou, Paris, 1999–2000, wo sich die hier vorgestellte Pink Bar von 2006 befindet), der Umbau des Maxim-Gorki-Theaters (Petit-Quevilly, 2000), das internationale Kommunikationszentrum von Renault (Boulogne, 2004), ein Entwurf für die Docks Quai Rambaud (Lyon, 2004) und das Theater von Saint-Nazaire (2004). Aktuellere Projekte sind die Bar Alvéole, Fondation d'Entreprise Ricard (Paris, 2007–08), der Umbau eines früheren Pariser Lagerhauses am Hafen zum Insitut Français de la Mode (2007–09) sowie das FRAC Centre in Orléans (2009–), alle in Frankreich.

DOMINIQUE JAKOB, née en 1966, est diplômée d'histoire de l'art de l'Université de Paris I (1990) et d'architecture de l'École d'architecture Paris-Villemin (1991). Elle a enseigné à l'École spéciale d'architecture (1998–99) et à l'École d'architecture Paris-Villemin (1994–2000). Né en Nouvelle-Zélande en 1961, **BRENDAN MACFARLANE** est B.Arch. de SCI-Arc (1984), et M.Arch. de Harvard GSD (1990). Il a enseigné à l'École d'architecture de Paris-La Villette (1995–96), à l'Institut Berlage d'Amsterdam (1996), à l'École d'architecture Bartlett de Londres (1996–98) et à l'École spéciale d'architecture à Paris (1998–99). De 1995 à 1997, MacFarlane a été critique de projets à l'Architectural Association de Londres. Jakob et MacFarlane ont fondé leur agence à Paris en 1992 et ont aussi été cofondateurs, avec Emmanuelle Marin-Trottin et David Trottin, de l'agence d'organisation d'expositions et de conférences Périphériques (1996–98). Parmi leurs principaux projets : la maison T (La-Garenne-Colombes, France, 1994, 1998) ; le restaurant Georges (Centre Pompidou, Paris, 1999–2000) dans lequel est situé le Pink Bar (2006) publié ici ; la restructuration du théâtre Maxime-Gorki (Petit-Quevilly, France, 1999–2000) ; le centre international de communication de Renault (Boulogne, France, 2004) ; une réhabilitation de docks avec les pavillons du quai Rambaud (Lyon, 2004) ; le théâtre Fanal (Saint-Nazaire, 2004). Parmi les projets récents : le bar Alvéole à la Fondation d'entreprise Ricard (Paris, 2007–08) ; la transformation d'un dock au bord de la Seine à Paris en Insitut français de la mode (2007–09) ; et le FRAC centre (Orléans, 2009–).

PINK BAR
Centre Pompidou, Paris, France, 2006

Centre Pompidou, Place Georges Pompidou, 75004 Paris, France, +33 1 44 78 47 99
Area: 22 m². Client: Georges Restaurant. Cost: €100 000

Returning to the Georges Restaurant run by the Costes family that they designed on the top floor of the Piano and Rogers Centre Pompidou in 2000, Jakob+Mac-Farlane made new use of a volume previously used for the cloakroom and restrooms. As they explain: "This new 'Pink' space, as second generation project, is conceived as a resultant element based on the same grid of the original restaurant project. Instead of deforming the grid to create the surfaced volumes, we carved out a resultant volume from a 3D matrix of 40 cubic centimeters, a micro division of the original building grid at the Centre Pompidou. This matrix is built from 10-millimeter aluminum sheets using laser cutting technology." Furniture for the Pink Bar was designed by Jakob+MacFarlane and produced by Cappellini, while lighting was done by iGuzzini.

In dem von der Familie Costes geführten Restaurant Georges, das sie 2000 im obersten Geschoss des Centre Pompidou von Piano und Rogers entworfen hatten, gestalteten Jakob+MacFarlane einen früher für Garderoben und Toiletten genutzten Bereichs um. Sie erläutern den Entwurf wie folgt: „Dieser neue rosafarbene Bereich, ein Projekt der zweiten Generation, wurde als Element auf dem gleichen Raster der ursprünglichen Restaurantplanung konzipiert. Anstatt das Raster zu verformen, um die erforderlichen Flächen zu gewinnen, schnitten wir ein weiteres Volumen aus einer 3-D-Matrix von 40 cm³ – ein kleiner Teil des ursprünglichen Rasters des Centre Pompidou. Diese Matrix besteht aus 10 mm starken Aluminiumplatten, die mit Lasertechnologie geschnitten wurden." Die Möbel für die Pink Bar wurden von Jakob+MacFarlane entworfen und von Cappellini produziert, die Beleuchtung stammt von iGuzzini.

De retour au Georges, le restaurant géré par la famille Costes qu'ils avaient conçu au dernier étage du Centre Pompidou par Piano et Rogers en 2000, Jakob et MacFarlane ont réutilisé un volume affecté au vestiaire et aux toilettes. «Ce nouvel espace Rose, projet de seconde génération, est un élément résultant de la trame du projet d'origine du restaurant. Au lieu de déformer cette trame pour créer des volumes, nous avons creusé le volume résultant dans une matrice en 3D de 40 cm³, en une microdivision de la trame originale du Centre Pompidou. Cette matrice est en tôle d'aluminium de 10 mm d'épaisseur découpée au laser»; Le mobilier du bar a également été conçu par les deux architectes et produit par Cappellini, tandis que l'éclairage a été réalisé par iGuzzini.

The bar structure and furniture were all custom-designed by the architects for this location on the top floor of the Centre Pompidou in Paris.

Die Barkonstruktion und die Möbel wurden von den Architekten speziell für dieses Lokal auf dem obersten Geschoss des Centre Pompidou in Paris entworfen.

La structure et le mobilier du bar ont été spécialement dessinés par les architectes pour ce lieu situé au dernier niveau du Centre Pompidou à Paris.

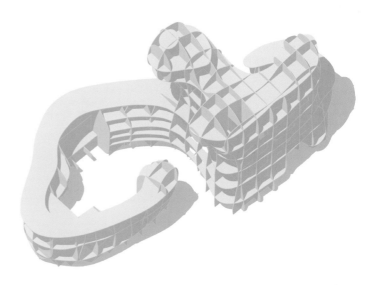

The drawing above shows the structure that is covered with a smooth, visible metallic skin. Bar stools, poufs, and tables were manufactured by Cappellini.

Diese Zeichnung zeigt die Konstruktion, die mit einer glatten Metallhaut verkleidet ist. Barstühle, Hocker und Tische wurden von Cappellini gefertigt.

Le dessin montre la structure qui a été recouverte d'une peau métallique lisse. Les tabourets, les poufs et les tables ont été fabriqués par Cappellini.

JOHNSEN SCHMALING ARCHITECTS

Johnsen Schmaling Architects
1699 North Astor Street
Milwaukee, WI 53202
USA

Tel: +1 414 287 9000
Fax: +1 414 287 9025
E-mail: info@johnsenschmaling.com
Web: www.johnsenschmaling.com

Brian Johnsen received his M.Arch degree from the University of Wisconsin in Milwaukee in 1997. Sebastian Schmaling received his M.Arch at Harvard GSD in 2002. Schmaling, originally from Berlin, had previously attended the University of Wisconsin, where he received another M.Arch degree (1996), and the Technische Universität Berlin, Germany (Vordiplom, Diplom-Ingenieur, 1994). He was a cofounder of **JOHNSEN SCHMALING ARCHITECTS** in 2003 with Brian Johnsen. Their work includes the Storewall (corporate headquarters, Milwaukee, 2005); the Camouflage House (Green Lake, 2006); the Blatz Milwaukee (transformation of former downtown brewery, 2006); Celeste 1218, an "urban loft" (Milwaukee, 2007); the Cafe Luna + Bar (Milwaukee, 2007–08, published here); and the Ferrous House (Spring Prairie, 2008), all in Wisconsin, USA.

Brian Johnsen erhielt 1997 seinen M. Arch. an der University of Wisconsin in Milwaukee. Sebastian Schmaling machte 2002 seinen M. Arch. an der Harvard Graduate School of Design. Der ursprünglich aus Berlin stammende Schmaling hatte zuvor an der University of Wisconsin (M. Arch. 1996) und an der Technischen Universität Berlin (Vordiplom, Diplom-Ingenieur, 1994) studiert. Mit Brian Johnsen gründete er 2003 das Büro **JOHNSEN SCHMALING ARCHITECTS**. Zu dessen ausgeführten Projekten zählen die Firmenzentrale von Storewall (Milwaukee, 2005), das Camouflage House (Green Lake, 2006), Blatz Milwaukee (Umbau einer früheren Brauerei im Stadtzentrum, 2006), Celeste 1218, ein „städtisches Loft" (Milwaukee, 2007), das Cafe Luna + Bar (Milwaukee, 2007–08, hier veröffentlicht) und das Ferrous House (Spring Prairie, 2008), alle in Wisconsin.

Brian Johnsen est M.Arch (Université du Wisconsin, Milwaukee, 1997). Sebastian Schmaling est M.Arch de la Graduate School of Design de l'Université de Harvard (2002). Schmaling, Berlinois d'origine, avait préalablement étudié à l'Université du Wisconsin où il avait obtenu un second M.Arch (1996), et à l'Université technique de Berlin (Vordiplom, Diplom-Ingenieur, 1994). Il a fondé l'agence **JOHNSEN SCHMALING ARCHITECTS** en 2003 avec Brian Johnsen. Parmi leurs travaux : le Storewall, siège social (Milwaukee, Wisconsin, États-Unis, 2005) ; la maison Camouflage (Green Lake, Wisconsin, 2006) ; le Blatz Milwaukee, transformation d'une ancienne brasserie du centre-ville (Milwaukee, 2006) ; le Celeste 1218, un « loft urbain » (Milwaukee, 2007) ; le Cafe Luna + Bar (Milwaukee, 2007–08, publié ici) ; et la maison Ferrous (Spring Prairie, 2008).

CAFE LUNA + BAR

Milwaukee, Wisconsin, USA, 2007–08

*First Place Riverwalk, 106 West Seeboth, Milwaukee, WI 53204, USA, +1 414 223 1558, www.cafelunalounge.com
Area: 251 m². Client: Megan McCormick. Cost: not disclosed*

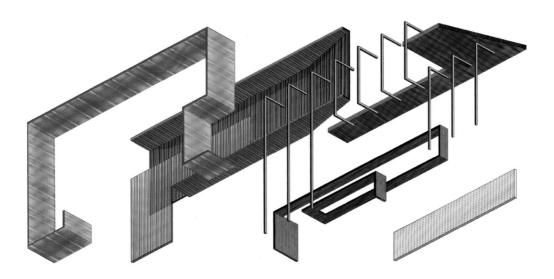

Located on the southern edge of downtown Milwaukee, the Cafe Luna + Bar overlooks the Milwaukee River and is inserted into what the architects call an "unexceptional commercial development." Indeed, the mediocre quality of the environment led the architects to seek "a high level of tactility, visual complexity, and drama." A textured wood-slat wall leads from the building lobby into the bar, wrapping the space like "heavy stage curtains." A mezzanine seating area is supported by thin structural steel columns. Back-lit cellular plastic panels animate the entire space with a deep red light and provide its main source of light. These panels also serve to conceal the necessary technical spaces of the bar. The architects conclude: "At night, the bar emits its mysterious glow through a series of large custom sliding doors into Milwaukee's somber nights, subtly marking the resurgence of this downtown neighborhood."

Das am südlichen Rand des Zentrums von Milwaukee gelegene Cafe Luna + Bar hat Ausblick auf den Milwaukee River und liegt in einem Gebiet, das Architekten als „unspektakuläre kommerzielle Bebauung" bezeichnen. In der Tat veranlasste die mäßige Qualität des Umfelds die Architekten dazu, sich um „ein hohes Niveau an taktiler Wirkung, optischer Komplexität und Dramatik" zu bemühen. Eine strukturierte Wand aus Holzleisten führt von der Empfangshalle des Gebäudes in die Bar und umgibt den Raum wie ein „schwerer Bühnenvorhang". Ein Zwischengeschoss mit Sitzplätzen wird von dünnen Stahlstützen getragen. Hinterleuchtete Lochplatten aus Kunststoff erfüllen den ganzen Raum mit tiefrotem Licht und dienen als Hauptlichtquelle. Außerdem verbergen sie die notwendigen technischen Einrichtungen der Bar. „Nachts strömt aus der Bar geheimnisvolles Licht durch mehrere große, speziell angefertigte Schiebetüren in Milwaukees dunkle Nächte und kündet von der Wiederbelebung dieses innerstädtischen Quartiers."

Situé à la limite sud du centre de Milwaukee, le Cafe Luna + Bar domine la rivière Milwaukee et s'insère dans ce que les architectes appellent « un quartier commercial banal ». La qualité médiocre de cet environnement les a conduits à rechercher « un degré élevé de tactilité, de complexité visuelle, et de spectaculaire ». Un mur texturé en lamelles de bois conduit du hall d'entrée de l'immeuble au bar et enveloppe l'espace à la manière « de lourds rideaux de scène ». La mezzanine garnie de sièges est soutenue par de fines colonnes d'acier structurel. Les panneaux en plastique cellulaire rétroéclairés animent l'ensemble du volume d'une lumière rouge dense et constituent la principale source d'éclairage. Ces panneaux servent également à cacher les espaces techniques nécessaires. « Le soir venu, le bar émet une mystérieuse lueur dans la nuit sombre de Milwaukee à travers une série de grandes portes coulissantes, signalant subtilement la résurgence de ce quartier du centre », concluent les architectes.

The drawing above shows the red "light ribbon" designed by the architects that wraps through the space (right). The Enzo Bar Stools are by Privacotta, Cube Lounge Chairs by West Elm, and the lounge tables were custom-designed by the architects.

Die Zeichnung oben zeigt das von den Architekten gestaltete rote „Lichtband", das sich durch den Raum windet (rechts). Die Barhocker Enzo stammen von Privacotta, die Sessel Cube von West Elm, die Tische wurden von den Architekten entworfen.

Le dessin ci-dessus précise le rôle du « ruban de lumière » rouge conçu par les architectes pour envelopper l'espace (à droite). Les tabourets de bar Enzo sont de Privacotta, et dans le lounge, les fauteuils Cube sont de West Elm. Les tables ont été spécialement dessinées par les architectes.

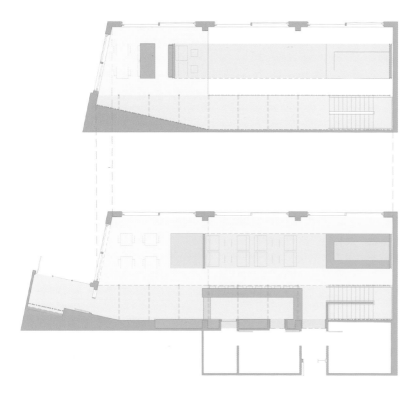

The comprehensive design of the space encompasses the lighting and the selection of furniture.

Die eindrucksvolle Raumgestaltung, einschließlich Beleuchtung und Wahl der Möblierung, wurde konsequent durchgehalten.

Plein de force, ce projet englobe l'éclairage et la sélection du mobilier.

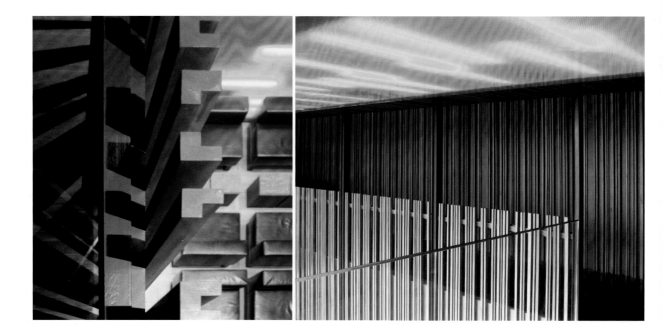

SFJONES ARCHITECTS

SFJones Architects
4218 Glencoe Avenue
Studio 2
Marina Del Rey, CA 90292
USA

Tel: +1 310 822 3822
Fax: +1 310 306 4441
E-mail: mailbox@sfjones.com
Web: www.sfjones.com

STEPHEN FRANCIS JONES received his B.Arch degree from the University of Florida (1982–86) and his M.Arch from the University of California, Los Angeles (UCLA; 1988–92). He began his career in Boston, working with Jung/Brannen Associates, designing high-rise buildings. He has been the principal and lead designer of his own firm for 19 years and worked on a wide variety of projects, including a cogeneration plant in Sacramento, California, and mixed-use housing in Barcelona, Spain. Recent projects include Hamasaku (Los Angeles, 2000); Lucky Strike Bowling Lanes (Hollywood, 2003); Chinois (Santa Monica, 2004); Kumo (West Hollywood, 2007, published here); the Veggie Grill (El Segundo, 2008); the Grill on the Alley (Thousand Oaks, 2008); and Anisette (Santa Monica, 2008), all in California, USA.

STEPHEN FRANCIS JONES erhielt seinen B. Arch. an der University of Florida (1982–86) und seinen M. Arch. an der University of California, Los Angeles (UCLA, 1988–92). Er begann seine berufliche Tätigkeit in Boston, wo er im Büro Jung/Brannen Associates Hochhäuser plante. Seit 19 Jahren ist er Leiter und Chefdesigner seiner eigenen Firma und hat sehr verschiedene Projekte realisiert, darunter ein Heizkraftwerk in Sacramento, Kalifornien, und Wohnbauten mit gemischter Nutzung in Barcelona. Zu den neueren Projekten zählen Hamasaku (Los Angeles, 2000), Lucky Strike Bowling Lanes (Hollywood, 2003), Chinois (Santa Monica, 2004), Kumo (West Hollywood, 2007, hier vorgestellt), der Veggie Grill (El Segundo, 2008), der Grill on the Alley (Thousand Oaks, 2008) und Anisette (Santa Monica, 2008), alle in Kalifornien.

STEPHEN FRANCIS JONES est B.Arch de l'Université de Floride (1982–86) et M.Arch de l'Université de Californie à Los Angeles (UCLA ; 1988–92). Il a entamé sa carrière à Boston, dans l'agence Jung/Brannen Associates, et conçu des immeubles de grande hauteur. Il est le dirigeant et le principal architecte de son agence, fondée il y a dix-neuf ans, et a travaillé sur des projets très variés, dont une usine de cogénération à Sacramento, Californie, et des immeubles mixtes à Barcelone. Parmi les réalisations récentes, tous en Californie, figurent le Hamasaku (Los Angeles, 2000) ; le bowling Lucky Strike (Hollywood, 2003) ; le Chinois (Santa Monica, 2004) ; le Kumo (West Hollywood, 2007, publié ici) ; le Veggie Grill (El Segundo, 2008) ; le Grill on the Alley (Thousand Oaks, 2008) ; et l'Anisette (Santa Monica, 2008).

KUMO

West Hollywood, California, USA, 2007

8360 Melrose Avenue, Los Angeles, CA 90069, USA, +1 323 651 5866, www.kumo-la.com
Area: 288 m². Client: Michael Ovitz. Cost: $1.6 million

Stephen Jones was the lead designer for this restaurant, located at 8360 Melrose Avenue in Los Angeles, working with his project team of Vikki Tucker and Yuwen Peng. The word *kumo* means cloud in Japanese and the owner requested a design that would resemble a cloud. "We started by examining what a white cloud is: reflected light on water molecules suspended in the sky," says Jones. Glass droplet chandeliers hang over the booths and the dark floors are hardly visible. As Jones says: "This creates the illusion that the dining experience is floating through the nighttime stratosphere." A semicircular stainless-steel and acrylic "cloud bar" continues the metaphor. An acrylic-lined wall with water running down it divides the private dining area. A large red mural by Chiho Aoshima in the private dining area contrasts with an otherwise "colorless" environment. "The absence of color allowed us to explore form, texture, and lighting on a tabula rasa," concludes Jones.

Stephen Jones war der verantwortliche Planer dieses in Los Angeles, 8360 Melrose Avenue, gelegenen Restaurants, an dem er mit Vikki Tucker und Yuwen Peng zusammenarbeitete. Das japanische Wort *kumo* bedeutet Wolke, und der Besitzer forderte einen Entwurf, der einer Wolke ähnelte. „Wir begannen mit der Untersuchung, woraus eine weiße Wolke besteht – aus reflektiertem Licht auf Wassermolekülen, die am Himmel hängen", sagt Jones. Über den Sitzgruppen hängen Lüster aus Glastropfen, und die dunklen Fußböden sind kaum sichtbar. Wie Jones sagt, „erzeugt dies die Illusion, als ob man beim Erlebnis des Speisens durch die nächtliche Stratosphäre schwebt". Eine halbkreisförmige „Wolkenbar" aus Edelstahl und Acryl setzt die Metapher fort. An einer mit Acryl verkleideten Wand läuft das Wasser herunter; sie dient zur Abgrenzung des privaten Speisebereichs. Ein großes, rotes Wandbild von Chiho Aoshima im privaten Essraum bildet einen Kontrast zum ansonsten „farblosen" Umfeld. „Die Abwesenheit von Farbe machte es möglich, dass wir uns ausschließlich mit Form, Struktur und Beleuchtung auseinanderzusetzen hatten", erläutert Jones.

Stephen Jones a été le responsable de ce projet de restaurant installé 8360 Melrose Avenue à Los Angeles, en collaboration avec Vikki Tucker et Yuwen Peng. *Kumo* signifie « nuage » en japonais et le propriétaire souhaitait que le nuage soit le thème de son établissement. « Nous avons commencé par étudier ce qu'est un nuage blanc : de la lumière réfléchie sur des molécules d'eau en suspension dans le ciel », explique Stephen Jones. Dans le restaurant, des lustres en gouttes de verre sont suspendus au-dessus des alvôves, et les sols de couleur foncée sont à peine perceptibles. L'architecte précise que c'est là « ce qui crée l'illusion de prendre son repas en suspension dans la stratosphère nocturne ». Un « bar nuage », semi-circulaire, en acier inoxydable et acrylique, exploite également cette métaphore. Un mur doublé d'acrylique sur lequel s'écoule de l'eau isole la salle à manger privée. Dans cette pièce, une grande fresque murale de tonalité rouge réalisée par l'artiste Chiho Aoshima contraste avec l'environnement voulu « incolore ». « L'absence de couleur nous a permis d'explorer la forme, la texture et l'éclairage en partant de zéro », conclut Stephen Jones.

In the dining area, chandeliers are by Eurofase (Ether 90). The banquettes are by Décor Fabrics (Los Angeles).

Die Kronleuchter im Speisebereich stammen von Eurofase (Ether 90), die Sitzbänke von Décor Fabrics (Los Angeles).

Dans la partie salle à manger, les lustres sont d'Eurofase (Ether 90), les banquettes de Décor Fabrics (Los Angeles).

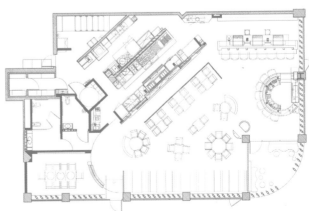

JOUIN MANKU

Agence Jouin Manku
8 Passage de la Bonne Graine
75011 Paris
France

Tel: +33 1 55 28 89 20 / Fax: +33 1 58 30 60 70
E-mail: agence@jouinmanku.com / Web: www.jouinmanku.com

Born in Nantes, France, in 1967, **PATRICK JOUIN** studied at the École Nationale Supérieure de Création Industrielle (ENSCI) in Paris and received his diploma in 1992. He worked in 1992 as a designer at the Compagnie des Wagons-Lits, and for the two following years at Tim Thom, Thomson Multimedia, under Philippe Starck, who was then Artistic Director of the brand. From 1995 to 1999, Patrick Jouin was a designer in Philippe Starck's Paris studio. He has designed numerous objects and pieces of furniture, while his architectural work includes the Alain Ducasse au Plaza Athénée Restaurant (Paris, 2000); 59 Poincaré Restaurant (Paris, 2000); Plastic Products Factory (Nantes, 2001); Plaza Athénée Bar (Paris, 2001); Spoon Byblos Restaurant (Saint-Tropez, 2002); Chlösterli Restaurants & Club, Spoon des Neiges Restaurant (Gstaad, Switzerland, 2004); Terrasse Montaigne, Plaza Athénée (Paris, 2005); and the Gilt Restaurant and Bar (New York, New York, 2005), all in France unless stated otherwise. **SANJIT MANKU** was born in 1971 in Nairobi, Kenya. He received his B.Arch degree from Carleton University (Ottawa, Canada, 1995) and was a designer in the office of Yabu Pushelberg (New York, 1996–2001). Sanjit Manku joined Patrick Jouin in 2001 and became a partner in 2006. During this period he has worked on interior and architecture projects, including the Mix restaurants in New York (2003) and Las Vegas (2004), as well as private houses in London and Kuala Lumpur (Malaysia, 2004–08), and hotels in England and France. Recently, Jouin Manku have completed Alain Ducasse at the Dorchester (London, UK, 2007); Le Jules Verne, Eiffel Tower (Paris, France, 2007); and the Auberge de l'Ill, Illhaeusern (France, 2007), all published here.

PATRICK JOUIN, geboren 1967 im französischen Nantes, studierte an der École Nationale Supérieure de Création Industrielle (ENSCI) in Paris und erhielt 1992 sein Diplom. Er arbeitete 1992 als Designer für die Compagnie des Wagons-Lits und in den darauffolgenden zwei Jahren bei Tim Thom, Thomson Multimedia, für Philippe Starck, der damals künstlerischer Leiter dieser Firma war. Von 1995 bis 1999 war Patrick Jouin Designer in Philippe Starcks Pariser Atelier. Er hat zahlreiche Objekte und Möbelstücke entworfen. Zu seinen Architekturprojekten zählen u. a. das Restaurant Alain Ducasse au Plaza Athénée (Paris, 2000), das Restaurant 59 Poincaré (Paris, 2000), eine Kunststofffabrik (Nantes, 2001), die Bar Plaza Athénée (Paris, 2001), das Restaurant Spoon Byblos (Saint-Tropez, 2002), die Restaurants und der Klub Chlösterli sowie das Restaurant Spoon des Neiges (Gstaad, Schweiz, 2004), Terrasse Montaigne, Plaza Athénée (Paris, 2005), und das Gilt Restaurant mit Bar (New York, 2005). **SANJIT MANKU** wurde 1971 in Nairobi, Kenia, geboren. Er erhielt seinen B. Arch. an der Carleton University (Ottawa, Kanada, 1995) und arbeitete als Designer im Büro von Yabu Pushelberg (New York, 1996–2001). Sanjit Manku ging 2001 zu Patrick Jouin und wurde 2006 sein Partner. Er hat an Architektur- und Innenarchitekturprojekten gearbeitet, u. a. den Mix Restaurants in New York (2003) und Las Vegas (2004) sowie an Einfamilienhäusern in London und Kuala Lumpur (Malaysia, 2004–08) und Hotels in England und Frankreich. Kürzlich haben Jouin Manku das Alain Ducasse im Dorchester Hotel (London, 2007) ausgeführt, ferner das Jules Verne im Eiffelturm (Paris, 2007) und die Auberge de l'Ill, Illhaeusern (Frankreich, 2007), die alle hier vorgestellt sind.

Né à Nantes en 1967, **PATRICK JOUIN** a étudié à l'École nationale supérieure de création industrielle (ENSCI) à Paris dont il est sorti diplômé en 1992. Il a ensuite travaillé pour la Compagnie des Wagons-Lits, puis les deux années suivantes pour Tim Thom, département de design de Thomson Multimédia, animé par Philippe Starck, alors directeur artistique de la marque. De 1995 à 1999, il a été designer chez celui-ci. Il a conçu de nombreux objets et meubles. Ses interventions architecturales comprennent : le restaurant du Plaza Athénée pour Alain Ducasse (Paris, 2000), le restaurant 59 Poincaré (Paris, 2000) ; une usine de produits en plastique (Nantes, 2001) ; le bar du Plaza Athénée (Paris, 2001) ; le restaurant Spoon Byblos (Saint-Tropez, 2000) ; le restaurant et club Chlösterli et le restaurant Spoon des Neiges (Gstaad, Suisse, 2004) ; la Terrasse Montaigne, Plaza Athénée (Paris, 2005) ; le Gilt Restaurant and Bar (New York, 2005). **SANJIT MANKU**, né en 1971 à Nairobi (Kenya), est B.Arch de l'Université Carleton (Ottawa, Canada, 1995) et a travaillé pour Yabu Pushelberg à New York (1996–2001). Il a rejoint Patrick Jouin en 2001 dont il est devenu associé en 2006. Pendant cette période, il a travaillé sur des projets d'architecture et d'aménagement intérieur dont les restaurants Mix de New York (2003) et Las Vegas (2004), ainsi que des résidences privées à Londres et à Kuala Lumpur (Malaisie, 2004–08), et des hôtels en Grande-Bretagne et en France. Récemment, Jouin Manku a achevé le restaurant Alain Ducasse au Dorchester (Londres, G.-B., 2007) ; le Jules Verne à la tour Eiffel (Paris, 2007) ; et l'Auberge de l'Ill à Illhaeusern (France, 2007), tous publiés ici.

ALAIN DUCASSE AT THE DORCHESTER

London, UK, 2007

Park Lane, London W1K 1QA, UK, +44 207 629 8866, www.alainducasse-dorchester.com
Area: 270 m². Clients: Alain Ducasse Entreprise and Dorchester Hotel. Cost: not disclosed
Team: Marie Deroudhile, Virginie Renaut, Jean-Baptiste Auvray

Below, the main dining room with a view of the VIP room (right) enclosed by a luminous column made of cracked optical fiber and natural sheer cotton strands. The space features chairs (Mobilia Italia) and service stations (Laval) custom-designed by Jouin Manku.

Unten: Der große Speisesaal mit Blick in den VIP-Raum (rechts) hinter einer leuchtenden Säule aus gebrochenen optischen Fasern und unbehandelten Baumwollsträngen. Der Bereich ist mit eigens entworfenen Stühlen (Mobilia Italiana) und Bedienungstheken (Laval) von Jouin Manku ausgestattet.

Ci-dessous, la salle principale et le salon VIP (à droite) inséré dans une colonne de lumière faite de fibre optique brisée et de torons de coton naturel. Les sièges (Mobilia Italia), et les dessertes de service (Laval) ont été spécialement dessinées par Jouin Manku.

A hotel as prestigious as the Dorchester on Park Lane in London combined with the famous French chef Alain Ducasse had to add up to a special occasion, and Ducasse called again here, as he has done in the past, on his favorite designer, Patrick Jouin. Seating 88 people, the restaurant opened in November 2007. In describing his scheme, Patrick Jouin asked: "How can you create luxury not from gold and crystal but from ordinary and sometimes coarse materials that are put together with careful consideration? The new restaurant for Alain Ducasse at the Dorchester Hotel in London is a work based on the notion that luxury is more about how things are put together than about what they are made from. Can an interpretation of an English garden placed inside a four-star hotel become luxurious?" The dining room overlooks Park Lane and Hyde Park, and is marked by a surprising round curtain made of scrim and optical fibers enclosing a VIP dining area for six people. The garden theme is evoked in a green wall designed by Jouin, while dividers made of leather and felt provide privacy for the tables. A total of 30,000 green balls of silk suspended from warm gray lacquered walls again echo the idea of a garden. Chairs in leather and wood, designed by Patrick Jouin and manufactured by Mobilia Italia, are used.

Die Verbindung eines so renommierten Hotels wie des Dorchester an der Park Lane in London und des berühmten französischen Küchenchefs Alain Ducasse musste zu einem besonderen Ereignis werden. Ducasse wandte sich hier, wie auch schon in der Vergangenheit, an den von ihm bevorzugten Architekten Patrick Jouin. Das Restaurant mit Platz für 88 Gäste wurde im November 2007 eröffnet. Bei der Beschreibung seines Entwurfs stellte Patrick Jouin die Frage: „Wie lässt sich Luxus statt mit Gold und Kristall mit gewöhnlichen und manchmal groben Materialien erzeugen, die nach sorgfältigen Überlegungen zusammengestellt werden? Das neue Restaurant für Alain Ducasse im Dorchester Hotel in London basiert auf der Vorstellung, dass Luxus eher davon abhängt, wie die Dinge kombiniert wurden, als von dem Material, aus dem sie bestehen. Kann die Interpretation eines englischen Gartens, der in ein Viersternehotel gesetzt wurde, zum Luxus werden?" Der Speisesaal hat Ausblick zur Park Lane und in den Hyde Park und zeichnet sich durch einen erstaunlichen, runden Vorhang aus Stoff und Glasfaser aus, der einen VIP-Speisebereich für sechs Personen einschließt. Das Gartenthema wird durch eine grüne, von Jouin gestaltete Wand angedeutet. Trennwände aus Leder und Filz sichern den Tischen ihre Privatsphäre. Insgesamt 30 000 grüne Seidenbälle wurden an den grau lackierten Wänden aufgehängt und erzeugen ebenfalls die Atmosphäre eines Gartens. Die Stühle aus Leder und Holz wurden von Patrick Jouin entworfen und von Mobilia Italia produziert.

L'association d'un hôtel aussi prestigieux que le Dorchester à Londres et du célèbre chef français Alain Ducasse devait être un événement, et Ducasse a fait appel une fois encore à son designer favori, Patrick Jouin. Conçu pour quatre-vingt-huit couverts, le restaurant a été inauguré en novembre 2007. Dans la description de son travail, Patrick Jouin se posait cette question : « Comment créer le luxe non avec de l'or et du cristal, mais à partir de matériaux ordinaires et parfois bruts, que l'on rapproche avec une attention particulière ? Le nouveau restaurant Alain Ducasse au Dorchester est une œuvre reposant sur l'idée que le luxe dépend davantage de la façon dont les éléments sont mis en dialogue que des matériaux avec lesquels ils sont faits. L'interprétation d'un jardin anglais à l'intérieur d'un hôtel quatre étoiles peut-elle devenir une image de luxe ? » La salle à manger, qui donne sur Hyde Park et Park Lane, se singularise par un étonnant rideau rond en canevas et fibres optiques qui délimite une salle à manger VIP pour six personnes. Le thème du jardin est évoqué par un grand mur vert conçu par Jouin, tandis que des partitions en cuir et feutre assurent l'intimité entre les tables. Trente mille boules de soie verte suspendues à des murs laqués d'un gris chaud renvoient à l'idée de jardin. Les sièges en bois et en cuir ont été dessinés par Patrick Jouin et fabriqués par Mobilia Italia.

Left, the main dining room with a glimpse on Hyde Park. Right, the Park Lane Room, including custom-designed chairs and lighting elements (Jouin Manku). Below, left, a design detail on the door to the main dining room and, right, a custom-designed cloud-like lighting element with metal leaves, measuring 12 meters in length.

Links: Der große Speisesaal mit Ausblick auf den Hyde Park. Rechts: Der Raum Park Lane mit speziell angefertigten Stühlen und Beleuchtungskörpern (Jouin Manku). Unten, links: Ein Entwurfsdetail an der Tür zum großen Speisesaal und (rechts) ein hierfür entworfenes, wolkenartiges Beleuchtungselement von 12 m Länge mit Metallblättern.

À gauche, la salle principale d'où l'on entrevoit Hyde Park. À droite, le salon Park Lane, dont les sièges et les éléments d'éclairage ont été spécialement conçus par Jouin Manku. Ci-dessous, à gauche, détail de la porte de la salle principale et, à droite, un élément d'éclairage en feuilles de métal mesurant 12 m de long.

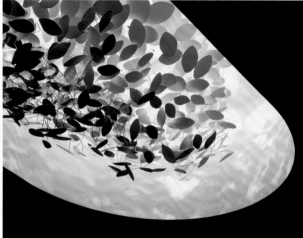

LE JULES VERNE

Eiffel Tower, Paris, France, 2007

Tour Eiffel, Avenue Gustave Eiffel, 75007 Paris, France, +33 1 45 55 61 44, www.lejulesverne-paris.com
Area: 425 m². Client: Millenia (Groupe Alain Ducasse, Sogeres). Cost: not disclosed
Team: Claudia Del Bubba, Ramy Fischler, Richard Perron

SETE, the company that operates the Eiffel Tower, selected L'Affiche (Groupe Sodexho) and Groupe Alain Ducasse to modernize its restaurants in 2006. The Jules Verne was inaugurated on December 22, 2007, after just 120 days of construction work. A fiber optic network on the ceiling that "recalls the streets of Paris," carbon-fiber chairs by Pininfarina, and other touches certainly make it clear that this place is firmly in the 21st century despite the 19th-century structure of the Eiffel Tower. Arriving visitors come out of the elevator, 125 meters above the ground, and look through a window directly into the kitchen. Jouin has played on the idea that the restaurant is a kind of vessel that might have been evoked in the novels of Jules Verne. "You climb aboard the Eiffel Tower as if you were embarking on a journey," says Patrick Jouin, who, like Jules Verne, was born in Nantes. The kitchen, with its staff of 47 people, is surrounded by a luminous glass wall with an aluminum honeycomb structure that is a central feature of the restaurant design. The new graphics of the restaurant were created by Pierre Tachon (Soins Graphiques), and the lighting was designed by Hervé Descottes (L'Observatoire International).

SETE, die Betreiberfirma des Eiffelturms, beauftragte 2006 L'Affiche (Groupe Sodexho) und Groupe Alain Ducasse mit der Modernisierung ihrer Restaurants. Das Jules Verne wurde am 22. Dezember 2007 nach einer Bauzeit von nur 120 Tagen eröffnet. Ein Netz aus Glasfaser an der Decke „erinnert an die Straßen von Paris". Stühle aus Kohlenfaserstoff von Pininfarina und andere Elemente zeigen eindeutig, dass dieser Ort fest im 21. Jahrhundert verankert ist, obgleich die Konstruktion des Eiffelturms aus dem 19. Jahrhundert stammt. Die Gäste fahren mit dem Aufzug 125 m hinauf und schauen durch ein Fenster direkt in die Küche. Jouin hat, angeregt durch die Romane von Jules Verne, mit dem Gedanken gespielt, dass das Restaurant ein Art Schiff sei: „Man steigt auf den Eiffelturm, als würde man sich zu einer Reise einschiffen", sagt Patrick Jouin, der – ebenso wie Jules Verne – in Nantes geboren wurde. Die Küche, in der 47 Personen arbeiten, ist von einer leuchtenden Glaswand sowie einer Wabenkonstruktion aus Aluminium umgeben und stellt ein zentrales Element des Restaurants dar. Das neue grafische Erscheinungsbild des Restaurants stammt von Pierre Tachon (Soins Graphiques), die Beleuchtung von Hervé Descottes (L'Observatoire International).

SETE, la société qui gère la tour Eiffel, a choisi en 2006 L'Affiche (Groupe Sodexho) et le Groupe Alain Ducasse pour moderniser ses restaurants. Le Jules Verne a été inauguré le 22 décembre 2007, après cent vingt jours de chantier seulement. Un réseau de fibres optiques au plafond qui « rappelle les rues de Paris », des fauteuils en fibre de carbone de Pininfarina et d'autres détails montrent clairement que ce lieu est déjà fermement ancré dans le XXIe siècle bien qu'il se trouve dans une construction datant du XIXe. Les hôtes, qui arrivent par l'ascenseur à 125 m au-dessus du sol, ont une vision directe sur les fourneaux. Jouin a joué sur l'idée que le restaurant était une sorte de vaisseau qui pourrait évoquer certains romans de Jules Verne. « Vous grimpez à bord de la tour Eiffel comme si vous embarquiez pour un voyage », dit Jouin, qui, comme Jules Verne, est né à Nantes. La cuisine, et son équipe de quarante-sept personnes, est entourée d'un mur de verre lumineux à structure d'aluminium en nid d'abeille qui est l'un des principaux points d'attraction du projet. La nouvelle identité graphique a été créée par Pierre Tachon (Soins Graphiques), et l'éclairage conçu par Hervé Descottes (L'Observatoire International).

Above right, view of the kitchen from the entrance to the restaurant. Right, view of a table with chairs designed by Patrick Jouin (Pininfarina) and a custom-designed lighting element (Patrick Jouin).

Oben, rechts: Blick auf die Küche vom Restauranteingang aus. Rechts: Tisch und Stühle nach einem Entwurf von Patrick Jouin (Pininfarina) und ein eigens entworfenes Lichtelement (Patrick Jouin).

Ci-dessus à droite, vue de la cuisine depuis l'entrée du restaurant. À droite, une table et des fauteuils dessinés par Patrick Jouin (Pininfarina) et un luminaire de plafond, lui aussi spécifiquement conçu par le designer.

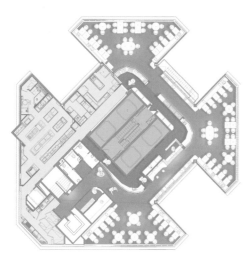

Above, a plan of the restaurant. The
strength of the design relies on the
coherence of objects and décor,
for the most part designed by Jouin
Manku for the Jules Verne restaurant
in the Eiffel Tower.

Oben: Grundriss des Restaurants.
Die Stärke des Entwurfs beruht auf
der Einheitlichkeit des Dekors und
der Objekte, die zum größten Teil
von Jouin Manku für das Restaurant
Jules Verne im Eiffelturm entworfen
wurden.

Ci-dessus, le plan du restaurant.
La force du projet repose sur la
cohérence du décor et des objets,
conçus pour la plupart spécifiquement par Jouin Manku pour le restaurant Jules Verne de la tour Eiffel.

A view of the service bar and lounge
area with a sommelier cabinet on
the right and dining area in the background. The carpet was designed by
Patrick Jouin (Tai Ping).

Blick auf Bar und Lounge mit einem
Schrank für den Sommelier rechts
und einem Essbereich im Hintergrund. Die Teppiche wurden von
Patrick Jouin (Tai Ping) entworfen.

Vue du bar de service et du lounge
avec un cabinet de sommelier à
droite. Au fond, une salle à manger.
La moquette a été dessinée par
Patrick Jouin (Tai Ping).

AUBERGE DE L'ILL

Illhaeusern, France, 2007

2, rue de Collonges au Mont d'Or, 68970 Illhaeusern, France, +33 3 89 71 89 00, www.auberge-de-l-ill.com
Area: 250 m². Client: Haeberlin family. Cost: not disclosed. Team: Laurent Janvier, Marie Deroudhile, Helicia Bonneville

The Auberge de l'Ill, located near the Ill River in Alsace, has existed since 1879, and has had three Michelin stars since 1967. Patrick Jouin attempted to create a design related to the history of the region, its soil, and the "family spirit" of the Haeberlins. He wrapped the front of the restaurant in horizontal wood "blades" in the tradition of local tobacco drying sheds. A corridor entrance leads to the greeting desk in a glazed space. From here, guests pass into a deep red-colored lounge with sofas, armchairs, and ottomans designed by Jouin for Cassina, and photos of the Haeberlin family. Two dining rooms dubbed La Véranda and La Salle à Manger follow, lit by "hand-blown glass reeds that grow on polished stainless-steel pools of water, just as though the river had flowed into the restaurant." The two other rooms, La Salle Alsacienne and Le Pigeonnier, are more rustic in their style, clad in wood planks, and they are separated by a "nut and chestnut branch sliding fence." Sophisticated LED lighting that changes color during the evening complements the actual design work.

Die am Fluss Ill im Elsass gelegene Auberge de l'Ill existiert seit 1879 und führt seit 1967 drei Michelin-Sterne. Patrick Jouin bemühte sich um eine Gestaltung, die auf die Geschichte der Region, das Land und den „Geist der Familie" Haeberlin Bezug nimmt. Er verkleidete die Frontseite des Restaurants mit horizontalen hölzernen „Sparren" in der Tradition der dortigen Schuppen zum Trocknen des Tabaks. Der Eingang durch einen Korridor führt zur Empfangstheke in einem verglasten Raum. Von hier gehen die Gäste weiter in eine dunkelrote Lounge mit Sofas, Sesseln und Ottomanen, die Jouin für die Firma Cassina entwarf, sowie Fotos der Familie Haeberlin. Es folgen zwei Speiseräume mit Namen La Véranda bzw. La Salle à Manger, die von „handgeblasenen, gläsernen Schilfrohren beleuchtet werden, die aus Wasserbecken aus poliertem Edelstahl herauswachsen – als wäre der Fluss in das Restaurant eingedrungen". Die beiden anderen Räume, La Salle Alsacienne und Le Pigeonnier, sind in rustikalerem Stil gehalten, mit Holzbrettern verkleidet und durch einen „verstellbaren Zaun aus Nuss- und Kastanienholz" voneinander getrennt. Ausgeklügelte LED-Beleuchtung, deren Farbe sich im Verlauf des Abends verändert, vervollständigt die neue Ausstattung.

L'Auberge de l'Ill, au bord de l'Ill en Alsace, existe depuis 1879 et arbore trois macarons Michelin depuis 1967. Patrick Jouin a voulu créer un décor en relation avec l'histoire de la région, son terroir et « l'esprit de famille » des propriétaires, les Haeberlin. Il a enveloppé la façade du restaurant de « lames » de bois horizontales dans la tradition des séchoirs à tabac de la région. Un corridor d'entrée conduit à l'accueil installé dans un espace vitré. De là, les hôtes accèdent à un salon rouge sombre dont les canapés, fauteuils et ottomans ont été dessinés par Jouin pour Cassina et qui est décoré de photos de la famille Haeberlin. Deux salles à manger appelées La Véranda et La Salle à Manger suivent, éclairées par des « roseaux de verre soufflé qui jaillissent de bassins d'acier inoxydable poli, comme si la rivière avait envahi le restaurant ». Les deux autres salles, La Salle Alsacienne et Le Pigeonnier sont de style plus rustique ; elles sont lambrissées de planches de bois et séparées par une « barrière coulissante de branches de noyer et de châtaignier ». un éclairage sophistiqué à base de LEDs qui change de couleurs pendant la soirée complète ce décor.

Above, the entrance to the restaurant and the Red Lounge with Haeberlin family portraits. Right, the main dining room with a custom-designed glass screen (MTM Tisca), custom chairs and dessert carts (Laval), and floor lamp (Les Héritiers).

Oben: Der Eingang zum Restaurant und die rote Lounge mit Porträts der Familie Haeberlin. Rechts: Der große Speisesaal mit einer hierfür entworfenen Glaswand (MTM Tisca) und extra angefertigten Stühlen und Dessertwagen (Laval) sowie Stehlampe (Les Héritiers).

Ci-dessus, l'entrée du restaurant et le Salon rouge décoré de portraits de la famille Haeberlin. À droite, la salle à manger principale. L'écran de verre a été spécialement créé pour cette salle (MTM Tisca), ainsi que les sièges, les dessertes (Laval) et les lampadaires (Les Héritiers).

Left page, the Pigeonnier lounge and fireplace. Above, a glass screen custom-designed by Patrick Jouin (Murano Due) encloses the VIP area in the main dining room.

Linke Seite: Die Lounge Pigeonnier mit Kamin. Oben: Eine von Patrick Jouin hierfür entworfene Glaswand (Murano Due) fasst den VIP-Bereich im großen Speisesaal ein.

Page de gauche, le salon du Pigeonnier et sa cheminée. Ci-dessus, un écran de verre dessiné par Patrick Jouin (Murano Due) encercle le salon VIP installé à l'intérieur de la salle à manger principale.

MARCIO KOGAN

Marcio Kogan
Alameda Tietê 505
01417–020 Cerqueira César
São Paulo, SP
Brazil

Tel: +55 11 3081 3522
Fax: +55 11 3063 3424
E-mail: info@marciokogan.com.br
Web: www.marciokogan.com.br

Born in 1952, **MARCIO KOGAN** graduated in 1976 from the School of Architecture at Mackenzie University in São Paulo. He received an IAB (Brazilian Architects Institute) Award for UMA Stores (1999 and 2002); Coser Studio (2002); Gama Issa House (2002), and Quinta House (2004). He also received the Record House Award for Du Plessis House (2004) and BR House (2005). In 2002, he completed a Museum of Microbiology in São Paulo and in 2003 he made a submission for the World Trade Center Site Memorial. He worked with Isay Weinfeld on the Fasano Hotel in São Paulo (2001–03) and also participated with Weinfeld in the 25th São Paulo Biennale (2002) with the project for a hypothetical city named Happyland. Kogan is known for his use of boxlike forms, together with wooden shutters, trellises, and exposed stone. Along with the Neogama BBH Plug Bar (São Paulo, Brazil, 2006, published here), Kogan's current residential projects are the E-Home, a "super-technological" house (Santander, Spain, 2007); an "extreme house" on an island in Paraty (Rio de Janeiro, Brazil, 2007); the Warbler House (Los Angeles, California, 2008); a villa in Milan (Italy, 2008); as well as two other houses, in Brasília (Brazil). His office is also working on a "Green Building" in New Jersey (USA, 2008).

MARCIO KOGAN, geboren 1952, beendete 1976 sein Architekturstudium an der Mackenzie-Universität in São Paulo. Er erhielt Preise des IAB (Instituto do Arquitetos do Brazil) für die UMA-Geschäfte (1999 und 2002), das Studio Coser (2002) sowie die Häuser Gama Issa (2002) und Quinta (2004). Für die Häuser Du Plessis (2004) und BR (2005) wurde ihm außerdem der Record House Award verliehen. Im Jahr 2002 baute er ein Museum für Mikrobiologie in São Paulo, und 2003 reichte er einen Vorschlag für das Mahnmal auf dem Gelände des World Trade Center ein. Mit Isay Weinfeld arbeitete er am Hotel Fasano in São Paulo (2001–03) und nahm auch mit Weinfeld an der 25. Biennale von São Paulo (2002) teil mit einem Entwurf für eine hypothetische Stadt namens Happyland. Kogan ist bekannt für seine kistenförmigen Bauten mit hölzernen Läden, Gittern und unbehandeltem Naturstein. Außer der Neogama BBH Plug Bar (São Paulo, 2006, hier vorgestellt) zählen zu Kogans aktuellen Wohnprojekten das E-Home, ein Supertechnologiehaus (Santander, Spanien, 2007), ein Extremhaus auf einer Insel in Paraty (Rio de Janeiro, 2007), das Haus Warbler (Los Angeles, Kalifornien, 2008), eine Villa in Mailand (2008) sowie zwei weitere Häuser in Brasília. Sein Büro arbeitet auch an einem „grünen Gebäude" in New Jersey (2008).

Né en 1952, **MARCIO KOGAN**, diplômé en 1976 de l'École d'architecture de l'Université Mackenzie à São Paulo, reçoit en 1983 un prix de l'IAB (Instituto do Arquitetos do Brazil) pour les magasins UMA (1999 et 2002) ; le studio Coser (2002) ; la maison Gama Issa (2002) ; et la maison Quinta (2004), tous à São Paulo. Il a également reçu le prix Record House pour la maison Du Plessis (2004) et la maison BR (2005). En 2002, il achève le musée de Microbiologie à São Paulo, et, en 2003, il participe au concours pour le mémorial du World Trade Center. Il a collaboré avec Isay Weinfeld au projet du Fasano Hotel (2001–03) et à l'occasion de la 25e Biennale de São Paulo (2002) où ils ont proposé une cité utopique nommée Happyland. Kogan est connu pour son utilisation de formes en boîtes, de volets en bois, de treillis et de pierres apparentes. Parmi ses projets, en dehors du Neogama BBH Plug Bar (São Paulo, 2006, publié ici), figurent la E-Home, une maison « supertechnologique » (Santander, Espagne, 2007) ; une « maison extrême » sur une île à Paraty (Rio de Janeiro, 2007) ; la maison Warbler (Los Angeles, États-Unis, 2008) ; une villa è Milan (2008) ; et deux autres maisons à Brasília. Son agence travaille également à un projet d'immeuble « vert » dans le New Jersey (2008).

NEOGAMA BBH PLUG BAR

São Paulo, Brazil, 2006

Av. Mofarrej, 1174 Vila Leopoldina, São Paulo, SP CEP 05311 000, Brazil, +55 11 2148 1900, www.neogamabbh.com.br
Area: 120 m². Client: Neogama BBH. Cost: $40 000. Team: Oswalo Pessano, Bruno Gomes, Studio MK27 team

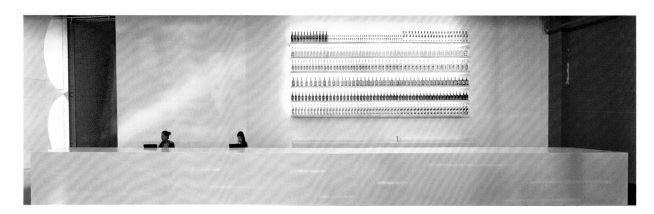

This unusual project involves the creation of a greeting desk for the advertising agency Neogama BBH that can be used as a bar at night or on the occasion of company receptions. Its carefully aligned and back-lit bottles have the look of a work of art in themselves, while LEDs and lighting effects on the long white counter and walls emphasize this impression. This is a very minimalist intervention, yet one that is fundamentally surprising. Marcio Kogan wrote the following text as he designed the installation: "Saturday morning. I take advantage of these moments of stillness at the office to get my things up-to-date. I start drawing the bar-reception area for Neogama BBH. A fruit truck announces, rather stridently, I don't know how many boxes of strawberries for 4 *reais*. 100 decibels louder than the delicate ears of *Homo sapiens* can withstand. I become super-irritated. I think of a plastic monolith having projected texts that form magically on a white surface. I begin tracing some lines of rather elongated proportions. I pause one second to think of the house I did for Claudia and Alexandre. There was a deep empathy from the first moment we met. I return to my butter-paper. I wonder if the Johnny B. Good lamp, by Ingo Maurer, would be good suspended over the counter. I turn on the radio: corruption, kidnappings, prison uprisings, cars, male and female bombs, etc… I turn off the radio as quickly as I can. The truck has already gone. Silence. In the next building a lyric singer is rehearsing a wonderful aria. The climate changes completely. It seems as if I went from the Fourth world to Venice. I look through the window and, in spite of the pretty brunette walking along the sidewalk, I immediately return to the sad reality of this dear city. Again, I analyze the drawings, like them, and decide to present this project, except that the LEDs will announce boxes of strawberries. Silently."

Dieses ungewöhnliche Projekt besteht in der Gestaltung einer Empfangstheke für die Werbeagentur Neogama BBH, die nachts oder zu Firmenveranstaltungen als Bar genutzt werden kann. Die ordentlich aufgereihten und hinterleuchteten Flaschen sehen für sich wie ein Kunstwerk aus, wobei LED-Leuchten und Lichteffekte an der langen, weißen Theke und den Wänden diesen Eindruck verstärken. Es handelt sich um einen sehr minimalistischen, jedoch völlig überraschenden Eingriff. Marcio Kogan schrieb, als er diese Installation gestaltete, folgenden Text: „Samstagmorgen. Ich nutze diese Momente der Stille im Büro, um meine Dinge aufzuarbeiten. Ich beginne mit dem Aufzeichnen des Empfangs-/Barbereichs für Neogama BBH. Ein Obstwagen bietet in durchdringendem Ton ich weiß nicht wie viele Erdbeerkisten zu vier reais an – 100 Dezibel lauter, als die Ohren des Homo sapiens aushalten können. Ich bin sehr genervt. Ich denke an einen Monolithen aus Kunststoff, auf dessen weiße Fläche geheimnisvoll wirkende Texte projiziert werden. Ich fange an, Linien in verlängerten Proportionen zu ziehen. Dann mache ich eine Sekunde Pause, um über das Haus nachzudenken, das ich für Claudia und Alexandre geplant habe. Vom ersten Moment an, als wir uns trafen, empfanden wir eine große Sympathie füreinander. Ich kehre zurück zu meinem Pauspapier. Ich überlege, ob die über der Theke aufgehängte Leuchte Johnny B. Good von Ingo Maurer gut aussehen würde. Ich schalte das Radio ein: Korruptionsfälle, Entführungen, Gefängnisrevolten, rasende Autos, Männer, Frauen etc. … So schnell ich kann, mache ich das Radio wieder aus. Der Obstwagen ist schon weg. Stille. Im Nachbargebäude übt ein Sänger eine wunderbare Arie. Das Klima verändert sich total. Es scheint, als wäre ich aus der Vierten Welt nach Venedig gekommen. Ich schaue durchs Fenster und kehre, anstatt die hübsche Brünette auf dem Bürgersteig zu betrachten, sofort zur traurigen Realität dieser geliebten Stadt zurück. Erneut analysiere ich die Zeichnungen, die mir gefallen, und beschließe, diesen Entwurf einzureichen, nur werden jetzt die LEDs Erdbeerkisten anbieten. Aber leise."

Cet étonnant projet portait sur la création d'une banque d'accueil pour l'agence de publicité Neogama BBH capable de servir de bar de nuit, ou d'être utilisée lors de réceptions données par l'entreprise. Les alignements de bouteilles rétroéclairées prennent une allure d'œuvre d'art, impression renforcée par des LEDs et des effets lumineux tout au long du comptoir blanc et des murs. Il s'agit d'une intervention très minimaliste, mais de celles qui surprennent. Marcio Kogan a rédigé ce texte pendant son travail de conception : « Samedi matin. J'ai profité de ces moments de calme au bureau pour remettre mes pensées au point. J'ai commencé à dessiner la zone de bar-réception pour Neogama BBH. Un camion de livraison de fruits hurle, à pleine puissance, je ne sais combien de cartons de fraises pour quatre réaux. Cent décibels de plus que ce que les délicates oreilles de l'*Homo sapiens* peuvent supporter. Je deviens superirrité. Je pense à un monolithe de plastique qui projetterait magiquement des textes sur une surface blanche. Je commence par quelques lignes dans des proportions assez allongées. Je m'arrête une seconde pour penser à la maison que j'ai faite pour Claudia et Alexandre. Je ressentis une empathie profonde dès le premier moment de notre rencontre. Je retourne à mon calque. Je me demande si la lampe Johnny B. Good, par Ingo Maurer, ferait bien suspendue au-dessus du comptoir. J'allume la radio : corruption, kidnappings, soulèvements en prison, voitures, bombes humaines mâles et femelles, etc. J'éteins la radio aussi vite que possible. Le camion est déjà parti. Silence. Dans l'immeuble voisin, un chanteur lyrique répète un air magnifique. Le climat change complètement. C'est comme si je passais du tiers-monde à Venise. Je regarde par la fenêtre et, en dépit de la mignonne petite brune qui marche sur le trottoir, je reviens immédiatement à la triste réalité de cette chère ville. Une fois encore, j'analyse les dessins, je les aime, et je décide de présenter ce projet, si ce n'est que les LEDs viendront annoncer la vente de cartons de fraises. Silencieusement. »

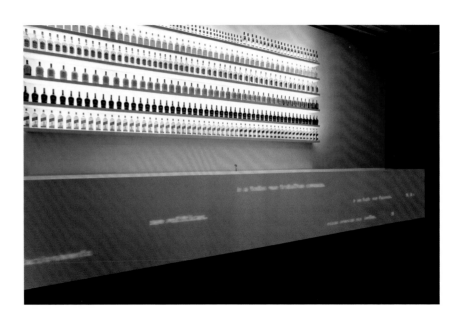

The basic element of the design is a white Corian counter with LEDs and a bottle rack made of wood and laminated plastic with backlighting.

Das Grundelement des Entwurfs ist eine weiße Theke aus Corian mit LED-Modulen und einem hinterleuchteten Flaschenregal aus Holz und laminiertem Kunststoff.

L'élément essentiel du projet est un comptoir en Corian blanc éclairé de LEDs et des rangements pour bouteilles rétro-éclairés en bois et plastique lamifié.

KENGO KUMA

Kengo Kuma & Associates
2–24–8 BY-CUBE 2F Minamiaoyama
Minato-ku
Tokyo 107–0062
Japan

Tel: +81 3 3401 7721 / Fax: +81 3 3401 7778
E-mail: kuma@ba2.so-net.ne.jp / Web: www.kkaa.co.jp

Born in 1954 in Kanagawa, Japan, **KENGO KUMA** graduated in 1979 from the University of Tokyo with a M.Arch degree. In 1985–86, he received an Asian Cultural Council Fellowship Grant and was a Visiting Scholar at Columbia University. In 1987, he established the Spatial Design Studio, and in 1991 he created Kengo Kuma & Associates. His work includes the Gunma Toyota Car Show Room (Maebashi, 1989); Maiton Resort Complex (Phuket, Thailand, 1991); Rustic, Office Building (Tokyo); Doric, Office Building (Tokyo); M2, Headquarters for Mazda New Design Team (Tokyo), all in 1991; Kinjo Golf Club, Club House (Okayama, 1992); Karuizawa Resort Hotel (Karuizawa, 1993); Kiro-san Observatory (Ehime, 1994); the Japanese Pavilion for the Venice Biennale (Venice, Italy, 1995); Atami Guest House, Guest House for Bandai Corp (Atami, 1992–95); Tomioka Lakewood Golf Club House (Tomioka, 1993–96); and the Toyoma Noh-Theater (Miyagi, 1995–96); all in Japan unless stated otherwise. He has also completed the Stone Museum (Nasu, Tochigi, 2000); a Museum of Ando Hiroshige (Batou, Nasu-gun, Tochigi, 2000); the Great (Bamboo) Wall Guest House (Beijing, China, 2002); One Omotesando (Tokyo, 2003); LVMH Osaka (2004); the Nagasaki Prefecture Art Museum (2005); the Fukusaki Hanging Garden (Osaka, 2005); and the Zhongtai Box, Z58 building (Shanghai, China, 2003–06). Recent work includes the Tobata C Block Project (Kitakyushu, Fukuoka, 2005–07); and the Steel House (Bunkyo-ku, Tokyo, 2005–07), both in Japan; as well as Sakenohana (London, UK, 2007) and Jugetsudo (Paris, 2008, both published here).

KENGO KUMA, geboren 1954 im japanischen Kanagawa, machte 1979 an der Universität Tokio seinen M. Arch. Von 1985 bis 1986 erhielt er ein Stipendium des Asian Cultural Council und war als Gaststipendiat an der Columbia University. 1987 gründete er das Spatial Design Studio und 1991 das Büro Kengo Kuma & Associates. Zu seinen Werken zählen der Showroom von Toyota in Gunma (Maebashi, 1989), die Ferienanlage Maiton (Phuket, Thailand, 1991), die Bürogebäude Rustic und Doric sowie M2, die Zentrale für das neue Mazda-Designteam (alle Tokio, 1991), das Klubhaus des Golfklubs Kinjo (Okayama, 1992), ein Ferienhotel in Karuizawa (1993), das Observatorium Kiro-san (Ehime, 1994), der Japanische Pavillon auf der Biennale von Venedig (1995), das Gästehaus der Firma Bandai (Atami, 1992–95), das Klubhaus des Golfklubs Lakewood (Tomioka, 1993–96), und das No-Theater Toyoma (Miyagi, 1995–96). Er hat außerdem ausgeführt: das Steinmuseum (Nasu, Tochigi, 2000), ein Museum für Ando Hiroshige (Batou, Nasu-gun, Tochigi, 2000), das Gästehaus Great (Bamboo) Wall (Peking, 2002), One Omotesando (Tokio, 2003), LVMH Osaka (2004), das Kunstmuseum der Präfektur Nagasaki (2005), den hängenden Garten Fukusaki (Osaka, 2005) und die Zhongtai Box, Gebäude Z58 (Shanghai, 2003–06). Zu den neueren Projekten gehören der Tobata C Block (Kitakyushu, Fukuoka, 2005–07) und das Stahlhaus (Bunkyo-ku, Tokio, 2005–07) sowie das Sakenohana (London, 2007) und das Jugetsudo (Paris, 2008, beide hier veröffentlicht).

Né en 1954 à Kanagawa au Japon, **KENGO KUMA** est diplômé de l'Université de Tokyo (1979). En 1985–86, il bénéficie d'une bourse de l'Asian Cultural Council et devient chercheur invité à l'Université Columbia. En 1987, il crée le Spatial Design Studio, et, en 1991, Kengo Kuma & Associates. Parmi ses réalisations : le Show Room Toyota de Gunma (Maebashi, 1989) ; le Maiton Resort Complex (Phuket, Thaïlande, 1991) ; l'immeuble de bureaux Rustic (Tokyo, 1991) ; l'immeuble de bureaux Doric (Tokyo, 1991) ; M2, siège du département de design de Mazda (Tokyo, 1991) ; le Club House du Kinjo Golf Club (Okayama, 1992) ; le Karuizawa Resort Hotel (Karuizawa, 1993) ; l'Observatoire Kiro-san (Ehime, Japon, 1994) ; le pavillon japonais pour la Biennale de Venise (Italie, 1995) ; l'Atami Guest House pour Bandaï Corp (Atami, 1992–95) ; le Club House du Tomioka Lakewood Golf (Tomioka, 1993–96) ; et le théâtre Nô Toyoma (Miyagi, 1995–96). Il a également réalisé le musée de la Pierre (Nasu, Tochigi, 2000) ; un musée consacré à Ando Hiroshige (Batou, Nasu-gun, Tochigi, 2000) ; la Great (Bamboo) Wall Guest House (Pékin, Chine, 2002) ; l'immeuble One Omotesando (Tokyo, 2003) ; l'immeuble LVMH Osaka (Japon, 2004) ; le Musée d'art de la préfecture de Nagasaki (2005) ; le jardin suspendu de Fukusaki à Osaka (Japon, 2005) ; et la Zhongtai Box, immeuble Z58 (Shanghaï, Chine, 2003–06). Plus récemment se sont ajoutés le projet Tobata C Block (Kitakyushu, Fukuoka, 2005–07) ; la Steel House (Bunkyo-ku, Tokyo, 2005–07), tous deux au Japon ; le Sakenohana (Londres, G. B., 2007) et le salon de thé Jugetsudo (Paris, 2008), tous deux publies ici.

SAKENOHANA

London, UK, 2007

23 St James's Street, London SW1A 1LP, UK, +44 207 925 8988, www.sakenohana.com
Area: 590 m². Client: Hakkasan Ltd. Cost: £2.625 million
Collaboration: Denton Corker Marshall (Co-Architect)

Located in Saint James Street, London, this Japanese restaurant occupies a former banking hall in a rather nondescript modern building. "At the beginning of the project," says Kengo Kuma, "the client requested a design that was not slick." His response was to integrate a traditional Japanese wood framework forming the ceiling and covering the entire space. "It is like a forest inside a building," he comments. The ground-floor dining area and reception space is formed by this bamboo framework. "My intention was to bring trees into the artificial London cityscape," says Kengo Kuma. On the southern side, some shade from the sun was necessary. The architect rejected the use of rice paper as being too "fashionable" and instead, "referring to the traditional Japanese *sudo*, we made an operable double-layer screen with the thinnest bamboo rods, which produce moiré-like wood-grain in daylight."

Dieses in der Saint James Street in London gelegene japanische Restaurant befindet sich in der ehemaligen Schalterhalle einer Bank in einem ziemlich unbedeutenden modernen Gebäude. „Am Anfang dieses Projekts", sagt Kengo Kuma, „wünschte der Bauherr keinen Hochglanzentwurf". Seine Reaktion darauf war eine traditionelle japanische Holzkonstruktion, welche die Decke bildet und den gesamten Raum überdeckt. „Sie ist wie ein Wald in einem Gebäude", erläutert er. Der Speiseraum im Erdgeschoss und der Empfangsbereich werden von diesem Bambusskelett eingefasst. „Mein Ziel war es, diese Bäume in die künstliche Stadtstruktur Londons einzufügen", sagt Kengo Kuma. An der Südseite war ein Sonnenschutz erforderlich. Der Architekt lehnte die Verwendung von Reispapier ab, das er als zu „modisch" betrachtete, und wählte stattdessen „das traditionelle japanische *sudo*. Wir fertigten eine verstellbare, zweischichtige Zwischenwand aus dünnsten Bambusstäben, die bei Tageslicht eine Art gemasertes Moiré bildet."

Situé sur Saint James Street, à Londres, ce restaurant japonais occupe un ancien hall de banque dans un immeuble moderne assez banal. « Au départ », explique Kuma, « le client souhaitait un projet qui ne soit pas lisse et mode. » La réponse de l'agence fut l'intégration d'une ossature japonaise traditionnelle en bois qui forme le plafond et recouvre la totalité du volume. « C'est comme une forêt à l'intérieur d'un immeuble », dit-il. La réception et la salle à manger du rez-de-chaussée sont délimitées par cette ossature en bambou. « Mon intention était d'insérer des arbres dans le paysage urbain londonien », poursuit l'architecte. « Côté sud, il était nécessaire de protéger la salle du soleil. Kuma écarta le papier de riz jugé trop « élégant » et, par référence au *sudo* traditionnel japonais, nous avons fabriqué un écran double épaisseur mobile à l'aide de tiges de bambou extrêmement fines qui produisent un effet presque moiré à la lumière du jour. »

The fan-shaped plan of the restaurant (below). The woodwork of the restaurant recalls traditional Japanese architecture, but creates an open, modern space.

Unten: Der fächerförmige Grundriss des Restaurants. Die Holzelemente erinnern an traditionelle japanische Architektur, bilden aber auch einen offenen, modernen Raum.

Ci-dessous : le plan en éventail du restaurant. La forte présence du bois rappelle l'architecture japonaise traditionnelle mais crée néanmoins un espace ouvert et moderne.

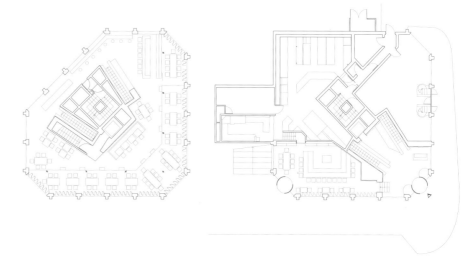

JUGETSUDO

Paris, France, 2008

Jugetsudo by Maruyama Nori, 95 rue de Seine, 75006 Paris, France, +33 1 46 33 94 90, www.jugetsudo.fr
Floor area: 75 m². Client: Maruyama Nori Co. Ltd. Cost: not disclosed. Local architects: MCH

At the counter, the Sen Chairs were designed by Kengo Kuma and manufactured by Knoll. The Hinoki wood counter was designed by Kengo Kuma and manufactured by Nomurakougeish, as were the shelves and suspended bamboo feature.

Die Sen-Stühle an der Theke stammen von Kengo Kuma und wurden von Knoll produziert. Die Theke aus Hinoki-Holz wurde ebenfalls von Kengo Kuma entworfen und von Nomurakougeish hergestellt wie auch die Regale und die hängenden Bambuselemente.

Les chaises Sen (derrière le comptoir) ont été dessinées par Kengo Kuma et fabriquées par Knoll. Le comptoir en bois d'hinoki également dessiné par Kuma, a été fabriqué par Nomurakougeish, de même que les étagères et les éléments décoratifs en bambou suspendus.

This is a tearoom located at the corner of the rue de Seine and the rue des Quatre Vents in Paris. The main space is on the ground level, with an old stone basement below. The Japanese elements in the design, and in particular the hanging bamboo, with stone arrangements along the bottom of the storefront windows, immediately set this space apart from other, more obviously French décors in neighboring boutiques. "I wanted to create a space like a bamboo thicket," says the architect Kengo Kuma. "In the thicket floats a different kind of air and light from those of our daily lives. At the centre of this unique space, we placed a solid, jointless board of Japanese cypress. Cypress was a special tree in that it was believed to smoothen the things put on it. Our idea was that people could feel the nature of Japan on that board. In the underground lies a stone tearoom. In the stone cave that rests in Paris underground the teas might show another quality." The client's motto, blending a sense of tradition with one of "renewal," seems to fit well with this small but very attractive space.

Dies ist eine Teestube an der Ecke der Rue de Seine und der Rue de Quatre Vents in Paris. Der Hauptraum liegt im Erdgeschoss über einem alten Natursteinfundament. Die japanischen Elemente des Entwurfs, besonders der hängende Bambus und das Natursteinarrangement unter den Schaufenstern des Lokals, heben diesen Raum deutlich von anderen, französisch inspirierten Dekors in den benachbarten Läden ab. „Ich wollte einen Raum schaffen, der einem Bambusdickicht gleicht", sagt der Architekt Kengo Kuma. „Darin herrschen eine andere Luft und ein anderes Licht als in unserem Alltag. In den Mittelpunkt dieses einzigartigen Raums setzten wir ein massives, fugenloses Brett aus japanischem Zypressenholz. Die Zypresse war ein besonderer Baum, weil man glaubte, sie würde die Dinge glätten, die man darauf stellte. Unsere Idee war, dass die Menschen die Natur Japans an diesem Brett spüren können. Im Untergeschoss befindet sich ein steinerner Teeraum. In diesem Steingewölbe im Pariser Untergrund kann der Tee eine andere Qualität annehmen." Der Vorstellung des Bauherrn von einer Verbindung aus Tradition und „Erneuerung" scheint dieser kleine, aber sehr attraktive Raum durchaus zu entsprechen.

Ce salon de thé a ouvert à l'angle de la rue de Seine et de celle des Quatre-Vents à Paris. Le volume principal du rez-de-chaussée se prolonge en sous-sol par une cave voûtée en pierre. Les éléments japonais du projet et, en particulier, les bambous suspendus ou la présence de galets dans les vitrines distinguent immédiatement ce lieu de la décoration tellement plus française des boutiques avoisinantes. «Je voulais créer un espace qui évoque un bosquet de bambous», a expliqué Kengo Kuma. «Dans un bosquet flotte toujours un air et une lumière différents de ce que nous vivons au quotidien. Au centre de cet espace très particulier, nous avons placé des planches de cyprès japonais massif, sans joint. Le cyprès jouissait jadis d'un statut spécial, car on croyait qu'il donnait de la douceur à tout ce qui était posé sur lui. Notre idée a été que les visiteurs pourraient ressentir la nature même du Japon en marchant sur ces planches. En sous-sol, se trouve un salon de thé aux murs en pierre apparente. Dans cette cave minérale nichée dans le sous-sol parisien, les thés peuvent faire montre d'autres qualités.» Le propos du client – fusionner le sens de la tradition avec celui du «renouveau» – semble avoir bien été traduit dans cet espace petit, mais très séduisant.

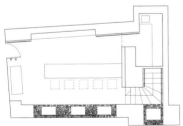

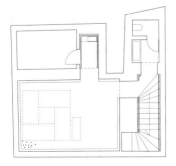

CHRISTIAN LIAIGRE

Bureau d'études Christian Liaigre
122 rue de Grenelle
75007 Paris
France

Tel: + 33 1 45 56 16 42
Fax: + 33 1 45 51 33 99
E-mail: etudes@christian-liaigre.fr
Web: www.christian-liaigre.fr

CHRISTIAN LIAIGRE was born in 1943 in Niort in the west of France, near the Atlantic, and is today one of the most reputed French interior designers. He says his work was influenced by the proximity to the sea and nature. He studied at the École Nationale Supérieure des Arts Decoratifs and at the École Nationale Supérieure des Beaux-Arts (both in Paris). Liaigre raised horses in the Vendée region of France (1969–75), and created collections of objects for design firms such as Nobilis (1978–85), before creating his own firm in 1985 on Rue de Varenne in Paris. Since 1986, he has opened shops under his own name in London, Bangkok, and Saint Barts. He has completed interiors and furniture for private residences for clients such as Rupert Murdoch, Calvin Klein, and Karl Lagerfeld; offices for the Crédit Mutuel de Paris; as well as the Montalembert Hotel in Paris (1986); the Mercer in New York (1997); and the Market Restaurant in Paris (2001). He also designed a yacht for Rupert Murdoch (2006). His firm presently consists of a team of 12 interior designers. Aside from the Buddakan Restaurant in New York (with Gilles & Boissier, New York, 2006), he also participated in the decoration of the Puerta América Hotel (Madrid, Spain, 2005).

CHRISTIAN LIAIGRE wurde 1943 in Niort im Westen Frankreichs am Atlantik geboren und gehört heute zu den bekanntesten französischen Innenarchitekten. Er sagt, dass seine Architektur von der Nähe zum Meer und zur Natur beeinflusst sei. Er studierte an der École Nationale Supérieure des Arts Decoratifs und an der École Nationale Supérieure des Beaux-Arts (beide in Paris). Liaigre züchtete Pferde in der französischen Region Vendée (1969–75) und sammelte Objekte für Designfirmen wie Nobilis (1978–85), bevor er 1985 sein eigenes Büro in der Rue de Varenne in Paris gründete. Seit 1986 hat er unter seinem eigenen Namen Geschäfte in London, Bangkok und Saint Barts eröffnet. Für Auftraggeber wie Rupert Murdoch, Calvin Klein und Karl Lagerfeld hat er Innenräume und Möbel für Einfamilienhäuser gestaltet sowie Büros für Crédit Mutuel de Paris und das Hotel Montalembert in Paris (1986), Mercer in New York (1997) und das Market Restaurant in Paris (2001) geplant. Er hat auch eine Jacht für Rupert Murdoch (2006) ausgestattet. Seine Firma besteht zurzeit aus einem Team von 12 Innenarchitekten. Außer am Restaurant Buddakan in New York (mit Gilles & Boissier, New York, 2006) war er auch an der Ausstattung des Hotels Puerta América (Madrid, 2005) beteiligt.

CHRISTIAN LIAIGRE est né en 1943 à Niort, dans le département des Deux-Sèvres, et est l'un des architectes d'intérieur français les plus connus. Selon lui, son travail a été influencé par la proximité de la mer et de la nature. Après l'École nationale supérieure des arts décoratifs et l'École nationale supérieure des beaux-arts (toutes deux à Paris), Christian Liaigre a élevé des chevaux en Vendée (1969–75), et créé des collections d'objets pour des maisons comme Nobilis (1978–85), avant de créer son agence en 1985, rue de Varenne à Paris. Depuis 1986, il a ouvert des magasins à son nom à Londres, Bangkok et Saint- Barthélemy. Il a réalisé des aménagements intérieurs et des mobiliers destinés à des résidences privées pour des clients comme Rupert Murdoch, Calvin Klein et Karl Lagerfeld ; les bureaux du Crédit mutuel de Paris et l'hôtel Montalembert à Paris (1986) ; l'hôtel Mercer à New York (1997) ; et le restaurant Market à Paris (2001). Il a également conçu un yacht pour Rupert Murdoch (2006). Son agence compte actuellement douze architectes d'intérieur. En dehors du restaurant Buddakan à New York (avec Gilles & Boissier, New York, 2006), il a également participé à la décoration de l'hôtel Puerta América (Madrid, 2005).

LA SOCIÉTÉ

Paris, France, 2008–09

4 Place Saint-Germain-des-Prés, 75006 Paris, France, +33 1 53 63 60 60
Area: not disclosed. Clients: Jean-Louis Costes, Alex Denis, Bruce Dauer and Giovanni Bouard
Cost: not disclosed

This large restaurant is set on the ground floor of the building of the Société d'Encouragement pour l'Industrie Nationale at number 4, Place Saint-Germain-des-Prés just opposite the Saint-Germain church. It also occupies the site of the former Bilboquet jazz club, whose entrance was on the Rue Saint-Benoît. Allying the talents of Jean-Louis Costes, one of the famous Costes brothers whose restaurants mark the French capital, and the designer Christian Liaigre, who sought here to create a space "outside of fashion and trends," this new restaurant is quite sure to become a fixture of the Paris scene, in the spirit of the neighboring Deux Magots café. Described by the designer as having "British and bohème influences," La Société places an emphasis on a dark, solid design, with touches of white marble and other materials that reinforce the timeless impression of the space. Works of art by Fabrice Langlade, Gérard Traquandi, Jacques Martinez, Marc Rebolo, Marine Class, Mathieu Levy, Sara Favriau, and Sophie Lafont are scattered throughout the restaurant.

Dieses große Restaurant befindet sich im Erdgeschoss des Gebäudes der Société d'encouragement pour l'Industrie Nationale an der Place Saint Germain-des-Prés Nr. 4, genau gegenüber der Kirche Saint-Germain. Es nimmt auch das Gelände des früheren Jazzklubs Bilboquet ein, dessen Eingang an der Rue Saint-Benoît lag. In Zusammenarbeit mit dem begabten Jean-Louis Costes, einem der durch ihre Pariser Restaurants berühmt gewordenen Brüder Costes, schuf der Architekt Christian Liaigre hier einen Ort, „jenseits von Mode und Trends". Dieses neue Restaurant wird mit Sicherheit zu einem festen Treffpunkt der Pariser Szene im Geist des benachbarten Cafés Deux Magots werden. Das La Société, dem eine „britische und bohemienhafte" Gestaltung zugeschrieben wird, zeigt eine betont dunkle, solide Ausstattung mit Spuren von weißem Marmor und anderen Materialien, welche die zeitlose Wirkung des Raums verstärken. Kunstwerke von Fabrice Langlade, Gérard Traquandi, Jacques Martinez, Marc Rebolo, Marine Class, Mathieu Levy, Sara Favriau und Sophie Lafont sind im ganzen Restaurant verteilt.

Ce vaste restaurant vient d'ouvrir au rez-de-chaussée de la Société d'encouragement pour l'industrie, 4 place Saint-Germain-des-Prés, juste en face de la célèbre église. Il occupe également l'ancien club de jazz, le Bilboquet, dont l'entrée se trouvait rue Saint-Benoît. Ce nouveau lieu a réuni les talents de Jean-Louis Costes, l'un des célèbres frères Costes dont les restaurants ont depuis longtemps fait date dans la capitale française, et le décorateur Christian Liaigre qui a cherché à créer un espace « hors des modes et des tendances ». Cette nouvelle adresse est à peu près certaine de devenir un des hauts lieux de la scène parisienne, dans l'esprit du café voisin Les Deux Magots. Décrit par Liaigre comme inspiré « d'influences britannique et bohème », La Société fait appel à des tonalités sombres, un style épuré, non sans quelques ponctuations de marbres et d'autres matériaux intéressants qui renforcent une impression d'intemporalité. Des œuvres d'art signées Fabrice Langlade, Gérard Traquandi, Jacques Martinez, Marc Rebolo, Marine Class, Mathieu Levy, Sara Favriau et Sophie Lafont sont disposées çà et là dans le restaurant.

Left, a solid Calacata marble champagne bucket carved by Sophie
Lafont. This angle shows the main
space of the restaurant leading from
the Place Saint-Germain toward the
Rue Saint-Benoît.

Links: Ein massiver Sektkübel, von
Sophie Lafont aus Calacatta-Marmor
gemeißelt. Die Aufnahme aus diesem
Blickwinkel zeigt den großen Saal des
Restaurants, der von der Place Saint-
Germain zur Rue Saint-Benoit reicht.

À gauche, un seau à champagne en
marbre de Calacata massif sculpté
par Sophie Lafont. La prise de vue
montre le volume principal du restaurant entre la place Saint-Germain et
la rue Saint-Benoît.

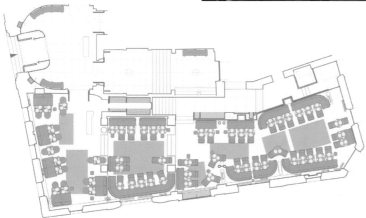

The end of the main room with its
piano for evening concerts. This
space is visible in the floor plan,
on the right, published here.

Das Ende des großen Saals mit
dem Klavier für Abendkonzerte.
Dieser Bereich ist rechts auf dem
hier gezeigten Grundriss erkennbar.

À l'extrémité de la salle principale,
un piano est prévu pour des concerts
en soirée. Ce même espace est
représenté sur la partie droite du
plan au sol ci-contre.

The essentially dark atmosphere of the restaurant is complemented by works of art that are for the most part white. The feeling of the space is convivial, and borders on the electric when evening crowds animate the space.

Die überwiegend dunkle Atmosphäre des Restaurants wird durch größtenteils weiße Kunstwerke ausgeglichen. Die Wirkung des Raums ist heiter und höchst anregend, wenn viele Menschen ihn beleben.

Le traitement du restaurant dans des tonalités essentiellement foncées se complète d'œuvres d'art, pour la plupart de couleur blanche. Il en émane un sentiment de convivialité qui s'intensifie lorsque la clientèle s'y presse le soir.

Above, the white marble champagne bar located near the entrance to the restaurant. Below, the contrast of materials and colors, ranging from black to white, is mastered by Christian Liaigre.

Oben: Die Sektbar in weißem Marmor liegt am Eingang zum Restaurant. Unten: Der Kontrast der Materialien und der Farben, die von Schwarz bis Weiß reichen, ist Christian Liaigre großartig gelungen.

Ci-dessus, le bar à champagne en marbre blanc, à proximité de l'entrée. Ci-dessous, les contrastes de matériaux et de couleurs, qui vont du blanc au noir, ont été superbement maîtrisés par Christian Liaigre.

MAKE ARCHITECTURE

MAKE Architecture
2138 Hyperion Avenue, Studio A
Los Angeles, CA 90027
USA

Tel: +1 323 669 0278
Fax: +1 323 669 0282
E-mail: admin@makearch.com
Web: www.makearch.com

William Beauter attended the State University of New York as an undergraduate and received his M.Arch degree from the Georgia Institute of Technology (1997). He worked on restaurant, hospitality, and office projects with Henry Schwab Architects and the Hauseman Group before joining PFVS Architects in Atlanta, Georgia. In 1999, he took a job as a project architect for Clive Wilkinson Architects in Los Angeles. He created **MAKE ARCHITECTURE** with Jess Mullen-Carey in 2000 "as a collaborative studio engaging a variety of single-family and multi-family residences, retail centers, and communal spaces." Jess Mullen-Carey graduated from Cornell University and worked with Gordon Architects in Buffalo, New York, before signing up with System Design in Los Angeles in 1996. Two years later, he went to work with Clive Wilkinson Architects as a project coordinator, where he met William Beauter. Their projects include the Bodega Wine Bar (Santa Monica, 2006, published here); Peach House (San Gabriel, 2007, published here); Western Retail Center and Car Wash (Torrance, 2008); 39th Street Residence (Manhattan Beach, 2008); Calle Anita Residence (Temecula, 2008); Pacific Amphitheater Backstage Production Buildings (Costa Mesa, 2008); Twentieth-Century Fox Visual Services Library (Los Angeles, 2008); New Regency Entertainment (Los Angeles, 2008); and for 2009, the Idaho Ave Condominiums (Los Angeles), all in California, USA.

William Beauter studierte die ersten Semester an der State University in New York und erhielt seinen M. Arch. am Georgia Institute of Technology (1997). Er arbeitete an Restaurant-, Hotel- und Bürobauten bei Henry Schwab Architects und der Hauseman Group und ging dann zu PFVS Architects in Atlanta, Georgia. 1999 wurde er Projektarchitekt bei Clive Wilkinson Architects in Los Angeles. 2000 gründete er mit Jess Mullen-Carey **MAKE ARCHITECTURE** „als kooperatives Atelier zur Planung von Ein- und Mehrfamilienhäusern, Einkaufszentren und Gemeinschaftseinrichtungen". Jess Mullen-Carey studierte an der Cornell University und arbeitete bei Gordon Architects in Buffalo, New York, bevor er 1996 zu System Design in Los Angeles ging. Zwei Jahre später wechselte er als Projektkoordinator zu Clive Wilkinson Architects, wo er William Beauter kennenlernte. Zu ihren Projekten zählen die Bodega Wine Bar (Santa Monica, 2006, hier veröffentlicht), das Peach House (San Gabriel, 2007, hier vorgestellt), das Western Retail Center and Car Wash (Torrance, 2008), ein Wohnhaus in der 39th Street (Manhattan Beach, 2008), das Wohnhaus Calle Anita (Temecula, 2008), das Kulissen- und Bühnenhaus des Pacific-Amphitheater (Costa Mesa, 2008), die Bibliothek von Twentieth-Century Fox Visual Services (Los Angeles, 2008), New Regency Entertainment (Los Angeles, 2008) und die Idaho Ave Condominiums (Los Angeles, 2009), alle in Kalifornien.

William Beauter a étudié à la State University de New York et a obtenu son diplôme de M.Arch du Georgia Institute of Technology (1997). Il a travaillé sur des projets de restaurants, d'hôtels et de bureaux pour Henry Schwab Architects et le groupe Hauseman, avant de rejoindre PFVS Architects à Atlanta, État de Géorgie. En 1999, il prend un poste d'architecte de projet chez Clive Wilkinson Architects à Los Angeles. Il a fondé **MAKE ARCHITECTURE** avec Jess Mullen-Carey en 2000, une « agence coopérative se consacrant à des projets de résidences familiales, de centres commerciaux et d'espaces communautaires ». Jess Mullen-Carey est diplômé de l'Université Cornell et a travaillé avec Gordon Architects à Buffalo, New York, avant d'entrer chez System Design à Los Angeles, en 1996. Deux ans plus tard, il a été engagé par Clive Wilkinson Architects en qualité de coordinateur de projet, ce qui lui a donné l'occasion de rencontrer William Beauter. Parmi leurs réalisations, toutes en Californie : le Bodega Wine Bar (Santa Monica, 2006, publié ici) ; la maison Peach (San Gabriel, 2007, publiée ici) ; le Western Retail Center et Car Wash (Torrance, 2008) ; la résidence de la 39th Street (Manhattan Beach, 2008) ; la résidence Calle Anita (Temecula, 2008) ; les immeubles de la Pacific Amphitheater Backstage Production (Costa Mesa, 2008) ; la bibliothèque des services visuels de la Twentieth Century Fox (Los Angeles, 2008) ; le New Regency Entertainment (Los Angeles, 2008) ; et, en 2009, un immeuble d'appartements en copropriété sur Idaho Ave (Los Angeles).

BODEGA WINE BAR

Santa Monica, California, USA, 2006

814 Broadway, Santa Monica, CA 90401, USA, +1 310 394 3504, www.bodegawinebar.com
Area: 251 m². Clients: Greg Seares and Jason McEntee. Cost: $150 000

The Bodega Wine Bar, consisting of seating for its clientele, bar service, and a kitchen, "offered an opportunity to create an interaction between the existing bow truss and brick building and the bustling street while carefully maintaining an intimate feel within the space," according to the architects. MAKE added a form in teak serving as the entry that projects beyond the building and extends to the interior raised lounge. They also used MDF (medium-density fiberboard) on exterior surfaces, and again extended it into the interior, where it is treated "with a range of finishes from matte to gloss and acts as a device to subtly define more intimate-feeling areas while maintaining visual connection throughout the space." A red-tinted glass along the street side gives a warm glow to the space and some privacy for diners.

Die Bodega Wine Bar besteht aus einem Gastraum, einer Bar und einer Küche und „bot die Gelegenheit, eine Wechselwirkung zwischen dem vorhandenen Backsteingebäude sowie der belebten Straße zu erzeugen, dabei aber im Raum eine intime Atmosphäre zu wahren", wie die Architekten es ausdrücken. MAKE fügte ein Element aus Teak hinzu, das als Eingang dient; es kragt aus dem Gebäude aus und erweitert sich innen zu einer erhöht liegenden Lounge. Für die Außenflächen verwendeten die Architekten MDF-Platten, ebenso im Innern, wo sie „unterschiedlich behandelt wurden, von matt bis glänzend, und auch dazu dienen, intimere Bereiche abzutrennen, aber dennoch Sichtverbindungen innerhalb des Raums zu wahren". Rot getöntes Glas an der Straßenseite verleiht dem Raum ein warmes Licht und den Gästen etwas Intimsphäre.

The Bodega Wine Bar, qui comprend un bar, une cuisine et une salle de restaurant « offrait l'opportunité d'une interaction entre l'immeuble en brique et charpente cintrée et la rue très animée, tout en préservant, à l'intérieur, un sentiment d'intimité», expliquent les architectes. MAKE a créé un élément en teck qui fait office d'entrée, se projette à l'extérieur et se prolonge à l'intérieur vers le salon en surélévation. L'agence a habillé l'extérieur de panneaux de médium que l'on retrouve également à l'intérieur, traités « dans une gamme de finitions allant du mat au brillant, ce qui permet de définir subtilement des zones d'atmosphère plus intime, tout en maintenant une connexion visuelle à travers l'espace tout entier ». Une vitrine en verre teinté rouge, donnant sur la rue, produit à l'intérieur une lumière chaleureuse, et renforce l'impression d'intimité ressentie par les clients.

Below, a floor plan and a view from the street, where laminated glass penetrates the façade (Colorpro). The red colors seen from the exterior dominate the interior décor.

Unten: Grundriss und Ansicht von der Straße, wo das Verbundglas die Fassade öffnet (Colorpro). Die von außen sichtbaren Rottöne beherrschen die Innenausstattung.

Ci-dessous, le plan au sol et une vue prise de la rue. Des panneaux de verre laminé rouge (Colorpro) ont été plaqués contre la façade. Le rouge domine également le décor intérieur.

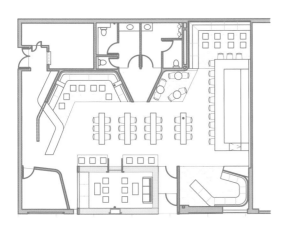

PEACH HOUSE
San Gabriel, California, USA, 2007

531 W Valley Blvd, San Gabriel, CA 91776, USA, +1 626 576 2400
Area: 42 m². Clients: Charlene Chin and Kai Liang. Cost: $75 000

The Peach House frozen yogurt shop is located in a simple, rectangular space in a commercial center at the corner of Valley Boulevard and New Avenue in San Gabriel. High gloss, repetitive rings made of MDF (medium-density fiberboard) define the walls and ceilings. The rings "peel away from the wall" to provide flat usable table surfaces. The reds and yellows employed in the small shop for the counter or entrance wall surface also run along the inner surfaces of the ribs, giving the whole a cheerful aspect. MAKE was also involved in the logo that refers directly to the architectural forms, and in the menu design for the Peach House. These two elements serve to underline the overall unity and identity of the small shop, which in its spatial configuration can be likened either to a take-out facility or to a bar.

Peach House, ein Laden, in dem gefrorener Joghurt verkauft wird, ist ein schlichter, rechteckiger Raum in einem Geschäftszentrum an der Ecke Valley Boulevard und New Avenue in San Gabriel. Viele glänzende Streifen aus MDF-Platten (mitteldichten Holzfaserplatten) überziehen Wände und Decken. Sie „lösen sich von der Wand" und bilden nutzbare Tischflächen. In diesem kleinen Laden verleihen die roten und gelben Farben der Theke und der Eingangswand dem ganzen Raum eine fröhliche Atmosphäre. MAKE war auch an der Gestaltung des Logos beteiligt, das sich unmittelbar auf die Architekturformen bezieht, sowie der Speisekarte von Peach House. Diese beiden Elemente dienen zur Betonung der Einheitlichkeit und Identität des kleinen Ladens, der in seiner räumlichen Gestaltung sowohl einem Verkaufsgeschäft als auch einer Bar ähnelt.

La boutique de «frozen yogurt», Peach House, occupe un simple espace rectangulaire dans un centre commercial situé à l'angle du Valley Boulevard et de New Avenue à San Gabriel. Les murs et les plafonds sont faits de plans vernis brillants et d'un dispositif répétitif d'anneaux en médium qui «se détachent du mur» pour créer le plan des tables. Les couleurs rouge et jaune du comptoir ou du mur de l'entrée se retrouvent sur la face intérieure des nervures, ce qui donne à l'ensemble un aspect chaleureux. MAKE a également réalisé un logo qui rappelle directement les formes architecturales et le style graphique du menu. Ces deux éléments soulignent l'unité d'ensemble et l'identité de cette petite boutique qui peut se comparer par sa configuration spatiale à un bar ou à une boutique de nourriture à emporter.

Panton Chairs by Verner Panton (Vitra) in yellow were chosen for Peach House. The laminated glass beneath the counter (next double page) is by Colorpro.

Panton-Stühle von Verner Panton (Vitra) in Gelb wurden für das Peach House gewählt. Das Verbundglas unter der Theke (folgende Doppelseite) stammt von Colorpro.

Les chaises Panton jaunes sont de Verner Panton (Vitra), le panneau de verre laminé derrière le comptoir (double page suivante) vient de Colorpro.

peach house

e and desserts

non fat frozen yogurt

		naked	dressed
house smoothie $3.95	original		
our house blend made to	small	$2.95	$4.75
	medium	$3.25	$6.95
razilian lemonade $1.85	big	$5.45	$——.85
imply sweet and creamy		additional toppings $.85	
de with real limes			
	peach or green tea	naked	dressed
d ice $5.48	small	$3.45	$5.25
2 toppings on a cloud of	medium	$3.75	$7.45
ed ice with sweetened	big	$5.95	
a swirl of original frozen		additional toppings $.85	

MAURICE MENTJENS

Maurice Mentjens Design
Martinusstraat 20
6123 BS Holtum
The Netherlands

Tel: +31 46 481 14 05
Fax: +31 46 481 14 06
E-mail: info@mauricementjens.com
Web: www.mauricementjens.com

MAURICE MENTJENS was born in Sittard in the province of Limburg, in the Netherlands, in 1964. He graduated from the Department of Jewelry and Product Design at the Academy of Visual Arts in Maastricht (1983–88), attended the Design Academy in Eindhoven (1988) and the Department of Interior and Product Design at the Academy of Visual Arts in Maastricht (1988–90). His most significant projects include: Ipanema (Bonnefantenmuseum, Maastricht, 2004, published here); Stash (Maastricht, 2004); Witloof (Maastricht, 2005, published here); Kiki 2 (Maastricht, 2005); Thaiphoon I and II parking garage and restaurant extension (Roermond, 2004 and 2006, published here); NWE Vorst (Tilburg, 2007); DSM Headquarters, meeting and reception room (Heerlen, 2007); Labels Store (Sittard, 2008); and Kymyka Shoe Store (Maastricht, 2009), all in the Netherlands.

MAURICE MENTJENS wurde 1964 in Sittard in der Provinz Limburg in den Niederlanden geboren. Er absolvierte sein Studium in der Abteilung für Schmuck- und Produktdesign der Akademie Beeldende Kunsten in Maastricht (1983–88), studierte an der Designakademie in Eindhoven (1988) und in der Abteilung für Innenarchitektur und Produktdesign der Akademie Beeldende Kunsten in Maastricht (1988–90). Zu seinen wichtigsten Projekten zählen die Lokale Ipanema (Bonnefanten-museum, Maastricht, 2004, hier veröffentlicht), Stash (Maastricht, 2004), Witloof (Maastricht, 2005, hier veröffentlicht), Kiki 2 (Maastricht, 2005), Thaiphoon I und II, Parkhaus und Restauranterweiterung (Roermond, 2004 und 2006, hier vorgestellt), NWE Vorst (Tilburg, 2007), der Sitzungs- und Empfangsraum der DSM-Hauptverwal-tung (Heerlen, 2007), der Labels Store (Sittard, 2008) und das Schuhgeschäft Kymyka (Maastricht, 2009), alle in den Niederlanden.

MAURICE MENTJENS, né à Sittard dans la province du Limburg aux Pays-Bas en 1964, est diplômé du Département de joaillerie et de design produits de l'Aca-démie des arts visuels de Maastricht (1983–88). Il a aussi étudié à l'Académie du design d'Eindhoven (1988) et au Département de Design intérieur et de produits à l'Académie des arts visuels de Maastricht (1988–90). Parmi ses projets les plus significatifs : l'Ipanema (Bonnefantenmuseum, Maastricht, 2004, publié ici) ; le Stash (Maastricht, 2004) ; le Witloof (Maastricht, 2005, publié ici) ; Kiki 2 (Maastricht, 2005) ; Thaiphoon I et II, parking et extension de restaurant (Roermond, 2004 et 2006, publié ici) ; NWE Vorst (Tilburg, 2007) ; le siège de DSM, salle de réunions et de réceptions (Heerlen, 2007) ; le magasin Labels (Sittard, 2008) ; et le magasin de chaus-sures Kymyka (Maastricht, 2009), tous aux Pays-Bas.

WITLOOF

Maastricht, The Netherlands, 2005

Sint Bernardusstraat 12, 6211 Maastricht, The Netherlands, +31 43 323 35 38, www.witloof.nl
Area: 108 m². Client: Witloof / Ad Fiddelers. Cost: €55 000

Located in the historic center of Maastricht, this restaurant is dedicated to Belgian cuisine. Maurice Mentjens explains: "My vision of the concept and design of Witloof was prompted by a visit to the cities of Antwerp and Ghent. The striking thing about Belgian cafés and restaurants is the often incongruous mix of styles and interior elements. You get the impression that everything has been built up bit by bit over the years, and that all sorts of bric-a-brac has been added. I did not want to translate this too literally to the new interior of Witloof. I came up with my own interpretation, in fact combining three interiors that typify Belgian restaurants." The restaurant is laid out with an entrance area designed like a "log cabin in the Ardennes," a white tile room "conjuring up memories of typical old chip shops," and a rear Salon with Baroque-style green wallpaper. Mentjens separates the first two spaces with a red neon light symbolizing the division between the Flemish and French-speaking areas of Belgium. A spiral staircase leads down to a black-painted cellar dating from the late Middle Ages.

Dieses im historischen Zentrum von Maastricht gelegene Restaurant widmet sich der belgischen Küche. Maurice Mentjens erläutert: „Meine Vorstellungen vom Konzept und der Ausstattung des Witloof gehen auf einen Besuch der Städte Antwerpen und Gent zurück. Das Besondere an belgischen Cafés und Restaurants ist die häufig widersprüchliche Mischung von Stilen und Elementen der Innenausstattung. Man hat den Eindruck, als sei alles Stück für Stück über die Jahre entstanden und aller nur mögliche Trödel hinzugefügt worden. Ich wollte dies nicht unmittelbar auf die neue Ausstattung des Witloof übertragen. So entschied ich mich für meine eigene Interpretation, eine Kombination dreier Innenräume, die für belgische Restaurants typisch sind." Das Restaurant hat einen Eingangsbereich, der wie ein „Blockhaus in den Ardennen" gestaltet ist, einen weiß gefliesten Raum, der „die Erinnerung an typische alte Pommesbuden heraufbeschwört", und einen rückwärtigen Salon mit grünen Barocktapeten. Mentjens teilt die beiden ersten Bereiche durch eine rote Neonbeleuchtung als Symbol für die Trennung in die flämisch und französisch sprechenden Regionen in Belgien. Eine Wendeltreppe führt hinunter zum schwarz gestrichenen Keller aus dem späten Mittelalter.

Situé au centre historique de Maastricht, ce restaurant s'est spécialisé dans la cuisine belge. « Ma vision du concept et du design du Witloof vient d'une visite des villes d'Anvers et de Gand. Ce qui frappe dans les cafés et restaurants belges est souvent un mélange incongru de styles et d'éléments de décoration intérieure. On a l'impression que tout s'est construit petit à petit, morceau par morceau, et que l'on y a ajouté tout un bric-à-brac. Je ne voulais pas traduire trop littéralement cette constatation dans les nouveaux aménagements du Witloof. J'en suis venu à ma propre interprétation combinant en fait trois types de décor typiques des restaurants belges », explique Maurice Mentjens. Le plan du restaurant présente une zone d'entrée conçue comme « un chalet dans les Ardennes », une pièce carrelée de blanc « rappelant des souvenirs de boutiques de frites typiques », et, dans le fond, un salon aux murs recouverts d'un papier peint vert de style baroque. Mentjens a séparé les deux premiers espaces par un tube au néon rouge qui symbolise la division entre les provinces francophones et néerlandophones belges. Un escalier en spirale conduit à une cave datant de la fin du Moyen Âge, peinte en noir.

The designer has created an unusual combination of what he perceives to be Belgian tradition, objects and wall coverings that are certainly old in their inspiration, and clean, modern furniture.

Der Architekt hat sich für eine ungewöhnliche Kombination entschieden: Objekte und Wandbekleidungen, die er für traditionell belgisch hält, und klares, modernes Mobiliar.

Le designer s'est livré à une combinaison inhabituelle d'éléments qu'il voit appartenir à la tradition belge, d'objets, de papiers peints d'inspiration ancienne et de meubles modernes aux lignes nettes.

IPANEMA, GRAND CAFÉ

Bonnefantenmuseum, Maastricht, The Netherlands, 2004

Avenue Ceramique 250, Ingang Maaspuntweg, 6201BS Maastricht, The Netherlands, +31 43 329 01 57, www.ipanema.nl
Area: 387 m². Clients: Jan-Willem Hermans and Sanne Ruers. Cost: € 100 000

Perspex plates applied to the windows of the Aldo Rossi building lend a cheerful atmosphere to the spaces, which are furnished in a modern, rather sparse way.

An den Fenstern angebrachte Acrylglasplatten erzeugen eine heitere Atmosphäre in den modern und eher sparsam möblierten Räumen. Das Gebäude wurde von Aldo Rossi geplant.

Des plaques de Perspex appliquées sur les fenêtres de l'immeuble dû à Aldo Rossi créent une atmosphère vivante dans cet espace meublé dans un style moderne, assez retenu.

A wooden floor and essentially open spaces give an air of simplicity to the design. Straight lines dominate the décor.

Holzboden und überwiegend offene Räume bilden ein schlichtes Ambiente. Gerade Linien bestimmen das Dekor.

Le sol en bois et des espaces très ouverts confèrent au projet une impression de grande simplicité. La ligne droite domine.

In a building designed by Aldo Rossi, with the furniture and the bar in the Grand Café by the same architect, Maurice Mentjens was asked to give the two large spaces a new feel with a small budget. With only indirect natural lighting available, Mentjens used Perspex (colored plastic) plates, and placed incandescent bulbs behind them for evening use. As he explains: "The idea for these Perspex plates came from the Richard Serra piece situated outside in front of the windows (large, rectangular steel plates set in a row like freestanding walls)." Rather than placing the bar in the middle of the space as Rossi had, the designer added a new white bar, dividing the area into two unequal parts. The wall, bench, and floor here are all made of the same wood. "The wall behind the bench opposite the bar is covered by Muurbloem ('Wall-flower')," explains Mentjens, "a hip Pippi Longstocking-style patchwork of modern and retro patterns." A stage contiguous with the floor extends into the audience area. The tower area of the museum is used for receptions, parties, and concerts. The wall is decorated with "swathes of heraldic colors" by the artist Fons Haagmans. A five-meter-high lamp illuminates this work and animates the tower space.

Maurice Mentjens erhielt den Auftrag, in einem von Aldo Rossi geplanten Gebäude, in dem auch die Bar im Grand Café mit von Rossi entworfenen Möbeln ausgestattet ist, zwei große Räume mit geringem Etat neu zu gestalten. Weil nur indirekte natürliche Belichtung möglich war, verwendete Mentjens Tafeln aus farbigem Acrylglas und brachte dahinter Glühlampen zur abendlichen Beleuchtung an. Er erläutert: „Die Idee für diese Acrylglastafeln stammt von Richard Serras Kunstwerk, das draußen vor den Fenstern steht (große, rechteckige Stahlplatten, die wie freistehende Mauern in einer Reihe aufgestellt sind)." Anstatt die Bar in die Mitte des Raums zu stellen, wie Rossi es getan hatte, fügte Mentjens eine neue, weiße Bar ein, die den Raum in zwei ungleiche Abschnitte teilt. Wand, Bank und Fußboden sind hier alle aus dem gleichen Holz. Die Wand hinter der Bank gegenüber von der Bar ist mit ‚Muurbloem' bedeckt,", erklärt Mentjens, „einem aktuellen Mix aus modernen und alten Mustern im Stil von Pippi Langstrumpf." Eine angrenzende Bühne erstreckt sich bis in den Zuschauerbereich. Der Raum im Turm des Museums dient für Empfänge, Partys und Konzerte. Die Wände wurden vom Künstler Fons Haagmans mit „breiten Streifen in heraldischen Farben" dekoriert. Eine 5 m hohe Lampe beleuchtet dieses Kunstwerk und belebt den Turmbereich.

Dans un immeuble conçu par Aldo Rossi, dont le bar et le mobilier du Grand Café sont réalisés par le même architecte, Maurice Mentjens a été chargé de redonner à deux grands volumes un esprit nouveau, pour un petit budget. Disposant seulement d'un éclairage naturel indirect, il a utilisé des panneaux de Perspex (plastique translucide de couleur) devant des lampes à incandescence pour éclairer les salles en soirée. « L'idée de ces panneaux de Perspex, explique l'architecte, est venue d'une œuvre de Richard Serra placée à l'extérieur, devant les fenêtres, composée de grandes plaques d'acier rectangulaires disposées en rang comme une succession de murs autoporteurs. » Plutôt que d'implanter le bar au centre de l'espace, comme l'avait fait Rossi, il a créé un nouveau comptoir blanc qui divise la salle en deux parties inégales. Le mur, les banquettes et le sol sont réalisés dans le même bois. « Le mur derrière la banquette, face au bar, est recouvert de *Muurbloem* (fleurs murales), un patchwork « hip », style Fifi Brindacier, constitué de motifs modernes et rétro. » Une scène dans le prolongement du sol s'avance dans la salle. La tour du musée est aménagée pour les réceptions et les concerts. Les murs y sont décorés de « bandeaux aux couleurs héraldiques » de l'artiste Fons Haagmans. Un luminaire de 5 m de haut éclaire cette intervention et anime le volume.

A five-meter-high lamp dominates the space where the artist Fons Haagmans has applied "heraldic colors" to the walls. Below, a plan shows this rounded space near the main dining room.

Eine 5 m hohe Leuchte beherrscht den Raum, in dem der Künstler Fons Haagmans „heraldische Farben" an den Wänden angebracht hat. Unten: Der Grundriss zeigt diesen runden Raum neben dem großen Speisesaal.

Un luminaire de 5 m de haut domine de sa présence cette salle aux murs peints par l'artiste Fons Haagmans à l'aide de « couleurs héraldiques ». Le plan ci-dessous décrit ce même espace circulaire proche de la salle à manger principale.

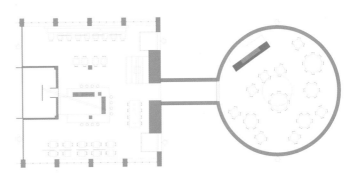

THAIPHOON I AND II

Roermond, The Netherlands, 2004–06

Zwartbroekstraat 31, 6041JL, Roermond, Limburg, The Netherlands, +31 47 533 31 35
Area: Thaiphoon I: 290 m²; Thaiphoon II: 52 m² (lounge); 486 m² (garage), Client: Peter Hendriks (Thaiphoon BV)
Cost: not disclosed

Maurice Mentjens decided to capture what he saw as the unique mixture of modern and traditional elements that is typical of Asia for this originally Thai restaurant. A wall with luminous colored beams that slowly change color "like the illuminated advertising displays in Tokyo and Bangkok" greets visitors at the bar, while the wall opposite is covered in snakeskin and flashing lights. The long wooden bar continues into a conservatory with a view into the white kitchen. The main dining room has red wood tables and more snakeskin on the walls. The conservatory at the back of this dining room has a glass roof and a wall with statues of Buddha. In 2006, the chef Mischa Trommelen decided to switch the focus of the restaurant to French food. Mentjens added a lounge and parking garage on that occasion. The surprising red garage is decorated with reproductions of 17th-century Dutch still-life paintings. A large-scale gold-lit fork marks the entrance to the restaurant, through a yellow glass mosaic tunnel. This tunnel leads to the new lounge, with one wall covered in green glass mosaics.

Für dieses ursprünglich als Thai-Restaurant geplante Lokal beschloss Maurice Mentjens, die seiner Meinung nach für Asien typische, einzigartige Mischung aus modernen und traditionellen Elementen einzufangen. Eine Wand mit bunt erleuchteten Balken, deren Farbe sich langsam verändert „wie die Leuchtreklamen in Tokio und Bangkok", empfängt die Besucher der Bar, während die gegenüberliegende Wand mit Schlangenhaut und blinkenden Leuchten überzogen ist. Die lange, hölzerne Theke führt bis in einen Wintergarten und gewährt Einblick in die in Weiß gehaltene Küche. Der große Speiseraum ist mit roten Holztischen und ebenfalls Schlangenhaut an den Wänden ausgestattet. Der Wintergarten hinter diesem Speiseraum hat ein Glasdach und eine Wand mit Buddhastatuen. 2006 beschloss der Chef Mischa Trommelen, das Restaurant auf französische Küche umzustellen. Mentjens ergänzte es bei der Gelegenheit um eine Lounge und ein Parkhaus. Dieses in auffälligem Rot gehaltene Gebäude ist mit Reproduktionen von holländischen Stillleben aus dem 17. Jahrhundert dekoriert. Eine riesige, golden beleuchtete Gabel bezeichnet den Eingang zum Restaurant, der durch einen Tunnel mit gelben Glasmosaiken führt und von dort aus weiter in die neue Lounge mit einer Wand aus grünen Glasmosaiken.

Maurice Mentjens a voulu capter ce mélange d'éléments modernes et traditionnels si caractéristique du pays d'Asie pour ce restaurant consacré à l'origine à la cuisine thaï. En entrant dans le bar, le client est accueilli par une ambiance lumineuse produite par des faisceaux lumineux muraux qui changent lentement de couleur, effet qui rappelle « les enseignes lumineuses de Tokyo et de Bangkok ». Le mur opposé, tendu de peau de serpent, est ponctué de lampes étincelantes. Le long bar en bois se prolonge jusque dans une sorte de serre d'où l'on a une vision sur la cuisine. La salle à manger principale, également tendue de serpent est équipée de tables en bois rouge. La serre au fond de cette salle possède un plafond de verre et un mur décoré de statues de Boudha. En 2006, le chef Mischa Trommelen a décidé de passer à la cuisine française. À cette occasion, Mentjens a ajouté un salon et un garage pour voitures curieusement décoré de reproductions de natures mortes hollandaises du XVIIe siècle. Une fourchette dorée surdimensionnée indique l'entrée du restaurant qui se fait par un tunnel en mosaïque de verre jaune, débouchant sur le nouveau salon dont un mur est traité en mosaïque de verre vert.

Gimlet Bar Stools (Moebles 133) are placed near the 12-meter-long oak bar. Custom-designed oak folding tables are fixed to the wall in the bar area. Seating at the rear is in black Tom Vac Chairs (Vitra).

Gimlet-Barhocker (Moebles 133) stehen an der speziell angefertigten, 12 m langen Bartheke aus Eiche; an der Wand dieses Raums sind eigens entworfene Klapptische aus Eiche angebracht. Die Sitzgruppe im Hintergrund besteht aus schwarzen Tom-Vac-Stühlen (Vitra).

Les tabourets de bar Gimlet (Moebles 133) sont alignés devant le bar en chêne de 12 m de long. Dans la même pièce, des tables pliantes spécialement conçues pour le lieu sont fixées au mur. Les sièges du fond sont les Tom Vac de Vitra.

The simplicity and continuity of the decor, with the repetitive use of the same chairs and stools, coupled with the oak tables, gives a feeling of solidity and modernity to the space.

Schlichtheit und Einheitlichkeit des Dekors sowie die Ausstattung mit gleichen Stühlen und Barhockern und den Eichentischen geben dem Raum ein solides und modernes Erscheinungsbild.

La simplicité et la continuité du décor, renforcées par le recours répétitif aux mêmes fauteuils et tabourets couplés à des tables en chêne, confèrent à cet espace un sentiment de solidité et de modernité.

Red Icon pendant lights (Kartell) and custom-designed red-stained oak tables are used in the restaurant area. Paintings from the Bonnefantenmuseum, Noortman Masterpaintings, and the Rijksmuseum were reproduced by Spectrum XL Printing (Voerendaal).

Rote Icon-Hängeleuchten (Kartell) und extra angefertigte, rot gebeizte Eichentische wurden im Restaurantbereich verwendet. Die Gemälde aus dem Bonnefantenmuseum, von Noortman Masterpaintings und aus dem Rijksmuseum wurden von Spectrum XL Printing (Voerendaal) reproduziert.

Les suspensions Red Icon (Kartell) et des tables en chêne teint en rouge spécialement conçues sont utilisées pour la salle du restaurant. Des peintures du Bonnefantenmuseum, de la galerie Noortman Masterpaintings et du Rijksmuseum ont été reproduites par Spectrum XL Printing (Voerendaal).

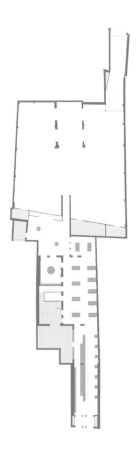

METRO ARQUITETURA

Metro Arquitetura
Av. João de Barros, 1527 Sl. 701
Espinheiro, Recife, PE, 52021–180
Brazil

Tel: +55 81 3426 5655
E-mail: metro@metro.arq.br
Web: www.metro.arq.br

João Domingos Azevedo was born in Recife, Brazil, in 1977 and graduated as an architect from the Universidade Federal de Pernambuco, the UFPE (2001). After graduation, he collaborated as a partner with Juliano Dubeux Arquitetos Associados for three years. In 2004 he founded his own office, **METRO ARQUITETURA**, which has worked on a number of projects in collaboration with other offices, such as Juliano Dubeux Arquitetos, Borsoi Arquitetura, and Pontual Arquitetos. Rafael Souto Maior was born in Recife in 1982 and Livia Brandão was born in Manaus in 1982; both graduated in Architecture from the UFPE in 2006 and joined Metro Arquitetura that year as partners. Juliano Dubeux, born in Recife in 1969, graduated from the UFPE in 1992. Dubeux was the founder and partner of two previous offices, DP&G and Astria Arquitetura, before creating his own office Juliano Dubeux Arquitetos Associados in 2000. In 2006, João Domingos Azevedo and Metro Arquitetura invited Juliano Dubeux to collaborate on the project for Club NOX (Recife, published here). Other work by Metro includes America (apartment building, Recife, under construction, with Juliano Dubeux and Borsoi Arquitetura); QG Building (Recife, under construction, with Juliano Dubeux and Borsoi Arquitetura); Veronese (apartment building, Recife, under construction, with Juliano Dubeux and Borsoi Arquitetura); Toquinho Village, Beach Bungalows (Toquinho Beach, 2007–); AACD Hospital Expansion (Recife, under construction, with Juliano Dubeux and Borsoi Arquitetura); NOSi Building + Data Center (Praia-Cabo Verde, 2007–); and the Pontes Office Building (Recife, 2009–), all in Brazil.

João Domingos Azevedo wurde 1977 in Recife, Brasilien, geboren und beendete 2001 sein Architekturstudium an der Universidade Federal de Pernambuco UFPE. Danach arbeitete er drei Jahre als Partner bei Juliano Dubeux Arquitetos Associados. 2004 gründete er sein eigenes Büro, **METRO ARQUITETURA**, das bei verschiedenen Projekten mit anderen Teams zusammengearbeitet hat, z. B. mit Juliano Dubeux Arquitetos, Borsoi Arquitetura und Pontual Arquitetos. Rafael Souto Maior wurde 1982 in Recife geboren, Livia Brandão 1982 in Manaus; beide beendeten 2006 ihr Architekturstudium an der UFPE und traten im gleichen Jahr als Partner bei Metro Arquitetura ein. Juliano Dubeux, 1969 in Recife geboren, studierte bis 1992 an der UFPE. Er war Gründer und Partner zweier früherer Büros, DP&G und Astria Arquitetura, bevor er im Jahr 2000 seine eigene Firma, Juliano Dubeux Arquitetos Associados, gründete. 2006 luden João Domingos Azevedo und Metro Arquitetura Juliano Dubeux zur Mitarbeit am Entwurf für den Club NOX (Recife, hier veröffentlicht) ein. Zu weiteren Werken von Metro zählen: America (Mehrfamilienhaus, Recife, im Bau, mit Juliano Dubeux und Borsoi Arquitetura), QG Building (Recife, im Bau, mit Juliano Dubeux und Borsoi Arquitetura), Veronese (Mehrfamilienhaus, im Bau, mit Juliano Dubeux und Borsoi Arquitetura), Strandbungalows Toquinho Village (Toquinho Beach, 2007–), Krankenhauserweiterung AACD (Recife, im Bau, mit Juliano Dubeux und Borsoi Arquitetura), NOSi Building + Data Center (Praia-Cabo Verde, 2007–) und das Bürogebäude Pontes (Recife, 2009–), alle in Brasilien.

João Domingos Azevedo né à Recife au Brésil en 1977 est architecte diplômé de l'Universidade Federal de Pernambuco, UFPE (2001). Après son diplôme, il est devenu partenaire de Juliano Dubeux Arquitetos Associados pendant trois ans. En 2004, il fonde sa propre agence, **METRO ARQUITETURA**, qui a travaillé sur un certain nombre de projets en collaboration avec d'autres structures comme Juliano Dubeux Arquitetos, Borsoi Arquitetura et Pontual Arquitetos. Rafael Souto Maior est né à Recife en 1982 et Livia Brandão à Manaus en 1982. Tous deux sont diplômés en architecture de l'UFPE (2006) et ont rejoint Metro Arquitetura la même année en tant que partenaires. Juliano Dubeux, né à Recife en 1969, diplômé de l'UFPE en 1992, avait été cofondateur de deux autres agences DP&G et Astria Arquitetura, avant de créer sa propre agence, Juliano Dubeux Arquitetos Associados en 2000. En 2006, João Domingos Azevedo et Metro Arquitetura ont invité Juliano Dubeux à collaborer au projet du Club NOX (Recife, publié ici). Parmi les autres réalisations de Metro, toutes au Brésil : America (immeuble d'appartements, Recife, en construction, avec Juliano Dubeux et Borsoi Arquitetura) ; l'immeuble QG (Recife, en construction, avec Juliano Dubeux et Borsoi Arquitetura) ; Veronese (immeuble d'appartements, Recife, en construction, avec Juliano Dubeux et Borsoi Arquitetura) ; Toquinho Village, bungalows de plage (Toquinho Beach, 2007–) ; l'extension de l'hôpital AACD (Recife, en construction, avec Juliano Dubeux et Borsoi Arquitetura) ; l'immeuble NOSi + Data Center (Praia-Cabo Verde, 2007–) ; et l'immeuble de bureaux Pontes (Recife, 2009–).

CLUB NOX

Recife, Brazil, 2006

Av Eng Domingos Ferreira, 2422 - Boa Viagem, Recife, PE CEP 51020–030, Brazil, +55 81 3326 3954, www.clubnox.com.br
Area: 1100 m². Client: Club NOX. Cost: $1 million. Collaborators: Rafael Souto Maior, Livia Brandão, Juliano Dubeux

Three young entrepreneurs, two of them DJs, commissioned Metro to create a bar and dance club on a main avenue in Recife. The architects conceived a "box of Cor-ten steel that wraps around a prism of glass that lets light of different colors escape from the interior." The glass prism corresponds to the lounge/bar area inside. The dance floor has a high ceiling with an upper membrane of translucent fiberglass strips that cross over each other and create a matrix of light and color. A tailor-made light system consisting of 256 RGB LEDs controlled by a DMX system can generate a total of 16 million different colors. The architects state: "The space remodels itself with light, making people dance and forget everything they left behind before entering the house." The sound system is designed for this large space, which can hold up to 900 people. By way of contrast, the lounge/bar is a "white, clean space, with sofas, tatami mats, wood, and green (plants). [...] Embraced by the glass prism that also illuminates the space with its colored light, the lounge is a resting area, a place to chat and eat, with softer music that slowly brings people back to the real world."

Drei junge Unternehmer, zwei davon Discjockeys, beauftragten Metro mit der Planung einer Bar und eines Tanzklubs an einer Hauptstraße in Recife. Die Architekten entwarfen eine „Box aus Cor-Ten-Stahl, die ein Prisma aus Glas umgibt, durch das Licht in verschiedenen Farben nach außen fällt". Das gläserne Prisma entspricht der Form des Lounge-Bar-Bereichs im Innern. Die Tanzfläche hat eine hohe Decke mit einer Membrane aus durchscheinenden Glasfaserstreifen, die über Kreuz verlegt sind und ein Muster aus Licht und Farbe bilden. Ein speziell angefertigtes Lichtsystem aus 256 RGB-LED-Modulen, gesteuert von einem DMX-System, kann insgesamt 16 Millionen Farben erzeugen. Dazu erklären die Architekten: „Der Raum gestaltet sich selbst durch das Licht, er lässt die Menschen tanzen und alles hinter sich lassen, sobald sie das Gebäude betreten." Das Schallsystem wurde eigens für diesen Raum entwickelt, der bis zu 900 Personen aufnehmen kann. Im Gegensatz dazu ist der Lounge-Bar-Bereich „ein weißer, klarer Raum mit Sofas, Tatamimatten, Holz und Grünpflanzen. [...] Umfangen vom gläsernen Prisma, das auch den Raum mit seinem farbigem Licht erhellt, ist die Lounge ein Ort zum Ausruhen, wo man sich bei leiser Musik unterhalten und essen kann, der die Menschen wieder in die reale Welt zurückführt."

Trois jeunes hommes d'affaires, dont deux DJ, ont commandé à Metro la création de ce bar et *dance club* sur l'une des principales avenues de Recife. Les architectes ont conçu une « boîte en acier Corten qui enveloppe un prisme de verre laissant échapper vers l'extérieur des lumières multicolores. » Le prisme correspond à la zone du bar et du lounge. La piste de danse se trouve sous un très haut plafond tendu d'une membrane de bandes de fibre de verre translucide qui s'entrecroisent et créent une matrice de lumière et de couleurs. L'éclairage fait de 256 LEDs RGB contrôlé par un système DMX peut créer 16 millions de couleurs. Comme l'expliquent les architectes : « L'espace se remodèle de lui-même par le biais de la lumière. Les gens dansent et peuvent oublier tout ce qu'ils laissent derrière eux en franchissant la porte du club. » La sonorisation a été spécialement conçue pour ce vaste volume qui peut contenir jusqu'à 900 personnes. Par contraste, le lounge bar est « un espace blanc, épuré, décoré de sofas, de tatami, d'éléments en bois et de plantes vertes. [...] Entouré de ce prisme de verre qui illumine également l'espace de lumière colorée, le lounge est une zone de repos, un lieu ou bavarder et dîner, dont la musique plus douce ramène lentement les clients vers le monde réel. »

The fiberglass light membrane of the Club (Plus Engenharia) changes color, creating very different moods according to the moment.

Die Lichtmembrane aus Glasfaser (Plus Engenharia) wechselt ihre Farben und erzeugt unterschiedliche, zum Anlass passende Stimmungen.

La membrane de fibre de verre qui recouvre les plafonds du Nox (Plus Engenharia) change de couleur pour créer, selon l'heure, des atmosphères différentes.

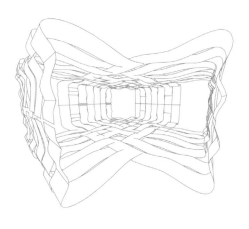

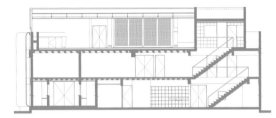

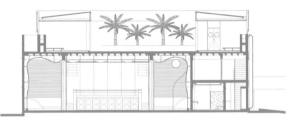

Above, elevations of the structure, and left, an exterior photo at night. Below, bar stools (Italica Design) and lounge sofa (LB Moveis) were designed by Metro Arquitetura.

Oben: Ansichten des Gebäudes. Links: Außenaufnahme bei Nacht. Unten: Die Barhocker (Italica Design) und das Lounge-Sofa (LB Moveis) wurden von Metro Arquitetura entworfen.

Ci-dessus, élévations de la structure et, à gauche, photo de nuit de l'extérieur. Ci-dessous, les tabourets de bar (Italica Design) et le sofa du lounge Sofa (LB Moveis) ont été dessinés pas Metro Arquitetura.

On the open terrace, Saccaro Outdoor Sofas (Saccaro) are used. The basic floor plan is square (below, right).

Auf der Terrasse im Freien stehen Saccaro-Sofas (Saccaro). Unten, rechts: Der Grundriss ist im Grunde quadratisch.

Sur la terrasse ouverte, canapés d'extérieur de Saccaro. Le plan du club est un simple carré.

Acquadulza Wine Bar and Restaura...

SIMONE MICHELI

Simone Micheli Architectural Hero SRL
Via Aretina 197r/199r/201r
50136 Florence
Italy

Tel: +39 055 69 12 16
Fax: +39 055 650 44 98
E-mail: simone@simonemicheli.com
Web: www.simonemicheli.com

SIMONE MICHELI founded his architectural studio in 1990 and the design company Simone Micheli Architectural Hero in 2003. He is involved in architecture, interior design, exhibition design, graphic design, and communication. In 2008, he organized the exhibition "La casa italiana" for ICE and Fiera Verona, in collaboration with Abitare il Tempo – Acropoli, at the MuBE (Brazilian Museum of Sculpture) in São Paulo, Brazil. The same event was presented in 2009 in Mexico City, Monterrey (Mexico), and in Dallas (Texas). In 2008, he won the "Homes Overseas Award" London International Prize for the best residential real-estate development project, with Golfo Gabella Lake Resort for the Sist group. He was awarded "Interior designer of the year" at the International Design Awards 2008. His recent work includes the San Ranieri Hotel (Pisa, 2007); Golfo Gabella Lake Resort (Maccagno, Varese, 2007, with the Acquadulza Restaurant published here); the Sketch Lounge Bar (Merano, Bolzano, 2007, also published here); the Wellness Center of the Exedra Nice Hotel (Nice, France, 2008); the Paradiso Hotel (Maccagno, Varese, in progress); the Park Hotel (Arezzo, in progress); the Wellness Center of the Via Matteotti Hotel (Milan, in progress); and residences in Chioggia (Venice, in progress), all in Italy unless stated otherwise.

SIMONE MICHELI gründete 1990 sein Architekturbüro und 2003 die Planungsfirma Simone Micheli Architectural Hero. Seine Arbeitsgebiete sind Architektur, Innenarchitektur, Ausstellungsgestaltung, Gebrauchsgrafik und Kommunikation. 2008 organisierte er die Ausstellung „La casa italiana" für ICE und Fiera Verona in Zusammenarbeit mit Abitare il Tempo – Acropoli am Museo Brasileiro de Escultura in São Paulo, Brasilien. Die gleiche Ausstellung fand 2009 auch in Mexiko-Stadt, Monterrey (Mexiko) und Dallas (Texas) statt. 2008 gewann Micheli mit dem Golfo Gabella Lake Resort für die Sist-Gruppe den internationalen Londoner Preis Homes Overseas Award für den besten Entwurf einer Wohnsiedlung. Außerdem wurde er 2008 mit dem International Design Award als Innenarchitekt des Jahres ausgezeichnet. Zu seinen neueren Arbeiten zählen das Hotel San Ranieri (Pisa, 2007), Golfo Gabella Lake Resort (Maccagno, Varese, 2007, mit dem Restaurant Acquadulza, hier veröffentlicht), die Sketch Lounge Bar (Merano, Bolzano, 2007, ebenfalls hier gezeigt), das Wellnesszentrum des Hotels Exedra Nice (Nizza, 2008), das Hotel Paradiso (Maccagno, Varese, in Arbeit), das Park Hotel in Arezzo (im Bau), das Wellnesszentrum des Hotels Via Matteotti (Mailand, im Bau) und Wohnhäuser in Chioggia (Venedig, in Arbeit).

SIMONE MICHELI a fondé son studio d'architecture en 1990 et la société de design, Simone Micheli Architectural Hero, en 2003. Il se consacre à l'architecture, l'architecture intérieure, le design d'expositions, le design graphique et la communication. En 2008, il a organisé l'exposition « La casa italiana » pour ICE et la Foire de Vérone, en collaboration avec « Abitare il Tempo – Acropoli », au MuBE (Musée brésilien de la sculpture) à São Paolo. La même manifestation a été présentée en 2009 à Mexico, Monterrey (Mexique) et Dallas (Texas). En 2008, il a remporté le Homes Overseas Award, prix international de Londres pour le meilleur projet de promotion immobilière résidentielle avec le Golfo Gabella Lake Resort pour le groupe Sist. Il a été nommé « Interior designer of the Year (designer d'intérieur de l'année) » aux International Design Awards 2008. Parmi ses interventions récentes, essentiellement en Italie : l'hôtel San Ranieri (Pise, 2007) ; le Golfo Gabella Lake Resort (Maccagno, Varese, 2007, dont le restaurant Acquadulza, publié ici) ; le Sketch Lounge Bar (Merano, Bolzano, Italie, 2007, également publié ici) ; le centre de remise en forme de l'Exedra Nice Hôtel (Nice, France, 2008) ; l'hôtel Paradiso (Maccagno, Varese, en cours) ; le Park Hotel (Arezzo, en cours) ; le centre de remise en forme de l'hôtel Via Matteotti (Milan, en cours) ; et des résidences à Chioggia (Venise, en cours).

ACQUADULZA WINE BAR AND RESTAURANT

Maccagno, Varese, Italy, 2007

Lungolago Girardi, 4, Maccagno 21010, Italy, +39 032 92 28 20 49, www.acquadulza.com
Area: 320 m². Client: Sist Group. Cost: €650 000

Located in the Golfo Gabella Lake Resort on Lake Maggiore, the Acquadulza bar, wine "butega," and restaurant, whose interior was designed by Simone Micheli, "is characterized by a wide, open space that, thanks to transparent glass diaphragms with sand-blasted rounded shapes, is harmoniously split into a number of contiguously linked settings that amplify the versatile character and interactive nature of the structure," according to the architect. Guests arrive in the "butega" area dedicated to the "tasting of typical local products" and proceed to the restaurant. Here a bar made of black lacquered wood and satin-finished stainless steel permits the exhibition of wines. Both this space and the restaurant have gneiss floors and exposed, white stone walls with some "raw" plaster and round mirrors back-lit with blue lights. The white plasterboard ceiling "brings to mind the ancient vaults of the Renaissance," while the furniture includes black wood and silver metal tables or silver chairs finished in black leather. The 70-square-meter bar is dominated by a "fluid retro bar in shiny lacquered acid green MDF (medium density fiberboard)." The Acquadulza bar, wine "butega," and restaurant is described by Simone Micheli as "a story of beauty that seeks to link the contents and the tastes of tradition to a volumetric present, in order to fascinate and involve visitors."

Das im Golfo Gabella Lake Resort am Lago Maggiore gelegene Lokal Acquadulza mit Bar, Wein-„butega" und Restaurant, dessen Innenausstattung von Simone Micheli ausgeführt wurde, zeichnet sich in den Worten des Architekten „durch einen weiten, offenen Bereich aus, der dank sandgestrahlter, transparenter Glaswände in abgerundeter Form harmonisch in verschiedene zusammenhängende Bereiche aufgeteilt ist, die den vielseitigen und interaktiven Charakter des Gebäudes verstärken". Die Gäste kommen in der „butega" an, wo sie „typische lokale Produkte probieren", und gehen weiter in das Restaurant. Hier stellt eine Bar aus schwarz lackiertem Holz und gebürstetem Edelstahl Weine zur Schau. Dieser Bereich wie auch das Restaurant haben Fußböden aus Gneis und weiße Natursteinwände mit rau verputzten Bereichen und runden, blau hinterleuchteten Spiegeln. Die weiß verputzte Decke „erinnert an die alten Gewölbe der Renaissance", während die Möblierung aus silbrigen, mit schwarzem Leder bezogenen Stühlen und Tischen aus schwarzem Holz und silbrigem Metall besteht. Der 70 m² große Barraum wird beherrscht von einer „durchgehenden Retro-Bartheke aus glänzenden, leuchtend grünen MDF (mitteldichten Faserplatten)". Das Acquadulza wird von Simone Micheli beschrieben als „eine Geschichte der Schönheit, die traditionelle Inhalte und Geschmäcker mit zeitgenössischer Raumgestaltung verbindet, um Besucher zu faszinieren und einzubeziehen".

Situé dans l'ensemble touristique du golfe de Gabella sur le lac Majeur, le bar Acquadulza, bar à vin, « butega » et restaurant, dont l'intérieur a été conçu par Simone Micheli, « est caractérisé par un vaste espace ouvert qui, grâce à des diaphragmes en verre transparent et sablé aux formes arrondies, se fractionne harmonieusement en un certain nombre de lieux contigus et reliés, qui amplifient le caractère souple et interactif de l'ensemble », explique l'architecte. Les hôtes passent dans la partie « butega » consacrée à « la dégustation de produits locaux typiques », avant d'accéder au restaurant. Là, un bar en bois laqué noir et acier inoxydable satiné a été aménagé pour la présentation des vins. Cet espace, de même que le restaurant, possède des sols en gneiss, des murs en pierre apparente décorés de plâtre « brut » et des miroirs ronds rétro-éclairés par des néons bleus. Le plafond en panneaux de plâtre blanc « rappelle les anciennes voûtes de la Renaissance ». Le mobilier se compose de tables en bois noir et métal, et de sièges en cuir noir à piètement argenté. Le bar de 70 m² est dominé par un « mur de fond fluide en médium laqué vert acide brillant ». Cette réalisation est présentée par son auteur comme « une narration sur la beauté qui cherche à lier le contenu et les goûts de la tradition dans un présent volumétrique qui fascine et implique les visiteurs ».

The chairs and poufs for the restaurant were designed by Simone Micheli (Fornasarig Sedie Friuli). Lights are by Targetti Sankey. To the right, the bar area of the restaurant.

Die Stühle und Hocker für das Restaurant wurden von Simone Micheli entworfen (Fornasarig Sedie Friuli). Die Leuchten sind von Targetti Sankey. Rechts, die Bar des Restaurants.

Les sièges et poufs du restaurant ont été dessinés par Simone Micheli (Fornasarig Sedie Friuli). Les éclairages sont de Targetti Sankey. À droite, la partie bar du restaurant.

The essentially dark atmosphere of Acquadulza is brightened by touches of light and color. Below, the floor plan of the 320-square-meter restaurant.

Die überwiegend dunkle Atmosphäre des Acquadulza wird durch Spuren von Licht und Farbe aufgehellt. Unten: Der Grundriss des 320 m² großen Restaurants.

L'atmosphère plutôt sombre de l'Acquadulza est allégée par des touches de couleur et de lumière. Ci-dessous, le plan au sol de ce restaurant de 320 m².

A curved ceiling and stone walls form the dining space, where dark furniture emphasizes the lighting pattern.

Eine gekrümmte Decke und Natursteinwände bilden den Speiseraum, in dem dunkle Möbel das Beleuchtungssystem hervorheben.

Dans la salle à manger, plafonds cintrés et murs en pierre apparente. Le mobilier de couleur sombre met en valeur le système d'éclairage.

SKETCH LOUNGE BAR

Merano, Bolzano, Italy, 2007

Passeggiata lungo Passirio 40, 39012 Merano, +39 047 321 18 00, www.sketch.bz
Area: 400 m². Client: Aukenthauer Family. Cost: € 700 000

Located in the Aurora Hotel, the entrance to the Sketch Lounge Bar is marked by a glass entry door and sliding glass frame allowing for open-air seating. The architect states that near the entrance "the space is almost completely occupied by an enormous bar counter covered in shiny stainless steel and mirrors with circular glazing surrounded by small points of flashing blue LED lights. A retro-counter takes up the entire wall and becomes a large, shiny, fuchsia laminated container marked by a long eyelet covered in an illuminated mirror with blue LED lights containing moveable transparent glass shelves to stock bottles and glasses." The opposite wall is clad in flexible plasterboard, while the brushed oak floor has pulsating lights. Video projectors hidden in the bar counter animate the wall surface. Fuchsia-colored or stainless-steel cylindrical poufs serve as either seats or tables. A second stainless-steel bar and a DJ box covered in white laminate, together with the lighting, ensure that the space is full of surprises, both in the choice of materials and the forms. In his rather emphatic style, the architect states that Sketch "is a new spatial fragment that is able to provide the user with a new kind of experience linked to the world of beauty, truth, and emotion."

Der Eingang zu der im Hotel Aurora gelegenen Sketch Lounge Bar erfolgt durch große gläserne Schiebetüren, sodass man auch im Freien sitzen kann. Der Architekt erklärt, am Eingang werde „der Raum fast vollständig von einer gewaltigen Bartheke eingenommen, die mit glänzendem Edelstahl und kreisförmigen Spiegeln überzogen ist, die von kleinen blauen LED-Strahlern umgeben sind. Eine Theke im Retro-Stil nimmt die gesamte Wand ein und wird zu einem großen, glänzenden, weinrot lackierten Container mit einer langen Öffnung, die von einem erleuchteten Spiegel mit blauen LED-Leuchten bedeckt ist und verstellbare, transparente Glasregale für Flaschen und Gläser enthält." Die gegenüberliegende Wand ist mit Gipskartonplatten verkleidet; der geschliffene Eichenboden ist mit flackernden Leuchten augestattet. In der Bartheke verborgene Videoprojektoren beleben die Wandfläche. Zylindrische, weinrote oder stählerne Hocker dienen als Sitze oder auch Tische. Eine zweite Bartheke aus Edelstahl und eine mit weißem Laminat überzogene Discjockeybox sowie die Art der Beleuchtung verleihen dem Raum weitere überraschende Effekte, sowohl in der Materialwahl als auch in ihren Formen. In seiner etwas pathetischen Ausdrucksweise erklärt der Architekt, dass Sketch „ein neues Raumfragment darstellt, das dem Nutzer eine neue Form der Erfahrung bietet, die ihn mit der Welt der Schönheit, Wahrheit und Emotion verbindet".

Située dans l'hôtel Aurora, l'entrée du Sketch Lounge se signale par une porte de verre et une partition coulissante également en verre qui ouvre sur une terrasse où l'on peut aller s'asseoir. Près de l'entrée, « l'espace est presque entièrement occupé par un énorme bar recouvert d'acier inoxydable brillant et des miroirs à cadres de verre circulaires à ponctuations lumineuses de LEDs bleu « flashy ». Une longue niche-comptoir occupe un mur tout entier, vaste présentoir en lamifié rose fuchsia brillant pris dans l'épaisseur du mur habillé de miroir éclairé de LEDs, équipé d'étagères mobiles en verre transparent contenant verres et bouteilles », explique l'architecte. Le mur opposé est habillé de panneaux de plâtre incurvés et le sol en chêne brossé est parsemé de sources lumineuses en pulsation. Des vidéoprojecteurs dissimulés dans le bar animent la surface du mur. Des poufs cylindriques fuchsia ou en acier inox font office de sièges ou de tables. Un second bar en acier inoxydable, une tribune plaquée de laminé blanc pour le DJ et l'éclairage sont des exemples des multiples surprises que réserve ce lieu, à la fois dans le choix des matériaux et celui des formes. S'exprimant dans son style assez emphatique, l'architecte précise que le Sketch est « un nouveau fragment d'espace capable d'offrir un nouveau type d'expérience liée au monde de la beauté, de l'authenticité et de l'émotion ».

Above, Ella poufs designed by Simone Micheli (Adrenalina). Lights are by Fabbian Illuminazione.

Oben: Von Simone Micheli entworfene Ella-Hocker (Adrenalina). Die Leuchten sind von Fabbian Illuminazione.

Ci-dessus, poufs Ella dessinés par Simone Micheli (Adrenalina). L'éclairage est de Fabbian Illuminazione.

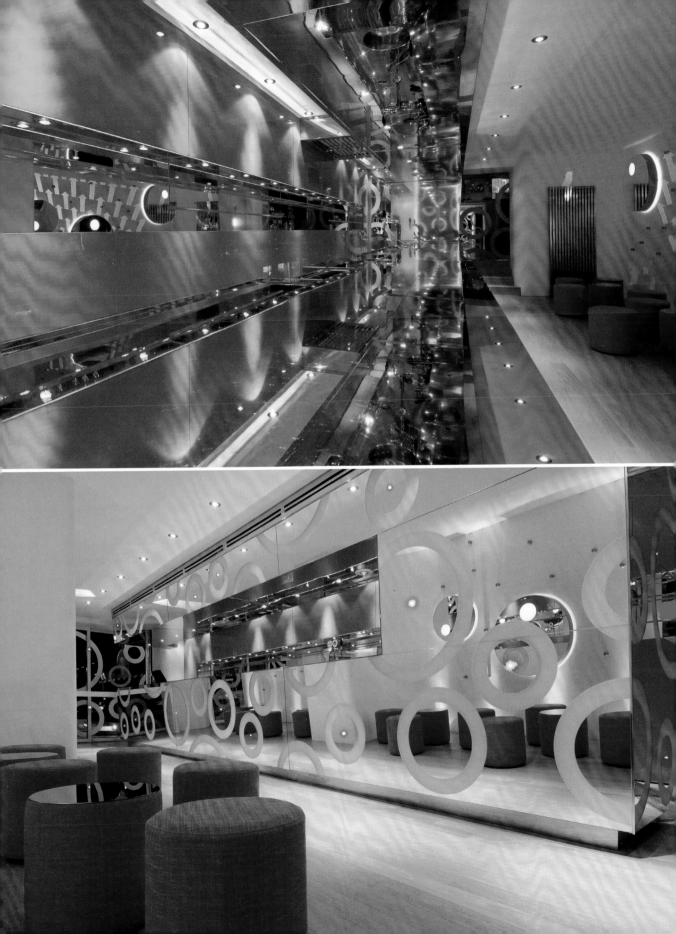

Special "illuminating bodies" designed by Micheli (Segno) create an unusual colored atmosphere. The plan shows the division of the bar into several spaces.

Spezielle, von Micheli entworfene „Beleuchtungskörper" (Segno) erzeugen eine ungewöhnliche farbige Atmosphäre. Der Grundriss zeigt die Aufteilung der Bar in mehrere Bereiche.

Des « corps illuminés » dessinés par Micheli (Segno) créent une étrange atmosphère colorée. Le plan montre la division du bar en plusieurs zones.

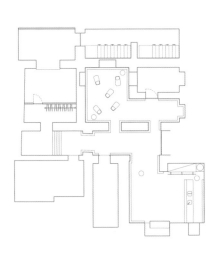

MOON DESIGN

Moon Design
Lijnzaadstraat 5
8860 Lendelede
Belgium

Tel: +32 496 12 98 97
E-mail: info@moon-design.eu
Web: www.moon-design.eu

Gerd Couckhuyt was born in 1970 in Belgium. He has received degrees from the School of Art, Stedelijke Leergangen Izegem (1999), and in Interior Design (1998) and Lighting Design (1999) from the Vormingsinstituut (Roeselare); and a further degree in Sculpture from the Academy of Art (Roeselare, 2004–05). He describes himself as a "self-employed interior designer." His work in 2007 included the interior design of the Claire Shoe Store (Roeselare); the Atmosphere Wellness Center (Wielsheke); the Zuri Club (Knokke, published here); a private house in Sint-Denijs-Westrem; and another house in Oostduinkerke, all in Belgium. Gerd Couckhuyt is the designer for **MOON DESIGN**, which was created in 2006, where Philip Meurisse is a product developer and Cinthy Couckhuyt the manager.

Gerd Couckhuyt wurde 1970 in Belgien geboren. Er studierte an der Kunsthochschule Stedelijke Leergangen Izegem (Abschluss 1999) sowie Innenarchitektur (Abschluss 1998) und Lichtdesign (Abschluss 1999) am Vormingsinstituut (Roeselare). Außerdem studierte er Bildhauerei an der Kunstakademie in Roeselare (2004–05). Er beschreibt sich selbst als „selbstständigen Innenarchitekten". Zu seinen Arbeiten von 2007 zählen die Innenausstattung des Schuhgeschäfts Claire (Roeselare), das Atmosphere Wellnesscenter (Wielsheke), der Klub Zuri (Knokke, hier veröffentlicht), Privathäuser in Sint-Denijs-Westrem und in Oostduinkerke, alle in Belgien. Gerd Couckhuyt ist der Planer des 2006 gegründeten Büros **MOON DESIGN**, Philip Meurisse der Produktdesigner und Cinthy Couckhuyt die Leiterin.

Gerd Couckhuyt est né en 1970 en Belgique. Il est diplômé de l'École d'art Stedelijke Leergangen Izegem (1999), d'architecture intérieure (1998) et de conception d'éclairage (1999) du Vormingsinstituut (Roeselare) ainsi que de sculpture (Académie d'art de Roeselare, 2004–05). Il se présente comme un « architecte d'intérieur indépendant ». En 2007, il a réalisé le magasin de chaussures Claire (Roeselare) ; le Centre de remise en forme Atmosphère (Wielsheke) ; le club Zuri (Knokke, publié ici) ; une résidence privée à Sint-Denijs-Westrem ; une autre maison à Oostduinkerke, le tout en Belgique. Gerd Couckhuyt est designer pour **MOON DESIGN**, agence fondée en 2006, au sein de laquelle Philip Meurisse est développeur produits, et dont Cinthy Couckhuyt tient la direction.

ZURI

Knokke, Belgium, 2007

Casino Knokke, Zeedijk Albertstrand 510, 8300 Knokke, Belgium, +32 50 60 55 04, vip@zuri.be, www.zuri.be.
Area: 300 m². Clients: Carl Pollyn and Chris Muylle. Cost: € 1.3 million

"A couple of years ago I had an idea in my head about creating a totally white bar. There wasn't really any location or space determined, nor a time to execute it," says Gerd Couckhuyt. He created Zuri in the space of the former Number One disco and Bis bar in the Casino in Knokke. Couckhuyt was given just six weeks for the demolition of the old facilities and the creation of Zuri. "The main idea," he says, "was to create two spaces: a day space and a night space with back-to-back bars divided by a screen parallel to the coast line." The entrance to the club is a black tunnel that contrasts strongly with the white interior. He used RGB "Modular Lighting Instruments" he had designed for the space for the changing light scheme. Calling on his multiple talents, Couckhuyt also created the furniture. "Moon, my own company, under which I developed this concept," he says, "also worked out the newly created furniture. Next to custom-made sofas, the new 'Zuri lounger' and 'Zuri barchair' came into being. The existing 'Island' and 'Rock Mutant' from the Moon collection were also integrated in this project." In what he calls a "spacy" environment, the designer integrated the sound systems into the walls and ceilings, rendering them almost invisible.

„Vor einigen Jahren kam mir der Gedanke, eine völlig weiße Bar zu planen. Es gab eigentlich keinen bestimmten Ort oder Raum dafür und auch keinen Termin, um sie auszuführen", sagt Gerd Couckhuyt. Er realisierte Zuri im Raum der ehemaligen Disko Number One und der Bar Bis im Kasino von Knokke. Couckhuyt hatte nur sechs Wochen Zeit zum Abräumen der alten Einrichtungen und für die Ausstattung von Zuri. „Der Hauptgedanke war", sagt er, „zwei Räume zu schaffen: einen für den Tag und einen für die Nacht, mit Rücken an Rücken gesetzten Theken und einer parallel zur Küste gestellten Zwischenwand." Der Eingang zum Klub führt durch einen schwarzen Tunnel, der einen starken Kontrast zum weißen Innenraum darstellt. Couckhuyt verwendete RGB-Leuchten, „Modular Lighting Instruments", die er für diesen Raum zur Veränderung der Lichtverhältnisse entworfen hatte. Dank seiner vielfachen Begabung plante Couckhuyt auch die Möblierung. „Moon, meine eigene Firma, in der ich dieses Konzept entwickelt habe", sagt er, „schuf auch das Design der neuen Möblierung: Außer den eigens angefertigten Sofas entstanden auch der neue ‚Zuri Lounger' und der ‚Zuri Barstuhl'. Die schon existierenden ‚Island' und ‚Rock Mutant' der Moon-Kollektion wurden ebenfalls in diesen Entwurf aufgenommen." In diese, vom Architekten als „ausgeflippt" bezeichnete Umgebung integrierte er in Wänden und Decken eine fast unsichtbare Tonanlage.

« Il y a quelques années, j'ai eu l'idée de créer un bar entièrement blanc. Rien n'était déterminé, ni le lieu, ni l'espace, ni le moment », explique Gerd Couckhuyt qui a finalement créé Zuri dans l'espace occupé naguère par la discothèque Number One et le bar Bis du casino de Knokke. Six semaines seulement lui ont été accordées pour démolir les anciennes installations et créer les nouvelles. « L'idée centrale », poursuit-il, « était de créer deux espaces : un de jour et un de nuit, dont les bars seraient dos à dos, séparés par un écran parallèle à la côte. » L'entrée se fait par un tunnel noir qui contraste fortement avec l'intérieur totalement blanc. Pour la programmation lumineuse, il s'est servi des Modular Lighting Instruments RGB qu'il a conçus lui-même. Mobilisant ses multiples talents, Couckhuyt a dessiné le mobilier. « Moon, ma propre entreprise, à travers laquelle j'ai mis au point ce concept, a également sorti ses nouvelles créations sur le mobilier. Aux canapés sur mesure se sont ajoutés un nouveau Zuri lounger et un Zuri barchair. Les modèles Island et Rock Mutant de la collection Moon ont été aussi retenus. » Dans ce qu'il appelle un environnement « spatial », le designer a intégré dans les murs et les plafonds une sonorisation qui est ainsi pratiquement invisible.

The entry and "nightspace" with the Zuri Lounger by Gerd Couckhuyt (Moon Design).

Der Eingang und der „Nachtraum" mit dem Zuri Lounger von Gerd Couckhuyt (Moon Design).

L'entrée et « l'espace-nuit » meublé du fauteuil Zuri de Gerd Couckhuyt (Moon Design).

"Day space" with the Zuri Bar Stool by Gerd Couckhuyt (Moon Design). Strong and changing colors mark the design and give variety to the volumes.

Der „Tagesraum" mit dem Barhocker Zuri von Gerd Couckhuyt (Moon Design). Starke und wechselnde Farben charakterisieren die Gestaltung und verleihen den Bereichen Vielfalt.

« L'espace-jour ». Les tabourets de bar Zuri de Gerd Couckhuyt (Moon Design). Des couleurs fortes et changeantes personnalisent ce projet et apportent de la variété aux volumes.

Above, "night space", with Rock Mutant and Zuri Lounger furniture by Couckhuyt and Moon Design.

Oben: Der „Nachtraum", mit Rock Mutant und Zuri Lounger von Couckhuyt und Moon Design möbliert.

Ci-dessus, « l'espace-nuit », meublé de fauteuils Rock Mutant et Zuri de Couckhuyt et Moon Design.

OFFICE DA

Office dA
1920 Washington Street #2
Boston, MA 02118
USA

Tel: +1 617 541 5540
Fax: +1 617 541 5535
E-mail: da@officeda.com
Web: www.officeda.com

Nader Tehrani was born in England in 1963 and is of Iranian descent. He received a B.F.A. (1985) and a B.Arch (1986) from the Rhode Island School of Design; and an M.Arch in Urban Design from the Harvard GSD in 1991. He teaches at MIT as an Associate Professor of Architecture, and has taught at the Harvard GSD, Rhode Island School of Design, and Georgia Institute of Technology, where he served as the Thomas W. Ventulett III Distinguished Chair in Architectural Design. Monica Ponce de Leon was born in 1965 in Venezuela. She received a B.A. from the University of Miami in 1989 followed by an M.Arch in Urban Design from the Harvard GSD in 1991. Ponce de Leon is a Professor at the Harvard GSD and became the Dean of the A. Alfred Taubman College of Architecture and Urban Planning at the University of Michigan in the fall of 2008. They formed their partnership in 1991 in Boston. In 2006, **OFFICE DA** designed the main library for the Rhode Island School of Design in Providence. In addition, Office dA won the first place award in the Villa Moda Competition for a mixed-use building in Kuwait, which includes housing, retail, multiplex, convention area, and sport facilities. Office dA recently completed the first LEED-certified, multi-housing building in Boston, the Macallen Building, with over 140 environmentally sensitive condominium units. Helios House, the first LEED-rated gas station, was completed in Los Angeles in 2007, and they have also realized Banq (Boston, Massachusetts, 2006–08, published here).

Der aus einer iranischen Familie stammende Nader Tehrani wurde 1963 in England geboren. Er erwarb 1985 den B.F.A. und 1986 den B.Arch. an der Rhode Island School of Design sowie 1991 den M.Arch. in Städtebau an der Harvard Graduate School of Design. Am Massachusetts Institute of Technology lehrt er als Privatdozent Architektur, zuvor unterrichtete er an der Harvard GSD, der Rhode Island School of Design und dem Georgia Institute of Technology, wo er als Inhaber des Thomas-W.-Ventulett-III-Lehrstuhls architektonisches Entwerfen lehrte. Monica Ponce de Leon wurde 1965 in Venezuela geboren. Sie erwarb 1989 den B.Arch. an der University of Miami und 1991 den M.Arch. an der Harvard GSD. Dort ist sie Professorin und wurde im Herbst 2008 Dekanin des A. Alfred Taubman College of Architecture and Urban Planning an der University of Michigan. Die Partnerschaft wurde 1991 in Boston gegründet. 2006 plante **OFFICE DA** die Hauptbibliothek für die Rhode Island School of Design in Providence. Außerdem gewann das Büro den ersten Preis im Villa-Moda-Wettbewerb für einen Mehrzweckbau in Kuwait, der Wohnungen, Einzelhandelsgeschäfte, ein Multiplexkino, Kongressräume und Sporteinrichtungen enthält. Kürzlich vollendete Office dA in Boston das Macallen Building, das erste nach LEED (Leadership in Energy and Environmental Design) zertifizierte Mehrfamilienhaus mit über 140 umweltfreundlichen Eigentumswohnungen. Helios House, die erste LEED-zertifizierte Tankstelle, wurde 2007 in Los Angeles errichtet, außerdem gestaltete Office dA das hier vorgestellte Restaurant Banq (Boston, Massachusetts, 2006–08).

D'origine iranienne, Nader Tehrani est né en Grande-Bretagne en 1963. Il est B.F.A. (1985), B.Arch (1986) de la Rhode Island School of Design, et M.Arch d'urbanisme de la Harvard GSD (1991). Professeur associé d'architecture au MIT, il a enseigné à la Harvard GSD, à la Rhode Island School of Design et au Georgia Institute of Technology où il a occupé la « Thomas W. Ventulett III Distinguished Chair » de projet architectural. Monica Ponce de Leon, née en 1965 au Venezuela est B.A. (Université de Miami, 1989) et M.Arch en urbanisme de la Harvard GSD (1991). Elle est professeure à la Harvard GSD et doyenne du « A. Alfred Taubman College of Architecture and Urban Planning » à l'Université du Michigan depuis l'automne 2008. Ils se sont associés en 1991 à Boston. En 2006, **OFFICE DA** a conçu la bibliothèque principale de la Rhode Island School of Design à Providence, et a remporté le premier prix pour le concours de la Villa Moda portant sur un immeuble mixte au Koweït (logements, commerces, « multiplexe », espaces pour les congrès et installations sportives). Office dA a récemment achevé le premier immeuble d'appartements certifié LEED à Boston, le Macallen Building, qui compte plus de cent quarante appartements de qualité durable. Leur Helios House, première station d'essence certifiée LEED, a été achevée à Los Angeles en 2007, ainsi que le Banq (Boston, Massachusetts, 2006–08, publié ici).

BANQ

Boston, Massachusetts, USA, 2006–08

1375 Washington St., Boston MA 02118, USA, +1 617 451 0077
Area: 446 m². Client: SOWA Restaurant Group. Cost: not disclosed

View of the dining area. The floor, tables, and banquettes were custom-designed by Office dA, and fabricated by Homeland Builders in Plyboo Neapolitan Plywood.

Blick in den Speiseraum: Boden, Tische und Sitzbänke wurden hierfür von Office dA entworfen und von Homeland Builders aus Plyboo Neapolitan Funierholz gefertigt.

Vue de la salle à manger. Le sol, les tables et les banquettes ont été spécialement conçus par Office dA, et fabriqués par Homeland Builders en contreplaqué Plyboo Neapolitan.

This restaurant is located in the former banking hall of the Penny Savings Bank. The name "Banq" is naturally a play on this original location. The front section of the space, near Washington Street, is a bar, with a larger hall to the rear serving as the dining area. The mechanical facilities for the restaurant are located in an irregular, striated, birch plywood-slatted ceiling, with areas that "drip" or "slump" to reveal exit signs or lighting fixtures. Continued in the wood used for the actual restaurant space, the "striations of the ground, the furnishings, and the ceiling all conspire to create a total effect, embedding the diners into the grain of the restaurant," declare the architects. The ceiling is kept at a small remove from the historic walls of the building. The architects have also developed the design of the bathrooms of the restaurant around the oval theme generated by the sinks and toilets.

Dieses Restaurant befindet sich in der ehemaligen Schalterhalle der Penny Savings Bank. Der Name „Banq" ist natürlich ein Wortspiel mit dem Ursprung seines Standorts. Der vordere Teil des Raums an der Washington Street ist eine Bar, dahinter liegt ein größerer Speisesaal. Die technischen Einrichtungen des Restaurants sind in einer frei geformten, gerippten Lamellendecke aus Birkenfurnier untergebracht, mit Bereichen, die „herunterhängen" oder „abstürzen", um Ausgangsschilder oder Leuchtkörper anzubringen. Das Holz setzt sich im Speisesaal fort; „die Streifenbildung auf dem Boden, an der Möblierung und der Decke bewirkt einen Gesamteffekt, der die Gäste in die Struktur des Restaurants einbezieht", erklären die Architekten. Die Decke ist leicht abgesetzt von den historischen Wänden des Gebäudes. Die Planer haben auch die Toiletten des Restaurants mit ovaler Anordnung der Waschbecken und Klosetts gestaltet.

Ce restaurant occupe l'ancien hall des guichets de la Penny Savings Bank, d'où le nom de « Banq ». La partie avant donnant sur Washington Street est un bar, le vaste hall à l'arrière ayant été transformé en salle à manger. Une bonne partie des installations techniques est dissimulée dans le plafond strié en contreplaqué de bouleau de profil organique irrégulier, dont certaines zones « plongent » ou « dégringolent » pour dégager la signalétique de sortie ou les luminaires. À travers le bois utilisé pour l'espace du restaurant, les « striations du sol, le mobilier et le plafond, tout conspire à créer un effet global qui plonge les clients dans le grain du restaurant », précisent les architectes. Le plafond est légèrement détaché des murs anciens et historiques de l'immeuble. Office dA a également conçu les toilettes du restaurant sur le thème de l'ovale des lavabos et des cuvettes.

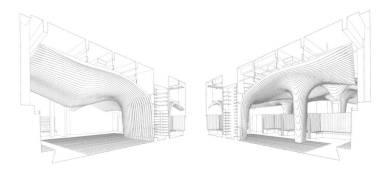

Drawings above show the articulation of the restaurant spaces relative to the building envelope. The bar visible on the right was custom-designed by Office dA and fabricated by Homeland Builders in solid walnut, Brookline veneered quartered walnut, clear white glass, and stainless steel.

Die Zeichnungen oben zeigen die Gliederung der Restaurantbereiche innerhalb der Gebäudehülle. Die Bar rechts wurde von Office dA entworfen und von Homeland Builders aus massivem Walnussholz, radial geschnittenem Walnussfurnier aus Brookline, Klarglas und Edelstahl gefertigt.

Les dessins ci-dessus montrent l'articulation des espaces du restaurant par rapport à l'enveloppe de l'immeuble. Le bar (à droite) a été dessiné par Office dA et fabriqué par Homeland Builders en noyer massif, noyer plaqué sur quartier Brookline, verre clair et acier inoxydable.

KATRIN OLINA

Katrin Olina Ltd.
P.O. Box 498
121 Reykjavik
Iceland

Tel: +354 692 1231
E-mail: info@katrin-olina.com
Web: www.katrin-olina.com

KATRIN OLINA, who describes herself as a "multidisciplinary artist," was born in Akureyri, Iceland. She studied industrial design at the École Supérieure de Design Industriel in Paris (1990–95). She worked in product development for Philippe Stark in Paris (1996) and Ross Lovegrove (London, 1997), before creating a partnership with Michael Young (MY Studio Ltd, Reykjavik, 1998–2005). She was Director of Studies at the Iceland Academy of the Arts (Reykjavik, 2000–04) and founded Katrin Olina Ltd. in Hong Kong, China, in 2007. She has worked on the Dr. James, Cosmetic Surgery clinic (Taipei, Taiwan, 2005, interior concept and design, collaboration with Michael Young); Skin, Aesthetic Cosmetic Surgery clinic (Florence, Italy, 2007, interior concept and design, collaboration with Michael Young); she designed the official poster for the 2007 Montreux Jazz Festival; created environmental graphics covering a surface of 150 square meters at the Regza Bar (100% Design, Tokyo, 2008); and the Cristal Bar (Hong Kong, China, 2008, published here). She has participated in numerous exhibitions, including a 2008 installation at the Reykjavik Art Museum.

KATRIN OLINA, die sich selbst als „multidisziplinäre Künstlerin" bezeichnet, wurde in Akureyri in Island geboren und studierte Industriedesign an der Ecole Supérieure de Design Industriel in Paris (1990–95). Sie arbeitete in der Produktentwicklung für Philippe Starck in Paris (1996) und Ross Lovegrove in London (1997), bevor sie eine Partnerschaft mit Michael Young einging (MY Studio Ltd., Reykjavik, 1998–2005). Sie war als Studienleiterin an der Iceland Academy of the Arts tätig (Reykjavik, 2000–04) und gründete 2007 das Büro Katrin Olina Ltd. in Hongkong, China. Zu ihren Arbeiten zählen die Klinik Dr. James Cosmetic Surgery (Taipeh, Taiwan, 2005, Innenarchitektur, in Zusammenarbeit mit Michael Young) und Skin, eine Klinik für ästhetische kosmetische Chirurgie (Florenz, 2007, Innenarchitektur, in Zusammenarbeit mit Michael Young). Sie gestaltete das offizielle Plakat für das Jazzfestival 2007 in Montreux, schuf Umweltgrafiken für eine 150 m² große Fläche in der Regza Bar (100 % Design, Tokio, 2008) und plante die Cristal Bar (Hongkong, China, 2008, hier veröffentlicht). Sie war in zahlreichen Ausstellungen vertreten, u. a. mit einer Installation 2008 im Kunstmuseum von Reykjavik.

KATRIN OLINA, qui se présente comme une « artiste multidisciplinaire », est née à Akureyri en Islande. Elle a étudié le design industriel à l'École supérieure de Design industriel à Paris (1990–95), puis a travaillé à la mise au point de produits chez Philippe Stark à Paris (1996) et Ross Lovegrove à Londres (1997), avant de s'associer avec Michael Young (MY Studio Ltd, Reykjavik, 1998–2005). Elle a été directrice des études à l'Académie d'Islande des arts (Reykjavik, 2000–04) et a fondé Katrin Olina Ltd. à Hongkong en 2007. Parmi ses réalisations : la clinique de chirurgie esthétique du Dr. James (Taipei, Taiwan, 2005, concept intérieur, design en collaboration avec Michael Young) ; Skin, clinique de chirurgie esthétique (Florence, Italie, 2007, concept intérieur, design en collaboration avec Michael Young) ; l'affiche officielle pour le Festival de jazz de Montreux en 2007 ; un environnement graphique de 150 m² pour le Regza Bar (100 % Design, Tokyo, 2008) ; et le Cristal Bar (Hongkong, 2008, publié ici). Elle a participé à de nombreuses expositions, dont une installation au Musée d'art de Reykjavik en 2008.

CRISTAL BAR

Hong Kong, China, 2008

9/F, 33 Wellington Street, The Loop, Central, Hong Kong, China, +852 2521 8999
Area: 111 m². Client: Zenses Group. Cost: not disclosed
Architecture Consultant: Sebastien Saint Jean. Lighting Consultant: Anlighten Design Studio

Located on the ninth floor of a high rise in the Central district of Hong Kong, the Cristal Bar was a winner of the 2009 Forum Aid Awards in which the jury stated: "With every available surface covered with Olina's graphic art, the patterns become more than just decoration and create a dream-like, immersive environment. It is a simple idea to make a two-dimensional pattern the dominant design feature of a three-dimensional space, but the result is striking." "I think of this project as taking the Renaissance ideas of murals and bringing them to the 21st century. It's not a backdrop, it's not wallpaper, it's something else. It's storytelling in space," says Katrin Olina. She used film and printing technology from 3M to create a seamless graphic surface that totally immerses guests in her imagery. The bar has four areas—a central area with graphics depicting seaweed forms and "hybrid water creatures," two adjacent rooms that are red in tone, and a final area with turquoise-green walls with "flowers" and "feathery forms." "The bar's graphic installation is intended to be a door to the subconscious," explains Olina. "The piece takes viewers from the depths of a foggy alien forest to the bottoms of waters to the heights of heaven."

Die im neunten Stock eines Hochhauses im zentralen Distrikt von Hongkong gelegene Cristal Bar wurde 2009 mit dem Forum Aid Award ausgezeichnet. Die Jury begründete dies wie folgt: „Da jede verfügbare Fläche mit Olinas Grafiken versehen wurde, werden die Muster zu mehr als reiner Dekoration und erzeugen eine traumhafte Umgebung. Es ist eine einfache Idee, ein zweidimensionales Muster zum beherrschenden Merkmal eines dreidimensionalen Raums zu machen, aber das Ergebnis ist überwältigend." Katrin Olina sagt: „Ich betrachte dieses Projekt als Übertragung der Renaissancevorliebe für Wandgemälde in das 21. Jahrhundert. Es handelt sich nicht um einen Hintergrund, eine Tapete, sondern um etwas anderes. Es sind erzählte Geschichten im Raum." Sie verwendet 3M-Film- und Drucktechniken, um eine zusammenhängende grafische Fläche zu erzeugen, die die Gäste völlig in ihre Bildwelt eintauchen lässt. Die Bar besteht aus vier Bereichen – einem zentralen, in dem die Grafiken Algenformen und „hybride Wassergeschöpfe" zeigen, zwei anschließenden, in Rot gehaltenen Räumen und einem letzten mit türkisgrünen Wänden, die mit „Blumen" und „Federformen" überzogen sind. „Die grafische Ausstattung der Bar soll eine Tür zum Unterbewussten öffnen", erklärt Olina. „Die Bilder führen den Betrachter aus der Tiefe eines nebelhaften, außerirdischen Waldes auf den Grund der Gewässer und in himmlische Höhen."

Installé au neuvième étage d'un gratte-ciel du centre de Hongkong, le Cristal Bar a remporté le prix du Forum AID 2009, accompagné de ce commentaire du jury : « Chaque surface disponible étant recouverte des compositions graphiques d'Olina, les motifs deviennent bien davantage qu'une simple décoration et créent un environnement éthéré dans lequel on peut s'immerger. C'est une idée simple pour faire d'un motif bidimensionnel l'élément dominant d'un espace tridimensionnel, mais le résultat est frappant. » « Pour moi ce projet se rapproche des pratiques de la Renaissance sur les fresques murales, que j'introduis au XXIᵉ siècle. Ce n'est pas un fond, ce n'est pas du papier peint, c'est quelque chose d'autre. C'est faire raconter une histoire par le lieu », explique Katrin Olina. Elle a utilisé un film et une technologie d'impression 3M pour créer une surface graphique continue qui plonge totalement les clients dans son imagerie. Le bar est divisé en quatre zones : une zone centrale au décor à base de formes d'algues et de « créature aquatiques hybrides », deux salles adjacentes de tonalité rouge, et une zone à murs vert turquoise décorée de « formes de fleurs et de plumes ». « L'installation graphique du bar se propose d'ouvrir une porte au subconscient », explique l'artiste. « Il emporte les spectateurs des profondeurs d'une forêt extraterrestre brumeuse vers le fond des eaux et les sommets du paradis… »

The entire décor of the Cristal Bar is by Katrin Olina. The furniture is by Michael Young.

Das gesamte Dekor der Cristal Bar stammt von Katrin Olina, die Möblierung von Michael Young.

La totalité du décor du Cristal Bar est signée Katrin Olina. Le mobilier est de Michael Young.

The décor occupies the entire space, walls, ceiling, and even floors, transporting visitors into the imaginary world of Katrin Olina.

Das Dekor überzieht den gesamten Raum, Wände, Decke und sogar den Boden, und entführt die Besucher in Katrin Olinas Fantasiewelt.

Le décor qui occupe la totalité de l'espace, plafonds et sols compris, transporte les clients dans le monde imaginaire de Katrin Olina.

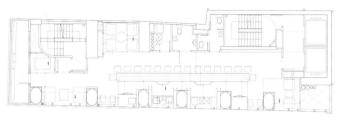

Strong colors ranging from greens to reds characterize the space and take on a life of their own, seemingly giving depth and movement to flat surfaces.

Die lebhaften Farben von Grün bis Rot prägen den Raum und übernehmen eine eigenständige Rolle; sie verleihen den ebenen Flächen Tiefe und Lebendigkeit.

L'espace se caractérise par des couleurs fortes – du rouge au vert – qui semblent mener leur vie propre et apportent de la profondeur et du mouvement aux surfaces planes.

OLSSONLYCKEFORS ARKITEKTER

OlssonLyckefors Arkitekter
Södra Viktoriagatan 44 A
41130 Göteborg
Sweden

Tel: +46 31 20 30 62
Fax: +46 31 20 30 61
E-mail: info@olssonlyckefors.se
Web: www.olssonlyckefors.se

Johan Olsson was born in 1972. He studied at the School of Architecture in Eindhoven (The Netherlands, 2004), founding **OLSSONLYCKEFORS** the year of his graduation. Andreas Lyckefors studied at the Chalmers Tekniska Högskola in Göteborg (Sweden, 1998) and received his M.Arch degree from the Technical University of Delft (The Netherlands, 2005). He worked briefly in the offices of Wingårdhs in Göteborg (1998) and OMA in Rotterdam (2003) before cofounding OlssonLyckefors in 2004. Their work includes the Peacock Dinner Clubs in Göteborg and Stockholm published here (2006 and 2007); a private house at Orust; the Taste International Restaurant (Göteborg, 2007); Villa Fördäcket (Göteborg, 2008); and Villa Skarenhed (Göteborg, 2008). Current work includes an office building in Karlstad; and an urban art space and pedestrian bridge in central Göteborg, all in Sweden. In 2007, they also designed the "Homeless" exhibition at Göteborg City Museum in collaboration with Nicklas Hultman. As the architects state: "The overall purpose of the office is not to specialize, because type or size doesn't really matter."

Der 1972 geborene Johan Olsson studierte Architektur in Eindhoven (Niederlande, 2004) und gründete **OLSSONLYCKEFORS** im Jahr seines Abschlusses. Andreas Lyckefors studierte an der Chalmers Tekniska Högskola in Göteborg (Schweden, 1998) und erhielt seinen M. Arch. an der Technischen Universität Delft (Niederlande, 2005). Für kurze Zeit arbeitete er in den Büros Wingårdhs in Göteborg (1998) sowie OMA in Rotterdam (2003) und gründete dann zusammen mit Olsson im Jahr 2004 OlssonLyckefors. Zu ihren Arbeiten zählen die Peacock Dinner Clubs in Göteborg und Stockholm, hier vorgestellt (2006 bzw. 2007), ein Privathaus in Orust, das Restaurant Taste International (Göteborg, 2007) sowie die Villen Fördäcket (Göteborg, 2008) und Skarenhed (Göteborg, 2008). Zu ihren aktuellen Planungen gehören ein Bürogebäude in Karlstad sowie ein städtischer Kunstbereich und eine Fußgängerbrücke im Zentrum von Göteborg, alle in Schweden. 2007 gestalteten sie auch die Ausstellung „Homeless" im Stadtmuseum Göteborg in Zusammenarbeit mit Nicklas Hultman. Wie die Architekten erklären, „ist das Gesamtziel des Büros nicht die Spezialisierung, weil Typen oder Größen eigentlich keine Rolle spielen".

Né in 1972, Johan Olsson a étudié à l'École d'architecture d'Eindhoven (Pays-Bas, 2004) et fondé **OLSSONLYCKEFORS** l'année de son diplôme. Andreas Lyckefors a étudié à la Chalmers Tekniska Högskola à Göteborg (Suède, 1998) et a passé son M.Arch à l'Université polytechnique de Delft (Pays-Bas, 2005). Il a brièvement travaillé dans les agences Wingårdhs à Göteborg (1998) et OMA à Rotterdam (2003) avant de cofonder OlssonLyckefors en 2004. Parmi les réalisations de l'agence : les Peacock Dinner Clubs à Göteborg et Stockholm publiés ici (2006 et 2007) ; une résidence privée à Orust ; le restaurant Taste International (Göteborg, 2007) ; la villa Fördäcket (Göteborg, 2008) ; et la villa Skarenhed (Göteborg, 2008). Les architectes travaillent actuellement sur un immeuble de bureaux à Karlstad ainsi qu'un espace d'art urbain et une passerelle piétonnière dans le centre de Göteborg. En 2007, ils ont également conçu l'exposition «Homeless» au musée municipal de Göteborg, en collaboration avec Nicklas Hultman. Les architectes précisent : «L'objectif de l'agence n'est pas de se spécialiser, car la typologie ou l'échelle n'ont pas réellement d'importance.»

PEACOCK DINNER CLUB

Göteborg, Sweden, 2006

Kunsportsavenyn 21, 41136 Göteborg, Sweden, +46 31 13 88 55, www.peacockdinnerclub.com/hamngatan
Area: 300 m². Client: Peacock Dinner Club. Cost: €300 000
Team: Frida Sjöstam (Project Architect)

The wall patterns were designed by Nicklas Hultman (Aröd Snickeri). Seating is designed by OlssonLyckefors (Aröd Snickeri).

Das Dekor der Wand wurde von Nicklas Hultman entworfen (Aröd Snickeri), die Sitze stammen von OlssonLyckefors (Aröd Snickeri).

Le décor des murs a été créé par Nicklas Hultman (Aröd Snickeri). Les sièges sont de OlssonLyckefors (Aröd Snickeri).

Right, an overall plan of the Club with the fan or peacock-tail pattern in evidence in the seating arrangements.

Rechts: Gesamtplan des Klubs, das Fächer- oder Pfauenschwanzmuster wird bei der Anordnung der Sitze deutlich.

À droite, une vue générale du club qui met en évidence la disposition en éventail des grandes banquettes.

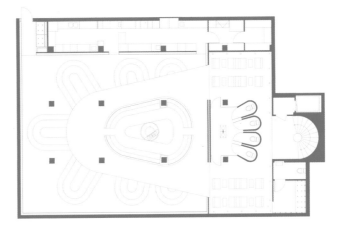

Once known as the Blue Peacock, this nightclub located underground on one of the main commercial avenues of Göteborg went out of business and was empty for seven years before a group of young businessmen who had experience in bars decided to revive it. Andreas Lyckefors explains: "They wanted a new dining concept, a restaurant and bar that seamlessly translate into a vibrating dancing scene as the night advances. The challenge was to create an exclusive restaurant but also a space that could become a house club later in the evening. In the end we put together a simple concept in an afternoon. We took a picture, cut it out and put it on a plan, elevating parts for seating around a lower central area, to be used for dancing later." Their design includes a white resin floor and a gold-laminated bar backed by a gold-sequined design. Black leather booths are arranged around the bar in the form of a peacock's tail, echoing the graphic design for the club created by Nicklas Hultman. The Peacock Club accommodates 70 people for dinner and up to 300 when it is used as a nightclub, with a minimal number of changes necessary in the décor. A lighting system that allows colors to change as the evening progresses is also part of the scheme.

Dieser früher unter dem Namen Blue Peacock bekannte Nachtklub liegt unter einer der Hauptgeschäftsstraßen Göteborgs. Er wurde geschlossen und stand sieben Jahre leer, bevor eine Gruppe junger Geschäftsleute mit Erfahrung im Barbetrieb beschloss, ihn wiederaufleben zu lassen. Andreas Lyckefors erklärt: "Sie wünschten ein neues Gastronomiekonzept, ein Restaurant und eine Bar, die sich im Verlauf der Nacht nahtlos in ein lebendiges Tanzlokal verwandeln. Die Herausforderung bestand darin, ein exklusives Restaurant, aber auch einen Raum zu schaffen, der am späten Abend zu einem Tanzklub werden kann. Schließlich stellten wir an einem Nachmittag ein einfaches Konzept zusammen. Wir nahmen ein Bild, schnitten es aus und legten es auf einen Grundriss, von dem wir Teile mit Sitzplätzen erhöht um einen zentralen, tiefer gelegenen Bereich anordneten, der später als Tanzfläche dienen konnte." Ihr Entwurf besteht aus einem weißen Kunstharzboden und einer in Gold beschichteten Bar in einem mit Goldpailletten überzogenen Raum. Schwarze Ledersitzgruppen sind in Form eines Pfauenschwanzes um die Bar angeordnet unter Bezugnahme auf das grafische Erscheinungsbild des Klubs von Nicklas Hultman. Der Peacock Club fasst 70 Personen zum Essen und bis zu 300, wenn er als Nachtklub genutzt wird, wobei nur geringe Veränderungen in der Ausstattung notwendig sind. Ein Beleuchtungssystem mit im Verlauf des Abends veränderlichen Farben gehört ebenfalls zum Entwurf.

Jadis connu sous le nom de Blue Peacock, ce club de nuit situé sous l'une des principales artères commerciales de Göteborg fut abandonné pendant sept ans avant qu'un groupe de jeunes hommes d'affaires qui avait l'expérience des bars décide de lui redonner vie. Andreas Lyckefors explique le projet : « Les commanditaires souhaitaient un nouveau concept de restauration, un bar restaurant qui, sans rupture trop marquée, se transforme en lieu de danse animé au fur et à mesure de l'avancée de la nuit. L'enjeu était de créer un restaurant exclusif, mais aussi un espace qui puisse servir de club de house music en fin de soirée. Finalement, nous avons trouvé un concept simple en un seul après-midi. Nous avons pris une photo, que nous avons découpée et posée sur un plan, en surélevant certaines parties où l'on puisse s'asseoir autour d'une zone centrale surbaissée, qui pouvait servir de piste de danse plus tard. » Le projet comprend également un sol en résine blanche et un bar en bois lamellé doré derrière lequel s'élève un élément décoratif recouvert de paillettes dorées. Les alcôves en cuir noir sont réparties autour du bar en forme de queue de paon, en écho à la décoration du club créé par Nicklas Hultman. Le Peacock Club peut recevoir soixante-dix personnes pour les repas et jusqu'à trois cents dans sa formule de night-club, avec un minimum de changements de décor. L'éclairage, dont les couleurs se modifient en cours de soirée, fait également partie du concept.

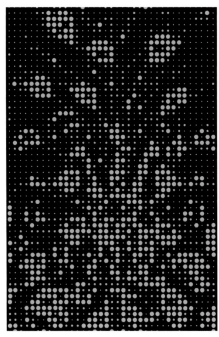

Bar stools are by Konstantin Grcic. The feel of the space is in good part generated by the surface treatments and in particular the wall patterns by Nicklas Hultman.

Die Barhocker stammen von Konstantin Grcic. Die Wirkung des Raums entsteht weitgehend durch die Oberflächenbehandlung und besonders das Wanddekor von Nicklas Hultman.

Les tabourets de bar sont de Konstantin Grcic. Le sentiment d'espace vient en grande partie du traitement des surfaces et en particulier des motifs muraux de Nicklas Hultman.

PEACOCK DINNER CLUB STOCKHOLM

Stockholm, Sweden, 2007

Tegnérgatan 37, 11161 Stockholm, Sweden, +46 31 13 88 55, www.peacockdinnerclub.com
Area: 450 m². Client: Peacock Club Stockholm. Cost: €500 000
Team: Frida Sjöstam (Project Architect)

As is the case in the Göteborg Club, here, seating is designed by Olsson-Lyckefors (Aröd Snickeri) and wall patterns by Nicklas Hultman (Aröd Snickeri).

Wie für den Klub in Göteborg wurden auch hierfür die Sitze von Olsson-Lyckefors (Aröd Snickeri) und das Wanddekor von Nicklas Hultman (Aröd Snickeri) entworfen.

Comme dans le club de Göteborg, les sièges ont été conçus par Olsson-Lyckefors (Aröd Snickeri) et le décor des murs par Nicklas Hultman (Aröd Snickeri).

The Peacock Dinner Club in Stockholm is underground like the one in Göteborg. Visitors enter the club via a descending ramp. "We wanted to create an environment that has an unrealistic and dreamlike sense to it," says Johan Olsson. Like the Göteborg facility, the Peacock Club Stockholm was designed to be converted from a restaurant into a nightclub later in the evening. The architects have used a system of perforated wood screens with LED lights that change in color as the evening progresses. Chain curtains and white plastered walls are also part of the décor. The club is centered around the bar, with seats that can be converted into the dance podium arranged in the shape of a horseshoe. Olsson says: "When Peacock is at its best it can be compared with a stormy ocean with people everywhere, dancing all over the place and on top of furniture. That is when the transformation is completed!"

Der Peacock Dinner Club in Stockholm liegt, ebenso wie der in Göteborg, im Untergeschoss. Gäste erreichen ihn über eine absteigende Rampe. „Wir wollten eine Umgebung schaffen, die unrealistisch und traumhaft wirkt", sagt Johan Olsson. Genau wie das Lokal in Göteborg wurde auch der Peacock Club in Stockholm so geplant, dass er am späteren Abend von einem Restaurant in einen Nachtklub verwandelt werden kann. Die Architekten verwendeten ein System aus gelochten, hölzernen Wandplatten mit LED-Leuchten, die ihre Farbe im Verlauf des Abends verändern. Kettenvorhänge und weiß verputzte Wände gehören ebenfalls zur Ausstattung. Die Sitzflächen des Klubs sind in Hufeisenform um die Bar im Zentrum angeordnet und können in eine Tanzfläche umgewandelt werden. Olsson sagt: „Peacock kann zu seiner besten Zeit mit einem stürmischen Ozean verglichen werden, wenn die Menschen überall, also auch auf den Möbeln tanzen. Dann ist die Umwandlung gelungen!"

Le Peacock Dinner Club de Stockholm est souterrain, comme celui de Göteborg. Les hôtes y accèdent par une rampe. « Nous souhaitions créer un environnement qui soit en quelque sorte irréel et marqué par le rêve », explique Johan Olsson. Comme à Göteborg encore une fois, le club devait pouvoir passer du statut de restaurant à celui de night-club plus tard dans la nuit. Les architectes ont utilisé un système d'écrans de bois perforés, parsemés d'ampoules LEDs, dont la lumière change au fil des heures. Des rideaux en maille métallique et des murs de plâtre blanc font également partie de ce décor. Le club est centré autour du bar et la zone des sièges se transforme en podium en forme de fer à cheval. Selon Olsson : « À ses meilleurs moments, le Peacock devient une sorte de tempête sur un océan, avec des gens de tous côtés, dansant n'importe où, y compris sur les meubles. C'est ce qui se produit lorsque la transformation est pleinement achevée. »

Wall patterns and the dark ambiance of the space create a mood for late evening entertainment.

Das Wanddekor und das dunkle Ambiente erzeugen eine geeignete Stimmung für nächtliche Unterhaltung.

Motifs muraux et ambiance sombre créent une atmosphère propice à la vie nocturne.

An overall view of the dining space (above) and the entrance to the Club (below). The tiles seen in the image below (right) are manufactured by e-kale.

Gesamtansicht des Speisesaals (oben) und Eingang zum Klub (unten). Die im Bild unten rechts erkennbaren Fliesen wurden von e-kale produziert.

Vue d'ensemble de la salle à manger (ci-dessus) et de l'entrée du club (ci-dessous). Le carrelage visible dans l'image ci-dessous (à droite) a été fabriqué par e-kale.

PACIFIC ENVIRONMENTS

Pacific Environments Architects
81 Grafton Road, Level 4
Grafton
Auckland
New Zealand

Tel: +64 9 308 0070
Fax: +64 9 308 0071
E-mail: info@pacificenvironments.co.nz
Web: www.pacificenvironments.co.nz

Born in 1959 in Wellington, New Zealand, Peter Eising obtained his B.Arch degree from the University of Auckland in 1984. From 1977 to 1984 he worked as a draftsman in the Ministry of Works and Development in Wellington. In 1988, he established Architects Patterson Limited with Andrew Patterson. He was a director of that firm until 2006, when he became the Director of **PACIFIC ENVIRONMENTS**. Lucy Gauntlett was born in 1981 in Melbourne, Australia. She graduated from the School of Architecture at Auckland University in 2004. She is also a professional photographer. Their work includes the Crater Lake House (Orakei, Auckland, 2004–06); Laidlaw Commercial Business Park (East Tamaki, Auckland, 2005–06); Tristar Gymnasium (Mount Roskill, Auckland, 2004–07); Saint Stephens Avenue Apartments (Parnell, Auckland, 2006–07); and the Yellow Tree House restaurant (Hokianga Harbour, Northland, 2008, published here). Their current work includes the Navy Training Facilities, Shakespeare's Point (Whangaparaoa Peninsula, Auckland, 2005–); and the Oceanic Artifacts Museum (Bora Bora, Tahiti, 2008–), all in New Zealand unless stated otherwise.

Der 1959 in Wellington, Neuseeland, geborene Peter Eising erwarb 1984 seinen B. Arch. an der University of Auckland. Von 1977 bis 1984 arbeitete er als Bauzeichner im Arbeits- und Entwicklungsministerium in Wellington. 1988 gründete er mit Andrew Patterson das Büro Architects Patterson Limited. Er war bis 2006 Leiter dieser Firma und übernahm dann die Leitung von **PACIFIC ENVIRONMENTS**. Lucy Gauntlett wurde 1981 in Melbourne, Australien, geboren und beendete 2004 ihr Studium an der Auckland University. Sie ist auch ausgebildete Fotografin. Zu den Werken des Büros gehören das Crater Lake House (Orakei, Auckland, 2004–06); der Gewerbepark Laidlaw (East Tamaki, Auckland, 2005–06); das Tristar Gymnasium (Mount Roskill, Auckland, 2004–07); die Apartments Saint Stephens Avenue (Parnell, Auckland, 2006–07) und das Restaurant Yellow Tree House (Hokianga Harbour, Northland, 2008, hier veröffentlicht). In Arbeit befinden sich die Marine-Ausbildungsanlage, Shakespeare's Point (Halbinsel Whangaparaoa, Auckland, 2005–) und das Oceanic Artifacts Museum (Bora Bora, Tahiti, 2008–), alle in Neuseeland, sofern nicht anders angegeben.

Né en 1959 à Wellington en Nouvelle-Zélande, Peter Eising est B.Arch de l'Université d'Auckland (1984). De 1977 à 1984, il a également travaillé comme dessinateur pour le Ministère des travaux et du développement à Wellington. En 1988, il fonde Architects Patterson Limited avec Andrew Patterson. Il dirige l'agence jusqu'en 2006, date à laquelle il devient directeur de **PACIFIC ENVIRONMENTS**. Lucy Gauntlett, née en 1981 à Melbourne (Australie), est diplômée de l'École d'architecture d'Auckland University (2004). Elle est également photographe professionnelle. Parmi leurs réalisations figurent : la maison de Crater Lake (Orakei, Auckland, 2004–06) ; le parc d'affaires Laidlaw (East Tamaki, Auckland, 2005–06) ; le gymnase Tristar (Mount Roskill, Auckland, 2004–07) ; un immeuble d'appartements sur Saint Stephens Avenue (Parnell, Auckland, 2006–07) et le Yellow Tree House Restaurant (Hokianga Harbour, Northland, 2008, publié ici). Ils travaillent actuellement à des installations de formation pour la Marine à Shakespeare's Point (Whangaparaoa Peninsula, Auckland, 2005–) et sur le projet du Musée des artefacts d'Océanie (Bora Bora, Tahiti, 2008–).

YELLOW TREE HOUSE

Hokianga Harbour, Northland, New Zealand, 2008

168 West Coast Road, RD1 Kohukohu Hokianga Northland, New Zealand, +64 9 405 5855, www.treehouse.co.nz
Floor Area: 44 m². Client: Yellow Pages Group. Cost: € 320 000

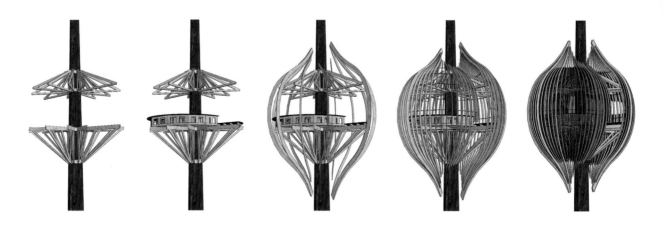

The surprising nautilis-shell design of the restaurant is fully visible in the drawings above, showing how the structure is wrapped around the tree.

Die erstaunliche Gestaltung des Restaurants in Form einer Nautilusschnecke ist in den Zeichnungen oben gut erkennbar; sie zeigen, wie das Gebäude sich um den Baum windet.

Ci-dessus : dessins de la structure de cet étonnant restaurant en forme de nautile et de son enveloppement autour du tronc d'un arbre.

The architects explain: "It's not often that a commission to design a tree house is offered, so when Colenso BBDO—on behalf of Yellow Pages—briefed Pacific Environments Architects for a 'reality' TV advert for an off-the-wall functioning restaurant, Pacific Environments jumped at the opportunity." The concept of this structure was to find all of the products and services required through Yellow Pages listings. A 40-meter-high redwood tree, 1.7 meters in diameter at its base, located north of Auckland, was selected for the project. The architects describe the site, in an open meadow near a stream at the edge of the woods, as "enchanted." Their design "has loose similarities to a sea shell with the open ends spiraling to the center. It's the tree house we all dreamed of as children but could only do as an adult fantasy." The access to the restaurant is through a 60-meter tree-top walkway. Despite its unexpected location, the restaurant seats 18 people and staff, and includes a bar. The architects also had to take into account camera angles for the advertisements to be filmed there. Kitchen and toilet facilities are located at ground level. The split-level floor of the restaurant is set no less than 10 meters above the ground. The structure was completed in December 2008.

Die Architekten erklären: „Es passiert nicht oft, dass einem der Entwurf für ein Baumhaus angeboten wird. Pacific Environments Architects ergriffen daher sofort die Gelegenheit, als Colenso BBDO ihnen – im Namen von Yellow Pages – den Auftrag für ein schräges, für einen ‚Reality-TV'-Spot vorgesehenes Restaurant erteilten." Das Konzept für dieses Gebäude bestand darin, alle erforderlichen Produkte und Dienstleistungen durch die Yellow Pages, die Gelben Seiten, zu finden. Für das Projekt wurde ein nördlich von Auckland stehender, 40 Meter hoher Redwoodbaum mit einem Basisdurchmesser von 1,7 Metern ausgewählt. Die Architekten schildern das an einem Fluss gelegene, offene Wiesengelände am Waldrand als „bezaubernd". Ihr Entwurf hat „entfernte Ähnlichkeit mit einer Meeresmuschel, deren Enden sich zum Mittelpunkt drehen. Es ist das Baumhaus, von dem wir alle als Kinder träumten, das wir aber erst als Erwachsenenfantasie verwirklichen konnten." Der Zugang zum Restaurant erfolgt über einen 60 m langen Fußweg auf die Höhe des Baumes. Trotz seiner ungewöhnlichen Lage bietet das Lokal Platz für 18 Gäste plus Bedienung und umfasst eine Bar. Die Architekten mussten auch die Position der Kamera für die Werbeaufnahmen berücksichtigen. Küche und Toiletten befinden sich auf Geländehöhe. Das Split-Level-Geschoss des Restaurants liegt 10 Meter über dem Boden. Im Dezember 2008 wurde das Gebäude fertiggestellt.

Dans leur présentation de ce projet, les architectes expliquent : « Il est rare de se voir proposer la commande d'une maison dans les arbres et lorsque l'agence Colins BBDO – pour leur client les Yellow Pages – nous a briefés pour une publicité pour la télévision autour d'une idée de restaurant suspendu, nous avons sauté sur cette opportunité. » Le concept de départ était de trouver dans les « Pages jaunes » tous les produits et services requis par la construction. Un arbre (redwood) de 40 m de haut et de 1,7 m de diamètre à sa base, a été repéré au nord d'Auckland et sélectionné pour l'opération. Les architectes présentent le site – une prairie ouverte au bord d'un ruisseau à la lisière des bois – comme un « lieu enchanté. » Leurs plans « présentent certaines similarités avec un coquillage en forme de spirale ouverte. C'est la maison dans les arbres dont nous avons tous rêvé quand nous étions enfants mais que nous ne pouvons réaliser que comme une fantaisie d'adulte. » L'accès au restaurant se fait par une passerelle de 60 m de long suspendue dans le haut des arbres. Malgré cette situation surprenante, le restaurant peut recevoir dix-huit personnes (clients et personnel) et comprend également un bar. Les architectes ont également dû prendre en compte les angles de prise de vue des caméras pour le tournage du film publicitaire prévu. La cuisine et les toilettes se trouvent au rez-de-chaussée. Le plancher à deux niveaux du restaurant se trouve à 10 m au-dessus du sol. L'ensemble a été achevé en décembre 2008.

Daylight views of the Yellow Tree
House and its dining space show its
open, airy design.

*Die Tageslichtaufnahmen des Yellow
Tree House und der Speiseraum zeigen die offene, luftige Gestaltung.*

*Vue de jour de la Yellow Tree House
et de l'espace des repas montrant
son aspect ouvert et aérien.*

Lighting is by ECC Lighting (Auckland), and acrylic floor lighting by PSP (Auckland). In these night views, the restaurant takes on an almost magical presence. Right, the architects' sketches of the structure.

Die Beleuchtung wurde von ECC Lighting (Auckland) ausgeführt, die Bodenbeleuchtung aus Acryl von PSP (Auckland). Auf diesen Nachtaufnahmen zeigt das Restaurant eine fast magische Präsenz. Rechts: Skizzen der Architekten vom Gebäude.

L'éclairage est de ECC Lighting (Auckland) et les spots de sol en acrylique de PSP (Auckland). Dans ces vues nocturnes, le restaurant projette une présence presque magique. À droite, des croquis structurels des architectes.

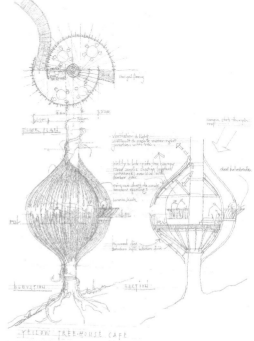

PENTAGRAM

Pentagram
11 Needham Road
London W11 2RP
UK

Tel: +44 207 229 3477
Fax: +44 207 727 9932
E-mail: email@pentagram.co.uk
Web: www.pentagram.com

PENTAGRAM is a design studio founded in 1972 by Alan Fletcher, Theo Crosby, Colin Forbes, Kenneth Grange, and Mervyn Kurlansky and currently has 17 design partners. Pentagram works in graphic design, identity, architecture, interiors, and products. They have designed packaging and products for companies such as Tesco, Boots, 3Com, Swatch, Tiffany & Co, Dell, Netgear, Nike, and Timex. They have also developed identities for Citibank, United Airlines, and the Co-Operative brand in the UK, as well as updating the visual identity of Saks Fifth Avenue. William Russell, who was responsible for the interiors of matter (London, UK, 2008, published here) studied architecture at the University of Newcastle-upon-Tyne and the Royal College of Art (RCA), working in Hong Kong for commercial architects RMJM between degrees. Having graduated from the RCA, he set up practice with David Adjaye, before establishing William Russell Architecture & Design in 2000. In 2005, he joined Pentagram's London office as a partner. Angus Hyland, who did the graphic design for matter, studied at the London College of Printing and the RCA. He graduated with an M. A. (RCA) in 1988. He ran his own studio in Soho for 10 years, working on a variety of projects, including book publishing, identities, fashion campaigns, commercials, record sleeves, and information design. In 1998, he became a partner in Pentagram's London offices.

PENTAGRAM ist ein Designstudio, das 1972 von Alan Fletcher, Theo Crosby, Colin Forbes, Kenneth Grange und Mervyn Kurlansky gegründet wurde und gegenwärtig 17 Designer beschäftigt. Pentagram arbeitet in den Bereichen Grafik, Image, Architektur, Innenausstattung und Produktgestaltung. Das Studio hat Verpackungen und Produkte für Firmen wie Tesco, Boots, 3Com, Swatch, Tiffany & Co, Dell, Netgear, Nike und Timex entworfen und grafische Erscheinungsbilder für Citibank, United Airlines und die Marke Co-Operative in Großbritannien gestaltet sowie dasjenige von Saks Fifth Avenue modernisiert. William Russell, der für die Innenausstattung von matter verantwortlich war (London, 2008, hier veröffentlicht), studierte Architektur an der University of Newcastle-upon-Tyne und am Royal College of Art (RCA); zwischendurch arbeitete er in Hongkong für das im kommerziellen Bereich tätige Architekturbüro RMJM. Nach Abschluss seiner Studien am RCA gründete er ein Büro zusammen mit David Adjaye und danach, im Jahr 2000, William Russell Architecture & Design. 2005 ging er als Partner zum Londoner Büro von Pentagram. Angus Hyland, der das grafische Erscheinungsbild für matter gestaltete, studierte am London College of Printing und am RCA. 1988 schloss er seine Studien mit einem M. A. vom RCA ab. Zehn Jahre lang unterhielt er ein eigenes Atelier in Soho und arbeitete an verschiedenen Projekten, u. a. verlegte er Bücher, gestaltete grafische Erscheinungsbilder, Werbekampagnen für Mode- und andere Firmen, Plattencover und Prospekte. 1998 wurde er Partner von Pentagram in London.

PENTAGRAM est un studio de design fondé en 1972 par Alan Fletcher, Theo Crosby, Colin Forbes, Kenneth Grange et Mervyn Kurlansky, qui compte actuellement dix-sept partenaires. Pentagram intervient dans les domaines du design graphique, de l'identité institutionnelle, de l'architecture, de l'architecture intérieure et du produit. L'agence a conçu des conditionnements et des produits pour des entreprises comme Tesco, Boots, 3Com, Swatch, Tiffany & Co, Dell, Netgear, Nike et Timex. Elle a également travaillé sur l'identité de Citibank, United Airlines et de la marque Co-Operative en Grande-Bretagne, ainsi que sur la modernisation de l'identité visuelle de Saks Fifth Avenue. William Russell, responsable de l'aménagement de matter (Londres, G.-B., 2008, publié ici) a étudié l'architecture à l'Université de Newcastle-upon-Tyne et au Royal College of Art (RCA). Entre ses deux diplômes, il a travaillé à Hongkong pour l'agence d'architecture RMJM. Diplômé du RCA, il a monté une agence avec David Adjaye, avant de fonder William Russell Architecture & Design en 2000. En 2005, il a rejoint le bureau de Londres de Pentagram comme partenaire. Angus Hyland, responsable du design graphique de matter, a étudié au London College of Printing et au RCA. Il possède un M. A. (RCA, 1988). Il a dirigé son propre studio à Soho pendant dix ans, intervenant sur des projets variés dans les domaines de l'édition, de l'identité de marque, des campagnes de mode, des films commerciaux, des pochettes de disques et de la signalétique. Il est devenu partenaire de Pentagram à Londres en 1998.

MATTER

London, UK, 2008

The O2, Peninsula Square London, SE10 0DY, +44 207 549 6686, www.matterlondon.com
Area: 2423 m². Client: Koobric UK Ltd. Cost: not disclosed
Team: Angus Hyland, Sarah Adams, Masumi Briozzo

The entrance to matter is marked by a large-scale back-lit logo that clients pass through to gain admittance. The triple-height "BodyKinetic" dance floor is the main space of the facility, crossed over at the top by a thin steel bridge. Variable lighting effects and projections provide most of the color in matter. Bars are located on the ground and first floors. The first floor has an island zinc bar located near a second, smaller dance floor, while concrete is used freely for benches, and even a cast-in-place DJ booth. The second floor features another dance floor with LED panels mirrored by LED screens on the ceiling, generating "a truly immersive environment." VIP guests are admitted to a private mezzanine level that overlooks the main dance floor. matter is located in the O2 Arena, the former Millennium Dome on the Greenwich peninsula in southeast London.

Der Eingang zu matter ist durch ein großformatiges, hinterleuchtetes Logo gekennzeichnet, das die Gäste durchschreiten müssen, um eintreten zu können. Die Tanzfläche „BodyKinetic" in dreifacher Raumhöhe ist der Hauptbereich des Lokals, über den oben eine schmale Stahlbrücke führt. Variable Beleuchtungseffekte und Projektionen übernehmen den Großteil der Farbgebung in matter. Die Bars befinden sich im ebenerdig und im ersten Obergeschoss. Dort befindet sich eine Thekeninsel aus Zink an einer zweiten, kleineren Tanzfläche. Beton wurde großzügig verwendet: für die Bänke und sogar für die Kabine aus Ortbeton für den Diskjockey. Im zweiten Obergeschoss befindet sich eine weitere Tanzfläche mit LED-Tafeln, die sich in LED-Flächen an der Decke spiegeln und „eine wahrhaft unwirkliche Umgebung" erzeugen. VIPs haben Zugang zu einem privaten Zwischengeschoss, von dem aus man die Tanzfläche überblickt. Das Lokal befindet sich in der O2 Arena, dem früheren Millennium Dome, auf der Greenwich-Halbinsel im Südosten Londons.

L'entrée du matter est signalée par un grand logo rétroéclairé que traversent les clients avant d'être admis. La piste de danse body-kinetic constitue l'espace principal, surplombé d'une mince passerelle métallique. Des effets de lumière variables et des projections fournissent l'essentiel de l'atmosphère chromatique. Les bars sont situés au rez-de-chaussée et à l'étage. Ce dernier est équipé d'un bar en zinc en îlot à proximité d'une seconde piste de danse plus petite. Les banquettes sont en béton de même que la cabine du DJ, coulée sur place. Le second étage propose également une piste de danse éclairée par des panneaux de LEDs reflétés par des écrans à LEDs suspendus au plafond, ce qui crée « un environnement d'immersion totale ». Les hôtes VIP ont droit à une mezzanine privée qui domine la piste principale. Le matter se trouve dans la O2 Arena, l'ancien Dôme du millénaire sur la péninsule de Greenwich dans le sud-est de Londres.

Above, the entrance to the former Millennium Dome and matter with its logo visible both on the walkway and as a lit symbol at night.

Oben: Der Eingang zum früheren Millennium Dome und zu matter. Das Logo ist am Zugang und als beleuchtetes Symbol bei Nacht sichtbar.

Ci-dessus, l'entrée de l'ancien Millennium Dome et du matter dont le logo est présent à la fois au sol et en enseigne lumineuse sur la façade.

The bridge design is by Pentagram. The Jarrah hardwood flooring by Junckers was installed by PICA Flooring. The vast space of matter is visible in the axonometric drawing below.

Die Brücke wurde von Pentagram entworfen. Der Hartholzboden aus Jarrah von Junckers wurde von PICA Flooring verlegt. Den großen Raum des matter zeigt die Axonometrie unten.

La conception du pont est de Pentagram. Le sol en parquet de bois de jarrah de Junckers a été posé par PICA Flooring. Le dessin axonométrique témoigne des imposantes dimensions du matter.

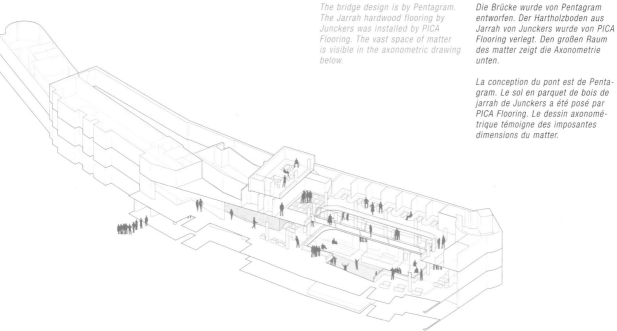

Leather upholstered banquette seating and diffused glass privacy screens designed by Pentagram. Left, a suspended metal bridge with metal mesh screens and floor-recessed RGB LED lights.

Die mit Leder gepolsterten Sitzbänke und die Trennwände aus Mattglas wurden von Pentagram entworfen. Links: Eine Hängebrücke aus Metall mit Metallgittern und in den Boden eingelassenen RGB-LED-Leuchten.

Les banquettes de cuir et les écrans de séparation en verre translucide ont été conçus par Pentagram. À gauche, une passerelle suspendue en métal à garde-corps en treillis métallique et éclairage par LEDs RGB intégrés au sol.

Precast GRC concrete cylinder tables, wall panels, stools, and bench seats by Pentagram. Folded sheet-steel powder-coated tables, acrylic cylinder pendent light with RGB LEDs, all by Pentagram. The tiled wall has RGB LED light tiles by Pilkington.

Die vorgefertigten zylinderförmigen Tische aus glasfaserbewehrtem Beton, Wandplatten, Hocker und Sitzbänke stammen von Pentagram, ebenso wie die Tische aus pulverbeschichtetem Stahlblech und die zylinderförmige Hängeleuchte aus Acryl mit RGB-LED-Modulen. Die geflieste Wand ist mit RGB-LED-Leuchten von Pilkington ausgestattet.

Tables cylindriques, panneaux muraux, tabourets et banc en béton préfabriqué GRC sont une création de Pentagram, de même que les tables en tôle d'acier pliée peinte par poudrage et les luminaires cylindriques suspendus en acryliques à LEDs RGB. Le mur carrelé est ponctué de carrelage lumineux de Pilkington à LEDs RGB.

PIERLUIGI PIU

Architetto Pierluigi Piu
Via Enrico Besta, 6
Cagliari 09129
Sardinia
Italy

Tel: +39 340 529 33 81
Fax: +39 178 276 98 02
E-mail: info@pierluigipiu.it
Web: www.pierluigipiu.it

PIERLUIGI PIU was born in Cagliari (Sardinia, Italy) in 1954. He studied at the University of Florence, Faculty of Architecture, and lived in that city until 1989. He created the design and production firm Atelier Proconsolo in Florence (1985–89). Since 1985, he has been an associate consultant for the Paris firm ACME Consultants (Association pour la Création et les Méthodes d'Evolution). He also worked with the Belgian architects Pierre Lallemand (Art & Build) and Steven Beckers, where he was directly involved in the complete refurbishment of the EEC Headquarters. Olivomare (London, UK, 2007, published here) won several prizes, including the "Russian International Architectural Award 2007" for its innovation in public interior spaces as well as the "International Design Award 2008" for interior design of commercial spaces. His most recent work (beginning in July 2008) is a new concept for the Mandarina Duck shops.

PIERLUIGI PIU wurde 1954 in Cagliari (Sardinien) geboren. Er studierte an der Architekturabteilung der Universität Florenz und lebte bis 1989 in dieser Stadt. Er gründete dort die Design- und Produktionsfirma Atelier Proconsolo (1985–89). Seit 1985 ist er assoziierter Berater der Pariser Firma ACME Consultants (Association pour la Création et les Méthodes d'Evolution). Er arbeitete auch mit den belgischen Architekten Pierre Lallemand (Art & Build) und Steven Beckers zusammen, mit denen er an der kompletten Umgestaltung des Hauptsitzes der Europäischen Kommission beteiligt war. Das Olivomare (London, 2007, hier veröffentlicht) gewann verschiedene Preise, darunter der Russian International Architectural Award 2007 für dessen innovativen öffentlichen Innenraum sowie der International Design Award 2008 für die Gestaltung von Gewerberäumen. Pius jüngste (im Juli 2008 begonnene) Arbeit ist ein neues Konzept für die Geschäfte der Mandarina-Duck-Kette.

PIERLUIGI PIU, né à Cagliari (Sardaigne, Italie) en 1954, a étudié à la Faculté d'architecture de l'Université de Florence où il a vécu jusqu'en 1989. Il a créé l'agence de design et de production Atelier Proconsolo à Florence (1985–89). Depuis 1985, il a été consultant associé pour l'agence parisienne ACME Consultants (Association pour la création et les méthodes d'évolution). Il a également travaillé avec les architectes belges Pierre Lallemand (Art & Build) et Steven Beckers, pour lesquels il a activement participé à la rénovation intégrale du siège de la Commission européenne. Le restaurant Olivomare (Londres, G.-B., 2007, publié ici) a remporté plusieurs prix, parmi lesquels le Russian International Architectural Award 2007 pour son innovation dans les espaces intérieurs publics ainsi que l'International Design Award 2008 pour le design intérieur des lieux commerciaux. Sa plus récente intervention (à partir de juillet 2008) a porté sur un nouveau concept de boutique pour Mandarina Duck.

OLIVOMARE RESTAURANT

London, UK, 2007

10 Lower Belgrave Street, London SW1W 0LJ, UK, +44 207 730 9022, www.olivorestaurants.com
Area: 109 m² dining room, bar, bathrooms. Client: Mauro Sanna, Oliveto & Olivo Ltd. Cost: £475 000
Collaboration: Zibi & Jack (Contractor), Jonathan Perrot (seats, cladding, doors),
Michael Blacker (Structural Engineer)

Lagò Chairs designed by Philippe Starck (Driade), Dissie tables by Llevore, Molina Alter (Arper), and Bigoli Lamps by Phay Halskada (Innermost) are used in the restaurant.

Die Lagò-Stühle wurden von Philippe Starck entworfen (Driade). Das Restaurant ist mit Dissie-Tischen von Llevore, Molina Alter (Arper), und Bigoli-Leuchten von Phay Halskada (Innermost) ausgestattet.

Petits fauteuils Lagò dessinés par Philippe Starck (Driade), tables Dissie de Llevore, Molina Alter (Arper) et luminaires Bigoli par Phay Halskada (Innermost).

Right, the exterior of Olivomare. Above, the fish wall pattern is a design by Pierluigi Piu based on drawings by M. C. Escher.

Rechts: Außenaufnahme des Olivomare. Oben: Das Fischmuster der Wand wurde von Pierluigi Piu entworfen; es basiert auf Zeichnungen von M. C. Escher.

À droite, la façade d'Olivomare. Ci-dessus, le motif aux poissons sur le mur a été créé par Pierluigi Piu à partir de dessins de M. C. Escher.

Located on Lower Belgrave Street in London, Olivomare is a seafood restaurant and its décor calls on sea-related themes. A side wall in the main dining room is clad in a pattern of laser-cut opaque laminated plastic that recalls the work of the artist M. C. Escher (1898–1972). Tubular, luminescent "tentacles" made of nylon mesh drop from the ceiling "evoking a stray shoal of jellyfish or anemones." Dizzie Chairs (Arper) and Lagò Chairs (Philippe Starck for Driade) are used. The basement kitchen is linked to the dining room via a staircase. The floors are finished in industrial opaque-white resin. The small rear dining room has abundant natural light brought in by a new skylight, while cladding here is characterized by a "wavy relief meant to evoke the sandy surface of the beach molded by the wind." The shop front was redesigned to integrate the neighboring shop, the Olivino Delicatessen, a complementary project that Pierluigi Piu also created, measuring just 40 square meters insofar as public space is concerned. A staircase protected by a glazed partition leads to the basement storage area, while a black-and-white layer of thick, opaque laminated plastic showing bottles and glasses occupies an entire wall. The area has a light-purple resin floor and a stainless-steel back counter with back-lit glazing and shelves for the merchandise (mostly wine).

Das in der Lower Belgrave Street in London gelegene Olivomare ist ein Fischrestaurant und sein Dekor auf Meeresthemen bezogen. Eine Seitenwand im großen Speisesaal ist mit einem Muster aus lasergeschnittenem opakem Kunststoff überzogen, das an die Werke des Künstlers M. C. Escher (1898–1972) erinnert. Röhrenförmige, leuchtende „Tentakel" aus Nylongeflecht hängen von der Decke und „erinnern an einen verirrten Schwarm von Quallen oder Seeanemonen". Dizzie-Stühle (Arper) und Lagò-Stühle (Philippe Starck für Driade) wurden ausgewählt. Die Küche im Untergeschoss ist über eine Treppe mit dem Speisesaal verbunden. Die Böden bestehen aus opakem, weißem Kunstharz. Der kleine, hintere Speiseraum erhält reichlich Tageslicht durch ein neues Oberlicht, während die Verkleidung hier als „welliges Relief, das an die vom Wind geformten Sandstrände erinnert", beschrieben wird. Die Vorderfront des Gebäudes wurde umgestaltet, um das benachbarte Geschäft, Olivino Delicatessen, einzubeziehen, ein zusätzlicher Auftrag – für eine Fläche von nur 40 m², was den öffentlichen Bereich betrifft –, der auch von Pierluigi Piu ausgeführt wurde. Eine von einer verglasten Trennwand geschützte Treppe führt zum Lagerraum im Untergeschoss, während ein schwarzweißer Überzug aus dickem Kunststoff die ganze Wand mit Flaschen und Gläsern bedeckt. Dieser Bereich hat einen hellvioletten Kunstharzboden und eine Theke aus Edelstahl mit hinterleuchteter Verglasung und Regalen für die Waren, vorwiegend Weine.

Situé Lower Belgrave Street à Londres, l'Olivomare est un restaurant de poissons dont le décor repose sur des thèmes liés à la mer. L'un des murs latéraux de la salle à manger principale est revêtu d'une composition de plaques de plastique lamellé opaque découpé au laser qui rappelle certaines œuvres de l'artiste M. C. Escher (1898–1972). Des « tentacules » tubulaires luminescentes en filets de Nylon descendent du plafond et « évoquent un « banc » de méduses ou d'anémones de mer ». Les sièges Dizie (Arper) et Lagò (Philippe Starck pour Driade) ont été choisis. La cuisine en sous-sol est reliée à la salle à manger par un escalier. Les sols sont en résine blanc opaque de finition industrielle. La petite salle à manger à l'arrière bénéficie d'un abondant éclairage naturel grâce à une nouvelle verrière. L'habillage de ses murs se caractérise par un « relief en vague qui rappelle le sable d'une plage modelée par le vent ». La partie donnant sur la rue a été redessinée pour intégrer une boutique voisine, l'Olivino Delicatessen – projet complémentaire également pris en charge par Pierluigi Piu – qui mesure à peine 40 m² dans sa partie accessible au public. Un escalier protégé par une séparation de verre conduit au stockage en sous-sol. Un mur entier est recouvert d'une épaisse strate de plastique noir et blanc montrant des bouteilles et des verres. Le sol est en résine violet pâle, le fond du comptoir est en en acier inoxydable à sections vitrées rétroéclairées et étagères de présentation des produits (essentiellement du vin).

The Corian, glass, and wood bar was custom-designed by Pierluigi Piu. The "Bottles and Glasses" (Tasselli/FAS) is also by the designer, as is the "Waves" design (Jonathan Perrot/ Elevation) for the walls (above).

Der Entwurf der Bar aus Corian, Glas und Holz stammt von Pierluigi Piu, ebenso der für „Bottles and Glasses" (Tasselli/FAS) und für „Waves" (Jonathan Perrot/Elevation) für die Wände (oben).

Le bar en Corian, verre et bois a été spécialement conçu par Pierluigi Piu, ainsi que les murs « bouteilles et verres » (Tasselli/FAS) et « vagues » (Jonathan Perrot/ Elevation).

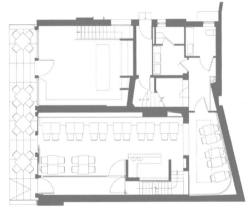

The "Coral Reef" wall design seen above and right is by Pierluigi Piu (Tasselli/FAS). These patterns contrast with the otherwise white décor and give it depth and presence.

Das oben und rechts abgebildete Muster „Coral Reef" stammt von Pierluigi Piu (Tasselli/FAS). Es bildet einen Kontrast zur ansonsten weißen Ausstattung und verleiht ihr Tiefe und Ausdruck.

Le mur « récif corallien » ci-dessus et à droite est de Pierluigi Piu (Tasselli/FAS). Ces motifs contrastent avec le décor par ailleurs très blanc tout en lui apportant une présence et une profondeur supplémentaires.

*The fish wall, left—and to the right,
a Slot washbasin (Antonio Lupi).*

*Das bereits vorher gezeigte Fisch-
muster – rechts das Waschbecken
Slot (Antonio Lupi).*

*Le « mur aux poissons » et, à droite,
le lavabo Slot (Antonio Lupi).*

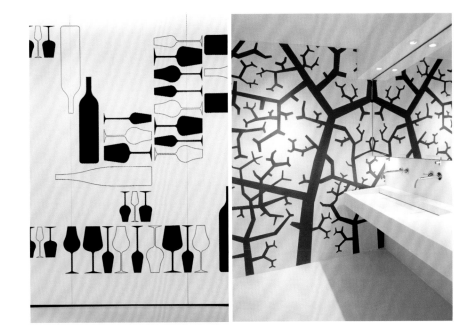

STUDIO ARNE QUINZE

Studio Arne Quinze
Walle 113a
8500 Kortrijk
Belgium

Tel: +32 56 24 05 90
Fax: +32 56 24 05 99
E-mail: info@studioarnequinze.tv
Web: www.studioarnequinze.tv

Born in 1971, Arne Quinze is the founder and artistic director of the Belgian conceptual architecture and design agency **STUDIO ARNE QUINZE** and furniture brand Quinze & Milan. While most biographies of architects or designers tend to emphasize their university degrees, Quinze's CV on his Web site reads in part: "Lacking a sterling education and shaped by the street life of his youth, Arne Quinze hung out with a motorcycle gang." Perhaps because he is self-taught, Arne Quinze seems to see no reason why design, architecture, and art cannot coexist and be created by the same person. His Primary Pouf (1999) was a commercial and aesthetic success, selling 15 000 pieces annually. Studio Arne Quinze were the designers of casual seating for the Koolhaas/OMA Seattle Central Library (Washington, 2004); a lounge and breakfast room for the Fox Hotel in Copenhagen (Denmark, 2005); furniture for the Stylesuite shop by Wiel Arets (Maastricht, The Netherlands, 2005); the Lime Bar (Porto Banuz, Spain, 2005); the renovation of a pharmacy in Oudenaarde (Belgium, 2006); and die kunstbar (Cologne, Germany, 2008, published here). Arne Quinze opened a large atelier and showroom in Kortrijk, Belgium (Gallery 113), in 2007. Quinze's 8000-square-meter wood installation Cityscape in Brussels remained in place for one year (2007–08).

Der 1971 geborene Arne Quinze ist der Gründer und künstlerische Leiter des belgischen Architektur- und Designbüros **STUDIO ARNE QUINZE** und der Möbelfirma Quinze & Milan. Während die meisten Architekten und Designer ihre akademischen Grade hervorheben, steht auf Quinzes Website in seinem Lebenslauf u. a.: „Arne Quinze verfügt über keine gediegene Ausbildung, sondern wurde in seiner Jugend vom Leben auf der Straße geprägt, er zog mit einer Motorradgang herum." Vielleicht weil er Autodidakt ist, gibt es für ihn keinen Grund, warum Design, Architektur und Kunst nicht von ein und derselben Person geschaffen werden können. Sein Hocker Primary Pouf (1999) war ein wirtschaftlicher und ästhetischer Erfolg; von ihm werden 15 000 Stück pro Jahr verkauft. Studio Arne Quinze gestaltete die bequemen Sitze in der von Koolhaas/OMA geplanten Zentralbibliothek in Seattle (Washington, 2004), die Lounge und den Frühstücksraum im Hotel Fox in Kopenhagen (2005), die Möblierung des Geschäfts Stylesuite von Wiel Arets (Maastricht, 2005), die Lime Bar (Porto Banuz, Spanien, 2005), den Umbau einer Apotheke in Oudenaarde (Belgien, 2006) und die kunstbar (Köln, 2008, hier veröffentlicht). 2007 eröffnete Arne Quinze ein großes Atelier mit Showroom in Kortrijk/Courtrai (Gallery 113). Quinzes 8000 m² große Holzinstallation „Cityscape" blieb ein ganzes Jahr hindurch in Brüssel stehen (2007/08).

Né en 1971, Arne Quinze est fondateur et directeur artistique de l'agence belge d'architecture conceptuelle et de design **STUDIO ARNE QUINZE** et de la marque de mobilier Quinze & Milan. Si la plupart des biographies d'architectes et de designers mettent en général l'accent sur les diplômes universitaires, le CV de Quinze publié sur son site Web est assez différent : « Sans éducation brillante, formé par la rue pendant sa jeunesse, Arne Quinze a traîné avec une bande de motards… » Peut-être du fait de cette formation autodidacte, il ne voit pas pourquoi le design, l'architecture et l'art ne pourraient coexister et être créés par la même personne. Son Primary Pouf (1999) a été un succès esthétique et commercial puisqu'il s'en vend chaque année quinze mille pièces. Studio Arne Quinze a dessiné les sièges de la Bibliothèque centrale de Seattle de Koolhaas/OMA (Washington, 2004) ; un salon et salle de petit déjeuner pour le Fox Hotel à Copenhague (Danemark, 2005) ; le mobilier pour la boutique Stylesuite de Wiel Arets (Maastricht, Pays-Bas, 2005) ; le Lime Bar (Porto Banuz, Espagne, 2005) ; la rénovation d'une pharmacie à Oudenaarde (Belgique, 2006) ; et die kunstbar (Cologne, Allemagne, 2008, publié ici). L'agence a ouvert un grand atelier et showroom, Gallery 113, à Courtrai (Belgique) en 2007. À Bruxelles, leur installation de 8000 m², en bois, Cityscape, est restée en place pendant une année (2007–08).

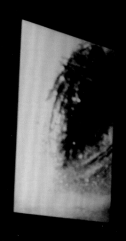

SURE

DISTRACTED

AN

EVERY

DIE KUNSTBAR

Cologne, Germany, 2008

Chargesheimerplatz 1, 50667 Cologne, Germany, +49 172 5279 845, www.diekunstbar.com
Area: 174 m². Client: not disclosed. Cost: not disclosed

The EYE. C.U installation consisting of 26 video screens is by Arne Quinze. Custom-designed Room 26 goatskin chairs, custom-designed benches and tables that make reference to wooden shipping crates are all manufactured by Quinze & Milan.

Die Installation „EYE. C.U" besteht aus 26 Videobildschirmen und stammt von Arne Quinze. Die speziell ange-fertigten Ziegenlederstühle Room 26, die Bänke und die Tische, die hölzer-nen Transportkisten ähneln, wurden alle von Quinze & Milan hergestellt.

L'installation d'Arne Quinze EYE. C.U se compose de vingt-six écrans vidéo. Les sièges Room 26 recouverts de peau de chèvre ainsi que les tables et bancs qui font référence à des caisses d'expédition en bois ont tous été fabriqués par Quinze & Milan.

Exterior view (right) and interior image
showing the EYE. C.U installation by
Arne Quinze.

Außenansicht (rechts) und Innenauf-
nahme der Installation „EYE. C.U"
von Arne Quinze.

Vue de l'extérieur (à droite) et intérieur de l'installation EYE. C.U d'Arne
Quinze.

This new bar is located near the central train station and cathedral of Cologne. After four years of planning, the concept for a bar, developed in collaboration with the private art association "Kölnischer Kunstverein," was brought to fruition. Each year, the association will select a different well-known artist to redesign the space or even the drink menu if they wish with the specific intention of not turning it into an art gallery, but rather a place where art lovers and others can meet. The first artist selected for die kunstbar is thus Arne Quinze. His installation, 'Eye. C.U', opened on November 14, 2008. Studio Arne Quinze used wooden boxes intended to transport art to cover the bar, in a metaphor for the "church not revealing what happens in the church as it is trying to hold on to its controlling role in society." In fact, with the proximity of Cologne cathedral, Arne Quinze dares passersby "to look for the seven differences between the church and 'EYE. C.U'. Once you come to think of it," he says, "there aren't many differences between the old religious predominance and the present domination of the camera. The religious suppressors in our society felt for centuries the necessity to keep people under their watch. Control and steering of the masses are keywords to keep a group under control for a desired social order. Nowadays cameras and digital techniques have superseded the church in an even more authoritative way. 'EYE. C.U' is the perfect symbolization of this process," he concludes.

Dieses neue Lokal liegt in der Nähe von Hauptbahnhof und Kölner Dom. Nach vier Jahren Planungszeit gelangte der in Zusammenarbeit mit dem privaten Kölnischen Kunstverein entstandene Entwurf zur Ausführung. Dieser Verein wird jedes Jahr einen anderen, bekannten Künstler auswählen für die Umgestaltung des Raums oder auch nur der Getränkekarte – in der erklärten Absicht, das Lokal nicht zu einer Kunstgalerie zu machen, sondern zu einem Ort der Begegnung für Kunstfreunde und andere Leute. Der erste für die kunstbar ausgewählte Künstler ist also Arne Quinze. Seine Installation „EYE. C.U" wurde am 14. November 2008 eröffnet. Studio Arne Quinze verwendete zum Transport von Kunstwerken bestimmte Holzkisten für die Ausstattung der Bar. Das steht als Metapher für „die Kirche, die um ihre Kontrolle über die Gesellschaft zu behalten, auch keinen Blick in ihr Inneres gewährt". In der Tat fordert Arne Quinze, durch die Nähe zum Dom bedingt, die Passanten auf, „nach den sieben Unterschieden zwischen der Kirche und „EYE. C.U" zu suchen. Wenn man darüber nachdenkt", sagt er, „gibt es keine großen Unterschiede zwischen der Vorherrschaft der Religion und der gegenwärtigen Herrschaft der Kamera. Über Jahrhunderte hielten es die religiösen Unterdrücker in unserer Gesellschaft für notwendig, die Menschen unter Beobachtung zu halten. Kontrolle und Steuerung der Massen sind die Stichworte, um eine Gruppe für eine angestrebte Gesellschaftsordnung zu kontrollieren. Heutzutage haben Kameras und digitale Techniken die Kirche in ihrer autoritären Haltung übertroffen „EYE. C.U" ist die perfekte Symbolisierung dieses Prozesses", folgert er.

Ce nouveau bar est situé près de la gare centrale et de la cathédrale de Cologne. C'est après quatre années de travaux préparatoires, que son concept mis au point avec l'association artistique Kölnischer Kunstverein a été mis en œuvre. Chaque année, en principe, l'association sélectionnera un artiste connu différent pour reconcevoir l'espace voire la carte des boissons. La contrainte est de ne pas transformer l'endroit en galerie d'art, mais en un lieu ou amateurs d'art et autres peuvent se retrouver. Le premier artiste choisi a été Arne Quinze. Son installation *EYE. C.U* a ouvert le 14 novembre 2008. Le Studio Arne Quinze s'est servi de caisses en bois pour le transport d'œuvres d'art pour habiller le bar, en une métaphore de « l'église, qui ne révèle pas ce qui se passe dans l'Église, tout en essayant de maintenir son contrôle sur la société ». Proche de la cathédrale de Cologne, Quinze incite les passants à « chercher les sept différences entre l'église et *EYE. C.U*. Quand vous y pensez bien, dit-il, il y a peu de différences entre la vieille domination de la religion et celle de la caméra aujourd'hui. Les oppresseurs religieux de notre société ont ressenti pendant des siècles la nécessité de garder les gens sous leur regard. Le contrôle et le pilotage des masses sont des mots clés pour maintenir le contrôle en vue de l'ordre social souhaité. Les caméras et les techniques numériques actuelles sont allées au-delà de l'Église de façon encore plus autoritaire. *EYE. C.U* est le symbole parfait de ce processus », conclut-il.

The goatskin chairs seen previously
and the EYE. C.U video installation by
Arne Quinze.

Die schon gezeigten Ziegenlederstühle und die Videoinstallation
„EYE. C.U" von Arne Quinze.

Les petits fauteuils tendus de peau
de chèvre et l'installation vidéo
EYE. C.U d'Arne Quinze.

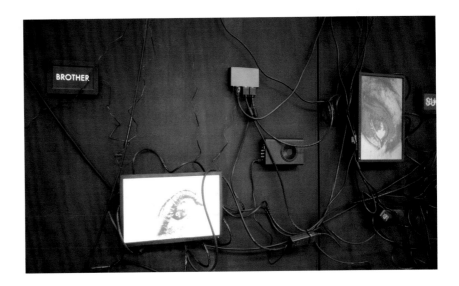

IMAAD RAHMOUNI

Imaad Rahmouni Architectures
8 Passage de la Bonne Graine
75011 Paris
France

Tel: +33 1 40 20 01 05
Fax: +33 1 40 21 01 07
E-mail: contact@imaadrahmouni.com
Web: www.imaadrahmouni.com

IMAAD RAHMOUNI received his degrees in Architecture from the École d'Architecture d'Alger (Algeria) in 1990, and the École d'Architecture Paris-Belleville (1995). From 1997 to 2000, he worked in the office of Philippe Starck (including work on the Taschen bookshop on the Rue de Buci in Paris). Recent work includes the Hotel Palais Namaskar (Marrakech, Morocco, 2007); offices for Publicis (Paris, France, 2007); the Klubb Rouge (Beijing, China, 2008, published here); the Hotel du Pacha (Marrakech, Morocco, 2008); and a competition for the urban design of a four-hectare area in Marrakech (Morocco, 2008). Current work includes the Hotel Ksar Menara (Marrakech, Morocco) and the Hotel G (Beijing, China).

IMAAD RAHMOUNI beendete 1990 sein Studium an der Ecole d'Architecture d'Alger (Algerien) und 1995 die Ecole d'Architecture Paris-Belleville. Von 1997 bis 2000 arbeitete er im Büro von Philippe Starck (u. a. an der Buchhandlung Taschen in der Rue de Buci in Paris). Zu seinen neueren Werken zählen das Hotel Palais Namaskar (Marrakesch, Marokko, 2007), Büros für Publicis (Paris, 2007), der Klubb Rouge (Peking, 2008, hier veröffentlicht), das Hotel du Pacha (Marrakesch, 2008) und ein städtebaulicher Wettbewerbsbeitrag für ein 4 ha großes Gelände in Marrakesch (2008). Aktuelle Projekte sind das Hotel Ksar Menara (Marrakesch) und das Hotel G (Peking).

IMAAD RAHMOUNI est diplômé en architecture de l'École d'architecture d'Alger (Algérie, 1990) et de l'École d'architecture Paris-Belleville (1995). De 1997 à 2000, il a travaillé pour Philippe Starck pour lequel il a collaboré au projet de la librairie Taschen, rue de Buci à Paris. Parmi ses travaux récents : l'hôtel Palais Namaskar (Marrakech, Maroc, 2007) ; des bureaux pour Publicis (Paris, 2007) ; the Klubb Rouge (Pékin, Chine, 2008, publié ici) ; l'Hôtel du Pacha (Marrakech, Maroc, 2008) ; la participation à un concours pour l'aménagement urbain d'un zone de 4 ha à Marrakech (Maroc, 2008). Il travaille actuellement sur les projets de l'hôtel Ksar Menara (Marrakech, Maroc) et de l'hôtel G (Pékin, Chine).

KLUBB ROUGE

Beijing, China, 2008

14th Floor, Block 3, China View, Gongti Donglu, Beijing, China, +86 10 6500 3333
Area: 1400 m². Clients: Mister Lim, N. Perrez. Cost: € 1.4 million

Located on the attic floor of the new China View Complex, this bar is centered around a light sculpture (designed and realized by the firm Andromeda) made of 650 irregular hand-blown Murano red glass spheres, 8000 LEDS, and 250 fiber-optic spotlights. Hanging from the ceiling over the main bar, the light fixture covers a total area of 88 square meters. The light generated by this sculpture is reflected in a steel plate, creating a "3D effect, contributing to creating an experience of immersion in the color red." The space has an opaque, gray resin floor, red mirrors on the bathroom walls, and furniture by Rahmouni, in beige and light brown leather and lacquered wood. A large wooden *mur à bougies* features an irregular geometric pattern of more than 100 candles. Opposite this wall, a large window allows guests to see the Chinese capital through a semi-transparent curtain. Seven fluidly shaped chandeliers in hand-blown red glass and a further six floor lamps complete the lighting installation. The Klubb also encompasses roof terraces and two mezzanines (one for a VIP area with a balcony that faces the main bar, and a cigar area, and one for Private Rooms).

Im Zentrum dieser im Dachgeschoss des neuen China View Complex gelegenen Bar befindet sich eine Lichtplastik aus 650 ungleichmäßigen, mundgeblasenen Kugeln aus rotem Muranoglas, 8000 LED-Modulen und 250 Strahlern aus optischen Fasern. Sie wurde von der Firma Andromeda gestaltet und ausgeführt. Dieses über der Haupttheke an der Decke hängende Element hat eine Oberfläche von insgesamt 88 m². Das von dieser Skulptur ausgehende Licht wird von einer Stahlplatte reflektiert, die „einen dreidimensionalen Effekt erzeugt und dazu beiträgt, dass man glaubt, in die Farbe Rot einzutauchen". Der Raum mit grauem Kunstharzboden ist mit Möbeln von Imaad Rahmouni aus beigefarbenem und hellbraunem Leder und lackiertem Holz möbliert. An den Toilettenwänden hängen rote Spiegel. Eine große, hölzerne „mur à bougies" zeigt ein unregelmäßiges geometrisches Muster aus über 100 Kerzen. Gegenüber von dieser Wand gewährt ein großes Fenster den Gästen durch einen halbtransparenten Vorhang Ausblick auf die chinesische Hauptstadt. Sieben schwungvoll geformte Kronleuchter aus mundgeblasenem rotem Glas und weitere sechs Stehlampen vervollständigen die Lichtinstallation. Der Klubb erstreckt sich auch auf Dachterrassen und zwei Mezzaningeschosse (eins als VIP-Bereich mit einem zur Haupttheke gerichteten Balkon und einem Raucherraum sowie eins für private Feiern).

Le plan de ce bar, situé au dernier étage du nouveau complexe China View, est centré sur une sculpture lumineuse – conçue et réalisée par la maison Andromeda –, composée de six cent cinquante sphères irrégulières soufflées à la bouche, en verre rouge de Murano, de huit mille LEDs et de deux cent cinquante points lumineux en fibre optique. Suspendue au plafond au-dessus du bar principal, cette structure recouvre une surface de 88 m². L'éclairage produit se reflète sur une plaque d'acier qui crée « un effet tridimensionnel, contribuant à générer une expérience d'immersion dans la couleur rouge ». Le sol est en résine opaque grise, des miroirs rouges ornent les murs des toilettes, et le mobilier dessiné par Imaad Rahmouni est en bois laqué et cuir beige et brun clair. Un grand « mur à bougies » en bois met en scène une centaine de bougies disposées selon un motif de forme irrégulière. Face à lui, une grande fenêtre permet aux clients d'apercevoir la capitale chinoise à travers un rideau semi-transparent. Sept chandeliers de forme fluide en verre soufflé rouge et six lampadaires de sol complètent l'éclairage. Le Klubb possède également deux terrasses et deux mezzanines, l'une destinée aux VIP – dotée d'un balcon face au bar principal et d'une pièce pour fumeurs de cigares –, et la seconde réservée à des salons privés.

The red chandeliers and main LED light sculpture (Andromeda, seen left and on the following double page) dominate the space and set its tone.

Die roten Kandelaber und die große LED-Lichtskulptur (Andromeda, links und auf der folgenden Doppelseite) beherrschen den Raum und prägen sein Erscheinungsbild.

Tous rouges, les lustres et la sculpture lumineuse à LEDs Andromeda (à gauche et double page suivante) dominent l'espace et donnent le ton général du décor.

Red lighting is diffused throughout
the space, giving it a warmth and
intimacy that befits the location.

Das rote, verstreute Licht wirkt warm
und intim und wertet den Raum auf.

L'éclairage rouge qui se diffuse
dans l'espace procure un sentiment
de chaleur et d'intimité qui convient
au lieu.

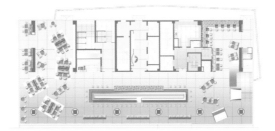

Floor plans show the disposition of the spaces and seating, with the central light sculpture (Andromeda) visible in the upper part of the photo below.

Die Grundrisse zeigen die Verteilung der Räume und Sitzgelegenheiten; die zentrale Lichtskulptur (Andromeda) ist im oberen Bereich der unteren Abbildung sichtbar.

Les plans montrent la disposition des espaces et des sièges. La sculpture lumineuse centrale Andromeda est visible en partie supérieure de la photo ci-dessous.

KARIM RASHID

*Karim Rashid Inc
357 West 17th Street
New York, NY 10011
USA*

*Tel: +1 212 929 8657
Fax: +1 212 929 0247
E-mail: office@karimrashid.com
Web: www.karimrashid.com*

The designer **KARIM RASHID** was born in Cairo, Egypt, in 1960. He received a B. A. in Industrial Design from Carleton University in Ottawa, Canada, in 1982 and completed postgraduate studies in Italy. He has created over 2500 objects for clients such as Alessi, Umbra, Prada, Issey Miyake, and Method. In explaining his approach, he refers to "sensual minimalism" or "affordable, democratic design for the masses." His work is represented in 15 museums worldwide and he has become a fixture in international awards for design. In March 2009, he stated: "I have 75 ongoing projects in over 35 different countries. Right now I am working on 18 different furniture collections, 3 lighting projects, a laptop, a line of luggage, a series of vibrators, a vodka bottle and a clothing line. I just finished the Prizotel in Bremen, the Market restaurant in Atlanta for Jean-Georges Vongerichten (published here), a retail store in Moscow, an airline lounge in Istanbul, a restaurant in NYC, a retrospective in Brazil, and an exhibition at the Museum of Arts and Design in New York. I am currently working on restaurants in Las Vegas, Singapore, and Portugal. I'm designing a casino in Serbia, condominiums in Russia, and a children's store in Moscow. My sixth book called KarimSpace featuring all my interior projects also releases this month (March 09)." He has also realized the Majik Café (Belgrade, Serbia, 2007–08, published here); and the Switch Restaurant (Dubai, UAE, 2009, published here).

Der Designer **KARIM RASHID** wurde 1960 in Kairo, Ägypten, geboren. Er erhielt 1982 seinen B. A. in Industriedesign an der Carleton University in Ottawa, Kanada, und absolvierte ein Postgraduate-Studium in Italien. Er hat über 2500 Objekte für Auftraggeber wie Alessi, Umbra, Prada, Issey Miyake und Method gestaltet. Seine Herangehensweise bezeichnet er als „sinnlichen Minimalismus" oder „erschwingliches, demokratisches Design für die Massen". Seine Arbeiten sind in 15 Museen weltweit ausgestellt, und er gehört zu den wiederholten Gewinnern internationaler Designpreise. Im März 2009 erklärte er: „Ich habe 75 Projekte in über 35 verschiedenen Ländern in Arbeit. Zurzeit arbeite ich an 18 verschiedenen Möbelserien, drei Beleuchtungsprojekten, einem Laptop, einer Gepäckserie, einer Serie von Vibratoren, einer Wodkaflasche und einer Modekollektion. Abgeschlossen habe ich gerade das Prizotel in Bremen, das Restaurant Market in Atlanta für Jean-Georges Vongerichten (hier veröffentlicht), ein Einzelhandelsgeschäft in Moskau, eine Flughafenlounge in Istanbul, ein Restaurant in New York City, eine Retrospektive in Brasilien und eine Ausstellung im Museum of Arts and Design in New York. Gegenwärtig arbeite ich an Restaurants in Las Vegas, Singapur und Portugal. Ich plane ein Kasino in Serbien, Eigentumswohnungen in Russland und ein Kinderkaufhaus in Moskau. Mein sechstes Buch mit dem Titel ‚KarimSpace', das alle meine Innenraumgestaltungen zeigt, wird diesen Monat (März 2009) ausgeliefert." Rashid hat auch das Café Majik (Belgrad, Serbien, 2007–08, hier veröffentlicht) und das Restaurant Switch (Dubai, Vereinigte Arabische Emirate, 2009, hier veröffentlicht) geplant und ausgeführt.

Le designer **KARIM RASHID** est né au Caire (Égypte) en 1960. Il a passé son B. A. de design industriel à Carleton University, Ottawa (Canada) en 1982 et achevé ses études supérieures en Italie. Il a créé plus de deux mille cinq cents objets pour des clients comme Alessi, Umbra, Prada, Issey Miyake et Method. Expliquant son approche, il se réfère à un « minimalisme sensuel » ou à un « design démocratique pour les masses, accessible ». Son travail est présent au sein de quinze musées dans le monde et il est devenu un habitué des prix internationaux de design. En mars 2009, il déclarait : « J'ai soixante-quinze projets en cours dans plus de trente-cinq pays. En ce moment, je travaille sur dix-huit lignes de meubles différentes, trois projets de luminaires, un ordinateur portable, une ligne de bagages, une série de vibrateurs, une bouteille de vodka et une ligne de vêtements. Je viens de terminer le Prizotel à Brême, le restaurant Market à Atlanta pour Jean-Georges Vongerichten (publié ici), un magasin à Moscou, un salon pour une compagnie aérienne à Istanbul, un restaurant à New York, une rétrospective au Brésil et une exposition au Museum of Arts and Design à New York. Je travaille aussi pour des restaurants à Las Vegas, Singapour et au Portugal. Je conçois un casino en Serbie, des appartements en Russie et un magasin pour enfants à Moscou. Mon sixième livre, intitulé *KarimSpace*, sur mes projets d'aménagement intérieur paraît également ce mois-ci (mars 09). » Par ailleurs, Karim Rashid a aussi réalisé le café Majik (Belgrade, Serbie, 2007–08, publié ici) et le restaurant Switch (Dubai, EAU, 2009, publié ici).

MAJIK CAFÉ

Belgrade, Serbia, 2007–08

Dzordza Vasingtona 38a, Belgrade, Serbia, +381 11 334 86 90, www.majikcafe.com
Area: 180 m². Client: Veselin Jevrosimovic. Cost: not disclosed

Karim Rashid explains that the design of the Majik Café restaurant in Belgrade stems from his philosophy of "creating a digipop digital nature and a seamless world that excites all the senses." Digital artwork made of RGB LED panels surrounds the bar, whose colors thus change continuously. A scrolling LED message board displays text messages sent by customers. Features such as profile mirrors with "data resonating from the eyes" in the restrooms or a full-length nude photo on the bathroom door ensure that every available space is used to render Majik dynamic and contemporary. The designer states: "The exterior is finished in polished stainless steel and mosaic tile. Icon-shaped windows and decorative ancient Serbian patterns are updated to create a kaleidoscopic, engaging, and inspiring fulgent space for lounging, dining, and drinking. The restaurant's message is East-meets-West digital freedom, where technology and new social behaviors are the global proponents of a new, singular, seamless world." The logo and branding of Majik are also by Karim Rashid.

Karim Rashid erläutert, dass der Entwurf für das Café Majik auf seiner Philosophie beruht, „ein digitales Digipop-Ambiente und eine ungetrübte Welt zu erschaffen, die alle Sinne ansprechen". Ein digitales Kunstwerk aus RGB-LED-Modulen umgibt die Bartheke, deren Farben sich ständig verändern. Eine LED-Informationstafel zeigt fortlaufend von den Besuchern übermittelte verbale Botschaften. Elemente wie Profilspiegel mit „Daten, die von den Augen ausgehen" im Waschraum oder ein Aktfoto in Lebensgröße an der Tür zu den Toiletten stellen sicher, dass jeder verfügbare Raum genutzt wurde, um Majik dynamisch und aktuell zu gestalten. Der Architekt erklärt: „Außen ist das Café mit poliertem Edelstahl und Mosaikfliesen verkleidet. Fenster in ungewöhnlichen Formen und dekorative alte serbische Muster werden benutzt, um einen kaleidoskopartigen, anregenden und inspirierenden, prächtigen Raum zum Verweilen, Speisen und Trinken zu bilden. Die Botschaft der Restaurants lautet: digitale Freiheit in der Begegnung von Ost und West, wobei Technologie und neue gesellschaftliche Verhaltensweisen die globalen Voraussetzungen für eine neue, einzigartige und grenzenlose Welt bilden." Auch das Logo und das grafische Erscheinungsbild des Majik stammen von Karim Rashid.

Karim Rashid explique que le projet du café restaurant Majik à Belgrade est issu de sa philosophie de « création d'une nature numérique « digipop » et d'un monde sans rupture qui exalte la totalité des sens ». Une œuvre d'art numérique en panneaux de LEDs RGB entoure le bar dont les couleurs varient en permanence. Un panneau à LEDs de messages défilants affiche des textos envoyés par les clients. De multiples détails, comme des miroirs en forme de profils « recevant des données en résonance du regard » dans les toilettes et une photo de nu toute hauteur sur leur porte, se multiplient pour faire du Majik un lieu dynamique et contemporain. « La façade extérieure est en acier inoxydable poli et mosaïque de carrelage. Des fenêtres en forme de cadres d'icônes et des motifs décoratifs serbes anciens ont été modernisés pour créer un espace kaléidoscopique resplendissant, chaleureux et motivant, où l'on vient se détendre, dîner et boire. Le message du restaurant est dans cette liberté de rencontre entre l'Orient et l'Occident quand la technologie et de nouveaux comportements sociaux deviennent les composants d'un monde neuf, singulier, sans rupture », ajoute Karim Rashid. Le logo et sa déclinaison sont également signés Karim Rashid.

Above, the exterior of the Majik Café. Right, Butterfly Chairs and Bokka Lamps, both by Karim Rashid (Magis) are used in the Café.

Oben: Außenansicht des Cafés Majik. Es ist mit Butterfly-Stühlen und Bokka-Leuchten, beide von Karim Rashid (Magis), ausgestattet (rechts).

Ci-dessus, l'extérieur du Majik Café. À droite, les sièges Butterfly et les lampes Bokka de Karim Rashid (Magis) sont très présents.

The custom-printed wallpaper is by Karim Rashid. Kant Stools by Karim Rashid (Casamania) and custom mirrors also by the designer can be seen above.

Die speziell hergestellte, bedruckte Tapete stammt von Karim Rashid. Oben sind die Kant-Hocker von Karim Rashid (Casamania) und die ebenfalls von ihm gestalteten Spiegel zu sehen.

Le papier peint a été spécialement dessiné par Karim Rashid. Ci-dessus, les tabourets Kant (Casamania) et les miroirs également créés par le designer.

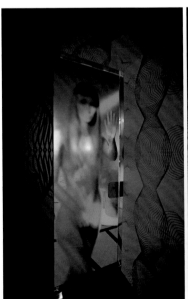
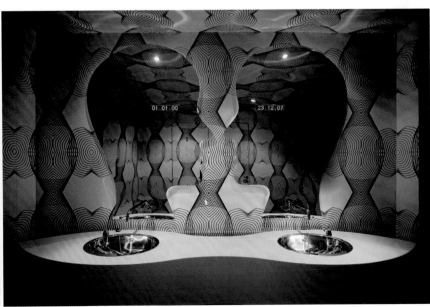

MARKET BY JEAN-GEORGES

Atlanta, Georgia, USA, 2008

Spice Market, W Atlanta Midtown, 188 14th Street, NE, Atlanta, GA 30361, USA, +1 404 549 5450, www.spicemarketatlanta.com
Area: 580 m². Client: Culinary Concepts by Jean-Georges. Cost: $1.35 million

Opened in November 2008, this two-level restaurant seats 200 and is located in the new W Atlanta-Buckhead Hotel. The client is the celebrity chef Jean-Georges Vongerichten. Karim Rashid states: "I designed Jean-Georges's Market to emulate stepping into the chic kitchen of a friend's house." He describes the space as "casual but artistic, minimal but human, sensual but informal." Undulating bamboo walls and a curved blue glass balustrade mark the main dining room. A Murano glass chandelier, organic cutouts in the walls, and a digital art mural in the stairway linking the two levels, mark the spaces. As Rashid states: "Market proves food and design are the two greatest connectors in our contemporary society." The bright colors and patterns that undulate through the space certainly give an impression of design continuity and an almost unworldly ethereality that seems typical of the current work of Karim Rashid.

Dieses zweigeschossige, im November 2008 eröffnete Restaurant fasst 200 Gäste und liegt im neuen W Atlanta-Buckhead Hotel. Bauherr ist der berühmte Küchenchef Jean-Georges Vongerichten. Karim Rashid berichtet: „Ich plante Jean-Georges' Market so, als betrete man die schicke Küche im Haus eines Freundes." Er beschreibt das Restaurant als „ungezwungen, aber künstlerisch, minimalistisch, aber menschlich, sinnlich, aber informell". Geschwungene Bambuswände und eine gekrümmte, blaue Glasbalustrade charakterisieren den großen Speisesaal. Ein Kronleuchter aus Muranoglas, organisch geformte Wandausschnitte und ein digitales Wandgemälde im Treppenhaus verbinden die beiden Ebenen und unterscheiden die Räume. Rashid erklärt: „Market beweist, dass Essen und Design die beiden großen Verbindungselemente unserer gegenwärtigen Gesellschaft darstellen." Die leuchtenden Farben und Muster, die durch den Raum schwingen, vermitteln zweifellos die Wirkung einer einheitlichen, fast überirdisch ätherischen Gestaltung, die offenbar für das aktuelle Werk von Karim Rashid typisch ist.

Ouvert en novembre 2008, ce restaurant de deux cents couverts répartis sur deux niveaux est situé à l'intérieur du nouvel W Atlanta-Buckhead Hotel. Le client est le célèbre chef Jean-Georges Vongerichten. Karim Rashid a précisé : « J'ai conçu le Market pour Jean-Georges, et pour donner l'impression d'entrer dans la cuisine chic d'une maison d'amis. » Il présente l'espace comme « simple mais artistique, minimaliste mais humain, sensuel mais informel ». Les murs ondulés en bambou et une balustrade incurvée en verre bleu personnalisent la salle à manger principale ainsi qu'un lustre en verre de Murano, des découpes de forme organique dans les murs et une fresque numérique murale dans l'escalier qui relie les deux niveaux. Comme le précise le designer : « Le Market prouve que la nourriture et le design sont les deux plus importants liens sociaux de la société contemporaine. » En parcourant cet espace, les couleurs vives et les motifs ondulants donnent une impression de continuité, venant souligner le caractère éthéré presque irréel qui semble caractéristique du travail récent de Karim Rashid.

Carpeting, tables, and wallpaper were all custom-designed by Karim Rashid for Market. The Alo Chairs (Magis) are also by the designer.

Teppich, Tische und Tapete wurden eigens für Market von Karim Rashid entworfen. Auch die Alo-Stühle (Magis) stammen von ihm.

La moquette, les tables et le papier peint ont été spécialement conçus par Karim Rashid pour le Market. Les fauteuils Alo (Magis) sont également dus au designer.

SWITCH RESTAURANT

Dubai, United Arab Emirates, 2009

The Dubai Mall, P.O. Box 113444, Dubai, UAE, +971 4 339 9131, www.meswitch.com
Area: 200 m². Client: Albassam Group. Cost: not disclosed

Located in the Dubai Mall, this restaurant and lounge seats 97 customers. It opened in February 2009. Karim Rashid states: "I wanted Switch to be a strong, symmetrical vision composed of a continuous, undulating wall that wraps around the space. The design creates an interesting texture for light and shadow, evoking the sand dunes in the desert. It is a unique environment of symmetry and balance that completely envelops the guests. The back-lit ceiling artwork consists of stylized inspirational Arabic phrases. The continuous wave seating provides an efficient and dynamic operating system. I wanted to create a powerful, clean space that offers a beautiful perspective. I wanted to create an oasis free from chaos." The wave and pattern effects employed by the designer create an almost surreal distance from ordinary spaces, transporting guests into what would appear to be another dimension, where food and design meet somewhere apart from the routine of daily existence.

Dieses Restaurant mit Lounge in der Dubai Mall hat Platz für 97 Gäste. Es wurde im Februar 2009 eröffnet. Karim Rashid sagt dazu: „Ich wollte Switch ein starkes, symmetrisches Erscheinungsbild geben, das aus einer durchgehenden, wellenförmigen Mauer besteht, die den Raum umgibt. Die Gestaltung bildet eine interessante Struktur, die Licht und Schatten aufnimmt und an Sanddünen in der Wüste erinnert. Es ist eine einzigartige Umgebung aus Symmetrie und Balance, die die Gäste völlig gefangennimmt. Das hinterleuchtete Kunstwerk an der Decke besteht aus stilisierten arabischen Sätzen. Die durchgehenden Wellensitze funktionieren als effizientes und dynamisches System. Ich wollte einen eindrucksvollen, klaren Raum schaffen, der eine schöne Aussicht bietet. Ich wollte eine Oase schaffen, die frei von Chaos ist." Die vom Architekten genutzten Effekte der Welle und des Dekors erzeugen eine fast surreale Distanz zu gewöhnlichen Räumen und versetzen die Besucher sozusagen in eine andere Dimension, in der sich Essen und Gestaltung irgendwo fern von der Routine des täglichen Lebens begegnen.

Ce restaurant-lounge de quatre-vingt dix-sept couverts, qui a ouvert en février 2009, est situé dans le Dubai Mall. « Je voulais, pour le Switch, cette vision forte et symétrique que donne le mur en ondulations continues qui enveloppe l'espace. Ce concept crée une texture intéressante pour l'ombre et la lumière et évoque les sables du désert. C'est un décor exceptionel, symétrique et équilibré, qui enveloppe les clients. L'œuvre artistique rétroéclairée suspendue au plafond fait appel à des textes arabes stylisés. La vague continue de la disposition des sièges constitue un système fonctionnel et dynamique. Je voulais créer un espace fort et net qui offre une superbe perspective, une oasis libérée de tout chaos », explique Karim Rashid. Les effets de vagues et de motifs utilisés installent une distance presque surréaliste par rapport à ce que l'on trouve habituellement dans ce genre de lieu et transportent les clients dans une autre dimension, où la gastronomie et le design se retrouvent loin de la routine quotidienne.

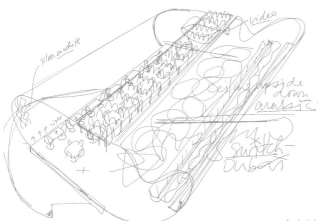

A sketch of the Switch Restaurant. Custom wall coverings by Karim Rashid were used here, the Sensual Styling Chair was also created by Rashid (Gamma State of the Art).

Eine Skizze des Restaurants Switch. Die hierfür gestaltete Wandverkleidung und der Stuhl Sensual Styling stammen ebenfalls von Karim Rashid (Gamma State of the Art).

Croquis du restaurant Switch. Karim Rashid a créé les motifs du décor mural ainsi que le fauteuil Sensual Styling (Gamma State of the Art).

THILO REICH/TRAN MAI HUY-THONG

Thilo Reich
Brunnenstr. 7 D
10119 Berlin
Germany

Tel: +49 176 20 56 21 28
E-mail: mail@thiloreich.com
Web: www.thiloreich.com

THILO REICH was born in 1981 in Stuttgart, Germany. He received his diploma in Architecture from the Technische Universität Berlin in 2009. He had an internship at Foster + Partners (London, 2000); and worked for Delugan Meissl in Vienna (2005–06). He worked as an architectural consultant at ABC-Art Berlin (2008). He completed the TRA Café (Berlin) in May 2009. The Chi Sing Restaurant (Berlin, 2008, published here) was the result of a collaboration with **TRAN MAI HUY-THONG**, born in Saigon, Vietnam, in 1979. Tran Mai Huy-Thong received his Master's degree in Fashion Design from the Saint Martins College of Art and Design (London, 2002), worked as a junior designer at Martin Margiela (Paris, 2002–03), as a senior designer at Strenesse Gabriele Strehle (Nördlingen, Germany, 2003–08), and is now Head of Women's Wear at René Lezard (Schwarzach, Germany, since October 2008).

THILO REICH wurde 1981 in Stuttgart geboren und erhielt 2009 sein Diplom in Architektur an der Technischen Universität Berlin. Er machte ein Praktikum bei Foster + Partners (London 2000) und arbeitete bei Delugan Meissl in Wien (2005–06), danach als Architekturberater bei ABC-Art in Berlin (2008). Im Mai 2009 vollendete er das Café TRA (Berlin). Das Restaurant Chi Sing (Berlin 2008, hier veröffentlicht) entstand in Zusammenarbeit mit **TRAN MAI HUY-THONG**, der 1979 in Saigon, Vietnam, geboren wurde. Er erhielt seinen Master in Modedesign am Saint Martins College of Art and Design (London, 2002), arbeitete als Juniordesigner bei Martin Margiela (Paris 2002–03) und als Seniordesigner bei Strenesse Gabriele Strehle (Nördlingen, Deutschland, 2003–08). Seit Oktober 2008 leitet er die Abteilung für Damenbekleidung bei René Lezard (Schwarzach, Deutschland).

THILO REICH, né en 1981 à Stuttgart, Allemagne, est diplômé en architecture de la Technische Universität de Berlin (2009). Il a effectué un stage chez Foster + Partners (Londres, 2000), et travaillé chez Delugan Meissl à Vienne (2005–06). Il a été consultant en architecture pour ABC-Art Berlin (2008). En mai 2009, il a achevé le café TRA (Berlin). Le restaurant Chi Sing (Berlin, 2008, publié ici) est le fruit d'une collaboration avec **TRAN MAI HUY-THONG**, né à Saïgon (Vietnam) en 1979. Tran Mai Huy-Thong a obtenu son mastère en design de mode au Saint Martins College of Art and Design (Londres, 2002), et a travaillé comme styliste junior chez Martin Margiela (Paris, 2002–03), puis comme styliste senior chez Strenesse Gabriele Strehle (Nördlingen, Allemagne, 2003–08). Il est actuellement responsable du prêt-à-porter féminin chez René Lezard (Schwarzach, Allemagne), depuis octobre 2008.

CHI SING RESTAURANT

Berlin, Germany, 2008

Rosenthaler Str. 62, 10119 Berlin, Germany, +49 30 20 08 92 84, www.chising-berlin.de
Area: 210 m². Client: Si An Gastronomie GmbH. Cost: €150 000
Collaboration: Tran Mai Huy-Thong

Silk origami "blossoms" hang from the ceiling and animate the space, which is a subtle mixture of traditional and modern elements. The varied chairs and objects recall the past, while the finishes and lighting have a decidedly modern air.

Seidene Origamiblüten hängen von der Decke und beleben den Raum, der eine subtile Mischung aus traditionellen und modernen Elementen darstellt. Die unterschiedlichen Stühle und Objekte nehmen auf die Vergangenheit Bezug, während die Wandbehandlung und die Beleuchtung entschieden modern sind.

Des « fleurs » de soie en origami suspendues au plafond animent le volume qui associe avec subtilité des éléments traditionnels et modernes. La variété des sièges et des objets rappelle le passé, tandis que les finitions et les éclairages sont résolument modernes.

Chi Sing (meaning Sister Sing) represents an intentional mixture of Asian and European culture, from cuisine to design. Thilo Reich states: "The space's interior reminds one of a dream; its playful, almost feminine, persona, shows an interesting contrast to Chi Sing's late 19th-century style, Wilhelmine façade." Using Western ideas of interior design, Thilo Reich and Tran Mai Huy-Thong also made use of the rules of feng shui. A total of 900 silk origami blossoms "rain down" from the ceiling and the entrance bar is also designed with reference to origami. Light gray shades dominate the color scheme, and filigree drawings on the gilt walls "add a warm touch to the room." A mixture of old gray-painted wooden chairs adds an unexpected charm and reference to the past. A downstairs area is described by the architect as "calm and dim" or "slightly meditative." The wall design is by Stefan Westerwelle and graphic design by Tomek Sadurski and Anna Mandoki.

Chi Sing (Schwester Sing) vertritt – von der Küche bis zur Gestaltung – eine bewusste Mischung aus asiatischer und europäischer Kultur. Thilo Reich erklärt: „Der Innenraum gleicht einem Traum; sein verspielter, fast femininer Charakter bildet einen interessanten Gegensatz zu Chi Sings wilhelminischer Fassade aus dem späten 19. Jahrhundert." Thilo Reich und Tran Mai Huy-Thong folgten westlichen Vorstellungen der Innenraumgestaltung, aber auch den Regeln des Feng-Shui. Insgesamt 900 seidene Origamiblüten „regnen" von der Decke herab, und auch die Bar am Eingang nimmt auf Origami Bezug. Schattierungen in Hellgrau bestimmen das Farbsystem, und filigrane Zeichnungen an den vergoldeten Wänden „geben dem Raum einen warmen Touch". Die Mischung alter, grau gestrichener Holzstühle strahlt einen unerwarteten Charme aus und stellt einen Bezug zur Vergangenheit her. Ein Bereich im Untergeschoss wird vom Architekten als „ruhig und dämmerig" oder „leicht meditativ" beschrieben. Die Wanddekoration stammt von Stefan Westerwelle, die Grafik von Tomek Sadurski und Anna Mandoki.

Le Chi Sing (« sœur Sing ») est un mélange volontaire d'éléments culturels asiatique et européen, allant de la cuisine au design. Selon Thilo Reich : « L'intérieur du volume évoque un rêve : il est joyeux, presque féminin, a du caractère, offre un contraste intéressant avec la façade « wilhelmienne » de l'immeuble qui date de la fin du XIXe siècle. » Travaillant à partir de concepts de décoration occidentale, Thilo Reich et Tran Mai Huy-Thong n'en ont pas moins fait appel aux principes du *feng shui*. Neuf cents fleurs en origami de soie « pleuvent » du plafond. Le bar de l'entrée est également une référence à la technique de l'origami. Le programme chromatique est dominé par des nuances de gris. Des dessins tracés sur les murs dorés « ajoutent une touche chaleureuse à la pièce ». Un mélange de vieilles chaises de bois peintes en gris offre une référence charmante et inattendue au passé. Un espace en sous-sol est décrit par l'architecte comme « calme et tamisé » ou « légèrement méditatif ». Le dessin mural est de Stefan Westerwelle et le travail graphique de Tomek Sadurski et Anna Mandoki.

The bar seen left evokes a folded form that might be reminiscent of origami but also brings to mind contemporary architecture. The overall space and its exterior (below) are both high and airy, making the origami hangings particularly effective.

Die links sichtbare Bar hat eine gefaltete Form, die an Origami erinnert, aber auch an sehr moderne Architektur. Der gesamte Raum und das Äußere (unten) erscheinen hoch und luftig, wodurch die hängenden Origami besonders zur Wirkung kommen.

Le bar (page de gauche), dont la forme évoque une feuille dépliée, pourrait rappeler l'origami japonais mais aussi l'architecture contemporaine. L'ensemble comme la façade sur la rue (ci-dessous) donnent une impression aérée et de grande hauteur qui rend la présence de l'origami suspendu particulièrement efficace.

ROBERTNEUN

ROBERTNEUN™
Baecker Buschmann Friedrich
Architektenpartnerschaft
Strassburger Str. 6–8
10405 Berlin
Germany

Tel: +49 30 84 71 26 66-0
Fax: +49 30 84 71 26 66-61
E-mail: info@robertneun.de
Web: www.robertneun.de

Thomas Baecker was born in New Haven, Connecticut, in 1969. He studied architecture at the Technische Universität Berlin (1990–98) and worked during the same period in the offices of Büttner Neuman Braun, Christoph Mäckler, and Eckert Negwer Suselbeek. He co-founded **ROBERTNEUN** in 2000. Nils Buschmann was born in 1972 in Frankfurt, Germany. He studied architecture at the Technische Universität Berlin (1993–2000) and worked during the same period in the offices of Augustin und Frank. He is another of the co-founders of ROBERTNEUN. Tom Friedrich was born in Bern, Switzerland, in 1972. He studied at the Hochschule der Künste in Berlin and at the Technische Universität Berlin (1993–2000), and worked in the offices of Kollhoff & Timmermann, Christoph Mäckler, Ortner & Ortner, and Heide von Beckerath Alberts. He became a partner of ROBERTNEUN in 2001. Their work includes the Giti Nourbakhsch Gallery (2006); the Tausend Bar (2007, published here); Weekend Club (2007); Nike Spirit Room III (2008); and the Tausend Restaurant (2009), all in Berlin.

Thomas Baecker wurde 1969 in New Haven, Connecticut, geboren. Er studierte Architektur an der Technischen Universität Berlin (1990–98) und arbeitete während dieser Zeit auch in den Büros Büttner Neumann Braun, Christoph Mäckler und Eckert Negwer Suselbeek. 2000 gründete er mit Nils Buschmann **ROBERTNEUN**. Buschmann wurde 1972 in Frankfurt am Main geboren. Er studierte Architektur an der Technischen Universität Berlin (1993–2000) und arbeitete während dieser Zeit in den Büros Augustin und Frank. Tom Friedrich wurde 1972 in Bern geboren. Er studierte an der Hochschule der Künste in Berlin und an der Technischen Universität Berlin (1993–2000) und arbeitete in den Büros Kollhoff & Timmermann, Christoph Mäckler, Ortner & Ortner und Heide von Beckerath Alberts. 2001 wurde er Partner bei ROBERTNEUN. Zu den Arbeiten des Büros zählen die Galerie Giti Nourbakhsch (2006), die Bar Tausend (2007, hier veröffentlicht), der Weekend Club (2007), der Nike Spirit Room III (2008) und das Restaurant Tausend (2009), alle in Berlin.

Thomas Baecker, né à New Haven, Connecticut, en 1969 a étudié l'architecture à la Technische Universität de Berlin (1990–98) et travaillé en même temps dans les agences de Büttner Neuman Braun, Christoph Mäckler et Eckert Negwer Suselbeek. Il est cofondateur de l'agence **ROBERTNEUN** en 2000. Nils Buschmann, né en 1972 à Francfort (Allemagne) a étudié l'architecture à la Technische Universität de Berlin (1993–2000) et travaillé concurremment dans l'agence Augustin und Frank. Il est un des cofondateurs de ROBERTNEUN. Tom Friedrich, né à Bern (Suisse) en 1972, a étudié à la Hochschule der Künste et à la Technische Universität de Berlin (1993–2000) et travaillé pour les agences Kollhoff & Timmermann, Christoph Mäckler, Ortner & Ortner, et Heide von Beckerath Alberts. Il est partenaire de ROBERTNEUN depuis 2001. Parmi leurs réalisations, toutes à Berlin : la galerie Giti Nourbakhsch (2006) ; le bar Tausend (2007, publié ici) ; le Weekend Club (2007) ; la Nike Spirit Room III (2008) et le restaurant Tausend (2009).

TAUSEND BAR

Berlin, Germany, 2007

Schifferbauerdamm 11, 10117 Berlin, +49 30 41 71 54 69, www.tausendberlin.com
Area: 600 m². Client: 101 Entertainment GmbH & Co KG. Cost: not disclosed

This bar is in an unusual location—within the viaduct arches of the Friedrichstrasse rapid-transit railway yard. The concrete walls of the bar are thus up to five meters thick, a fact that influenced the design, where it was necessary to avoid a "bunker" atmosphere. A large round light inspired by desk lamps marks one end of the bar and chromium-plated aluminum scales are used on the ceiling, with walls covered with colored glass intended to reflect light and to reduce the enclosed aspect of the space. The architects describe the lamp as a "magic object that determines the character of the entire space" through different effects ranging from cool to stroboscopic. A stage provides the possibility of live music. Smoked oak and roughly woven wool are amongst the materials used with the idea of giving a warm, "cozy" feel to the space.

Diese Bar befindet sich an einem ungewöhnlichen Ort – in den Arkaden des Eisenbahnviadukts an der Friedrichstraße. Die Betonwände der Bar sind daher bis zu 5 m stark – eine Tatsache, die den Entwurf beeinflusste, weil es nötig war, eine Bunkeratmosphäre zu vermeiden. Eine große, runde, von Schreibtischlampen inspirierte Leuchte betont eine Seite der Bar, während schuppenförmige, verchromte Aluminiumelemente an der Decke verwendet wurden. Die Wände sind mit farbigem Glas verkleidet, die das Licht reflektieren sollen, um die Wirkung der Eingeschlossenheit zu reduzieren. Die Architekten beschreiben die Lampe als „magisches Objekt, das den Charakter des gesamten Raums bestimmt" durch die verschiedenen Lichteffekte, die von kalt bis stroboskopisch reichen. Eine Bühne bietet Gelegenheit für Livemusik. Zu den verwendeten Materialien gehören Räuchereiche und grob gewebte Wolle, die dem Raum eine warme, „gemütliche" Wirkung geben sollen.

Ce bar s'est installé dans un lieu inhabituel : les arches du viaduc de la gare des chemins de fer régionaux de la Friedrichstrasse. Les murs de béton ont plus de 5 m d'épaisseur, ce qui a influencé le projet et demandé d'éviter de tomber dans une atmosphère de « bunker ». Un grand luminaire circulaire inspiré d'une lampe de bureau marque l'extrémité du bar. Les architectes le décrivent comme « un objet magique qui détermine le caractère de l'espace tout entier » par l'émission de différents effets, allant d'une lumière froide à des effets stroboscopiques. Des échelles en aluminium chromé recouvrent le plafond et les murs sont habillés de verre coloré pour refléter la lumière et diminuer l'aspect fermé du volume. Une petite scène a été prévue pour des musiciens. Le bois de chêne fumé et des étoffes de laine à tissage grossier font partie des matériaux utilisés pour créer une atmosphère chaleureuse, « cosy ».

Seating and tables are by ROBERTNEUN (Raumausstattung Heinisch). The bar (TMT Tischlerei Andreas Stachon) and the "light object" seen above are also by the designers (Lichtbau Scheider Moll).

Sitze und Tische stammen von ROBERTNEUN (Raumausstattung Heinisch), ebenso die Bar (TMT Tischlerei Andreas Stachon). Oben: Auch das „Lichtobjekt" wurde von den Architekten entworfen (Lichtbau Scheider Moll).

Les sièges et les tables sont de ROBERTNEUN (Raumausstattung Heinisch) de même que le bar (TMT Tischlerei Andreas Stachon) et « l'objet lumineux » photographié ci-dessus (Lichtbau Scheider Moll).

Glass and wood surfaces (TMT
Tischlerei Andreas Stachon) and
the mirrored ceiling (Artis Tischlerei)
are all designed by ROBERTNEUN.

Das Design der Glas- und Holzflächen
(TMT Tischlerei Andreas Stachon)
sowie der Spiegeldecke (Tischlerei
Artis) stammt von ROBERTNEUN.

Les plans en verre et en bois (TMT
Tischlerei Andreas Stachon) ainsi que
le plafond en miroirs (Artis Tischlerei)
ont tous été créés par ROBERTNEUN.

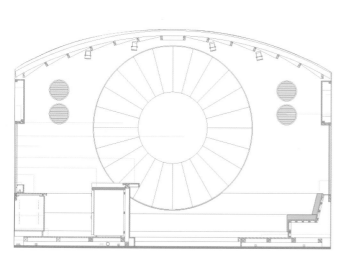

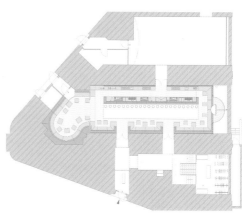

SERIE

Serie Architects London
Unit 4L Leroy House, 436 Essex Road
London N1 4EA, UK
Tel: +44 207 226 0022
E-mail: info@serie.co.uk, Web: www.serie.co.uk

Serie Architects Mumbai
317 A-Z Industrial Estate, G.K. Road, Lower Parel
Mumbai 400013, India
Tel: +91 22 40 04 69 52 / Fax: +91 22 40 04 69 53
E-mail: info@serie.co.in

SERIE (formerly Chris Lee Architects and Contemporary Urban) is an international practice based in London and Mumbai working in architecture, urbanism, and design. The practice provides full architecture, master planning, interior design, and furniture design services for the private and public sector. Christopher C. M. Lee received a B. A. from the National University of Singapore (1995) and graduated from the Architectural Association (AA) in London in 1998. He is presently Unit Master of Diploma Unit 6 at the AA. Kapil Gupta, who is based in Mumbai, graduated from the Sir J. J. College of Architecture (Mumbai, 1998) and completed postgraduate studies at the AA in London. He is the Director of Research and Publications at the Urban Design Research Institute in Mumbai. Their work includes Jewel Tech (Mumbai, 2002); Leo Burnett Office (Mumbai, 2003); Aluhwahlia Gallery (Mumbai, 2004); Thanks Boutique (Mumbai, 2005); Blue Frog Acoustic Lounge (Mumbai, 2007, published here); and, more recently, the deGustibus Hotels (2005–08); Birla Schools (2007–09); and Birla Medical Spa (2007–08), all in India.

SERIE (früher Chris Lee Architects und Contemporary Urban) ist ein international tätiges Büro mit Sitz in London and Bombay, das in den Bereichen Architektur, Städtebau und Design arbeitet und seine Dienste für Bauten, Bebauungspläne, Innenarchitektur und Möbeldesign im öffentlichen und privaten Sektor anbietet. Christopher C. M. Lee machte seinen B. A. an der staatlichen Universität Singapur (1995) und beendete 1998 sein Studium an der Architectural Association (AA) in London. Er ist zurzeit Unit Master of Diploma Unit 6 an der AA. Kapil Gupta, der in Bombay arbeitet, studierte am Sir J. J. College of Architecture (Bombay, 1998) und danach an der AA in London. Heute ist er Director of Research and Publications am Urban Design Research Institute in Bombay. Zu seinen Projekten gehören Jewel Tech (Bombay, 2002), Leo Burnett Office (Bombay, 2003), die Galerie Aluhwahlia (Bombay, 2004), die Boutique Thanks (Bombay, 2005), die Blue Frog Acoustic Lounge (Bombay, 2007, hier veröffentlicht) und als neuere Projekte die deGustibus Hotels (2005–08), die Birla-Schulen (2007–09) und das Birla Medical Spa (2007–08), alle in Indien.

SERIE (anciennement Chris Lee Architects and Contemporary Urban) est une agence internationale basée à Londres et Mumbai qui offre des services complets dans les domaines de l'architecture, de l'urbanisme, de l'architecture intérieure et de la conception de meubles, aussi bien pour le secteur public que privé. Christopher C. M. Lee est B. A. de l'Université nationale de Singapour (1995) et diplômé de l'Architectural Association (AA) de Londres en 1998. Il est actuellement responsable de l'unité de diplôme 6 à l'AA. Kapil Gupta, basé à Mumbai, diplômé du Sir J. J. College of Architecture (Mumbai, 1998), a achevé ses études supérieures à l'AA de Londres. Il est directeur de la recherche et des publications à l'Urban Design Research Institute à Mumbai. Parmi leurs réalisations, toutes en Inde : Jewel Tech (Mumbai, 2002) ; les bureaux de l'agence Leo Burnett (Mumbai, 2003) ; la galerie Aluhwahlia (Mumbai, 2004) ; la boutique Thanks (Mumbai, 2005) ; le salon acoustique Blue Frog (Mumbai, 2007, publié ici) ; et, plus récemment, les deGustibus Hotels (2005–08) ; les écoles Birla Schools (2007–09) ; et le spa médical Birla (2007–08).

BLUE FROG ACOUSTIC LOUNGE AND STUDIOS

Mumbai, India, 2007

D/2 Mathuradas Mills Compound, N.M. Joshi Marg, Lower Parel, Mumbai 400 013, India, +91 22 40 33 23 33, www.bluefrog.co.in
Area: 1000 m². Client: Blue Frog Media Pvt. Ltd. Cost: not disclosed

Cast concrete floors, molded plaster-board walls, and acoustic foam panels for the ceiling were used by the designers. The lighting design is by Abhay Wadhwa Associates.

Die Architekten verwendeten Gussbeton für die Böden, geformte Gipsplatten für die Wände und schallschluckende Schaumstoffelemente für die Decken. Die Lichtplanung stammt von Abhay Wadhwa Associates.

Les sols sont en béton coulé sur place, les murs en plâtre moulé et des panneaux acoustiques en mousse doublent le plafond. L'éclairage a été conçu par Abhay Wadhwa Associates.

Serie converted an industrial warehouse in the old mill district of Mumbai into a sound recording studio and acoustic lounge. The lounge consists of a restaurant, bar, and stage for live performances. One of the criteria was high acoustic quality. The architects explain: "The deep structure that was employed is of a cellular organization composed of circles, of varying sizes in plan approximating a horse-shoe configuration. The differential extrusions of these circles, encapsulated at different levels as tiered cylindrical seating booths, allow the eye level of diners and standing patrons to be distributed across staggered levels that increase in height away from the stage." The mahogany-paneled booths seat between 4 and 10 people and are arranged around an open center for the performances. Roof and glazing for the north-lit former warehouse were renovated. A poured-concrete floor and acoustically treated ceilings complete the installation.

Das Büro Serie baute ein Industrielagerhaus im alten Gewerbegebiet von Bombay in ein Tonstudio und eine Akustiklounge um. Letztere besteht aus einem Restaurant mit Bar und einer Bühne für Liveaufführungen. Ein wichtiges Kriterium war die Qualität der Akustik. Die Architekten erklären: „In dem tiefen Bauwerk wurden kreisförmige Raumzellen unterschiedlicher Größe auf einem nahezu hufeisenförmigen Grundriss angeordnet. Die verschiedenen Ausbuchtungen dieser Kreise, die auf unterschiedlichem Niveau aufgereihte zylindrische Sitznischen bilden, lenken den Blick der Speisenden und des stehenden Personals über die ansteigenden Ebenen zur Bühne." Die vier bis zehn Personen fassenden, mit Mahagoni verkleideten Nischen sind um einen zentralen Bereich für die Aufführungen angeordnet. Das Dach und die Verglasung des von Norden belichteten ehemaligen Lagerhauses wurden erneuert. Ein Boden aus Gussbeton und die mit Akustikelementen ausgestatteten Decken vervollständigen die Einrichtung.

Serie a reconverti cet ancien entrepôt industriel du vieux quartier des moulins à Mumbai en studio d'enregistrement et salon acoustique. Le lounge comprend un restaurant, un bar et une scène pour des spectacles en direct. L'un des critères du projet était d'atteindre un niveau élevé de qualité acoustique. Les architectes expliquent : « Le principe d'infrastructure que nous avons utilisé est celui d'une organisation cellulaire composée de cercles de différentes dimensions prenant approximativement en plan la forme d'un fer à cheval. Les extrusions différentielles de ces cercles délimitent, à différents niveaux, des alcôves cylindriques reliées entre elles, ce qui permet aux clients, qu'ils soient assis ou debout, d'orienter leur regard selon des niveaux en zigzag dont la hauteur augmente au fur et à mesure que l'on s'éloigne de la scène. » Les alcôves lambrissées d'acajou peuvent accueillir de quatre à dix personnes et sont disposées autour d'un espace central dans lequel se déroulent les performances. La toiture et les verrières de l'ancien entrepôt orientées au nord ont été rénovées. Un sol en béton coulé et des plafonds acoustiques complètent l'installation.

The furniture was custom-manufactured by the general contractor. The acoustics were designed by Munroe Acoustics.

Die Möbel wurden vom Generalunternehmer speziell für dieses Projekt gefertigt. Den Schallschutz planten Munroe Acoustics.

Le mobilier a été réalisé par l'entreprise générale. L'acoustique a été prise en charge par Munroe Acoustics.

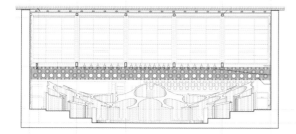

S Bar ►

PHILIPPE STARCK

Ubik
18/20 rue du Faubourg du Temple / 75011 Paris / France
Tel: +33 1 48 07 54 54 / Fax: +33 1 48 07 54 64
E-mail: info@philippe-starck.com / Web: www.starck.com

PHILIPPE STARCK was born in 1949 and attended the École Nissim de Camondo in Paris. Though he is, of course, best known as a furniture and object designer, his projects as an architect include the Café Costes (Paris, 1984); Laguiole Knife Factory (Laguiole, France, 1987); Royalton Hotel (New York, 1988); Nani Nani Building (Tokyo, 1989); Paramount Hotel (New York, 1990); Asahi Beer Hall (Tokyo, 1990); the Teatriz Restaurant (Madrid, 1990); and the Baron Vert building in Osaka (1990). He has also designed a number of private houses and apartment blocks, for example Lemoult in Paris (1987); the Angle in Antwerp (1991); apartment buildings in Los Angeles (1991); and a private house in Madrid (1991). He was responsible for the interior design of the Saint Martin's Lane and Sanderson Hotels in London (UK, 1999 and 2000); the Delano in Miami (1995); the Mondrian in Los Angeles (California, 1997); the Hudson in New York (New York, 2000); and the Clift in San Francisco (California, 2001). He has also worked on the design of condominium apartments in Toronto (75 Portland Street, Canada); the 24-story JIA boutique hotel in Hong Kong (China, 2004); and is also responsible for the Taschen bookstores in Paris (2002), Los Angeles (2004), and New York (2007). The Faena in Buenos Aires (2007) and the Fasano in Rio de Janeiro (Brazil, 2007), are more recent hotel ventures. In 2007, the Japanese restaurant Katsuya and the S Bar (published here) opened in Los Angeles, California, while Le Meurice opened in Paris, France. The 40,000-square-meter Alhondiga in Bilbao, Spain, a "place of discovery, exchange and living," opened in 2008. Starck's other ventures include his role as Creative Director of Yoo, a property development company, in which he is associated with the developer John Hitchcox and Jade Jagger.

PHILIPPE STARCK wurde 1949 geboren und studierte an der École Nissim de Camondo in Paris. Obgleich er am bekanntesten als Möbel- und Objektdesigner wurde, hat er auch viele Architekturprojekte realisiert. Dazu gehören das Café Costes (Paris, 1984), die Messerfabrik Laguiole (Laguiole, Frankreich, 1987), das Royalton Hotel (New York, 1988), das Nani Nani Building (Tokio, 1989), das Paramount Hotel (New York, 1990), die Asahi Beer Hall (Tokio, 1990), das Restaurant Teatriz (Madrid, 1990) und das Baron Vert Building in Osaka (1990). Er hat auch eine Reihe von Ein- und Mehrfamilienhäusern entworfen, z. B. Lemoult in Paris (1987), Angle in Antwerpen (1991) und Apartmenthäuser in Los Angeles (1991) sowie ein Privathaus in Madrid (1991). Er war verantwortlich für die Innengestaltung der Hotels Saint Martin's Lane und Sanderson in London (1999 und 2000), des Delano in Miami (1995), des Mondrian in Los Angeles (Kalifornien, 1997), des Hudson in New York (2000) und des Clift in San Francisco (Kalifornien, 2001). Außerdem hat er Eigentumswohnungen in Toronto (75 Portland Street, Kanada), das 24-geschossige JIA Boutique Hotel in Hongkong (China, 2004) gestaltet und ist verantwortlich für die Buchhandlungen Taschen in Paris (2002), Los Angeles (2004) und New York (2007). Das Faena in Buenos Aires (2007) und das Fasano in Rio de Janeiro (2007) sind die neuesten Hotelprojekte. 2007 wurden das japanische Restaurant Katsuya und die S Bar (hier vorgestellt) in Los Angeles und das Le Meurice in Paris eröffnet. Das 40 000 m² große Alhondiga in Bilbao, ein „Ort zum Entdecken, Austauschen und Leben", wurde 2008 eröffnet. Starck arbeitet außerdem als Kreativdirektor für Yoo, eine Bauträgergesellschaft, wo er mit den Investoren John Hitchcox und Jade Jagger zusammenarbeitet.

Né en 1949, **PHILIPPE STARCK** a suivi les cours de l'École Nissim de Camondo à Paris. Bien qu'il soit surtout connu comme designer de mobilier et d'objets, il a réalisé des projets architecturaux dont le café Costes (Paris, 1984); l'usine de coutellerie de Laguiole (Laguiole, France, 1987); le Royalton Hotel (New York, 1988); l'immeuble Nani Nani (Tokyo, 1989); le Paramount Hotel (New York, 1990); l'Asahi Beer Hall (Tokyo, 1990); le restaurant Teatriz (Madrid, 1990); et l'immeuble Baron Vert à Osaka (1990). Il a également conçu un certain nombre de résidences privées et d'immeubles d'appartements, par exemple la maison Lemoult à Paris (1987); la maison Angle à Anvers (1991); des immeubles de logements à Los Angeles (1991); et une résidence privée à Madrid (1991). Il a été responsable des aménagements intérieurs des hôtels Saint Martin's Lane et Sanderson à Londres (1999 et 2000); du Delano à Miami (1995); du Mondrian à Los Angeles (Californie, 1997); du Hudson à New York (New York, 2000); et du Clift à San Francisco (Californie, 2001). Il a également conçu des appartements en copropriété à Toronto (75 Portland Street, Canada); la boutique hôtel JIA de vingt-quatre niveaux à Hongkong (Chine, 2004); et a aménagé les librairies Taschen de Paris (2002), Los Angeles (2004) et New York (2007). Faena à Buenos Aires (2007) et Fasano à Rio de Janeiro (Brésil, 2007) sont ses plus récentes interventions dans le domaine de l'hôtellerie. En 2007, le restaurant japonais Katsuya et le S Bar (publié ici) ont ouvert leurs portes à Los Angeles, ainsi que les nouvelles salles de l'hôtel Meurice à Paris. Les 40 000 mètres carrés de l'Alhondiga à Bilbao, Espagne, « lieu de découverte, d'échange et de vie », a ouvert en 2008. Starck est, entre autres, directeur créatif de Yoo, une société de promotion immobilière à laquelle il est associé, avec le promoteur John Hitchcox et Jade Jagger.

S BAR

Los Angeles, California, USA, 2007

6304 Hollywood Blvd., Los Angeles, CA, USA, +1 323 957 2279, www.sbe.com
Area: 176 m². Client: SBE. Cost: not disclosed. Collaboration: SBE Design Team, Design ARC

The S Bar opened in October 2007 in Hollywood, at the intersection of Hollywood Boulevard and Vine Street, with the same client (SBE Restaurant & Nightlife Group) as Katsuya and near the Japanese restaurant. According to SBE: "The ambience of S Bar evokes the urban, eclectic style of an artist's warehouse gallery." The bar has four large-scale photographs of Versailles, each covering an entire wall, by the French photographer Patrick Tournebœuf. Starck has opted here for what he calls a "flea-market style" of seating with intentionally mismatched chairs and tables and upside-down lamps dangling from the ceiling. The bar and doorways are lit in blue neon light.

Die an der Kreuzung von Hollywood Boulevard und Vine Street in Hollywood gelegene S Bar wurde im Oktober 2007 vom gleichen Träger (SBE Restaurant & Nightlife Group) wie das Restaurant Katsuya und in dessen Nähe eröffnet. „Das Ambiente der S Bar erinnert an den urbanen, eklektischen Stil einer Kunstgalerie in einem ehemaligen Lagerhaus", heißt es bei SBE. Vier großformatige Fotografien von Versailles des französischen Fotografen Patrick Tournebœuf bedecken jeweils eine ganze Wand der Bar. Starck hat hier den von ihm so bezeichneten „Flohmarktstil" gewählt, mit bewusst nicht zusammenpassenden Stühlen und Tischen sowie Lampen, die verkehrt herum von der Decke hängen. Die Bar und der Eingang sind in blaues Neonlicht getaucht.

Le S Bar a ouvert ses portes à Hollywood en octobre 2007, au carrefour de Hollywood Boulevard et de Vine Street. Il appartient au même propriétaire (SBE Restaurant & Nightlife Group) que le restaurant Katsuya qui se trouve à proximité. Selon SBE : « L'ambiance du S Bar évoque le style urbain et éclectique d'un atelier entrepôt d'artiste. » Le bar est décoré de quatre photographies de très grand format de Versailles prises par le photographe français Patrick Tournebœuf, chacune recouvrant un mur entier. Starck a opté ici pour ce qu'il appelle « un style de marché aux puces », dans la sélection des sièges et des tables de toutes origines et des lampes suspendues par les pieds au plafond. Le bar et ses entrées sont éclairés au néon bleu.

Starck's current mode is eclectic and influenced by a "flea market" atmosphere as the upside down, hanging lamps seen here demonstrate.

Starcks gegenwärtiger Stil ist eklektisch und von einer „Flohmarkt"-Atmosphäre geprägt, wie die hier verkehrt aufgehängten Leuchten zeigen.

Le style actuel de Starck s'oriente vers l'éclectisme et a été influencé ici par l'atmosphère d'un marché aux puces, comme le montrent ces luminaires suspendues par les pieds.

Like the lamps, chairs and other objects are varied, almost as though they might have come from an old home, which certainly gives a comfortable atmosphere.

Wie die Leuchten sind auch die Stühle und anderen Objekte unterschiedlich, als ob sie aus einem alten Haus stammen, was zweifellos eine gemütliche Atmosphäre bewirkt.

Les lampes, les sièges et de multiples objets sont d'origines très variées, comme s'ils se trouvaient dans une maison ancienne, ce qui crée une atmosphère agréable et confortable.

BACCARAT MOSCOW

Moscow, Russia, 2008

19-21 Nikolskaya Street, Moscow 109012, Russia, +7 495 93 333 89, www.baccarat.com
Area: not disclosed. Client: Baccarat. Cost: not disclosed.

After the Paris restaurant on the Place des États-Unis opened in 2003, Baccarat opened a second "house" in February 2008 in Moscow, again working with the designer Philippe Starck. The glassmaker has a long history of collaboration with Russia, as a candelabra belonging to the last Tsar in the Paris museum of Baccarat demonstrates. Baccarat objects are displayed on the ground floor of the building. Baccarat furniture, mirrors, and crystal display windows, as well as a giant lit table with a crystal base, mark the space. In 1823, Karl Verrein opened a pharmacy on Nikolskaya Street. In March 1862, Verrein moved the pharmacy to the other side of Nikolskaya Street, to a house purchased from the merchant K. K. Schilbach. Verrein's son, Vladimir Karlovich, oversaw construction of the new building that would become a legendary pharmacy. The architect Adolf Erichson designed the Nikolskaya pharmacy, which took five years to build and was completed in 1895. The interior of the pharmacy was designed in the old German style, with a gallery highlighted by tall, architectural cabinets and stained wooden counters. The building's interiors are palatial, featuring a central staircase decorated with artificial marble and wrought iron. Starck's current style is ideally suited to this surprising historic and contemporary Moscow mixture.

Nach dem Pariser Lokal an der Place des Etats-Unis von 2003 eröffnete Baccarat im Februar 2008 in Moskau ein weiteres „Haus", wiederum in Zusammenarbeit mit dem Designer Philippe Starck. Die Glasfirma blickt auf eine lange Geschichte der Beziehungen zu Russland zurück, wie ein Kronleuchter aus dem Besitz des letzten Zaren im Pariser Baccarat-Museum beweist. Baccarat-Objekte werden im Erdgeschoss des Gebäudes ausgestellt. Der Raum wird von Baccarat-Möbeln, -Spiegeln und Ausstellungsvitrinen für Kristall sowie einem riesigen, beleuchteten Tisch mit Kristallbasis beherrscht. 1823 eröffnete Karl Verrein in der Nikolskaya-Straße eine Apotheke. Im März 1862 verlegte er sie auf die andere Straßenseite in ein von dem Kaufmann K. K. Schilbach erworbenes Haus. Verreins Sohn Wladimir Karlowitsch betreute den Neubau, der von Adolf Erichson entworfen wurde und nach fünf Jahren Bauzeit 1895 fertiggestellt wurde. Die Innenausstattung der legendären Apotheke erfolgte im altdeutschen Stil mit einer Galerie, hohen Einbauschränken und dunklen Holztheken. Das Innere des Hauses ist palastartig und hat eine zentrale, mit künstlichem Marmor und Schmiedeeisen dekorierte Treppe. Starcks aktuelle Gestaltungsweise passt hervorragend zu dieser erstaunlichen Mischung aus historischem und zeitgenössischem Moskauer Stil.

Après sa « vitrine » parisienne ouverte place des États-Unis en 2003, Baccarat a ouvert une seconde maison en février 2008 à Moscou, cette fois encore avec l'aide du designer Philippe Starck. Les cristalleries françaises ont une longue histoire de collaboration avec la Russie, comme en témoigne un candélabre ayant appartenu au dernier tsar de Russie et conservé au musée parisien de Baccarat. Des objets produits par la maison sont exposés au rez-de-chaussée du bâtiment : meubles, miroirs et vitrines pour cristaux, ainsi qu'une gigantesque table lumineuse à piètement de cristal. En 1823, Karl Verrein avait ouvert une pharmacie rue Nikolskaia. En mars 1862, il la transféra en face dans une maison achetée au négociant K. K. Schilbach. Le fils de Verrein, Vladimir Karlovitch, supervisa la construction d'un nouveau bâtiment qui allait devenir une pharmacie légendaire due à l'architecte Adolf Erichson. Les travaux durèrent cinq années et s'achevèrent en 1895. L'intérieur, de style allemand, était marqué par d'imposants comptoirs de bois teint et des vitrines très architecturées. Le décor intérieur, avec son escalier central en marbre artificiel et ferronnerie de fonte était palatial. Le style actuel de Starck est idéalement adapté à ce mélange surprenant qui évoque le Moscou d'hier et d'aujourd'hui.

Philippe Starck makes the most of the glass expertise of Baccarat in these rather grand spaces dominated by glass chandeliers.

Philippe Starck nutzte die Erfahrung von Baccarat mit Glas für diese großartigen Räume, die von gläsernen Kronleuchtern beherrscht werden.

Philippe Starck a tiré le maximum de l'expertise du cristal de Baccarat comme le montrent ces impressionnants volumes dominés par des lustres et chandeliers étincelants.

The crystalline transparency of the
space, most visibly present in the
numerous chandeliers, is also present
in the furnishings.

Die kristalline Transparenz des
Raums, die sich vor allem in den
zahlreichen Kadelabern ausdrückt,
zeigt sich auch am Mobiliar.

Le thème de la transparence cristal-
line si fortement exprimée dans les
multiples luminaires se retrouve
également dans le mobilier.

The grandiose past of Russia is not far removed from these images, but Starck also maintains a degree of distance, or humor, which has always characterized his designs.

Diese Bilder rufen durchaus die groß-artige Vergangenheit Russlands ins Gedächtnis, aber Starck wahrt auch eine gewisse Distanz – oder zeigt Humor, der stets seine Entwürfe aus-zeichnet.

Si l'évocation du passé grandiose de la Russie n'est pas absente de ces images, Starck sait conserver une certaine distance – ou un humour qui caractérise toujours ses projets.

SUPER POTATO

Super Potato Co., Ltd.
3–34–17 Kamikitazawa
Setagaya-ku
Tokyo 156–0057
Japan

Tel: +81 3 3290 0195
Fax: +81 3 3290 1650
E-mail: info@superpotato.jp
Web: www.superpotato.jp

SUPER POTATO was created in 1973. Its president is Takashi Sugimoto, who was born in Tokyo in 1945, and obtained his degree in Art from the Tokyo National University of Fine Arts and Music in 1968. Its major clients have included the Hankyu, Seibu, and Parco department stores in Japan, as well as the JR West and JR East rail lines. Other clients include Sony, Suntory, and Hyatt International. They have worked on "area-development and planning for shopping malls, development of new-style stores, restaurants, showrooms etc., planning and development of resorts, golf courses and clubs, hotels, halls," as well as the creation of the furniture or "utensils" required for their projects. Their recent work includes a Spa and Ball Room for the Century Hyatt Hotel, as well as the French restaurant Cuisine(s) Michel Troisgros (Tokyo, 2006); a lobby lounge and restaurant called "The Dining Room" for the Hyatt Regency (Hakone, Kanagawa, 2006); the Nedalny Vostok Restaurant (Moscow, Russia, 2006, published here); the Kriya Spa for the Grand Hyatt Bali (Bali, Indonesia, 2007); the China Kitchen Restaurant for the Hyatt Regency Delhi (Delhi, India, 2007); and the On the Bund Vue Restaurant in the Hyatt Regency Shanghai (Shanghai, China, 2007).

SUPER POTATO wurde 1973 gegründet und wird von Takashi Sugimoto geleitet, der 1945 in Tokio geboren wurde und 1968 sein Kunststudium an der Tokyo National University of Fine Arts and Music abschloss. Zu den wichtigsten Auftraggebern des Büros zählen die Kaufhäuser Hankyu, Seibu und Parco in Japan und die Eisenbahngesellschaften JR West und JR East, außerdem die Firmen Sony, Suntory und Hyatt International. Super Potatos Tätigkeit besteht in der „Erschließung und Planung von Shopping-Malls, modernen Geschäften, Restaurants, Showrooms sowie Freizeitanlagen, Golfplätzen und Klubs, Hotels und Hallen", aber auch in der Gestaltung von Möbeln oder „Utensilien" für diese Projekte. Zu den neueren Arbeiten zählen ein Bad und ein Ballsaal für das Century Hyatt Hotel sowie das französische Restaurant Cuisine(s) Michel Troisgros (Tokio, 2006), die Lounge und das Restaurant The Dining Room im Hotel Hyatt Regency (Hakone, Kanagawa, 2006), das Restaurant Nedalny Vostok (Moskau, 2006, hier veröffentlicht), das Kriya Spa für das Grand Hyatt Bali (Bali, Indonesien, 2007), das Restaurant China Kitchen für das Hyatt Regency Delhi (Delhi, Indien, 2007) und das Restaurant On the Bund Vue im Hyatt Regency Shanghai (Shanghai, China, 2007).

L'agence **SUPER POTATO** fut créée in 1973. Son président, Takashi Sugimoto, né à Tokyo en 1945, fut diplômé en art de l'Université nationale des beaux-arts et de musique de Tokyo, en 1968. Cette agence compte parmi ses plus importants clients les grands magasins japonais Hankyu, Seibu et Parco, ainsi que les compagnies de chemin de fer JR West et JR East, ou Sony, Suntory et Hyatt International. Super Potato travaille sur des projets « de développement de zones et d'urbanisme pour des centres commerciaux, sur des projets de développement vers des styles nouveaux de magasins, de *showrooms* et de restaurants. Elle œuvre également sur l'urbanisme et le développement de lieux touristiques, de terrains de golf et de clubs, d'hôtels, de halls de réception », ainsi que sur la création du mobilier ou des objets que nécessitent ses projets. Parmi ses récentes réalisations : une salle de bal et un spa pour le Century Hyatt Hotel, et le restaurant français Cuisine(s) Michel Troisgros (Tokyo, 2006) ; le hall de réception et le restaurant The Dining Room pour le Hyatt Regency (Hakone, Kanagawa, 2006) ; le restaurant Nedalny Vostok (Moscou, Russie, 2006, publié ici) ; le Kriya Spa pour le Grand Hyatt Bali (Bali, Indonésie, 2007) ; le restaurant China Kitchen pour le Hyatt Regency Delhi (Delhi, Inde, 2007) ; et le restaurant On the Bund Vue du Hyatt Regency Shanghaï (Shanghaï, Chine, 2007).

NEDALNY VOSTOK RESTAURANT

Moscow, Russia, 2006

15/2 Tverskoi Bulvar, Moscow, Russia, +7 495 694 06 41
Area: 748 m². Client: Novikov Restaurant Group
Cost: not disclosed

The client Arkady Novikov came to see the architects and explained that the similarity of Russian food in taste and preparation to that of Japan made Japanese cuisine popular in Moscow. Novikov and Super Potato principal Takashi Sugimoto discussed the restaurant concept and decided to base it in good part on Kamchatka crab—and to develop it as a "Russian restaurant in the Japanese style." Large quantities of food are prepared in a "kitchen factory" in front of the guests—the first full, open kitchen created in Moscow. The bright, open atmosphere of the restaurant does indeed seem to have something to do with both Russian and Japanese cultures, but it is really a fusion of these, together with knowledge and concern for cooking and the presentation of food.

Der Bauherr Arkadi Nowikow suchte die Architekten auf und erklärte ihnen, dass japanisches Essen in Moskau deshalb so beliebt ist, weil Geschmack und Zubereitung der russischen Küche ähneln. Nowikow und Super Potatos Chef Takashi Sugimoto diskutierten das Konzept und beschlossen, den Kamtschatka-Krebs als Grundlage zu nehmen und es als ein „russisches Restaurant im japanischen Stil" zu entwickeln. In einer „Küchenfabrik" werden Speisen in großer Zahl vor den Augen der Gäste zubereitet – es handelt sich um die erste völlig offene Küche in Moskau. Die fröhliche, offene Atmosphäre des Restaurants scheint in der Tat mit der russischen wie auch der japanischen Kultur zusammenzuhängen, es ist wirklich eine Fusion im Hinblick auf die Kenntnisse und die Liebe zum Kochen und die Präsentation der Speisen.

Le client, Arkady Novikov, est allé à la rencontre des architectes, et leur a expliqué que ce sont les similarités rassemblant les cuisines russe et japonaise, tant par le goût que par la préparation des aliments, qui ont rendu la cuisine japonaise si populaire à Moscou. Novikov et le directeur de Super Potato, Takashi Sugimoto, ont discuté ensemble du concept du restaurant et décidé de le faire reposer en grande partie sur des recettes à base de crabe du Kamchatka, et de développer un « restaurant russe de style japonais ». Les multiples plats sont préparés dans un « atelier cuisine » devant les clients, première cuisine entièrement ouverte créée à Moscou. L'atmosphère ouverte et lumineuse du lieu semble bien être en accord avec les deux cultures, russe et japonaise, mais exprime plutôt une fusion de celles-ci, ainsi que la connaissance des modes de cuisson et des styles de présentation des plats.

The bar/lounge with a fireplace was designed by Ryoichi Niwata (Hup Yew Sen). A specially designed crab tank (FabriSteel) can be seen on the right.

Die Bar/Lounge mit einem Kamin wurde von Ryoichi Niwata (Hup Yew Sen) geplant. Ein speziell entworfenes Aquarium für Krustentiere (FabriSteel) ist rechts zu sehen.

Le bar lounge à cheminée a été conçu par Ryoichi Niwata (Hup Yew Sen). À droite, un vivier à crustacés spécialement conçu pour l'endroit (FabriSteel).

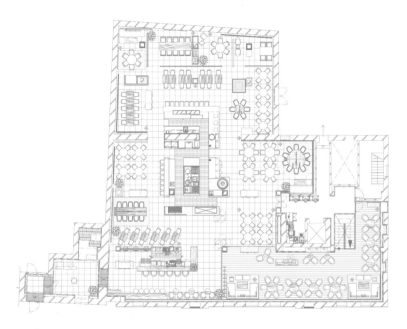

The sushi counter was designed by
Ryoichi Niwata (Hup Yew Sen). A floor
plan of the restaurant can be seen to
the left.

Die Sushi-Bar wurde ebenfalls von
Ryoichi Niwata (Hup Yew Sen) ent-
worfen. Links: Grundriss des
Restaurants.

Le bar à sushi a été dessiné par
Ryoichi Niwata (Hup Yew Sen).
À gauche, le plan d'ensemble du
restaurant.

Special heating lamps (right) were
provided by FabriSteel, while the
wooden dining tables were designed
by Ryoichi Niwata (Hup Yew Sen).

Spezielle Wärmelampen (rechts) wurden von FabriSteel geliefert, während
die hölzernen Speisetische von Ryoichi Niwata (Hup Yew Sen) stammen.

La lampe chauffante (à droite) vient
de FabriSteel. Les tables en bois sont
signées Ryoichi Niwata (Hup Yew Sen).

TIDY ARQUITECTOS

Tidy Arquitectos
Marchant Pereira 407
Providencia, Santiago de Chile
Chile

Tel: +56 2 223 8489
E-mail: info@tidy.cl
Web: www.tidy.cl

Albert Tidy was born in 1967 in Santiago, and graduated from the Universidad de Chile in 1992. In 1998, he graduated from Yale School of Architecture as a Fulbright Scholar, obtaining his M.Arch degree and the Samuel J. Fogelson Memorial Award for Excellence in Design. He has been an Associate Professor at the Universidad de Chile since 1999. Between 2005 and 2007, he served as Director at the school, and in 2007 he was named Director of the San Sebastian School of Architecture in Santiago, Chile. He founded **TIDY ARQUITECTOS** with his brother and partner Ian Tidy in 2000. Ian Tidy was born in 1974 and graduated from the Pontificia Universidad Católica de Chile in 2000. He currently teaches Interior Design and Object Design as an Associate Professor at the Universidad del Desarrollo (Santiago, 2007–08). His furniture design work has received recognition in numerous exhibitions and publications in Chile. They have completed the Organiko Restaurant (Providencia, Santiago, 2002); the Stryker Offices (Las Condes, Santiago, 2002); as well as a number of private houses, such as the Casa Muñoz (Tunquén, 2002–03); and the Amorio Restaurant (Santiago, 2005–06, published here), all in Chile. They have a number of projects underway for private houses, such as the Casa Martinez (Aculeo Lake, 2007–08).

Albert Tidy wurde 1967 in Santiago geboren und studierte bis 1992 an der Universidad de Chile. 1998 beendete er sein Studium als Fulbright-Stipendiat an der Yale School of Architecture mit dem M. Arch. und wurde mit dem Samuel J. Fogelson Memorial Award for Excellence in Design ausgezeichnet. Ab 1999 war er außerordentlicher Professor an der Architekturabteilung der Universidad de Chile. Von 2005 bis 2007 war er Direktor dieser Lehranstalt und wurde 2007 zum Direktor der Architekturhochschule San Sebastian in Santiago de Chile ernannt. Er gründete 2000 das Büro **TIDY ARQUITECTOS** mit seinem Bruder und Partner Ian Tidy. Dieser wurde 1974 geboren und beendete sein Studium an der Pontificia Universidad Católica de Chile im Jahr 2000. Gegenwärtig unterrichtet er als außerordentlicher Professor Innenarchitektur und Objektdesign an der Universidad del Desarrollo (Santiago, 2007–08). Seine Möbelentwürfe haben in zahlreichen Ausstellungen und Publikationen in Chile Anerkennung gefunden. Zu den ausgeführten Projekten des Büros zählen das Restaurant Organiko (Providencia, Santiago, 2002), das Bürogebäude Stryker (Las Condes, Santiago, 2002) und eine Reihe von Privathäusern, z. B. die Casa Muñoz (Tunquén, 2002–03) sowie das Restaurant Amorio (Santiago, 2005–06, hier veröffentlicht), alle in Chile. Mehrere Einfamilienhäuser befinden sich im Bau, u. a. die Casa Martinez (Aculeo Lake, 2007–08).

Albert Tidy, né en 1967 à Santiago, est diplômé de l'Universidad de Chile (1992). En 1998, boursier Fulbright, il a obtenu son M.Arch, puis le Samuel J. Fogelson Memorial Award for Excellence in Design de la Yale School of Architecture. Il est professeur associé à l'École d'architecture de l'Universidad de Chile depuis 1999. De 2005 à 2007, il a été directeur de l'école et, en 2007, a été nommé directeur de l'École d'architecture San Sebastian à Santiago du Chili. Il a fondé l'agence **TIDY ARQUITECTOS** avec son frère Ian Tidy en 2000. Ian Tidy, né en 1974 est diplômé de la Pontificia Universidad Católica de Chile (2000). Il enseigne actuellement l'architecture intérieure et le design d'objet comme professeur associé à l'Universidad del Desarrollo (Santiago 2007–08). Ses créations de meubles ont fait l'objet de nombreuses expositions et publications au Chili. Ensemble, ils ont réalisé, au Chili, le restaurant Organiko (Providencia, Santiago, 2002); les bureaux Stryker (Las Condes, Santiago, 2002); ainsi que de nombreuses résidences privées comme la maison Muñoz (Tunquén, 2002–03); et le restaurant Amorio (Santiago, 2005–06, publié ici). Ils travaillent actuellement à plusieurs projets de maisons dont la maison Martinez (Aculeo Lake, 2007–08).

AMORIO RESTAURANT

Bellavista, Santiago, Chile, 2005–06

Constitucíon 181, Providencia, Santiago, Chile, +56 2 777 1454, www.amorio.cl
Area: 350 m². Clients: Benjamín Vicuña, Gonzalo Valenzuela, Gustavo Page. Cost: $330 000
Team: Miguel Alemparte, Nicolás Alemparte

This project was awarded to the architects as a result of a private competition organized by a group of well-known Chilean actors. The brief was to create a bar and restaurant in an old two-story house in the "bohemian" neighborhood of Bellavista in Santiago without entirely removing its aged appearance. The Tidy brothers kept the exterior walls intact while reworking the interiors completely. The front of the house was carefully restored using the original materials, but a glazed opening was added to mark the entrance. An exterior balcony was also rebuilt. Inside, a large central bar is encountered at the access level, while the upper floor is completely bare of fixed objects, creating a "more informal environment."

Diesen Auftrag erhielten die Architekten als Ergebnis eines auf privater Basis von einer Gruppe bekannter chilenischer Schauspieler organisierten Wettbewerbs. Die Ausschreibung forderte die Einrichtung einer Bar und eines Restaurants in einem alten, zweigeschossigen Haus im Bohemeviertel Bellavista in Santiago, ohne das alte Erscheinungsbild des Gebäudes total zu verändern. Die Gebrüder Tidy bewahrten die Außenmauern, veränderten das Innere jedoch vollkommen. Die Vorderfront des Hauses wurde bei Erhalt der originalen Materialien sorgfältig restauriert, aber durch eine verglaste Öffnung zur Markierung des Eingangs ergänzt. Auch ein Außenbalkon wurde wiederhergestellt. Im Innern befindet sich auf der Eingangsebene eine große, zentrale Bar, während das Obergeschoss keine festen Einbauten hat und eine „informellere Umgebung" darstellt.

Ce projet a été confié aux architectes à l'issue d'un concours privé organisé par un groupe d'acteurs chiliens très connus. Le cahier des charges portait sur la création d'un bar et d'un restaurant dans une vieille maison à un étage du quartier « bohème » de Bellavista à Santiago, sans modifier entièrement son aspect ancien. Les frères Tidy ont conservé intact les murs extérieurs, tout en réaménageant entièrement l'intérieur. La façade a été soigneusement restaurée en réutilisant des matériaux d'origine, mais une ouverture vitrée signale désormais l'entrée. Un balcon a également été reconstruit. À l'intérieur, le vaste bar central occupe le rez-de-chaussée, tandis que l'étage est dégagé de tout mobilier fixe pour créer « un environnement moins formel ».

The exterior of the restaurant building before restoration (below) and after (left page). The architects' sketch shows the transformation of the old structure. Stools above are by Michael Thonet (Vienna).

Das Restaurantgebäude von außen vor der Restaurierung (unten) und danach (linke Seite). Die Skizze der Architekten zeigt die Veränderung des alten Bauwerks. Die Hocker oben stammen von Michael Thonet (Wien).

L'extérieur du restaurant avant (ci-dessous) et après sa restauration (page de gauche). Le croquis de l'architecte montre la transformation de l'ancien bâtiment. Les tabourets ci-dessus viennent de chez Michael Thonet (Vienne).

The bar and built-in furniture are by
the architects. Other furniture was
purchased in local flea markets and
restored.

Die Bar und die Einbaumöbel stammen
von den Architekten. Weitere Möbel
wurden auf örtlichen Flohmärkten
gekauft und restauriert.

Le bar et le mobilier intégré sont dus
aux architectes. Les autres meubles
ont été achetés sur des marchés aux
puces locaux et restaurés.

The two floors of the restaurant are
seen in the drawings (right). Below,
an overall view of the bar area with
its exposed brick walls.

*Rechts: Die Pläne zeigen beide
Ebenen des Restaurants. Unten:
Gesamtansicht des Barraums mit
dem offengelegten Mauerwerk.*

*À droite, plans des deux niveaux du
restaurant. Ci-dessous une vue d'ensemble du bar et ses murs de brique
apparente.*

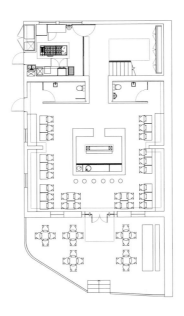
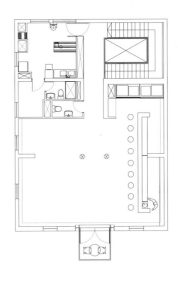

MARCEL WANDERS

Marcel Wanders studio
Westerstraat 187
1015 MA Amsterdam
The Netherlands

Tel: +31 20 422 13 39
Fax: +31 20 681 50 56
E-mail: joy@marcelwanders.com
Web: www.marcelwanders.com

MARCEL WANDERS was born in 1963 in Boxtel, the Netherlands. He graduated from the School of the Arts, Arnhem, in 1988. His reputation was launched by his iconic Knotted Chair, which he produced for Droog Design in 1996. He now works with the biggest European contemporary design manufacturers like B&B Italia, Bisazza, Poliform, Moroso, Flos, Boffi, Cappellini, Droog Design, and Moooi, of which he is also Art Director and co-owner. Additionally, he was the editor of the *International Design Yearbook 2005*. In the same year, together with chef Peter Lute, he created the LUTE SUITES hospitality concept. He also designed the interior of the restaurant Thor at the Hotel on Rivington in New York, including bar, lounge, and private club (2003–04, published here) and the interior of Blits, a new restaurant in Rotterdam (2005). Works by Marcel Wanders figure in the collections of the Museums of Modern Art in New York and San Francisco, the Victoria and Albert Museum in London, the Stedelijk Museum in Amsterdam, Museum Boijmans van Beuningen in Rotterdam, the Centraal Museum in Utrecht, and the Museum of Decorative Arts in Copenhagen.

MARCEL WANDERS wurde 1963 in Boxtel, Niederlande, geboren. 1988 beendete er sein Studium an der Kunsthochschule in Arnheim. Seinen Ruf begründete er mit dem zur Ikone gewordenen Knotted Chair, den er für 1996 für Droog Design entwarf. Er arbeitet heute für die größten europäischen Designproduzenten wie B&B Italia, Bisazza, Poliform, Moroso, Flos, Boffi, Cappellini, Droog Design sowie die Firma Moooi, deren Mitbesitzer und Art-Direktor er ist. Außerdem war er Herausgeber des *International Design Yearbook 2005*. Im gleichen Jahr schuf er, zusammen mit dem Chefkoch Peter Lute, das Hotelkonzept LUTE SUITES. Er gestaltete auch die Innenräume des Restaurants Thor im Hotel on Rivington in New York, einschließlich der Bar, der Lounge und des Privatklubs (2003–04, hier veröffentlicht), sowie die Räume des Blits, eines neuen Restaurants in Rotterdam (2005). Werke von Marcel Wanders wurden in die Sammlungen der Museums of Modern Art in New York und San Francisco, des Victoria and Albert Museum in London, des Stedelijk Museum in Amsterdam, des Museum Boijmans van Beuningen in Rotterdam, des Centraal Museum in Utrecht und des Kunstgewerbemuseums in Kopenhagen aufgenommen.

MARCEL WANDERS, né en 1963 à Boxtel, aux Pays-Bas, est diplômé de l'École des arts d'Arnhem (1988). Sa réputation doit initialement beaucoup à sa célèbre Knotted Chair, qu'il réalisa pour Droog Design en 1996. Il travaille maintenant pour les plus grandes maisons européennes comme B&B Italia, Bisazza, Poliform, Moroso, Flos, Boffi, Cappellini, Droog Design et Moooi, dont il est directeur artistique et copropriétaire. Par ailleurs, il a été rédacteur en chef de l'*International Design Yearbook 2005*. La même année, avec le chef, Peter Lute, il a créé le concept hôtelier des LUTE SUITES. Il a conçu l'aménagement du restaurant Thor pour l'Hotel on Rivington à New York, comprenant un bar, un lounge et un club privé (2003–04, publié ici) ; ainsi que celui du nouveau restaurant Blits à Rotterdam (2005). Des œuvres de Marcel Wanders figurent dans les collections des Musées d'art moderne de New York et de San Francisco, du Victoria and Albert Museum à Londres, du Stedelijk Museum à Amsterdam, du Museum Boijmans van Beuningen à Rotterdam, du Centraal Museum à Utrecht et du Musée des arts décoratifs de Copenhague.

THOR, THE HOTEL ON RIVINGTON

New York, New York, USA, 2003–04

107 Rivington Street, New York, NY 10002, USA, +1 212 796 8040, www.hotelonrivington.com/thor.html
Area: 336 m² restaurant, lounge, bar; 115 m² private club. Client: The Hotel on Rivington
Cost: not disclosed. Collaboration: Grzywinski Pons Architects

The Hotel on Rivington, a 21-story glass tower, opened in October 2004. The hotel restaurant, Thor (an acronym for the hotel's name), was designed by Marcel Wanders. The space includes a 6.4-meter-high glass ceiling that offers views of the Lower East Side. The space features wallpaper with an elaborate pattern in black, white, and yellow. The lounge, with its floor-to-ceiling windows, is accessible through an unpretentious side door and includes a Swarovski crystal-embedded bar and white walls with pebbles. Wanders and The Hotel on Rivington have done a good deal to make this formerly out-of-the-way area fashionable. The fact that the duplex penthouse in the hotel was meant to be designed by Zaha Hadid also helped to give the location a design pedigree, but the intervention of Wanders has given Thor a cosmopolitan cachet that ensured the success of the venue.

Das Hotel on Rivington, ein 21-geschossiger Glasturm, wurde im Oktober 2004 eröffnet. Das Hotelrestaurant Thor (ein Akronym des Hotelnamens) wurde von Marcel Wanders gestaltet. Der Bereich hat eine 6,4 m lange Glasdecke, die Ausblick über die Lower East Side bietet. Ein besonderes Merkmal ist die mit einem kunstvoll ausgearbeiteten Muster in Schwarz, Weiß und Gelb versehene Tapete. Die Lounge mit geschosshohen Fenstern wird durch eine unprätentiöse Seitentür betreten und hat eine Bar, in die Swarovski-Kristalle eingearbeitet sind, und weiße, mit Kieselsteinen bedeckte Wände. Wanders und das Hotel on Rivington haben viel unternommen, um diesen früher abgelegenen Bereich aufzuwerten. Die Tatsache, dass das zweigeschossige Penthouse im Hotel von Zaha Hadid gestaltet werden sollte, trug ebenfalls dazu bei, dem Ort eine Designeratmosphäre zu verleihen. Die Eingriffe von Wanders haben dem Thor eine kosmopolitische Prägung gegeben, die den Erfolg des Unternehmens gesichert hat.

L'Hotel on Rivington, tour de verre de vingt étages, a ouvert ses portes en octobre 2004. Le restaurant de l'hôtel, appelé Thor (acronyme fabriqué à partir du nom de l'hôtel), a été conçu par Marcel Wanders. Il comprend un plafond de verre à 6,4 m de haut qui offre une vue sur le Lower East Side. Les murs sont tendus d'un papier peint à motif complexe en noir, blanc et jaune. Le salon, aux fenêtres toute hauteur, est accessible par une porte latérale toute simple. Il est décoré d'un bar incrusté de cristaux de Swarovski et de murs blancs ornés de galets. Wanders et l'Hotel on Rivington ont beaucoup fait pour rendre populaire ce quartier un peu excentré. Le fait que la penthouse en duplex devait être conçue par Zaha Hadid a également aidé à redonner un peu de lustre au site, mais l'intervention de Wanders a certainement donné au Thor un cachet cosmopolite qui a assuré son succès.

Right page, a black steel Outhouse by Marcel Wanders dominates the restaurant space. The "new" antique tables and chairs were also designed by Wanders (Cappellini).

Rechts: Ein stählernes „Haus" von Marcel Wanders beherrscht den Restaurantbereich. Die „neuen" antiken Tische und Stühle wurden ebenfalls von Wanders entworfen (Cappellini).

Page de droite, une Outhouse en acier noir de Marcel Wanders domine le volume du restaurant. Les sièges et tables de style rétro ont également été dessinés par Wanders (Cappellini).

ISAY WEINFELD

Isay Weinfeld Arquiteto
Rua Andre Fernandes 175
04536–020 São Paulo, SP
Brazil

Tel: +55 11 3079 7581
Fax: +55 11 3079 5656
E-mail: info@isayweinfeld.com
Web: www.isayweinfeld.com

ISAY WEINFELD was born in 1952 in São Paulo, Brazil. He graduated from the School of Architecture at Mackenzie University in 1975. In an unusual mixture of careers, Weinfeld has also worked in cinema since 1974, making 14 short films that have received numerous international awards. In 1988, he wrote and directed his first full-length movie, *Fogo e Paixão*, considered to be one of the 10 best comedies produced that year worldwide. In 1989, the São Paulo Art Critics' Association awarded him the Prize for Best New Director. He has taught theory of architecture courses at the School of Architecture of Mackenzie University and was a Professor of Kinetic Expression at the School of Communications of the Fundação Armando Álvares Penteado. Weinfeld has completed dozens of private homes, commercial projects, banks, advertising agencies, discotheques, a bar, a restaurant, an art gallery, and the Hotel Fasano (São Paulo, 2001–03). He has worked with Marcio Kogan on numerous projects, including the 2001 exhibition "Arquitetura e Humor" at the Casa Brasileira Museum. Recent work includes the Mocotó Bar and Restaurant (London, UK, 2006–07, published here); the Sumaré House (São Paulo, 2007); and the Kesley Caliguere Antique Shop (São Paulo, 2007).

ISAY WEINFELD wurde 1952 in São Paulo geboren. Er beendete 1975 sein Architekturstudium an der Mackenzie University. Weinfeld ist in einer ungewöhnlichen Mischung von Berufen tätig gewesen. Er hat seit 1974 auch beim Kino gearbeitet und 14 Kurzfilme geschaffen, die zahlreiche internationale Auszeichnungen erhielten. 1988 schrieb er das Drehbuch und führte Regie bei seinem ersten Spielfilm *Fogo e Paixão*, der als eine der zehn weltweit besten Komödien jenes Jahrs beurteilt wurde. 1989 verlieh der Verband der Kunstkritiker von São Paulo ihm den Prize for Best New Director. Er hat Architekturtheorie an der Architekturabteilung der Mackenzie University gelehrt und war Professor für kinetischen Ausdruck an der Schule für Kommunikation der Fundação Armando Álvares Penteado. Weinfeld hat Dutzende von Einfamilienhäusern, kommerziellen Bauten, Banken, Werbeagenturen, Diskotheken, eine Bar, ein Restaurant, eine Kunstgalerie und das Hotel Fasano (São Paulo, 2001–03) ausgeführt. Mit Marcio Kogan hat er an zahlreichen Projekten zusammengearbeitet, u. a. 2001 an der Ausstellung „Arquitetura e Humor" im Museum Casa Brasileira. Zu seinen aktuellen Arbeiten zählen die Bar und das Restaurant Mocotó (London, 2006–07, hier veröffentlicht), das Haus Sumaré (São Paulo, 2007) und das Antiquitätengeschäft Kesley Caliguere (São Paulo, 2007).

ISAY WEINFELD, né en 1952 à São Paulo (Brésil), est diplômé de l'École d'architecture de l'Université Mackenzie (1975). Sa riche carrière l'a mené à s'intéresser également au cinéma depuis 1974. Il a réalisé quatorze courts métrages qui ont reçu de nombreux prix internationaux. En 1988, il a écrit et dirigé son premier long métrage *Fogo e Paixão*, considéré comme l'une des dix meilleures comédies produites dans le monde cette année-là. En 1989, l'Association des critiques d'art de São Paulo lui a remis son prix du « Meilleur nouveau metteur en scène ». Il a enseigné la théorie de l'architecture à l'École d'architecture de l'Université Mackenzie, et a été professeur d'expression cinétique à l'École de communication de la Fondation Armando Álvares Penteado. Weinfeld a réalisé des dizaines de résidences privées, de projets commerciaux, de banques, d'agences de publicité, de discothèques, un bar, un restaurant, une galerie d'art et l'hôtel Fasano (São Paulo, 2001–03). Il a collaboré avec Marcio Kogan sur de nombreux projets, dont la pièce « Arquitetura e Humor » au Musée de la Maison brésilienne (2001). Parmi ses récentes réalisations : le restaurant et bar Mocotó (Londres, G.-B., 2006–07 ; publié ici) ; la maison Sumaré (São Paulo, 2007) et le magasin d'antiquités Kesley Caliguere (São Paulo, 2007).

MOCOTÓ BAR AND RESTAURANT
London, UK, 2006–07

145 Knightsbridge, London SW1X 7PA, UK, +44 207 225 2300
Area: 600 m². Client: David Ponte. Cost: not disclosed
Team: Domingos Pascali, Elena Scarabotolo, Sophia Lin

Mocotó was a Brazilian restaurant (since closed) located in the Knightsbridge area of London. The restaurant, occupying the lower level, was complemented by a *boteco*, or relaxed bar, on the upper floor with large windows open to the street and a rough wood finish. Isay Weinfeld states: "The expression of architecture does not come from the obvious usage of Brazilian elements in construction. Design is rigorous, with the bar being somewhat rustic and the restaurant more discreet." In the restaurant, the more sophisticated atmosphere was marked by granite countertops or cinnamon wood floors. In the bar, tabletops made with cement tiles and old Brazilian benches made the more convivial atmosphere immediately tangible. A curtain designed by Isay Weinfeld ("Biombo" for Etel Interiores) linked the two spaces via an open space between the levels on the street side.

Mocotó war ein (seither geschlossenes) brasilianisches Restaurant im Gebiet Knightsbridge in London. Zu dem auf der unteren Ebene gelegenen Restaurant gehörte eine *boteco*, eine volkstümliche Bar im Obergeschoss mit großen, zur Straße orientierten Fenstern und einer groben Holzverkleidung. Isay Weinfeld erklärt: „Das architektonische Erscheinungsbild geht nicht auf die offensichtliche Verwendung brasilianischer Bauelemente zurück. Das Design ist streng, die Bar eher rustikal und das Restaurant zurückhaltender." In Letzterem wurde die elegantere Atmosphäre von der Thekenfläche aus Granit und den Böden aus Zimtholz bestimmt. In der Bar waren die Tischplatten mit Zementfliesen belegt, und alte brasilianische Bänke bewirkten eine eher gelockerte, sofort spürbare Atmosphäre. Ein von Isay Weinfeld entworfener Vorhang („Biombo" für Etel Interiores) verband beide Bereiche über einen Freiraum an der Straßenseite.

Le Mocotó était un restaurant brésilien (fermé depuis) situé dans le quartier de Knightsbridge à Londres. Il se complétait à l'étage d'un *boteco*, ou petit bar décontracté, décoré de finitions en bois brut et doté de grandes fenêtres donnant sur la rue. Isay Weinfeld explique : « L'expressivité de l'architecture ne vient pas de l'utilisation évidente d'éléments brésiliens dans la construction. Le design est rigoureux, le bar assez rustique et le restaurant plus discret. » L'atmosphère plus sophistiquée du restaurant s'appuyait sur des plans en granit et des sols en bois de cannelle. Dans le bar, les plateaux des tables en carreaux de ciment et de vieux bancs brésiliens rendaient l'atmosphère nettement plus conviviale. Un rideau dessiné par Isay Weinfeld (« Biombo » pour Etel Interiores) faisait le lien entre les deux salles grâce à un vide ouvert entre les niveaux le long de la rue.

Bar stools (Kiko Chair) are by Sergio Rodrigues, as are the Tião Chairs in the dining area. Old benches (Jacaré do Brasil) and old stools (Casa Antigua) are also used by the architect in this space.

Die Barhocker (Kiko Chair) stammen von Sergio Rodrigues, ebenso die Tião-Stühle im Speisesaal. Auch alte Bänke (Jacaré do Brasil) und alte Hocker (Casa Antigua) verwendete der Architekt für die Möblierung dieses Raums.

Les tabourets de bar (Kiko Chair) et les chaises Tião dans la salle à manger sont de Sergio Rodrigues. L'architecte a également meublé son espace de bancs (Jacaré do Brasil) et de vieux tabourets (Casa Antigua).

The wood panels were designed by Isay Weinfeld (Legno Marcenaria) as were the wall lamps (Cia de Illuminação).

Die Holztafeln wurden von Isay Weinfeld gestaltet (Legno Marcenaria), ebenso die Wandlampen (Cia de Illuminação).

Les panneaux de bois ont été dessinés par Isay Weinfeld (Legno Marcenaria) de même que les éclairages muraux (Cia de Illuminação).

The partition/curtain was designed by Isay Weinfeld for Mocotó and manufactured by Etel Interiores.

Die Trennwand/der Vorhang wurde von Isay Weinfeld für das Mocotó entworfen und von Etel Interiores hergestellt.

Le rideau/séparation a été conçu par Isay Weinfeld pour Mocotó et fabriqué par Etel Interiores.

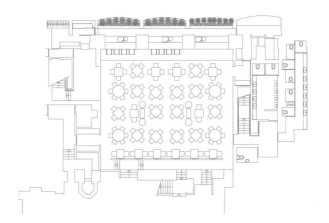

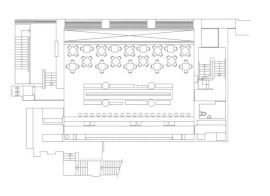

WONDERWALL /
MASAMICHI KATAYAMA

Wonderwall Inc.
3–4–10 Sendagaya
Shibuya-ku
Tokyo 151–0051
Japan

E-mail: contact@wonder-wall.com
Web: www.wonder-wall.com

Masamichi Katayama was born in Okayama, Japan, in 1966 and set up the firm H. Design Associates (1992–99), before creating **WONDERWALL** in 2000. As his firm description has it: "While respecting conventional and traditional aspects of architecture, he believes in breaking boundaries, and he is on a continual search for new ideas. Hence the name, Wonderwall: a continuous endless journey. Each project is conceived from scratch, rarely repeating details and ideas used in past projects. When designing retail spaces, not only does Katayama address all the elements of the interior, such as lighting, materials, and proportions, he also considers the actual experience of shopping." His work includes Pierre Hermé Paris (Tokyo, 2005); A Bathing Ape, Busy Work Shop (Hong Kong, 2006); Uniqlo (Soho, New York, 2006); A. P.C. Homme (Daikanyama, Tokyo, 2007); Uniqlo (Oxford Street, London, 2007); I. T. Pacific Place (Hong Kong, 2007); Tokyo Curry Lab and Kafka (Minato-ku, Tokyo, 2007, both published here); Bape Store (Harajuku, Tokyo, 2008); The Tokyo Towers/Sky Lounge and Guest Suites (Kachidoki, Tokyo, 2008); and Colette (Paris, 2008).

Masamichi Katayama wurde 1966 in Okayama geboren und gründete die Firma H. Design Associates (1992–99) sowie danach, im Jahr 2000, **WONDERWALL**. In der Beschreibung seiner Firma heißt es: „Während er konventionelle und traditionelle Aspekte der Architektur respektiert, will er auch Grenzen überschreiten und ist ständig auf der Suche nach neuen Ideen. Daher auch der Name Wonderwall: ein kontinuierlicher, nicht endender Weg. Jedes Projekt wird neu angegangen, nur selten werden Details und Ideen aus früheren Projekten verwendet. Wenn Katayama Geschäftsräume plant, kümmert er sich nicht nur um alle Elemente der Innenausstattung wie Beleuchtung, Materialien und Proportionen, sondern berücksichtigt auch das heutzutage erwartete Einkaufserlebnis." Zu seinen Arbeiten zählen: Pierre Hermé Paris (Tokio, 2005), A Bathing Ape, Busy Work Shop (Hongkong, 2006), Uniqlo (Soho, New York, 2006), A. P.C. Homme (Daikanyama, Tokio, 2007), Uniqlo (Oxford Street, London, 2007), I. T. Pacific Place (Hongkong, 2007), Tokyo Curry Lab und Kafka (Minato-ku, Tokio, 2007, beide hier veröffentlicht), Bape Store (Harajuku, Tokio, 2008), The Tokyo Towers/Sky Lounge und Gästesuiten (Kachidoki, Tokio, 2008) sowie Colette (Paris, 2008).

Masamichi Katayama né à Okayama en 1966 a créé l'agence H. Design Associates (1992–99) avant de fonder **WONDERWALL** en 2000. Selon la présentation de l'agence : « Tout en respectant les aspects conventionnels et traditionnels de l'architecture, il croit en la rupture des limites et est en quête permanente d'idées nouvelles. D'où le nom de Wonderwall : un voyage continu sans fin. Chaque projet est conçu à partir de zéro, et il est rare que des détails et des idées utilisés dans des projets antérieurs se voient répétés. Dans sa conception des aménagements d'un espace commercial, non seulement Katayama mobilise tous les éléments inérieurs comme l'éclairage, les matériaux et les proportions, mais il prend également en compte l'expérience même de l'acte d'achat. » Parmi ses réalisations, le magasin Pierre Hermé Paris (Tokyo, 2005) ; A Bathing Ape, Busy Work Shop (Hongkong, 2006) ; Uniqlo (Soho, New York, 2006) ; A. P.C. Homme (Daikanyama, Tokyo, 2007) ; Uniqlo (Oxford Street, Londres, 2007) ; I. T. Pacific Place (Hongkong, 2007) ; Tokyo Curry Lab et Kafka (Minato-ku, Tokyo, 2007, tous deux publiés ici) ; Bape Store (Harajuku, Tokyo, 2008) ; The Tokyo Towers/Sky Lounge and Guest Suites (Kachidoki, Tokyo, 2008) ; et Colette (Paris, 2008).

TOKYO CURRY LAB

Tokyo, Japan, 2007

2F Tokyo Tower, 4–2–8 Shiba-koen, Minato-ku, Tokyo 105–0011, Japan, +81 3 5425 2900, www.tokyocurrylab.jp
Area: 60 m². Client: Chance Lab Corporation. Cost: not disclosed
Collaboration (Lighting): Masaki Yasuhara (Plus y)

The smooth, modern appearance of the Tokyo Curry Lab plays on Japanese taste for fast food, but in this instance, the quality of the design and the nature of the food encourage passersby to take a more careful look.

Das glatte, moderne Erscheinungsbild des Tokyo Curry Lab spielt auf die japanische Vorliebe für Fast Food an, aber in diesem Fall regen die Qualität der Gestaltung und die Art der Speisen die Passanten zum genaueren Hinsehen an.

L'aspect moderne et épuré du Tokyo Curry Lab joue sur le goût des Japonais pour la nourriture rapide, mais ici la qualité du projet et la nature de la cuisine servie encouragent les passants à entrer.

Based on a concept of Kundo Koyama, the creator of Fuji TV's Iron Chef show, the Tokyo Curry Lab is intended as an "innovative lab for experimenting and inventing curry recipes." Located in the Tokyo Tower, an iconic 332-meter-high communications facility in Shiba Park, a "lab" area with colorful spice tubes is complemented by a dining counter located behind it. The designer says: "The serious yet humorous interior is intended for curry lovers who are serious at play." With its stainless-steel counter and animal graphics, this small space is both unexpected and coherent.

Das auf einem Konzept von Kundo Koyama, dem Schöpfer der Iron-Chef-Show von Fuji TV, beruhende Tokyo Curry Lab soll ein „innovatives Laboratorium zum Experimentieren und Erfinden von Curryrezepten" sein. Es befindet sich im Tokyo Tower, dem zur Ikone gewordenen, 332 m hohen Funk- und Fernsehturm im Shiba Park. Ein „Labor"-Bereich mit farbenfreudigen Gewürzbehältern wird ergänzt durch eine dahinter liegende Speisetheke. Der Architekt sagt: „Das seriöse und trotzdem humorvolle Interieur ist für Liebhaber des Curry bestimmt, die das Spiel ernsthaft betreiben." Dieser kleine Raum mit einer Theke aus Edelstahl und Tiergrafiken ist sowohl überraschend als auch konsequent.

D'après un concept de Kundo Koyama, créateur d'une célèbre émission de télévision, le Tokyo Curry Lab est un « laboratoire innovant au service de l'invention et de l'expérimentation de recettes au curry ». Installée dans la Tokyo Tower, une tour de télécommunications iconique de 332 m de haut dressée dans le parc Shiba, la zone de « lab » aux tubes d'épices colorés s'accompagne d'un comptoir où les clients viennent consommer. « Cet intérieur sérieux, mais non sans humour, est destiné aux amateurs de curry qui prennent leur passion au sérieux », explique l'architecte. Ce petit restaurant à comptoir en acier et décoré de reproductions d'animaux est à la fois cohérent et surprenant.

Glass tubes filled with spices form a partition near the continuous curvilinear dining counter, matched by an overhead ceiling protrusion.

Mit Gewürzen gefüllte Glasröhren bilden eine Trennwand neben der durchgehend gekrümmten Theke, deren Form von einem Vorsprung der Decke aufgenommen wird.

Des tubes en verre remplis d'épices forment une séparation près du comptoir de dégustation de forme curviligne, à laquelle répond celle du plafond.

KAFKA

Tokyo, Japan, 2007

Tokyo Midtown 3F, 9–7–4 Akasaka, Minato-ku, Tokyo 107-0052, Japan, +81 3 5413 7700
Area: 101 m². Client: D's Inc. Cost: not disclosed. Collaboration (Lighting): Masaki Yasuhara (Plus y)

Kafka is located in the Roppongi area of Tokyo and more precisely in the Tokyo Midtown complex. Masamichi Katayama says: "The overall design is a forward interpretation of the traditional Japanese concept of *wa*, or harmony." Katayama called on various artisans in the project, such as the potter Doichi Uchida, who designed the ceramic countertops in the main dining room, and the lacquer artist Akito Akagi, who created the lacquered table in the private dining room. The name of the restaurant is not related to the famous Prague-born author, but rather is a contraction of two Japanese words *kanno* (which means "possible") and *fukanno* (which means "not possible").

Das Kafka liegt im Bezirk Roppongi in Tokio, genauer gesagt in dem Komplex Midtown Tokyo. Masamichi Katayama sagt: „Die Gesamtgestaltung ist eine fortschrittliche Interpretation des traditionellen japanischen Begriffs *wa* oder Harmonie." Katayama bezog verschiedene Kunsthandwerker in das Projekt ein, etwa den Töpfer Doichi Uchida, der die Tischflächen aus Keramik im großen Speisesaal gestaltete, und den Lackkünstler Akito Akagi, der den Lacktisch im privaten Speiseraum schuf. Der Name des Restaurants bezieht sich nicht auf den berühmten Schriftsteller aus Prag, sondern ist eine Verschmelzung der beiden japanischen Wörter „kanno" (möglich) und „fukanno" (unmöglich).

Le Kafka est situé dans le quartier de Roppongi à Tokyo et plus précisément dans le complexe de Tokyo Midtown. «La conception d'ensemble est une interprétation avancée du concept japonais traditionnel de *wa*, ou harmonie», explique Masamichi Katayama qui a fait appel à divers artisans, dont le potier Doichi Uchida qui a créé les plans en céramique de la salle à manger principale, et au laqueur, Akito Akagi, auteur de la table en laque de la salle à manger privée. Le nom du restaurant est sans rapport avec le célèbre auteur praguois, mais est la contraction des deux mots japonais *kanno* («possible») et *fukanno* («impossible»).

The Kafka is a contemporary Japanese restaurant that aims to develop a fresh approach to traditional cooking. One of their specialties is yaki-ishi mushi, dishes cooked by the steam from liquid that is poured on a hot stone.

Das Kafka ist ein modernes japanisches Lokal, das eine neue Art der traditionellen Küche anbietet. Eine seiner Spezialitäten sind yaki-ishi mushi, im Dampf gegarte Speisen, die in flüssiger Form auf einen heißen Stein gegossen werden.

Le Kafka est un établissement japonais contemporain qui développe une approche nouvelle de la cuisine traditionnelle. L'une de ses spécialités est le yaki-ishi mushi, plat cuit à la vapeur dégagée par l'écoulement d'un liquide sur de la pierre brûlante.

The dark atmosphere of the restaurant is meant to provide a soothing "contemporary" feel, with a number of artworks heightening the impression that this place is exceptional.

Die dunkle Atmosphäre des Restaurants soll ein beruhigendes „zeitgemäßes" Befinden bewirken; zahlreiche Kunstwerke verstärken das Gefühl, dass dieser Ort etwas Besonderes darstellt.

L'atmosphère sombre du restaurant veut exprimer un sentiment de contemporanéité apaisante. La présence d'œuvres d'art renforce l'impression de se trouver dans un lieu exceptionnel.

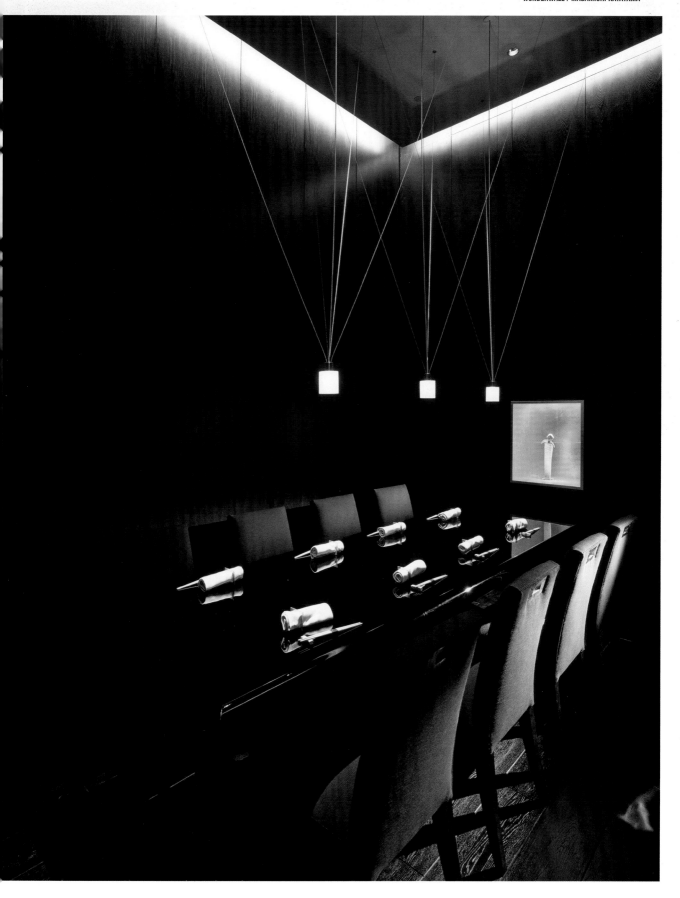

YABU PUSHELBERG

Yabu Pushelberg – Toronto
55 Booth Avenue
Toronto, Ontario M4M 2M3
Canada

Tel: +1 416 778 9779
Fax: +1 416 778 9747
E-mail: infoTO@yabupushelberg.com
Web: www.yabupushelberg.com

Based in Toronto and New York, **YABU PUSHELBERG** was founded in 1980 by George Yabu and Glenn Pushelberg. Their clients include Louis Vuitton, Bergdorf Goodman, Tiffany & Co., Carolina Herrera, Four Seasons Hotels & Resorts, W Hotels, Thompson Hotels, Park Hyatt International, Mandarin Oriental Hotel Group, Peninsula Hotels, and Saint Regis Hotels. With a staff of about 100, the firm offers interior design, technical, project administration, and even art consulting expertise. George Yabu received a B. A. in Applied Arts (Interior Design) from Ryerson Polytechnic (Toronto). He oversees the creation and development of design components on each firm project. Glenn Pushelberg also has a B. A. in Applied Arts from Ryerson Polytechnic. They are currently developing Four Seasons Hotels in New York, Toronto, Auckland, Bangalore, and Bora Bora. Their recent restaurants include the Blue Fin (New York); Maimon Wine & Grill (Tokyo); and the Peter Restaurant (Tokyo, Japan, 2007, published here).

Das in Toronto und New York ansässige Büro **YABU PUSHELBERG** wurde 1980 von George Yabu und Glenn Pushelberg gegründet. Zu seinen Auftraggebern gehören Louis Vuitton, Bergdorf Goodman, Tiffany & Co., Carolina Herrera, Four Seasons Hotels & Resorts, W Hotels, Thompson Hotels, Park Hyatt International, Mandarin Oriental Hotel Group, Peninsula Hotels und Saint Regis Hotels. Die Firma mit etwa 100 Mitarbeitern bietet Leistungen in Innenarchitektur, Technik, Projektleitung und sogar Beratung auf dem Gebiet der Kunst an. George Yabu erwarb den B. A. in angewandter Kunst (Innenarchitektur) am Ryerson Polytechnic (Toronto). Er überwacht die Entstehung und Entwicklung der Entwurfselemente von jedem Projekt der Firma. Glenn Pushelberg hat ebenfalls den B. A. in angewandter Kunst vom Ryerson Polytechnic. Gegenwärtig arbeitet das Büro an Four Seasons Hotels in New York, Toronto, Auckland, Bangalore und Bora Bora. Zu ihren neuesten Restaurants zählen das Blue Fin (New York), das Maimon Wine & Grill (Tokio) und das Restaurant Peter (Tokio, 2007, hier veröffentlicht).

Basée à Toronto et New York, l'agence **YABU PUSHELBERG** a été fondée en 1980 par George Yabu et Glenn Pushelberg. Ils comptent parmi leurs clients Louis Vuitton, Bergdorf Goodman, Tiffany & Co., Carolina Herrera, Four Seasons Hotels & Resorts, W Hotels, Thompson Hotels, Park Hyatt International, Mandarin Oriental Hotel Group, Peninsula Hotels et Saint Regis Hotels. Comptant environ cent collaborateurs, l'agence est spécialisée en architecture intérieure, aménagements techniques, gestion de projets et même conseil en acquisition d'œuvres d'art. George Yabu est B. A. en arts appliqués (architecture intérieure) de Ryerson Polytechnic (Toronto). Il supervise la création et la mise en place de chaque projet conçu par l'agence. Glenn Pushelberg est également B. A. en arts appliqués de Ryerson Polytechnic. Ils réalisent actuellement des projets pour le groupe Four Seasons Hotels à New York, Toronto, Auckland, Bangalore et Bora Bora. Ils ont récemment conçu les restaurants Blue Fin (New York), Maimon Wine & Grill (Tokyo) et le Peter (Tokyo, Japon, 2007, publié ici).

PETER RESTAURANT

Tokyo, Japan, 2007

The Peninsula Tokyo, 1–8–1 Yurakucho, Chiyoda-ku, Tokyo 100–0006, Japan, +81 3 6270 2888, www.peninsula.com
Area: 1036 m². Client: The Peninsula Tokyo. Cost: not disclosed

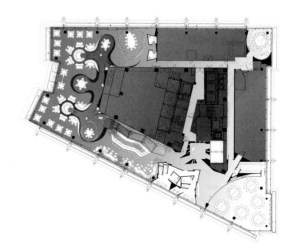

Dining tables are for the most part in macassar ebony veneer skin on MDF board and high-gloss PU coating (Gradation). Chairs are from Pan Interior Products.

Die meisten Speisetische bestehen aus Makassar-Ebenholz-Furnier auf MDF-Platte mit Hochglanzbeschichtung aus Polyurethan (Gradation). Die Stühle stammen von Pan Interior Products.

Les tables sont pour la plupart en placage d'ébène de macassar sur médium recouvert d'un vernis haute brillance PU (Gradation) Les fauteuils viennent de Pan Interior Products.

This restaurant, seating 128 clients in its main dining room, occupies the entire 24th floor of the Peninsula Tokyo Hotel and offers a 360° view of the Japanese capital and in particular of the gardens of the Imperial Palace. The facility includes two semi-private dining areas, one private dining room, and a banquet room accommodating up to 60 guests. Acrylic panels by the artist Marc Littlejohn complement curved windows. The restaurant is reached via custom-made elevators from the hotel lobby. The vestibule has walls made of folded black metal designed by D'Art. The architects state: "Inside the restaurant, a long bar of folded metal echoes the geometric motif of the vestibule, while organically shaped wooden bar stools and benches in a dark toffee-color sit in juxtaposition. Curvilinear pod chairs in dark bronze provide additional seating by the windows, while polished-chrome tree sculptures by Hirotoshi Sawada reference the Imperial Gardens and Hibiya Park below." An interactive video wall projects images of Hong Kong in this Chinese restaurant. Another artwork, made of metal strips, by Hirotoshi Sawada covers the ceiling of the banquet room.

Dieses Restaurant mit 128 Plätzen im großen Speisesaal nimmt das gesamte 24. Geschoss des Peninsula Hotels in Tokio ein und bietet einen 360°-Rundblick auf die japanische Hauptstadt und insbesondere die Gärten des Kaiserpalasts. Das Lokal enthält zwei halbprivate Speiseräume, einen privaten Speiseraum und einen Bankettsaal für 60 Gäste. Acryltafeln des Künstlers Marc Littlejohn schmücken die gebogenen Fenster. Das Restaurant wird über speziell angefertigte Aufzüge von der Hotelhalle erreicht. Seine Vorhalle hat Wände aus gefaltetem, schwarzem Metall, die von D'Art gestaltet wurden. Die Architekten erklären: „Im Restaurant nimmt eine lange Bar aus gefaltetem Metall das geometrische Motiv aus der Vorhalle auf, während braune, organisch geformte, hölzerne Barhocker und Bänke einen Kontrast dazu bilden. Dunkelbraune Schalensessel bieten zusätzliche Sitzplätze am Fenster. Glänzende, verchromte Baumskulpturen von Hirotoshi Sawada nehmen Bezug auf die kaiserlichen Gärten und den Hibiya Park." Eine interaktive Videowand projiziert Bilder von Hongkong in dieses chinesische Restaurant. Ein weiteres Kunstwerk aus Metallstreifen von Hirotoshi Sawada überzieht die Decke des Bankettsaals.

Ce restaurant de cent vingt-huit couverts en salle principale occupe la totalité du vingt-quatrième niveau du Peninsula Tokyo Hotel et offre une vue panoramique à 360 degrés sur la capitale japonaise et, en particulier, sur les jardins du Palais impérial. Les installations comprennent deux salles à manger semi-privées, une salle privée et une salle de banquet de soixante couverts. Des panneaux en acrylique de l'artiste Marc Littlejohn viennent en complément des baies cintrées. Des ascenseurs spécialement conçus conduisent les hôtes du hall de l'hôtel au restaurant. Les murs du vestibule sont en panneaux de métal noir plié conçus par D'Art. « À l'intérieur du restaurant, un long bar en métal plié fait écho au motif graphique du vestibule. Viennent s'y juxtaposer des tabourets en bois de forme organique et des banquettes de couleur caramel foncé. Des fauteuils curvilignes en bronze sombre offrent d'autres possibilités d'assise près des fenêtres, tandis que des sculptures d'arbre en chrome poli de Hirotoshi Sawada font référence aux jardins impériaux et au parc Hibiya en contrebas », expliquent les architectes. Un mur d'écrans vidéo interactifs projette des images de Hongkong dans ce restaurant chinois. Une autre œuvre d'art en bandeaux de métal, toujours d'Hirotoshi Sawada, orne le plafond de la salle des banquets.

The bar stools seen above are from Pan Interior Products, and the restaurant host stand (right) is in polished stainless steel and macassar ebony verneer (Gradation).

Die oben gezeigten Barhocker stammen von Pan Interior Products, der Empfangstisch (rechts) ist aus poliertem Edelstahl und Makassar-Ebenholz-Furnier (Gradation).

Les tabourets de bar ci-dessus sont de Pan Interior Products et le comptior d'accueil des hôtes est en acier inoxydable poli et placage d'ébène de macassar (Gradation).

CATE YOUNG

Cate Young Design (CYD)
30A Montague Street
Balmain, 2041 NSW
Australia

Tel: +61 2 9810 7311
Fax: +61 2 9810 3941
E-mail: cate@cyd.com.au
Web: www.cyd.com.au

Born in 1968, **CATE YOUNG** founded her own design firm at the age of 19. She created her current structure, CYD, in 1993, when she was given the commission to design the Sails Restaurant in Noosa on the coast of Queensland. Between 1997 and 2000, she was the Principal Interior Designer for the All Seasons Hotel Group, where she worked on the group's 33 existing hotels and the concept for three new ones. She created Australia's first design concept gallery "cyd.concept" in 2003. She admits to being influenced by the French designers Andrée Putman and Christian Liaigre. Recent work includes the Water Bar (2007, published here); the Quarantine Station Hotel (North Head, Manly, 2008); and the Sheraton Noosa Resort & Spa (2008), all in Sydney, Australia.

CATE YOUNG, geboren 1968, gründete im Alter von 19 Jahren ihre eigene Firma. Ihre jetzige Form unter dem Namen CYD erhielt das Unternehmen 1993, als Young den Auftrag erhielt, das Sails Restaurant in Noosa an der Küste von Queensland zu planen. Von 1997 bis 2000 war sie die leitende Innenarchitektin der All Seasons Hotel Group; sie arbeitete für die 33 bestehenden Hotels dieser Gruppe und plante drei neue. 2003 gründete sie Australiens erste Designgalerie „cyd.concept". Sie bekennt, dass sie von den französischen Designern Andrée Putman und Christian Liaigre beeinflusst wurde. Zu ihren neueren Arbeiten zählen die Water Bar (2007, hier veröffentlicht), das Quarantine Station Hotel (North Head, Manly, 2008) und das Sheraton Noosa Resort & Spa (2008), alle in Sydney, Australien.

Née in 1968, **CATE YOUNG** a fondé sa première agence de design à l'âge de dix-neuf ans. Elle a créé sa structure actuelle, CYD, en 1993, lorsqu'elle a reçu commande du restaurant Sails à Noosa sur la côte du Queensland. De 1997 à 2000, elle a été principale designer du groupe All Seasons Hotel pour lequel elle est intervenue sur les trente-trois hôtels et le concept de trois nouveaux établissements. Elle a créé la première galerie de design d'Australie « cyd.concept » en 2003. Elle reconnaît avoir été influencée par les designers français Andrée Putman et Christian Liaigre. Parmi ses récentes réalisations : le Water Bar (2007, publié ici) ; le Quarantine Station Hotel (North Head, Manly, 2008) ; et le Sheraton Noosa Resort & Spa (2008), toutes à Sydney, Australie.

WATER BAR

Sydney, Australia, 2007

Blue Hotel, Cowper Wharf Road, Woolloomooloo, NSW 2011, Australia, +61 2 9331 9000
Area: 728 m². Client: Taj Sydney. Cost: $400 000
Collaboration: Clive Lucas, Stapleton & Partners Pty Ltd., Heritage Consultants

The Water Bar is located on Finger Wharf at Woolloomooloo Bay in Sydney and was a refurbishment carried out in a listed building for the Taj Hotel and Palace Group. The spectacular 13-meter-high ceiling of this industrial space was one of the challenges met by Cate Young in responding to the client's brief to "bring back the space, create intimate and inviting zones with a hint of opulence to attract the A-list crowd." Cate Young explains: "Our design solution was translated directly from water, using a dark silvery palette to give the space light and shade, creating dramatic intimate zones which sit comfortably in the industrially sculptural interior." Swarovski crystal curtains were used in contract with glossy black lacquered surfaces and black mirrors. Young concludes: "High contrast noir lighting was used to create a sense of soft drama."

Die Water Bar liegt am Finger Wharf in der Woolloomooloo-Bucht in Sydney. Es handelte sich um den Umbau eines denkmalgeschützten Gebäudes für die Taj Hotel and Palace Group. Eine spektakuläre, 13 m hohe Decke und das industrielle Ambiente gehörten zu den Herausforderungen für Cate Young, denn der Auftraggeber forderte, „den Raum zurückzugewinnen, intime und einladende sowie auch elegante Bereiche zu schaffen, um anspruchsvolle Kunden anzulocken". Cate Young erläutert: „Unsere Entwurfslösung wurde unmittelbar vom Wasser bestimmt, indem wir eine dunkel-silbrige Farbpalette verwendeten, um dem Raum Licht und Schatten zu geben, eindrucksvolle, intime Bereiche zu schaffen, die sich in das industrielle, skulpturale Interieur einfügen." Vorhänge aus Swarovski-Kristall wurden als Kontrast zu den glänzend schwarz lackierten Flächen und schwarzen Spiegeln gewählt. Young fügt hinzu: „Stark kontrastierende, schwarze Leuchten schaffen eine sanfte Dramatik."

Le Water Bar est situé dans Finger Wharf à Woolloomooloo Bay, à Sydney. Il fait partie de l'opération de rénovation d'un bâtiment classé, menée par le groupe Taj Hotel and Palace. Un spectaculaire plafond de 13 m de haut et un volume d'origine industrielle faisaient partie des défis que devait relever Cate Young pour répondre au désir du client « de faire ressentir à nouveau l'espace, créer des zones intimes et accueillantes avec un soupçon d'opulence pour attirer le tout-Sydney ». Cate Young explique : « Notre solution est directement issue de l'eau. Nous utilisons une palette argent foncé pour donner à l'espace de la lumière et de l'ombre, en composant des zones spectaculaires intimes qui s'insèrent confortablement dans un intérieur sculptural d'origine industrielle. » Les rideaux en cristaux de Swarovski viennent contraster avec des plans laqués noir brillant et des miroirs noirs. « Une lumière noire à fort contraste a été utilisée pour créer un effet spectaculaire, mais non appuyé », conclut Young.

The Crystal Sculpture designed by CYD was manufactured by Turner Brothers (Swarovski). The Stainless-Steel Oblique Stools were designed by Korban Flaubert (Korban Flaubert).

Die von CYD gestaltete „Crystal Sculpture" wurde von Turner Brothers (Swarovski) hergestellt. Die Oblique Hocker aus Edelstahl entwarf Korban Flaubert (Korban Flaubert).

La sculpture en cristal conçue par CYD a été fabriquée par Turner Brothers (Swarovski). Les tabourets en acier inoxydable Oblique sont de Korban Flaubert (Korban Flaubert).

INDEX OF ARCHITECTS, BUILDINGS, AND PLACES

CREDITS

PHOTO CREDITS — **2** © James Silverman/www.jamessilverman.co.uk / **7–8** © Ezra Stoller / Esto / **9** © Inga Pollliweit / **10** © Richard Pare / **11** © Frank Oudeman / **12** © Nicolas Borel / **13** © Kozo Takayama / **14** © Peter Hebeisen / **17** left © Vincent Knapp / **17** right Nagi © / **18** © Banyan Tree Hotels & Resorts / **19** © Anna Kahn / **20** © Anders Sune Berg / **21** © Junkichi Tatsuki / **22** © Sebastián Sepúlveda Vidal / **23** © Guedes + DeCampos/F./S.Guerra/fabpics / **24** © James Silverman/www.jamessilverman.co.uk / **25** © Doug Edmunds / **26** © Daniel Sumesgutner / **28** © Eric Laignel / **29** © Virgile Simon Bertrand / **30** © Starck Network / **31** © John Horner / **32** © Lucy Gauntlett / **33** © Luke Hayes / **34** © Leonardo Finotti / **35** © Marcus Clinton Photography / **36** © Richard Bryant/arcaid.co.uk / **37** © Pedro Vanucchi / **38** © 3deluxe-biorhythm / **39** © Emanuel Raab / **41–43** © Gulliver Theis / **44** left © Oskar de Kiefte / **44** right © Paulien de Gaaij / **45–49** © CornbreadWorks / **50–53** © Banyan Tree Hotels & Resorts / **54** © Felipe Assadi + Francisca Pulido / **55–59** © Assadi + Pulido / **60** © Yuki Kuwana / **61–65** © Michael Weber Photography / **66** © Barkow Leibinger Architekten / **67–71** © Christian Richters / **72** © bel lobo & bob neri arquitetos / **73–75** © Anna Kahn / **76** © CBA / Christian Biecher & Associés / **77–83** © Luc Boegly / **84** © Buchner Bründler Architekten / **85–87** © Mark Niedermann / **88** © Studio Arthur Casas SP / **89–91** © Leonardo Finotti / **92** © CL3 Architects Limited / **93–99** © Eddie Siu / **100** © concrete architectural associates / **101–105** © concrete architectural associates/Photography by Frank Pinckers / **106–109** © Ewout Huibers/www.ewout.tv / **110** © Electric Dreams / **111–113** © Fredrik Sweger / **114** © Elenberg Fraser / **115–119** © Dianna Snape / **120** © Stuart Forbes Associates / **121–123** © Richard Bryant/arcaid.co.uk / **124** © Carlo Gavazzeni / **125–129** © Ramon Prat / **130** © gca arquitectes associats / **131, 133–135** © Jordi Miralles / **132** © David Cardelus / **136** © Patrick Swirc / **137–145** © Kang Xiaoxiang Courtesy by Gilles & Boissier / **146** © Stephanie Goto / **147–151** © Frank Oudeman / **152–157** © Ricky Ridecós / **158–163** © Golf Tuttler: Lai Xuzhu, Still Lifes exposed works by: Kevin Brest, Oak Taylor-Smith / **164** © Guedes + DeCampos / **165–169** © Guedes + DeCampos/F./S.Guerra/fabpics / **170** © Steve Double / **171–175** © Luke Hayes / **176–181** © Anders Sune Berg / **182** © Hosoya Schaefer Architects / **183–187** © Iwan Baan / **188** © Jakob+MacFarlane / **189–193** © Nicolas Borel / **194** © Johnsen Schmaling Architects / **195–199** © Doug Edmunds / **200** © SFJones Architects / **201–203** © Weldon Brewster / **204** © Jouin Manku / **205–217** © Eric Laignel / **218** © Marcio Kogan / **219–221** © Pedro Vannucchi / **222** © Courtesy of Kengo Kuma & Associates / **223–225** © Junkichi Tatsuki / **226–227** © André Morin / **228** © Peter Lindbergh / **229–233** © Eric Morin / **234–237** © MAKE Architecture / **238–241** © John Linden / **242** © Maurice Mentjens Design / **243–253** © Arjen Schmitz / **254** © Metro Arquitetura / **255–259** © Leonardo Finotti / **260** © Simone Micheli Architectural Hero / **261–269** © Jürgen Eheim / **270** © Moon Design / **271–277** © Filip Dujardin / **278** © Office dA / **279–283** © John Horner / **284** © Katrin Olina Ltd. / **285–289** © Harlim Djauhar Winata / **290** © OlssonLyckefors Arkitekter / **291–295** © James Silverman/www.jamessilverman.co.uk / **296–299** © Åke E:son Lindman / **300** © Pacific Environments NZ Ltd. Architects / **301–305** © Lucy Gauntlett / **306** © Pentagram / **307, 308** left, **309, 310** top and bottom left © Gavin Jackson/arcaid.co.uk / **308** right, **310** bottom right, **311** © Nick Turner / **312** © Architetto Pierluigi Piu / **313–319** © Giorgio Dettori / **320** © Studio Arne Quinze / **321–325** © Dave Bruel/Studio Arne Quinze / **326** © Imaad Rahmouni Architectures / **327–333** © Susetta Bozzi / **334** © Karim Rashid / **335–339** © Karim Rashid/Photography by Nebojsa Babic / **340–341** © Karim Rashid/Photography by Lauren Rubinstein / **344** © Tom Tomczyk / **345, 347** top left, **348, 349** © Stefan Ruhmke / **346–347, 347** top right © Prodevion GmbH/www.p-devion.de / **350** © ROBERTNEUN™ / **351–355** © Annette Kisling, Berlin / **356** © Serie Architects / **357–361** © Fram Petit/www.frampetit.com / **362–369** © Starck Network / **370** © Super Potato / **371–375** © Nedalny Vostok Restaurant / **376** © Tidy Arquitectos / **377–381** © Sebastián Sepúlveda Vidal / **382** © Marcel Wanders studio / **383–385** © Inga Powilleit / **386** © Isay Weinfeld Arquiteto / **387–391** © Leonardo Finotti / **392** © Wonderwall / **393–399** © Kozo Takayama / **400** © Chiun-Kai Shih / **401–405** © Evan Dion / **406** © Cate Young Design (CYD) / **407–411** © Marcus Clinton Photography

CREDITS FOR PLANS / DRAWINGS / CAD DOCUMENTS — **40, 43** © 3deluxe-biorhythm / **46–47, 49** © Architectuurbureau Sluijmer en Van Leeuwen / **56, 58** © Felipe Assadi + Francisca Pulido / **63** © AvroKO / **75** © bel lobo & bob neri arquitetos / **82** © CBA / Christian Biecher & Associés / **87** © Buchner Bründler Architekten / **95, 99** © CL3 Architects Limited / **113** © Electric Dreams / **129** © Studio Fuksas / **133, 134** © gca arquitectes associats / **151** © Stephanie Goto / **154, 156, 162** © Graft / **185, 187** © Hosoya Schaefer Architects / **193** © Jakob+MacFarlane / **196, 198** © Johnsen Schmaling Architects / **203** © SFJones Architects / **212** © Jouin Manku / **225, 227** © Courtesy of Kengo Kuma & Associates / **231** © Bureau d'études Christian Liaigre / **237** © MAKE Architecture / **253** © Maurice Mentjens Design / **257–259** © Metro Arquitetura / **264, 269** © Simone Micheli Architectural Hero / **276** © Moon Design / **283** © Office dA / **286, 289** © Katrin Olina Ltd. / **293** © OlssonLyckefors Arkitekter / **302, 304–305** © Pacific Environments NZ Ltd. Architects / **309** © Pentagram / **317** © Architetto Pierluigi Piu / **333** © Imaad Rahmouni Architectures / **342–343** © Karim Rashid / **355** © ROBERTNEUN™ / **361** © Serie Architects / **374** © Super Potato / **379–381** © Tidy Arquitectos / **391** © Isay Weinfeld Arquiteto / **402** © Yabu Pushelberg